Guide to
COLLEGE
READING

Guide to
COLLEGE
READING

SECOND EDITION

Kathleen T. McWhorter

NIAGARA COUNTY COMMUNITY COLLEGE

SCOTT, FORESMAN AND COMPANY
Glenview, Illinois
Boston
London

LIBRARY OF CONGRESS

Library of Congress Cataloging-in-Publication Data

McWhorter, Kathleen T.
    Guide to college reading / Kathleen T. McWhorter.—2nd ed.
        p.   cm.
    Bibliography: p.
    Includes index.
    ISBN 0-673-39665-7
    1. Reading (Higher education)   2. Developmental reading.
    3. College readers.   I. Title.
LB2395.3.M39   1989
428.4'07'11—dc19   88-20955
                                                    CIP

1 2 3 4 5 6 7 8 9 10 — MVN — 94 93 92 91 90 89 88

Printed in the United States of America

ACKNOWLEDGMENTS

The author wishes to thank the following authors and publishers for permission to reprint
their material in this text.

Selected Passages and Excerpts, Parts One–Five

Pages 13–14, 106, 117, 134–135   From Ross J. Eschelman and Barbara G. Cashion, *Sociology:
An Introduction*, ed., pp. 82–83 and 88–90. Copyright © 1985 by Ross J. Eschelman and
Barbara G. Cashion. Reprinted by permission of Scott, Foresman and Company.

Page 33   Two selections from *Roget's International Thesaurus.* Copyright © 1960 by Harper
& Row, Publishers, Inc. Reprinted by permission of the publisher.

Page 37   Pronunciation key, definition of "oblique": Copyright © 1980 by Houghton Mifflin
Company. Reprinted by permission from *The American Heritage Dictionary of the English
Language, New College Edition.*

Page 38   Definition of "greedy" and "green": From *Webster's New World Dictionary*, second
college edition. Copyright © 1970, 1972, 1974, 1976, 1978 by Simon & Schuster, Inc. Reprinted by permission of Simon & Schuster, Inc.

Pages 59–60, 109, 110, 111   From Jean Luttrell Weirich, *Personal Financial Management*, pp.
240–241, 155. Copyright © 1983 by Jean Luttrell Weirich. Reprinted by permission of Jean
Luttrell Weirich.

Pages 68, 112, 115   From James Geiwitz, *Psychology: Looking at Ourselves*, 2nd ed., pp.
200, 219, 276, 512, 513. Copyright © 1980 by James Geiwitz. Reprinted by permission of
James Geiwitz.

(continued on page 477)

To the Instructor

The continuing decline of basic skill competencies among students, coupled with the influx of nontraditional students, has resulted in growing numbers of developmental students on many college campuses. Colleges and universities are confronted with the choice of either preparing these developmental students for the requirements of college level work or losing them through attrition or failure. As a result, many institutions have initiated developmental reading courses targeted at students whose reading competency is below ninth-grade level. This text, then, is written to equip the developmental student with the basic reading skills needed to cope with the demands of academic work.

Many developmental college students share learning characteristics, attitudes, and motivational levels that differ significantly from those of the traditional college student. This text, because it was written specifically for developmental students, uses approaches, methodology, and reading materials that address these characteristics. This text adopts an encouraging, supportive, nonthreatening voice and an unassuming attitude toward learning. The text provides a variety of everyday examples and extensive exercises to encourage students to become involved and to apply the skills presented. The chapters are divided into numerous sections; exercises are frequent, but brief and explicit. The language and style are simple and direct; explanations are clear and often presented in step-by-step form. Reading topics and materials have been chosen carefully to relate to the

students' interests and background, while exhibiting potential for broadening their range of experience. Many developmental students have compensated for poor reading skills with alternate learning styles; they have become visual and auditory learners. To capitalize on this, a visual approach to learning, including drawings, diagrams, and visual aids to illustrate concepts, is used throughout the text.

The text is organized into six major sections, following the logical progression of skill development from words to sentences and then to paragraphs, articles, essays, and chapters. It also proceeds logically from literal comprehension to critical interpretation and reaction. Part One presents basic approaches to vocabulary development, including contextual aids, analysis of word parts, pronunciation, and the use of the dictionary and other reference sources. Part Two, "Strategies for Active Reading," emphasizes prereading techniques that prepare and enable the student to comprehend and to recall content. Concentration, previewing, activating background knowledge, and using guide questions are emphasized. This unit also contains a chapter on comprehension monitoring. The student is shown how to recognize comprehension signals, how to assess his or her comprehension, and how to strengthen it. Part Three is concerned with the development of literal comprehension skills. It provides extensive instruction and practice with sentence and paragraph comprehension and recognition of thought patterns. Part Four deals with skills for reading lengthy units of material—articles, essays, and textbook chapters. Here the emphasis is on recognition and use of organization and structure as a guide to effective reading and review. Critical reading and thinking are the focus of Part Five; it is concerned with the interpretive and analytical skills students need in order to interact with and evaluate written material. Each of these sections concludes with a unit titled "Making Your Skills Work Together" that integrates the skills taught in the section and provides reinforcement and application. Part Six, "Reading Selections," contains thirty articles, essays, and textbook excerpts chosen on the basis of interest and applicability to skills taught in the text. Each selection is prefaced by an interest-catching introduction, a vocabulary preview, and a previewing question. Literal and critical questions as well as a words-in-context exercise and vocabulary review follow each selection.

Several current methodological and pedagogical emphases are prevelant throughout the text. The integration of reading and writing skills is one major emphasis. Students are called upon to respond to exercises by writing sentences and paragraphs. Answers to most questions for each reading selection also require composition. Another emphasis is the treatment of reading as a thinking process—a process in which the student interacts with textual material and sorts, evaluates, and reacts to its organization and content. Students, for example, are shown how to define their purpose for reading, ask questions, identify and use organization and structure as a guide to understanding, make inferences, and interpret and evaluate what

they read. Comprehension monitoring is also addressed within the text. Through a variety of techniques, students are encouraged to be aware of and to evaluate and control their level of comprehension of the material they read.

Numerous changes and additions have been made in the second edition. Ten new reading selections were added on topics of current interest, including AIDS, stress management, and environmental protection. Part Two, "Strategies for Active Reading," contains two new chapters that emphasize reading as a thinking process. Chapter 4 discusses prereading strategies, including previewing, activating background knowledge, and developing guide questions. Chapter 5 introduces comprehension monitoring; students are taught to recognize positive and negative comprehension signals and several monitoring techniques are presented. A section on mapping as a visual means of organizing information has been added to Chapter 11. The chapter on sentence patterns has been revised to place more emphasis on strategies for reading complicated sentences. A section titled "Types of Supporting Details" has been added to Chapter 7. Additional exercises have been provided in Chapters 1, 2, 7, 8, and 12.

An Instructor's Manual, including an Answer Key, accompanies the text. Chapter Review Quizzes, each consisting of ten multiple choice items, are provided. The manual also describes in detail the basic features of the text and offers suggestions for structuring the course, for teaching developmental students, and for approaching each section of the text. Collaborative learning activities are suggested for each chapter.

I wish to express my gratitude to my reviewers for their excellent ideas, suggestions, and advice on the development of this text: Donna Wood, State Technical Institutes, Memphis, Tennessee; Miriam Walker, Eastern New Mexico University; Carolyn Scherm, West Georgia College; Lillian Lemke, Kean College; David Worley, Lincoln Memorial University; Gary Brown, San Diego State University; and Kathryn Welsch, Western Michigan University. My editor, Joseph Opiela, deserves special recognition and thanks for the guidance, support, and encouragement he has provided.

To the Student

College is very different from any other type of educational experience. It is different from high school, job training programs, adult education, or technical training programs. New and different types of learning are demanded, and you need new skills and techniques to meet these demands.

Here are a few statements about college. Treat them like a quiz, if you wish. Decide whether each statement is true or false, and write *T* for True or *F* for False in the space provided. Each statement will make you think about the reading and study demands of college. Check your answers by reading the paragraph following each item. As you work through this quiz, you will find out a little about what is expected of you in college. You will see whether or not you have an accurate picture of what college work involves. You will also see how this text will help you to become a better, more successful student.

_____ 1. For every hour I spend in class, I should spend one hour studying outside of class.
False. Many students feel that even one hour for each class (or fifteen hours per week for students carrying a fifteen credit-hour load) is a lot. Actually, the rule of thumb used by many instructors is two hours of study for each class hour. So you can see that you are expected to do a great deal of reading, studying, and learning on your own time.

THIS TEXT IS WRITTEN TO HELP YOU READ
AND LEARN IN THE EASIEST AND BEST WAY.

_____ 2. I should expect to read about 80 textbook pages per week in each of my courses.

True. A survey of freshman courses at one college indicated that the average course assignment was roughly eighty pages per week. This may seem like a lot of reading—and it is.

THIS TEXT WILL BUILD YOUR READING SKILLS TO HANDLE THIS TASK. IT WILL SUGGEST TECHNIQUES FOR UNDERSTANDING AND REMEMBERING WHAT YOU READ, IMPROVING YOUR CONCENTRATION, AND HANDLING DIFFICULT READING ASSIGNMENTS.

_____ 3. There are a lot of words I don't know, but my vocabulary is about as good as it needs to be.

False. For each college course you take, there will be new words to learn. Some will be everyday words; others will be specialized or technical.

PART ONE OF THIS BOOK WILL SHOW HOW TO DEVELOP YOUR VOCABULARY BY LEARNING NEW WORDS, FIGURING OUT WORDS YOU DON'T KNOW, AND USING REFERENCE SOURCES.

_____ 4. College instructors will tell me exactly what to learn for each exam.

False. College instructors seldom tell you exactly what to learn or review. They expect you to decide what is important and to learn that information.

PART THREE OF THIS TEXT WILL SHOW YOU HOW TO IDENTIFY WHAT IS IMPORTANT IN PARAGRAPHS, PASSAGES, ARTICLES, ESSAYS AND TEXTBOOK CHAPTERS.

_____ 5. The more facts I memorize, the higher my exam grades will be.

False. Learning a large amount of facts is no guarantee of a high grade in a course. Some instructors and the exams they give are concerned with your ability to see how facts and ideas fit together, or to evaluate ideas, make comparisons, and recognize trends.

PARTS THREE AND FOUR OF THIS TEXT WILL

SHOW YOU HOW TO ORGANIZE AND SEE RELA-
TIONSHIPS AMONG FACTS AND IDEAS.

_____ 6. The only assignments that instructors give are readings in the textbook.

False. Instructors often assign readings in a variety of sources including periodicals, newspapers, and reference and library books. These readings are intended to add to the information presented in your text and by your instructor.

PART FOUR OF THIS TEXT DISCUSSES HOW TO READ ARTICLES AND ESSAYS BY SHOWING YOU HOW THEY ARE ORGANIZED AND DISCUSSING THE MOST COMMON TYPES. PART SIX CONTAINS THIRTY READING SELECTIONS FOR PRACTICE AND SKILL APPLICATION.

_____ 7. Rereading a textbook chapter is the best way to prepare for an exam on that chapter.

False. Reading is actually one of the poorest ways to review. Besides, it's often dull and time consuming.

PART FOUR OF THIS TEXT PRESENTS FOUR MORE EFFECTIVE ALTERNATIVES: UNDERLINING AND MARKING, OUTLINING, MAPPING, AND SUMMARIZING.

_____ 8. College instructors expect me to react to, evaluate, and criticize what I read.

True. Beyond understanding the content of textbooks, articles, and essays, instructors also want their students to be able to criticize and evaluate ideas.

PART FIVE OF THIS TEXT WILL SHOW YOU HOW TO INTERPRET WHAT YOU READ, FIND THE AUTHOR'S PURPOSE, AND ASK CRITICAL QUESTIONS.

_____ 9. The best way to read a textbook assignment is to turn to the correct page, start reading, and continue reading until it is finished.

False. There are numerous things you can do before you read, while you read, and after you read that can improve your comprehension and retention.

PART TWO OF THIS TEXT DISCUSSES HOW TO BUILD YOUR CONCENTRATION, PREVIEW AND THINK ABOUT WHAT YOU WILL READ, AND USE

QUESTIONS TO GUIDE YOUR READING. PART FOUR DISCUSSES TECHNIQUES TO USE AFTER YOU READ TO STRENGTHEN COMPREHENSION AND RECALL.

———— 10. You can never know whether you have understood a textbook reading assignment until you take an exam on the chapter.
False. As you read, it is possible and important to keep track of and evaluate your level of understanding.
PART TWO OF THIS TEXT WILL SHOW YOU HOW TO MONITOR YOUR COMPREHENSION. YOU WILL ALSO LEARN TO RECOGNIZE COMPREHENSION SIGNALS AND HOW TO STRENGTHEN YOUR COMPREHENSION.

By analyzing the above statements and the correct responses, you can see that college is a lot of work, much of which you must do on your own. However, college is also a new, exciting experience that will acquaint you with new ideas and opportunities.

This text is written to help you get the most out of college and to take advantage of the opportunities it offers. Its purpose is to equip beginning college students with the reading skills necessary for academic success.

The text is organized into five instructional units: Part One: Vocabulary; Part Two: Strategies for Active Reading; Part Three: Comprehension; Part Four: Comprehension and Retention; and Part Five: Critical Reading and Thinking. A sixth unit, made up of thirty reading selections, gives you an opportunity to apply and practice skills using a wide range of articles, essays, and textbook excerpts.

The text contains numerous features to help you learn and to become a more successful student. These include:

- Numerous practical situations and everyday examples to explain techniques and help you maintain interest

- Diagrams and drawings to help you visualize how reading material is organized

- Numerous exercises to enable you to try out new techniques

- A chapter on how to monitor (keep track of) your own comprehension and learning

- A special section at the end of each unit, "Making Your Skills Work Together," that helps you combine and apply your skills

- An emphasis on reading as a thinking process—as a way of processing and sorting information

· A section on "Reading Technical Material"

· An integration of reading and writing skills—as you learn skills for reading, you see how that can help you become a better writer

· A section on "Mapping"—a visual means of organizing information

The opportunity of college lies ahead of you. The skills this text provides, along with plenty of hard work, will make your college experience a meaningful and valuable one.

Contents

Guide to
COLLEGE
READING

PART ONE

VOCABULARY:
The Key to Meaning

Joe and Sal were both taking a sociology course. Joe was doing well in the course, but Sal was not. In particular, Sal was having trouble with the vocabulary in the textbook. He complained, "I can't even pronounce some of these words, much less know what they mean! There are so many words I don't know that I can't look them all up. And to make things worse, the instructor uses these same words on exams."

Sal asked Joe if he were having the same trouble. Joe agreed that there were many new and difficult words, but he said he had worked out a way of handling them. He figured out the meanings of many words from the way they were used in a sentence. He also used word parts to figure out meanings. To pronounce hard words, he broke the words into syllables. Then he used a dictionary to check meanings or pronunciations of which he was unsure.

Joe has acquired a set of skills that are helping him to handle the vocabulary in college courses. These skills help him improve his overall, everyday vocabulary as well.

Vocabulary development is a skill worth the effort to improve. Your vocabulary affects not only your reading skills, but your speaking, listening, and writing skills as well. In speaking, the words you choose affect how well you are understood, the impression you make, and how people react to you. In writing, your vocabulary determines how clearly and accurately you can express your ideas to others. In listening, your vocabulary influences how much you understand in class lectures, speeches, and class discussions.

THIS PART OF THE TEXT WILL HELP YOU IMPROVE YOUR VOCABULARY SO THAT

1. You will be able to use several types of context clues to figure out the meanings of words you do not know. (Chapter 1)

2. You will be able to add words to your vocabulary by learning word parts. (Chapter 2)

3. You will be able to use a dictionary easily and rapidly. (Chapter 3)

4. You will know how to pronounce unfamiliar words. (Chapter 3)

5. You will be able to start and use a card system for learning new words. (Chapter 3)

Chapter 1

USING CONTEXT CLUES

THIS CHAPTER WILL SHOW YOU HOW TO

1. Figure out the meanings of words from their use in a sentence

2. Use four types of context clues

WHAT IS CONTEXT?

Read the following brief paragraph. Several words are missing. Try to figure out the missing words and write them in the blanks.

Most Americans can speak only one _____. Europeans, however, _____ several. As a result, Europeans think _____ are unfriendly and unwilling to communicate with them.

Did you insert the word *language* in the first blank, *speak* or *know* in the second blank, and *Americans* in the third blank? Most likely, you correctly identified all three missing words. You could tell from the sentence what word to put in. The words around the missing words (the sentence context) gave you clues to what word would fit and make sense. Such clues are called context clues.

While you are unlikely to find missing words on a printed page, you will often find words that you do not know. Context clues can help you to figure out the meanings of unfamiliar words.

Example:

> **Phobias**, such as fear of heights, water, or confined spaces, are difficult to eliminate.

From the sentence, you can tell that *phobias* means "fears of specific objects or situations."

Here's another example:

> The couple finally **secured** a table at the popular, crowded restaurant.

You can figure out that *secured* means "got or took ownership of" the table.

TYPES OF CONTEXT CLUES

There are four types of context clues to look for: (1) definition, (2) example, (3) contrast, and (4) inference.

Definition Clues

Many times a writer defines a word, directly or indirectly, immediately following its use. The writer may define a word directly by giving a brief definition or providing a synonym (a word that has the same meaning). Such words and phrases as *means, is, refers to*, and *can be defined as* are often used. Here are some examples:

> **Induction** refers to the <u>process of reasoning from the known to the unknown</u>.

> A **markdown** is a <u>reduction in the original selling price of a product</u>.

At other times, rather than formally define the word, a writer may provide clues or synonyms. Punctuation is often used to signal that a definition clue to a word's meaning is to follow. Punctuation also separates the meaning clue from the rest of the sentence. Three types of punctuation are used in this way. In the examples below, notice that the meaning clue is separated from the remainder of the sentence by punctuation.

1. Commas

   > <u>Contracts</u>, or enforceable, written agreements between two or more parties form the basis of civil law.

   > Hypochondria, <u>excessive worry over one's health</u>, is common among senior citizens.

2. Parentheses

The dynamo (an early form of the generator) was on display at the museum.

Some stores offer loss leaders (products on which the stores lose money) to gain new customers.

3. Dashes

Probability—the likelihood that an event will occur—is important in the field of statistics.

Myopia—nearsightedness—can cause a person to fail the vision test required to obtain a driver's license.

EXERCISE 1-1

Directions: *Read each sentence and write a definition or synonym for each boldface word or phrase. Use the definition context clue to help you determine word meaning.*

1. **Glogg**, a Swedish hot punch, is often served at holiday parties.

   _____

2. The judge's **candor**—his sharp, open frankness—shocked the jury.

   _____

3. A **chemical bond** is a strong attractive force that holds two or more atoms together.

   _____

4. **Lithium** (an alkali metal) is so soft it can be cut with a knife.

   _____

5. Hearing, technically known as **audition**, begins when a sound wave reaches the outer ear.

   _____

6. Five-line rhyming poems, or **limericks**, are among the simplest forms of poetry.

   _____

7. Our country's **gross national product**—the total market value of its national output of goods and services—is increasing steadily.

   _____

8. A **species** is a group of animals or plants that share similar characteristics and are able to interbreed.

_____

9. Broad, flat noodles that are served covered with sauce or butter are referred to as **fettucine**.

_____

10. Many diseases have **latent periods**, periods of time between the infection and the first appearance of a symptom.

_____

Example Clues

Writers often include examples that help to explain or clarify a word. Suppose you do not know the meaning of the word *toxic*, and you find it used in the following sentence:

> **Toxic** materials, such as arsenic, asbestos, pesticides, and lead, can cause bodily damage.

This sentence gives four examples of toxic materials. From the examples given, which are all poisonous substances, you could conclude that *toxic* means "poisonous."

Examples:

> **Unconditioned responses**, including heartbeat, blinking, and breathing, occur naturally in all humans.

> Mark experienced several **traumas** in early childhood, including the divorce of his parents and the death of his grandmother.

> Various **Slavic** languages, including Russian, Ukrainian, Polish, and Czech, are spoken in Toronto's ethnic districts.

> **Overt behaviors**—crying, laughing, or screaming—are sometimes misunderstood unless the motives behind them are learned.

EXERCISE 1-2

Directions: *Read each sentence and write a definition or synonym for each boldface word or phrase. Use the example context clue to help you determine meaning.*

1. Many **pharmaceuticals**, including morphine and penicillin, are not readily available in some countries.

_____

2. The child was **reticent** in every respect; she would not speak, refused to answer questions, and avoided looking at anyone.

   _____

3. Most **condiments**, such as pepper, mustard, and catsup, are used to improve the flavor of foods.

   _____

4. Instructors provide their students with **feedback** through test grades and comments on papers.

   _____

5. **Physiological needs**—hunger, thirst, and sex—promote survival of the human species.

   _____

6. Clothing is available in a variety of **fabrics**, including cotton, wool, polyester, and linen.

   _____

7. In the past month, we have had almost every type of **precipitation** —rain, snow, sleet, and hail.

   _____

8. **Involuntary reflexes**, like breathing and heartbeat, are easily measured.

   _____

9. The student had a difficult time distinguishing between **homonyms** —words such as *see* and *sea*, *wore* and *war*, and *deer* and *dear*.

   _____

10. Abstract paintings often include such **geometrics** as squares, cubes, and triangles.

    _____

Contrast Clues

It is sometimes possible to determine the meaning of an unknown word from a word or phrase in the context that has an opposite meaning. Notice, in the following sentence, how a word opposite in meaning from the boldface word provides a clue to its meaning:

One of the dinner guests **succumbed** to the temptation to have a second piece of cake, but the others resisted.

Although you may not know the meaning of *succumbed*, you know that the one guest who succumbed was different from the others who resisted. The word *but* suggests this. Since the others resisted a second dessert, you can tell that the one guest gave in and had one. Thus, *succumbed* means the opposite of *resist*.

Examples:

During the ceremony, the graduates were quiet, but afterward they became **boisterous**.

I **loathe** dogs even though most of my family loves them.

The student **ironically** called the test simple, but the rest of the class really believed it was simple.

All of the furniture in the dining room seemed dull and unpolished except the china cabinet, which had quite a **luster** to it.

EXERCISE 1-3

Directions: *Read each sentence and write a definition or synonym for each boldface word. Use the contrast clue to help you determine meaning.*

1. Some city dwellers are **affluent**; others live in or near poverty.

   _____

2. I am certain that the hotel will hold our reservation, but if you are **dubious**, call to make sure.

   _____

3. Although most experts **concurred** with the research findings, several strongly disagreed.

   _____

4. The speaker **denounced** certain legal changes but praised other reforms.

   _____

5. The woman's parents **thwarted** her marriage plans but encouraged her to leave home.

   _____

6. In medieval Europe, **peasants** led difficult lives, whereas the wealthy landowners lived in luxury.

   _____

7. When the couple moved into their new home they **revamped** the kitchen and bathroom, but did not change the rest of the rooms.

_____

8. The young nurse was **bewildered** by the patient's symptoms, but the doctor realized she was suffering from a rare form of leukemia.

_____

9. My husband was **pessimistic** about my chances of winning the lottery, but I was certain I would win.

_____

10. The mayoral candidate praised the town council, while the mayor **deprecated** it.

_____

Inference Clues

Many times you can figure out the meaning of an unknown word by using logic and reasoning skills. For instance, look at the following sentence:

Bob is quite **versatile**; he is a good student, a top athlete, an excellent car mechanic, and a gourmet cook.

You can see that Bob is successful at many different types of activities, and you could reason that *versatile* means "capable of doing many things competently."

Examples:

An **unscrupulous** shop owner tried to sell as an antique a glass vase that had been made last year.

After I sampled six different types of pizza, my appetite was completely **satiated**.

In order to **economize**, he decided to begin doing his own car repairs.

If the child was not so **gullible**, I could not have convinced him that the moon is made of cheese.

EXERCISE 1-4

Directions: *Read each sentence and write a definition or synonym for each boldface word. Try to reason out the meaning of each word using information provided in the context.*

1. The **wallabies** at the zoo looked like kangaroos.

   _____

2. The foreign students quickly **assimilated** many aspects of American culture.

   _____

3. On hot, humid summer afternoons, I often feel **languid**.

   _____

4. Some physical fitness experts recommend jogging or weight lifting to overcome the effects of a **sedentary** job.

   _____

5. The legal aid clinic was **subsidized** by city and county funds.

   _____

6. When the bank robber reached his **haven**, he breathed a sigh of relief and began to count his money.

   _____

7. The teenager was **intimidated** by the policeman walking the beat and decided not to spray paint the school wall.

   _____

8. The vase must have been **jostled** in shipment because it arrived with several chips in it.

   _____

9. Although she had visited the fortune teller several times, she was not sure she believed in the **occult**.

   _____

10. If the plan did not work, the colonel had a **contingency** plan ready.

    _____

EXERCISE 1-5

Directions: *Read each sentence and write a definition or synonym for each boldface word. Use the context clue to help you determine meaning.*

1. The economy was in a state of continual **flux**; inflation increased one month and decreased the next.

   _____

2. The grand jury **exonerated** the police officer of any possible misconduct or involvement in illegal activity.

   _____

3. Art is always talkative, but Ed is usually **taciturn**.

   _____

4. Many **debilities** of old age, including poor eyesight and loss of hearing, can be treated medically.

   _____

5. Police **interrogation**, or questioning, can be a frightening experience.

   _____

6. The soap opera contained numerous **morbid** events: the death of a young child, the suicide of her father, and the murder of an older brother.

   _____

7. Peter, who spent long hours in exhausting practice, finally learned to type; Sam's efforts, however, were **futile**.

   _____

8. Although the farm appeared **derelict**, we discovered that an elderly man lived there.

   _____

9. The newspaper's error was **inadvertent**; the editor did not intend to include the victim's name.

   _____

10. To save money, we have decided to **curtail** the number of tapes we buy each month.

    _____

11. The mechanic **scalded** his hand from water or steam released from the hot radiator.

    _____

12. The businesswoman's **itinerary** outlined her trip and listed Cleveland as her next stop.

    _____

13. **Theologies**, such as Catholicism, Buddhism, and Hinduism, are discussed at great length in the class.

    _____

14. Steven had very good **rapport** with his father, but was unable to get along well with his mother.

_____

15. The duchess had a way of **flaunting** her jewels so that everyone could see and envy them.

_____

EXERCISE 1-6

Directions: *Read each of the following passages and use context clues to figure out the meaning of each boldface word or phrase. Write a synonym or brief definition for each in the space provided.*

Can looking at a color affect your behavior or **alter** your mood? Some researchers are **skeptical**, but others believe color can influence how you act and feel. A number of experiments have been conducted that **demonstrate** the effects of color. In 1979 a psychologist named Schauss **evaluated** the effect of the color pink. He found that the color relaxed the subjects so much that they could not perform simple strength tests as well as they did when looking at other **hues**. The officer in charge of a U.S. Navy **brig** in Washington noticed Schauss's findings and allowed Schauss to test his calm-color **hypothesis** on inmates. Today, many **institutions**, such as jails, juvenile correction facilities, and holding centers, put individuals in pink rooms when their tempers **flare**.

No one is certain how color affects behavior. Schauss **conjectures** that a person's response to color is determined in the brain's **reticular formation**, a relay station for millions of the body's nerve impulses. Another researcher **speculates** that **perception** of color by the eye **spurs** the release of important chemicals in the body.

alter _____

skeptical _____

demonstrate _____

evaluated _____

hues _____

brig _____

hypothesis _____

institutions _____

flare _____

conjectures _____

reticular formation _____

speculates _____

perception _____

spurs _____

The most important set of symbols is language. **Language**, among humans, refers to the systematized usage of speech and hearing to convey or express feelings and ideas. It is through language that our ideas, values, beliefs, and knowledge are **transmitted**, expressed, and shared. Other **media** such as music, art, and dance are also important means of communication, but language is uniquely flexible and precise. It permits us to share our experiences in the past and present, to **convey** our hopes for the future, and to describe dreams and fantasies that may bear little **resemblance** to reality. Some scientists have questioned whether thought is even possible without language. Although language can be used **imprecisely** and seem hard to understand, it is the chief factor in our ability to transmit culture.

language _____

transmitted _____

media _____

convey _____

resemblance _____

imprecisely _____

Social norms are another element of culture. **Norms** are rules of conduct or social expectations for behavior. These rules and social expectations **specify** how people should and should not behave in various social situations. They are both **prescriptive** (they tell people what they should do) and **proscriptive** (they tell people what they should not do). . . .

An early American sociologist, William G. Sumner (1840–1910), identified two types of norms, which he labelled "folkways" and "mores." They are **distinguished** not by their content, but by the degree to which group members are **compelled** to conform to them, by their degree of importance, by the **severity** of punishment if they are violated, or by the intensity of feeling associated with adherence to them. Folkways are customs or conventions. They are norms in that they provide rules for conduct, but violations of folkways bring only mild censure. . . .

Mores are considered more important than folkways, and reactions to their **violation** are more serious. They are more likely than folkways to involve clear-cut distinctions between right and wrong, and they are more closely associated with the values a society considers important.

norms _____

specify _____

prescriptive _____

proscriptive _____

distinguished _____

compelled _____

severity _____

violation _____

THE LIMITATIONS OF CONTEXT CLUES

There are two limitations to the use of context clues. First, context clues seldom lead to a complete definition. Second, sometimes a sentence does not contain clues to a word's meaning. In these cases you will need to draw upon other vocabulary skills. Chapters 2 and 3 will provide you with these skills.

SUMMARY

One way to figure out the meaning of an unknown word is to use context clues—to study the way the word is used in the sentence and paragraph in which it is found. The four types of context clues discussed in this chapter were as follows:

- Definition—a brief definition of or synonym for a word
- Example—specific instances or examples that clarify a word's meaning
- Contrast—a word or phrase of opposite meaning
- Inference—the use of reasoning skills to figure out word meanings

Chapter 2

RECOGNIZING THE STRUCTURE OF WORDS

THIS CHAPTER WILL SHOW YOU HOW TO

1. **Figure out words you do not know**

2. **Use prefixes, roots, and suffixes**

USING WORD PARTS TO EXPAND YOUR VOCABULARY

Suppose that you came across the following sentence in a human anatomy textbook:

Trichromatic plates are used frequently in the text to illustrate the position of body organs.

If you did not know the meaning of *trichromatic*, how could you determine it? There are no clues in the sentence context. One solution is to look the word up in a dictionary. An easier and faster way is to break the word into parts and analyze the meanings of the parts. Many words in the English language are made up of word parts called prefixes, roots, and suffixes. These word parts have specific meanings that, when added together, can help you determine the meaning of the word as a whole.

The word *trichromatic* can be divided into three parts, its prefix, root, and suffix.

- Prefix—tri- ("three")

- Root—chrome ("color")

- Suffix—-atic ("characteristic of")

You can see from this analysis that *trichromatic* means "having three colors."

Here are a few other examples of words that you can figure out by using prefixes, roots, and suffixes:

> The parents thought the child was **unteachable**.
> un- = not
> teach = help someone learn
> -able = able to do something
> unteachable = not able to be taught

> The student was a **nonconformist**.
> non- = not
> conform = go along with others
> -ist = one who does something
> nonconformist = someone who does not go along with others

The first step in using the prefix-root-suffix method is to become familiar with the most commonly used word parts. The prefixes and roots listed in Tables 2-1 and 2-2 will give you a good start in determining the meanings of thousands of words without looking them up in the dictionary. For instance, more than 10,000 words can begin with the prefix non-. Not all these words are listed in a collegiate dictionary, but they would appear in an unabridged dictionary (see Chapter 3). Another common prefix, *pseudo-*, is used in more than 400 words. A small amount of time spent learning word parts can yield a large payoff in new words learned.

Before you begin to use word parts to figure out new words, there are a few things you need to know:

1. In most cases, a word is built upon at least one root.

2. Words can have more than one prefix, root, or suffix.
   a. Words can be made up of two or more roots (geo/logy).
   b. Some words have two prefixes (in/sub/ordination).
   c. Some words have two suffixes (beauti/ful/ly).

3. Words do not always have a prefix and a suffix.
   a. Some words have neither a prefix nor a suffix (read).
   b. Others have a suffix but no prefix (read/ing).
   c. Others have a prefix but no suffix (pre/read).

4. Roots may change in spelling as they are combined with suffixes. Some common variations are included in Table 2-2.

Table 2-1 COMMON PREFIXES

Prefix	Meaning	Sample Word
Prefixes referring to amount or number		
bi	two	bimonthly
centi	hundred	centigrade
deci	ten	decimal
equi	equal	equidistant
micro	small	microscope
milli	thousand	milligram
mono	one	monocle
multi	many	multipurpose
poly	many	polygon
semi	half	semicircle
tri	three	triangle
uni	one	unicycle
Prefixes meaning "not" (Negative)		
a	not	asymmetrical
anti	against	antiwar
contra	against, opposite	contradict
dis	apart, away, not	disagree
in/il/ir/im	not	illogical
mis	wrongly	misunderstand
non	not	nonfiction
un	not	unpopular
pseudo	false	pseudoscientific
Prefixes giving direction, location, or placement		
circum	around	circumference
com/col/con	with, together	compile
de	away, from	depart
ex/extra	from, out of, former	ex-wife
hyper	over, excessive	hyperactive
inter	between	interpersonal
intro/intra	within, into, in	introduction
post	after	posttest
pre	before	premarital
re	back, again	review
retro	backward	retrospect
sub	under, below	submarine
super	above, extra	supercharge
tele	far	telescope
trans	across, over	transcontinental

Table 2-2 COMMON ROOTS

Root	Meaning	Sample Word
aud/audit	hear	audible
aster/astro	star	astronaut
bio	life	biology
cap	take, seize	captive
chron(o)	time	chronology
corp	body	corpse
cred	believe	incredible
dict/dic	tell, say	predict
duc/duct	lead	introduce
fact/fac	make, do	factory
graph	write	telegraph
geo	earth	geophysics
log/logo/logy	study, thought	psychology
mit/miss	send	dismiss
mort/mor	die, death	immortal
path	feeling	sympathy
phono	sound, voice	telephone
photo	light	photosensitive
port	carry	transport
scop	seeing	microscope
scrib/script	write	inscription
sen/sent	feel	insensitive
spec/spic/spect	look, see	retrospect
tend/tent/tens	stretch or strain	tension
terr/terre	land, earth	territory
theo	god	theology
ven/vent	come	convention
vert/vers	turn	invert
vis/vid	see	invisible
voc	call	vocation

5. Sometimes, you may identify a group of letters as a prefix or root but find that it does not carry the meaning of the prefix or root. For example, in the word *internal*, the letters *inter* should not be confused with the prefix *inter-*, meaning "between." Similarly, the letters *mis* in the word *missile* are part of the root and are not the prefix *mis-*, which means "wrong; bad."

PREFIXES

Prefixes appear at the beginnings of many English words. They alter the meaning of the root to which they are connected. In Table 2-1, thirty-six common prefixes are grouped according to meaning.

EXERCISE 2-1

Directions: *Use the list of common prefixes in Table 2-1 to determine the meaning of each of the following words. Write a brief definition or synonym for each. If you are unfamiliar with the root, you may need to check a dictionary.*

1. interoffice _____
2. supernatural _____
3. nonsense _____
4. introspection _____
5. prearrange _____
6. reset _____
7. subtropic _____
8. transmit _____
9. multidimensional _____
10. imperfect _____

EXERCISE 2-2

Directions: *Write a synonym for each word in heavier type (boldface).*

1. an **atypical** child _____
2. to **hyperventilate** _____
3. an **extraordinary** request _____
4. **semisoft** cheese _____
5. **antisocial** behavior _____
6. to **circumnavigate** the globe _____
7. a **triweekly** delivery _____
8. an **uneventful** weekend _____
9. a **disfigured** face _____
10. to **exhale** smoke _____

EXERCISE 2-3

Directions: *Read each of the following sentences. Use your knowledge of prefixes to complete the incomplete word.*

1. A text titled *Botany* was _____ titled *Understanding Plants*.

2. The politician delivered his speech in a dull _____ tone.

3. The new sweater had a snag, and I returned it to the store because it was _____ perfect.

4. The flood damage was permanent and _____ reversible.

5. I was not given the correct date and time; I was _____ informed.

6. People who speak several different languages are _____ lingual.

7. A musical _____ lude was played between the events in the ceremony.

8. I decided the magazine was uninteresting, so I _____ continued my subscription.

9. Merchandise that does not pass factory inspection is considered _____ standard and sold at a discount.

10. The tuition refund policy approved this week will apply to last year's tuition as well; the policy will be _____ active to January 1 of last year.

11. The elements were _____ acting with each other when they began to bubble and their temperature rose.

12. _____ ceptives are widely used to prevent unwanted pregnancies.

13. All of the waitresses were required to wear the restaurant's _____- form.

14. The _____ viewer asked the presidential candidates unexpected questions about important issues.

15. The draperies were _____ colored from long exposure to the sun.

EXERCISE 2-4

Directions: *Use your knowledge of prefixes to figure out the missing word in each sentence. Write the word in the space provided.*

1. Our house is a duplex. The one next door with three apartments is a _____.

2. A preparation applied to the skin to reduce or prevent perspiration is called an _____.

3. A person who cannot read or write is called _____.

4. I did not use my real name; instead I gave a _____.

5. If someone seems to have greater powers than do normal humans, he or she might be called _____ .

6. A friend who criticizes you too often without reason is _____ .

7. If you plan to continue to take college courses after you graduate, you would be taking _____ courses.

8. Substances that fight bacteria are known as _____ drugs.

9. The branch of biology that deals with very small living organisms is _____ .

10. In the metric system a(an) _____ is one one–hundredth of a meter.

11. One one–thousandth of a second is called a _____ .

12. The tape showed an instant _____ of the touchdown.

13. A disabling physical handicap is often called a _____ .

ROOTS

Roots carry the basic or core meaning of a word. Hundreds of root words are used to build words in the English language. Thirty of the most common and most useful are listed in Table 2-2. Knowledge of the meanings of these roots will enable you to unlock the meanings of many words. For example, if you know that the root *dic/dict* means "tell or say," then you would have a clue to the meanings of such words as *dictate* (speak for someone to write down), *dictation* (words spoken to be written down), and diction (wording or manner of speaking).

EXERCISE 2-5

Directions: *Use the list of common roots in Table 2-2 to determine the meanings of the following words. Write a brief definition or synonym for each, checking a dictionary if necessary.*

1. dictaphone _____

2. biomedicine _____

3. photocopy _____

4. porter _____

5. visibility _____

6. credentials _____

7. speculate _____

8. terrain _____

9. audition _____

10. sentiment _____

11. astrophysics _____

12. capacity _____

13. chronicle _____

14. corporation _____

15. facile _____

16. autograph _____

17. sociology _____

18. phonometer _____

19. sensation _____

20. vocal _____

21. geography _____

22. portable _____

23. asteroid _____

24. versatile _____

25. visionary _____

EXERCISE 2-6

Directions: *Complete each of the following sentences with one of the words listed below.*

apathetic	extensive	prescribed	tendon
captivated	extraterrestrial	scriptures	verdict
deduce	graphic	spectators	visualize
dictated	phonics	synchronized	

1. The jury brought in its _____ after one hour of deliberation.

2. Religious or holy writings are called _____.

3. She closed her eyes and tried to _____ the license plate number.

4. The _____ watching the football game were tense.

5. The doctor _____ two types of medication.

6. The child's list of toys he wanted for his birthday was _____.

7. The criminal appeared _____ when the judge pronounced sentence.

8. The runners _____ their watches before beginning the race.

9. The textbook contained numerous _____ aids, including maps, charts, and diagrams.

10. The study of the way different parts of words sound is _____.

11. The athlete strained a(n) _____ and was unable to continue training.

12. The movie was about a(n) _____, a creature not from earth.

13. The district manager _____ a letter to her secretary who then typed it.

14. Through his attention—grabbing performance, he _____ the audience.

15. By putting together the clues, the detective was finally able to _____ who committed the crime.

SUFFIXES

Suffixes are word endings that often change the part of speech of a word. For example, adding the suffix *y* to the noun *cloud* produces the adjective *cloudy*. Accompanying the change in part of speech is a shift in meaning. (*Cloudy* means "resembling clouds; overcast with clouds; dimmed or dulled as if by clouds.")

Often, several different words can be formed from a single root word with the addition of different suffixes.

Examples:

Root: class
root + suffix = class/ify, class/ification, class/ic

Root: right
root + suffix = right/ly, right/ful, right/ist, right/eous

If you know the meaning of the root word and the ways in which different suffixes affect the meaning of the root word, you will be able to figure out a word's meaning when a suffix is added. A list of common suffixes and their meanings appears in Table 2-3.

You can expand your vocabulary significantly by learning the variations in meaning that occur when suffixes are added to words you already know. When you find a word that you do not know, look for the root word. Then, using the sentence the word is in (called its context; see Chapter 1), figure out what the word means with the suffix added. Occasionally you may find that the spelling of the root word has been changed. For instance, a final *e* may be dropped, a final consonant may be doubled, or a final *y* may be changed to *i*. Consider the possibility of such changes when trying to identify the root word.

Table 2-3 COMMON SUFFIXES

Suffix	Sample Word
Suffixes that refer to a state, condition, or quality	
able	touchable
ance	assistance
ation	confrontation
ence	reference
ible	tangible
ion	discussion
ity	superiority
ive	permissive
ment	amazement
ness	kindness
ous	jealous
ty	loyalty
y	creamy
Suffixes that mean "one who"	
ee	tutee
eer	engineer
er	teacher
ist	activist
or	advisor
Suffixes that mean "pertaining to or referring to"	
al	autumnal
ship	friendship
hood	brotherhood
ward	homeward

Examples:

The article was a **compilation** of facts.
        root   + suffix
        compil(e) + -ation = something that has been compiled, or put
                                together into an orderly form

We were concerned with the **legality** of our decision to change addresses.
        root + suffix
        legal + -ity   = pertaining to legal matters

Our college is one of the most **prestigious** in the state.
        root   + suffix
        prestig(e) + -ious = having prestige or distinction

EXERCISE 2-7

Directions: *For each of the words listed, add a suffix so that the word will complete the sentence. Write the new word in the space provided. Check a dictionary if you are unsure of the spelling.*

1. converse
   Our phone _____ lasted ten minutes.

2. assist
   The medical _____ labeled the patient's blood samples.

3. qualify
   The job applicant outlined his_____ to the interviewer.

4. intern
   The doctor completed her _____ at Memorial Medical Center.

5. eat
   We did not realize that the blossoms of the plant could be
   _____.

6. audio
   She spoke so softly that she was not _____.

7. season
   It is usually very dry in July, but this year it has rained constantly. The weather isn't very _____.

8. permit
   The professor granted her _____ to miss class.

9. instruct
   The lecture on Freud was very _____.

10. remember
    The wealthy businessman donated the building in _____ of his deceased father.

11. mortal
    The _____ rate in Ethiopia is very high.

12. president
    The _____ race held many surprises.

13. feminine
    She called herself a _____, although she never actively supported the movement for equal rights for women.

14. hazard
    The presence of toxic waste in the lake is _____ to health.

15. destine
    The young man felt it was his _____ to become a priest.

EXERCISE 2-8

Directions: *For each word listed below, write as many new words as you can create by adding suffixes.*

1. compare _____

2. adapt _____

3. right _____

4. identify _____

5. will _____

6. prefer _____

7. notice _____

8. like _____

9. pay _____

10. promote _____

HOW TO USE WORD PARTS

Think of roots as being at the root or core of a word's meaning. There are many more roots than are listed in Table 2-2. You already know many of these, because they are everyday words. Think of prefixes as word parts that are added before the root to qualify or change its meaning. Think of suffixes as add-ons that make the word fit grammatically into the sentence in which it is used.

When you come upon a word you do not know, keep the following pointers in mind:

1. First, look for the root. Think of this as looking for a word inside a larger word. Often a letter or two will be missing.

Examples:	un/utter/able	post/operat/ive
	defens/ible	non/adapt/able
	inter/colleg/iate	im/measur/ability
	re/popular/ize	non/commit/tal

2. If you do not recognize the root, then you will probably not be able to figure out the word. The next step is to check its meaning in a dictionary. For tips on locating words in a dictionary rapidly and easily, see Chapter 3.

3. If you did recognize the root word, next look for a prefix. If there is one, determine how it changes the meaning of the word.

Examples:	un/utterable	post/operative
	un- = not	post- = after

4. Locate the suffix, if there is one, and determine how it further adds to or changes the meaning of the root word.

Examples:	unutter/able	postoperat/ive
	-able = able to	-ive = state or condition

5. Next, try out the meaning in the sentence in which the word was used. Substitute your meaning for the word and see whether the sentence makes sense.

   Examples: Some of the victim's thoughts were **unutterable** at the time of the crime.
   unutterable = not able to be spoken

   My sister was worried about the cost of **postoperative** care.
   postoperative = state or condition after an operation

EXERCISE 2-9

Directions: *Use the steps listed previously to determine the meaning of each boldface word. Circle the root in each word and then write a brief definition of the word that fits its use in the sentence.*

1. The doctor felt the results of the x-rays were **indisputable**.

   _____

2. The **dissimilarity** among the three brothers was surprising.

   _____

3. The **extortionist** demanded two payments of $10,000 each.

   _____

4. It is **permissible** to camp in most state parks.

   _____

5. The student had **retentive** abilities.

   _____

6. The **profiteer** was fined for failing to file an income tax return last year.

   _____

7. We were surprised by her **insincerity**.

   _____

8. The child's **oversensitivity** worried his parents.

   _____

9. The English instructor told Peter that he had written a **creditable** paper.

   _____

10. The rock group's agent hoped to **repopularize** their first hit song.

    _____

11. The gambler was filled with **uncertainty** about the horse race.

    _____

12. The **nonenforcement** of the speed limit led to many deaths.

    _____

13. The effects of the disease were **irreversible**.

    _____

14. The mysterious music seemed to **presignify** the murder of the movie's heroine.

    _____

15. The **polyphony** filled the concert hall.

_____

16. Sailors used to think the North Sea **unnavigable**.

_____

17. She received a **dishonorable** discharge from the Marines.

_____

18. The criminal was **unapologetic** to the judge about the crimes he had committed.

_____

19. A systems analysis revealed that the factory was **underproductive**.

_____

20. He rotated the dial **counterclockwise**.

_____

SUMMARY

When context does not give enough clues to the meaning of an unknown word, it is helpful to break the word into word parts. The beginnings, middles, and endings of words are called prefixes, roots, and suffixes. Learning the meanings of the most common prefixes, roots, and suffixes will provide a basis for analyzing thousands of English words.

Chapter 3

LEARNING NEW WORDS

THIS CHAPTER WILL SHOW YOU HOW TO

1. Use dictionaries and the thesaurus

2. Pronounce unfamiliar words

3. Develop a system for learning new words

Most people think they have just one level of vocabulary and that this can be characterized as high or low, strong or weak. Actually, everyone has at least four levels of vocabulary, and each varies in strength:

1. Words you use in everyday speech or writing

   Examples: decide, death, daughter, damp, date

2. Words you know but seldom or never use in your own speech or writing

   Examples: document, disregard, destination, demon, dense

3. Words you've heard or seen before but cannot define completely

   Examples: denounce, deficit, decadent, deductive, decisive

4. Words you've never heard or seen before

   Examples: doggerel, dogma, denigrate, deleterious, diatropism

In the spaces provided, list five words in each of these four categories. It will be easy to think of words for Category 1. Words for Categories 2–4 may be taken from the following list:

contort	connive	fraught
continuous	congruent	gastronome
credible	demean	havoc
activate	liberate	impertinent
deletion	heroic	delicacy
focus	voluntary	impartial
manual	resistance	delve
garbanzo	alien	attentive
logic	meditate	osmosis

Category 1	*Category 2*	*Category 3*	*Category 4*
_____	_____	_____	_____
_____	_____	_____	_____
_____	_____	_____	_____
_____	_____	_____	_____
_____	_____	_____	_____

To build your vocabulary, try to shift as many words as possible from a less-familiar to a more-familiar category. This task, however, is not an easy one. You must start noticing words. Then you must question, check, and remember their meanings. Finally, and most important, you must use these new words often in your speech and writing.

This chapter will help you improve your word awareness by (1) discussing the use of reference sources, (2) showing you how to pronounce difficult words, and (3) presenting an index card system for learning new words.

WORD INFORMATION SOURCES

Three written sources are most useful in improving one's vocabulary: (1) the dictionary, (2) subject area dictionaries, and (3) the thesaurus.

The Dictionary

THE COLLEGIATE DICTIONARY

The dictionary is an essential tool for every college student. If you do not already own a collegiate dictionary, buy one as soon as possible. You will need a dictionary to complete the exercises in this chapter.

Inexpensive paperback editions of the collegiate dictionary are available and recommended. Do not buy a condensed pocket dictionary. These versions do not contain enough words and will not provide you with sufficient information to suit your needs in college courses. Most college bookstores stock several collegiate dictionaries. Among the most widely used are *The American Heritage Dictionary of the English Language*, *Webster's New Collegiate Dictionary*, and *Webster's New World Dictionary of the American Language*.

THE UNABRIDGED DICTIONARY

Libraries own large, complete dictionaries, called unabridged dictionaries. These often have thousands of pages. They contain much more information on each word than collegiate dictionaries. You may need to refer to an unabridged dictionary to find an unusual word, an unusual meaning of a word, or to check the various prefixes or suffixes that can be used with a particular word.

Subject Area Dictionaries

Many subject areas have specialized dictionaries that list most of the important words used in that field. These dictionaries give specialized meanings for words and suggest how and when to use the words. For the field of nursing, for instance, there is *Taber's Cyclopedic Medical Dictionary*. Other subject area dictionaries include *A Dictionary of Anthropology*, *The New Grove Dictionary of Music and Musicians*, and *A Dictionary of Economics*.

Find out whether there is a subject area dictionary for the subjects you are studying. Most such dictionaries are available only in hardback and are likely to be expensive. However, many students find them worth the initial investment. Most libraries have copies of specialized dictionaries in the reference section.

EXERCISE 3-1

Directions: *Find the name of a subject area dictionary for each of the fields listed below.*

1. psychology _____

2. law _____

3. statistics _____

The Thesaurus

A thesaurus is a dictionary of synonyms. It groups words together that have similar meanings. A thesaurus is particularly useful to:

- Locate a precise, exact term to fit a particular situation

- Find an appropriate descriptive word

- Find a word to replace one that is overused or unclear

- Find a word that conveys a more specific shade of meaning

Suppose you are looking for a more precise word for the expression *will tell us about* in the following sentence:

In class today, our chemistry instructor **will tell us about** our next assignment.

The thesaurus lists the following synonyms for "tell—explain":

.10 **explain, explicate, expound,** exposit; **give the meaning,** tell the meaning of; **spell out,** unfold; **account for,** give reason for; **clarify, elucidate,** clear up, **make clear,** make plain; **simplify,** popularize; **illuminate,** enlighten, **shed** or **throw light upon;** rationalize, euhemerize, demythologize, allegorize; tell or show how, show the way; **demonstrate, show, illustrate,** exemplify; decipher, crack, unlock, find the key to, unravel, **solve** 487.2; explain oneself; explain away.

.11 **comment upon,** commentate, remark upon; **annotate,** gloss; **edit,** make an edition.

.12 **translate, render,** transcribe, transliterate, put or turn into, transfuse the sense of; construe; English.

.13 **paraphrase, rephrase, reword, restate,** rehash; give a free or loose translation.

Read the above entry and underline words or phrases that you think would be more descriptive than *tell about.* You might underline words and phrases such as *comment upon, illustrate, demonstrate,* and *spell out.*

The most widely used thesaurus is *Roget's Thesaurus.* Inexpensive paperback editions are available in most bookstores.

When you first consult a thesaurus, you will have to become familiar with its format and learn how to use it. The following is a step-by-step approach:

1. Start with the extensive index in the back to locate the word you are trying to replace. Following the word, you will find the number(s) of the section(s) in the main part of the thesaurus that list the synonyms of that word.

2. Turn to those sections, scanning each list and jotting down all the words you think might work.

3. Test each of the words you selected in the sentence in which you will use it. The word should fit the context of the sentence.

4. Select the word that sounds right and fits best with what you have said.

5. Choose only words with which you are familiar and whose shades of meaning you know. Check words of which you are unsure in a dictionary before using them. Remember, misusing a word is often a more serious error than using a word that is overused or not descriptive.

EXERCISE 3-2

Directions: *Use a thesaurus to choose a more precise or descriptive word to replace the boldface word or phrase in each sentence. Write the word in the space provided.*

1. Although the movie was **good**, it lasted only an hour.

   _____

2. The judge **looked at** the criminal as she pronounced the sentence.

   _____

3. The accident victim was awarded a **big** cash settlement.

   _____

4. The lottery winner was **happy** to win the $100,000 prize, but he was surprised to learn that a sizable portion had already been deducted for taxes.

   _____

5. On the first day of class, the instructor **talked to** the class about course requirements.

   _____

USING YOUR DICTIONARY

The first step in using your dictionary is to become familiar with the kinds of information it provides. In the following sample entry, each kind of information is marked:

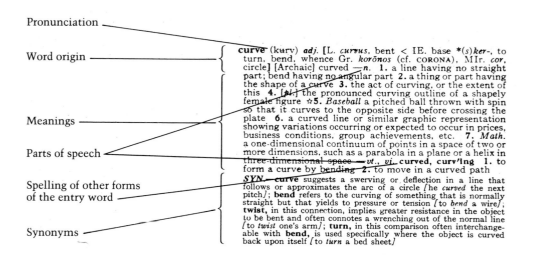

Pronunciation

Word origin

Meanings

Parts of speech

Spelling of other forms of the entry word

Synonyms

curve (kʉrv) *adj.* [L. *curvus*, bent < IE. base *(s)ker-, to turn, bend, whence Gr. *korōnos* (cf. CORONA), MIr. *cor*, circle] [Archaic] curved —*n.* **1.** a line having no straight part; bend having no angular part **2.** a thing or part having the shape of a curve **3.** the act of curving, or the extent of this **4.** [*pl.*] the pronounced curving outline of a shapely female figure ☆**5.** *Baseball* a pitched ball thrown with spin so that it curves to the opposite side before crossing the plate **6.** a curved line or similar graphic representation showing variations occurring or expected to occur in prices, business conditions, group achievements, etc. **7.** *Math.* a one-dimensional continuum of points in a space of two or more dimensions, such as a parabola in a plane or a helix in three-dimensional space —*vt., vi.* **curved, curv'ing 1.** to form a curve by bending **2.** to move in a curved path
SYN.—**curve** suggests a swerving or deflection in a line that follows or approximates the arc of a circle [he *curved* the next pitch]; **bend** refers to the curving of something that is normally straight but that yields to pressure or tension [to *bend* a wire]; **twist**, in this connection, implies greater resistance in the object to be bent and often connotes a wrenching out of the normal line [to *twist* one's arm]; **turn**, in this comparison often interchangeable with **bend**, is used specifically where the object is curved back upon itself [to *turn* a bed sheet]

You can see that a dictionary entry provides much more than definitions alone. Information is provided as well on word pronunciation, part of speech, word history, and special uses.

EXERCISE 3-3

Directions: *Use the sample dictionary entry above to complete the following items.*

1. Find three meanings for *curve* and write a sentence using each.

_____

_____

_____

2. Explain what *curve* means when used in *baseball*.

_____

3. Explain how the meaning of *curve* differs from the meaning of the word *bend*.

_____

In the past, you may have found parts of the dictionary confusing or difficult to use. Many students complain about the numerous symbols and abbreviations that are used. Actually, once you are familiar with its format, you will see that the dictionary is systematic, highly organized, and provides a great deal of information about each word. The following is a brief review of the parts of a dictionary entry most often found confusing.

Abbreviations

All dictionaries provide a key to abbreviations used in the entry itself as well as some commonly used in other printed material. Most often this key appears on the inside front cover or on the first few pages of the dictionary.

EXERCISE 3-4

Directions: *Find the meaning of each of the following symbols and abbreviations in a dictionary and write it in the space provided.*

1. v.t._____

2. < _____

3. c._____

4. Obs._____

5. Fr._____

6. pl._____

Word Pronunciation

After each word entry, the pronunciation of the word is given in parentheses.

Examples:

helmet (hĕl′mĭt)   connection (kə-nĕk′shən)
apologize (ə-pŏl′ə-jīz)   orchestra (ôr′kĭ-strə)

This part of the entry shows how to pronounce a word by spelling it the way it sounds. Different symbols are used to indicate certain sounds. Until you become familiar with this symbol system, you will need to refer to the pronunciation key. Most dictionaries include a pronunciation key at the bottom of each page or every other page. Here is a sample key from the *American Heritage Dictionary*:

ă pat/ā pay/âr care/ä father/b bib/ch church/d deed/ĕ pet/ē be/f fife/g gag/h hat/hw which/ĭ pit/ī pie/îr pier/j judge/k kick/l lid,
needle/m mum/n no, sudden/ng thing/ŏ pot/ō toe/ô paw, for/oi noise/ou out/ o͝o took/ o͞o boot/p pop/r roar/s sauce/sh ship, dish/
t tight/th thin, path/*th* this, bathe/ŭ cut/ûr urge/v valve/w with/y yes/z zebra, size/zh vision/ə about, item, edible, gallop, circus/

The key shows the sound the symbol stands for in a word you already
know how to pronounce. For example, suppose you are trying to pronounce the word *helix* (hē′lĭks). The key shows that the letter *e* in the first
part of the word sounds the same as the *e* in the word *be*. The *i* in *helix* is
pronounced the same way as the *i* in *pit*.

To pronounce a word correctly, you must also accent (stress, or say
more heavily) the appropriate part of the word. In a dictionary respelling,
an accent mark (′) usually follows the syllable, or part of the word, that is
stressed most heavily.

Examples:

audience ôd′ē-ən(t)s
football fo͝ot′bôl
homicide hôm′ĭ-sīd
hurricane hûr′ĭ-kān
literature lĭt′ər-ə-cho͝or
soporific sôp-ə-rĭf′ĭk

Some words have two accents—a primary stress and a secondary
stress. The primary one is stressed more heavily and is printed in darker
type than the secondary accent.

Example: interstate ĭn′ter-stāt′

Try to pronounce each of the following dictionary respellings, using
the pronunciation key:

dĭ-vûr′sə-fī   bo͝osh′əl
chăl′ənj   bär′bĭ-kyoo

EXERCISE 3-5

Directions: *Use the pronunciation key above to sound out each of the fol-*
lowing words. Write the word, spelled correctly, in the space provided.

1. kə-mĭt′ _____

2. kăp′chər _____

3. bə-räm′ə-tər _____

4. sĕksh′ə-wəl _____

5. ī-dĕn′tə-fĭ-kā′shən _____

6. ĭn-dĭf′ər-əns _____

7. lûr′nĭd _____

8. lĭk′wĭd _____

9. nōō′səns _____

10. fär′mə-sē _____

Multiple Meanings

Most words have more than one meaning. When you look up the meaning of a new word, you must choose the meaning that fits the way the word is used in the sentence context. The following sample entry for the word *green* contains many meanings for the word.

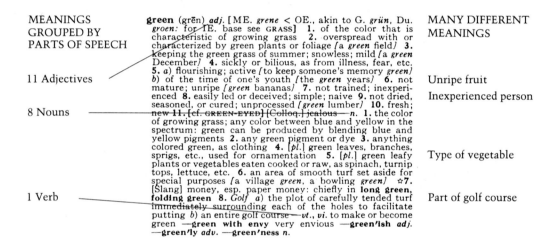

The meanings are grouped by part of speech and are numbered consecutively in each group. Generally, the most common meanings of the word are listed first, with more specialized, less common meanings appearing toward the end of the entry. Now, find the meaning that fits the use of the word *green* in the following sentence.

> The local Vietnam Veteran's organization held its annual fundraising picnic on the village **green**.

In this sentence, *green* refers to "an area of grass used for special purposes." Since this is a specialized meaning of the word, it appears toward the end of the entry.

Here are a few suggestions for choosing the correct meaning from among those listed in an entry:

1. If you are familiar with the parts of speech, try to use these to locate the correct meaning. For instance, if you are looking up the meaning of a word that names a person, place, or thing, you can save time by reading only those entries given after *n.* (noun).

2. For most types of college reading, you can skip definitions that give slang and colloquial (abbreviated *colloq.*) meanings.

3. If you are not sure of the part of speech, read each meaning until you find a definition that seems correct.

4. Test out your choice by substituting the meaning in the sentence with which you are working. Substitute the definition for the word and see whether it makes sense in the context (see Chapter 1).

Suppose you are looking up the word *oblique* to find its meaning in this sentence:

My sister's **oblique** answers to my questions made me suspicious.

o·blique (ō-blēk′, ə-; *Military* ō-blīk′, ə-) *adj. Abbr.* **obl.** **1. a.** Having a slanting or sloping direction, course, or position; inclined. **b.** *Geometry.* Designating lines or planes that are neither parallel nor perpendicular. **2.** Indirect or evasive in execution, meaning, or expression; not straightforward. **3.** Devious, misleading, or dishonest: *oblique answers.* **4.** Not direct in descent; collateral. **5.** *Botany.* Having sides of unequal length or form: *an oblique leaf.* **6.** *Grammar.* Designating any noun case except the nominative or the vocative. **7.** *Rhetoric.* **Indirect** *(see).* —*n.* **1.** An oblique thing, such as a line, direction, or muscle. **2.** *Nautical.* The act of changing course by less than 90 degrees. —*adv. Military.* At an angle of 45 degrees: *Right oblique, march!* [Middle English *oblike,* from Latin *oblíquus†.*] —**o·blique′ly** *adv.* —**o·blique′ness** *n.*

The second definition fits the way *oblique* is used in the sentence.

EXERCISE 3-6

Directions: *Write an appropriate meaning for the boldface word in each of the following sentences. Use the dictionary to help you find the meaning that makes sense in the sentence.*

1. The last contestant did not have a **ghost** of a chance.

   _____

2. The race car driver won the first **heat**.

   _____

3. The police took all possible **measures** to protect the witness.

   _____

4. The orchestra played the first **movement** of the symphony.

_____

5. The plane stalled on the **apron**.

_____

Spelling

The entry gives the correct spelling of a word. It also shows how the spelling changes when a word is made plural or endings (suffixes—see Chapter 2) are added, as in the following examples.

Word	*Word + Ending*
budget	budgetary
	budgeter
exhibit	exhibitor
	exhibition
fancy	fancily
	fanciness
	fancier

Other Aids

Many dictionaries (especially hardback editions) also contain numerous useful lists and tables. These are usually printed at the end of the dictionary. Frequently included are tables of weights and measures and of periodic elements in chemistry, biographical listings for famous people, a pronouncing gazetteer (a geographical dictionary), and lists of standard abbreviations, colleges, and signs and symbols.

EXERCISE 3-7

Directions: *Use a dictionary to answer each of the following items. Write your answer in the space provided.*

1. What parts of speech can the word *interior* be used as?

_____

2. How is the word *exacerbate* pronounced? Record its phonetic spelling.

_____

3. Which part of the word *opinion* is stressed (accented)?

_____

4. How many different meanings can you think of for the word *pitch*? Write as many as you can think of. Then check to see how many meanings are given in the dictionary.

_____

_____

_____

Locating Words Rapidly

Most dictionaries include guide words to help you locate words rapidly. At the top of each dictionary page are two words in dark print, one in the left corner and one in the right. The guide word on the left is the first entry on that page. The right-hand guide word is the last entry. All the words on that page come between the two guide words in alphabetical order.

To find quickly whether a word is on a certain page, look at the guide words. If the word you are looking for comes between the two guide words on the page alphabetically, then scan that page until you find the word. If the word does not come between those guide words, you need not look at that page at all.

Suppose you are looking up the word *loathsome*. The guide words on a particular page are *livid* and *lobster*. You know that the word *loathsome* will be on that page because, alphabetically, *loathsome* comes after *livid* and before *lobster*.

EXERCISE 3-8

Directions: *Read each entry word and the pair of guide words that follows it. Decide whether the entry word would be found on the dictionary page with those guide words. Write* yes *or* no *in the space provided.*

Entry Word	*Guide Words*	
1. grotesque	gritty—ground	_____
2. stargaze	standard—starfish	_____
3. ridicule	ridgepole—rigid	_____
4. exponent	expletive—express	_____
5. dissident	displease—dissidence	_____

PRONOUNCING UNFAMILIAR WORDS

Most college students, at one time or another, meet words that they are unable to pronounce. To pronounce an unfamiliar word, sound it out syllable by syllable. (Knowing how to divide words into syllables is useful for typing term papers and other written materials. When you have to break a word at the end of a line, it must be split between syllables.)

Here are a few simple rules for dividing words into syllables:

1. Each syllable is a separate, distinct speech sound. Pronounce the following words and try to hear the number of syllables in each.

   Examples:

expensive	ex/pen/sive	= 3 syllables
recognize	rec/og/nize	= 3 syllables
punctuate	punc/tu/ate	= 3 syllables
complicated	com/pli/cat/ed	= 4 syllables

2. Each syllable has at least one vowel and usually one or more consonants. (The letters *a, e, i, o, u,* and sometimes *y* are vowels. All other letters are consonants.)

   Examples: as/sign   re/act   cou/pon   gen/er/al

3. Divide words before a single consonant.

   Examples: hu/mid   pa/tron   re/tail   fa/vor

4. Divide words between two consonants appearing together.

   Examples: pen/cil   lit/ter   lum/ber   sur/vive

5. Divide words between prefixes (word beginnings) and roots (base words) and/or between roots and suffixes (word endings).

   Examples:

   Prefix + Root
   pre/read   post/pone   anti/war
   Root + Suffix
   sex/ist   agree/ment   list/ing

   (For a more complete discussion of prefixes, roots, and suffixes, see Chapter 2.)

6. Divide compound words between the individual words that form the compound word.

   Examples:

house/broken	house/hold	space/craft
green/house	news/paper	sword/fish

7. Divide words between two vowel sounds that appear together.

Examples: te/di/ous   ex/tra/ne/ous

EXERCISE 3-9

Directions: *Use slash marks(/) to divide each of the following words into syllables.*

1. polka
2. pollute
3. ordinal
4. hallow
5. judicature

6. innovative
7. obtuse
8. germicide
9. futile
10. extoll

11. tangelo
12. symmetry
13. telepathy
14. organic
15. hideous

16. tenacity
17. mesmerize
18. intrusive
19. infallible
20. fanaticism

A SYSTEM FOR LEARNING NEW WORDS

As you read textbook assignments and reference sources and while listening to your instructors' class presentations, you are constantly exposed to new words. Unless you make a deliberate effort to remember and use these words, many of them will probably fade from your memory. One of the most practical and easy-to-use systems for expanding your vocabulary is the index card system. It works like this:

1. Whenever you hear or read a new word that you intend to learn, jot it down in the margin of your notes or mark it some way in the material you are reading.

2. Later, write each word on the front of an index card. Then look up the meaning of the word and write this on the back of the card. Also record a phonetic key for the word's pronunciation, its part of speech, other forms the word may take, and a sample sentence or example of how the word is used. Your cards should look like the one in Figure 3-1 on page 44.

3. Once a day, take a few minutes to go through your pack of index cards. For each card, look at the word on the front and try to recall its meaning on the back. Then check the back of the card to see whether you were correct. If you were unable to recall the meaning or if you confused the word with another word, retest yourself. Shuffle the cards after each use.

4. After you have gone through your pack of cards several times, sort the cards into two piles, words you know and words you have not learned. Then, putting the known words aside, concentrate on the words still to be learned.

5. Once you have learned the entire pack of words, review them often to refresh your memory.

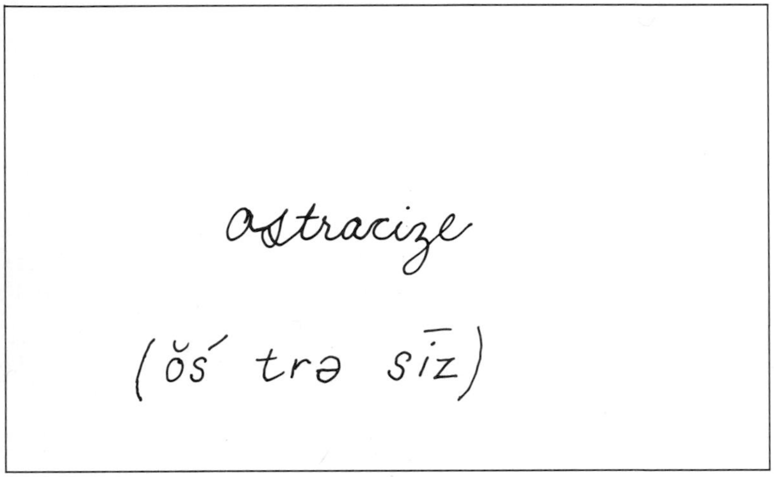

ostracize

(ŏs´ trə sīz)

Front

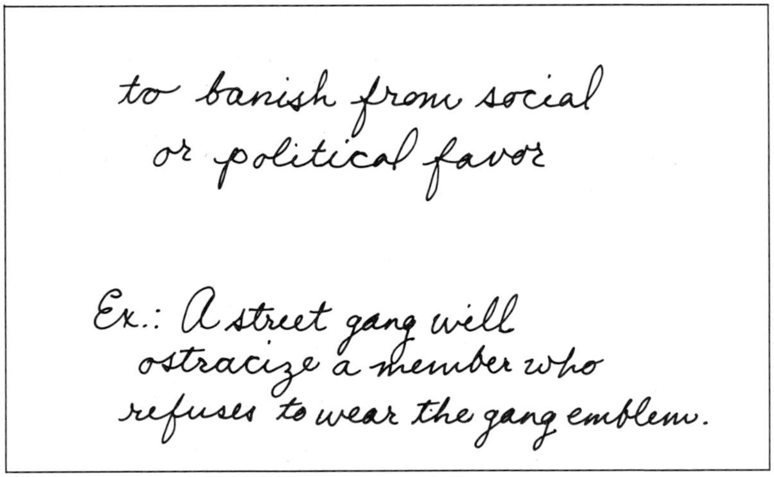

to banish from social or political favor

Ex.: A street gang will ostracize a member who refuses to wear the gang emblem.

Back

Figure 3-1 Sample index card.

This index card system is effective for several reasons. First, it can be reviewed in the spare time that is often wasted waiting for a class to begin, riding a bus, and so on. Second, the system enables you to spend time learning what you do *not* know rather than wasting time studying what you already know. Finally, the system overcomes a major problem that exists in learning information that appears in list form. If the material to be learned is presented in a fixed order, you tend to learn it in that order and may be unable to recall individual items when they appear alone or out of order. By shuffling the cards, you scramble the order of the words and thus avoid this problem.

EXERCISE 3-10

Directions: *Make a set of at least twenty word cards, choosing words from one of your textbooks or from one of the reading selections in the back of this book. Then, study the cards using the method described in this chapter.*

SUMMARY

A good vocabulary is essential to effective speaking, writing, listening, and reading. This chapter focused on techniques for strengthening your word awareness and building a strong vocabulary. The first two sections of the chapter discussed the use of reference sources—collegiate and unabridged dictionaries, subject area dictionaries, and the thesaurus. The next section offered tips and summarized basic rules for pronouncing unfamiliar words. The last section suggested an index card system for learning new words.

PART ONE REVIEW

MAKING YOUR SKILLS WORK TOGETHER

A COMBINED APPROACH TO VOCABULARY

Throughout this unit you have learned several ways to approach words you do not know. In Chapter 1 you learned how to look for meaning clues in the sentence context. In Chapter 2 you saw that breaking a word into parts can help you discover its meaning. Finally, in Chapter 3 you learned how to use various information sources to unlock word meaning and a card system for learning new words.

While each of these skills is effective by itself, each becomes more useful when used in combination with others. You will find that various combinations of techniques work better than any one by itself. The combination you use, however, depends on the situation. For instance, one time you might use context and then a dictionary. Another time you might use context and word parts. Context, however, is always the final test of whether you have correctly defined a word. To be correct, a definition must make sense in the context.

Let us consider an example in which combined skills are more effective than context alone. In figuring out the meaning of the word *unassuming* in the following sentence, both context and word parts are useful:

The bank executive's **unassuming** attitude toward her customers made them think of her as an ordinary person.

Context alone suggests that the executive had an attitude that made customers think of her as an ordinary person, but this still does not give you enough information. Using word parts, you can see the prefix *un-* (meaning "not") and the root word *assume*. By combining these clues, you can figure out that the executive did not assume too much about her position or herself. Thus, *unassuming*, in the above context, means "not forward" or "modest."

Here's another example:

The security wall surrounding the building made it **impenetrable.**

Context tells you that *impenetrable* refers to a condition of the building. Using word parts, you know this:

prefix: im- = not
root: penetr(ate) = force a way through
suffix: -able = able to
impenetrable = not able to force a way through

In some situations it may be necessary to check a dictionary for an exact meaning once you have found a meaning clue in the context. Once you have a meaning clue, you will find that reading through the numerous definitions listed is much easier and faster than if you have no idea what you are looking for. Then, once you have used an effective combination of methods to determine a word's meaning, be sure not to forget it. Jot the new word onto an index card and use the card system to place that word in your permanent store of word meanings.

EXERCISE 1

Directions: *Read each sentence and write a definition or synonym for each boldface word. Use a combination of skills to determine meaning.*

1. The class was **demoralized** when everyone failed the first exam.

   _____

2. The film we saw in class today was **noncontroversial**.

   _____

3. In spite of close **surveillance**, three inmates managed to escape.

   _____

4. The union leader **exculpated** himself from blame for the strike by saying he had encouraged members to return to work.

   _____

5. At eighty years of age, my grandmother still moves with **alacrity**.

   _____

6. There was no need to **recapitulate** the speaker's faults; they were clear to everyone.

   _____

7. The teen-ager's **puerile** remarks offended his parents' guests.

   _____

8. **Dehydrated** food often lacks flavor.

   _____

9. Sam's **maladroit** behavior surprised everyone at the concert.

   _____

10. The government **imposed** controls that froze prices and wages.

    _____

PART TWO

READING AS THINKING

Rhonda is taking an anatomy and physiology course, a required course in nursing. She reads all assignments and spends long hours studying. She rereads assignments, underlines, and studies her notes. In fact, she spends more time preparing for each weekly quiz than most other students in the class. Before each quiz she feels confident; she has studied and feels she knows the material. When the instructor returns the weekly quiz, Rhonda is always surprised and disappointed. She thought she did well, but she receives a failing grade of 50 or 60. She cannot understand why she has failed the quizzes, since she studied the material.

Rhonda decided to visit the college's learning center. The first thing the instructor asked her to do was locate in her textbook the correct answer to each quiz item. When Rhonda had difficulty doing this, the instructor questioned her on portions of the textbook. The instructor realized that Rhonda did not understand and had not thought about what she had read. The instructor asked Rhonda several questions about how she read the chapters and discovered that Rhonda did not use an active approach to studying. She did nothing before beginning to read to sharpen her mind and make reading easier. She read mechanically, from beginning to end and she did not check her understanding of the material. She did not realize her comprehension was poor or incomplete. The instructor then made suggestions for strategies to help Rhonda get involved with what she was reading, and showed her how to keep track of her level of comprehension.

The purpose of this part of the book is to help you develop skills to approach reading as a thinking process. You will learn various techniques that will increase your comprehension. You will also learn how to keep track of your level of understanding and what to do if it is poor or incomplete.

**THIS PART OF THE TEXT WILL HELP YOU
IMPROVE YOUR SKILLS SO THAT:**

1. **You will start with a positive attitude (Chapter 4).**

2. **You can maintain a high level of concentration (Chapter 4).**

3. **You will be able to learn what a chapter or article is about before you read it (Chapter 4).**

4. **You can discover what you already know about a subject (Chapter 4).**

5. **You can use questions to guide your reading (Chapter 4).**

6. **You can keep track of your level of understanding (Chapter 5).**

7. **You can correct weak or poor comprehension (Chapter 5).**

Chapter 4

PREREADING STRATEGIES

THIS CHAPTER WILL SHOW YOU HOW TO

1. **Start with a positive attitude**

2. **Control your concentration**

3. **Preview before reading**

4. **Activate your background knowledge**

5. **Develop questions to guide your reading**

Would you like to get more out of what you read for the time you spend? Do you want to avoid spending unnecessary time rereading and reviewing? This chapter will discuss five techniques that can make an immediate, noticeable change in how well you understand and remember what you read. Because each is done *before* you actually begin reading, they are called *pre*reading strategies. As you work through this chapter you will see that there is more to reading an assignment than opening your book to the correct page, checking its length, and beginning to read.

START WITH A POSITIVE ATTITUDE

Regardless of all the techniques and habits you develop, reading will always be difficult if you approach it as something you dislike. If you expect reading to be tiring and boring, it will be. On the other hand, if you approach reading positively, you will be more successful. To read with a positive attitude, try the following:

1. Accept responsibility for your own learning. In college it is up to you to learn what has been taught in class and what is included in assigned textbook chapters. This takes a lot of work, and nobody makes you do it. If you fail an exam, you cannot blame your instructor for not teaching or the textbook for being too difficult. Think of reading and studying as tasks you must do to succeed in college. Try not to think of reading and studying as tasks that prevent you from doing things that are more fun.

2. Plan on spending time. Reading is not a task that you can rush through. Taking your time will pay off in increased comprehension.

3. Think of reading as a way of sifting and sorting out information that you need to learn from that which is less important. Actively search for key ideas as you read. Try to connect these ideas with what your instructor is discussing in class.

4. Think of reading as the writer's way of communicating a message to you, the reader. Look for clues about the writer's personality, his or her attitudes, opinions, and beliefs. This will put you in touch with the writer as a person and will help you understand his or her message. Part Four of this book will offer suggestions to help you do this.

CONTROL YOUR CONCENTRATION

Do you have difficulty concentrating? If so, you are like many other college students. Many say that concentration is the main reason they cannot read or study effectively. Building concentration involves two steps: (1) controlling your surroundings and (2) focusing your attention.

Controlling Your Surroundings

Poor concentration is often the result of distractions caused by the time and place you have chosen to study. Here are a few ideas to help you overcome poor concentration:

1. Choose a place to read that is relatively free of interruptions. If people interrupt you at home or in the dormitory, try the campus library.

2. Find a place free of distractions and temptations. Avoid places with outside noises, friends close at hand, a television set or an interesting project to complete.

3. Read in the same place each day. Eventually you will get in the habit of reading there and concentration will become easier, almost automatic.

4. Do not read where you are too comfortable. It is easy to lose concentration, become drowsy, or fall asleep when you are too relaxed.

5. Choose a time of day when you are mentally alert. It is easier to concentrate if you are not exhausted, hungry, or drowsy.

Focusing Your Attention

Even if you follow the above suggestions, you may still find it difficult to become organized and stick with your reading. This often takes much self-discipline, but the following suggestions may make this easier:

1. Set goals and time limits for yourself. Before you begin a reading assignment, decide how long it should take, and check to see that you stay on schedule. Before you begin an evening of homework, write down what you plan to do and how long each assignment should take. Sample goals for an evening are shown in Figure 4-1, on page 56.

2. Choose and reserve blocks of time each day for reading and study. Write down what you will study in each time block each day/evening. Working at the same time each day establishes a routine, and makes concentration a bit easier.

3. Vary your reading. For instance, rather than spending an entire evening on one subject, work for one hour on each of three subjects.

4. Reward yourself for accomplishing things as planned. Delay entertainment until after you have finished studying. Use such things as ordering a pizza, calling a friend, or watching a TV program as rewards after you have completed several assignments.

5. Plan frequent breaks. Do this at sensible points in your reading —between chapters or after major chapter divisions.

6. Keep physically as well as mentally active. Try highlighting, un-

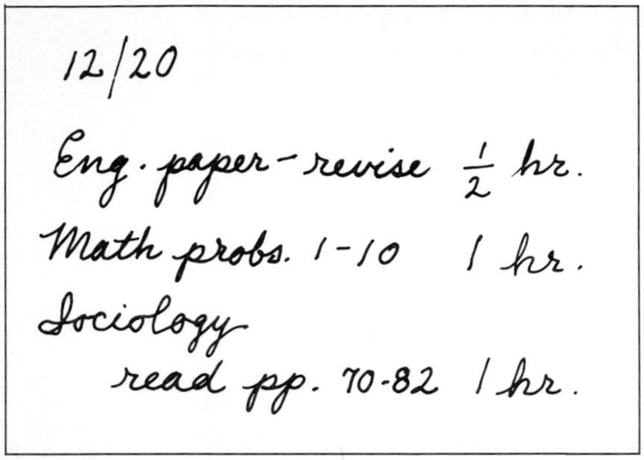

12/20

Eng. paper—revise $\frac{1}{2}$ hr.

Math probs. 1-10   1 hr.

Sociology
     read pp. 70-82 1 hr.

Figure 4-1   Goals and time limits.

derlining, or making summary notes as you read (see Chapter 10).
These activities will force you to pay attention to the assignment.

EXERCISE 4-1

Directions: *Answer each of the following questions as honestly as you
can. They will help you analyze problems with concentration. You may
want to discuss your answers to some items with others in your class.*

1. Where do you read and study? _____

   What interruptions, if any, might occur? _____

   _____

2. Do you need to find a better place? _____

   If so, list a few alternatives. _____

   _____

3. What is the best time of day for you to read? (If you don't know, experiment with different times until you begin to see a pattern.)

   _____

4. How long do you normally read without a break?

   _____

5. What type of distractions bother you the most?

   _____

6. How many different assignments do you work on in one evening?

   _____

7. What types of rewards might work for you?

_____

EXERCISE 4-2

Directions: *As you read your next textbook assignment, either for this course or another, be alert for distractions. Each time your mind wanders, try to identify the source of distraction. List in the space provided the cause of each break in your concentration and a way to eliminate each, if possible.*

_____

_____

_____

EXERCISE 4-3

Directions: *Before you begin your next study session, make a list in the space provided of what you intend to accomplish and how long you should spend on each task.*

	Assignment	Time
1.	_____	_____
2.	_____	_____
3.	_____	_____

PREVIEWING

Would you cross a city street without checking for traffic first? Would you pay to see a movie you had never heard of and knew nothing about? Would you buy a car without test driving it or checking its mechanical condition?

Most likely you answered "no" to each of these questions. Now answer a related question, one that applies to reading: should you read an article or textbook chapter without knowing what it is about or how it is organized? You can probably guess that the answer is "no." This section explains a technique called previewing.

Previewing is a way of familiarizing yourself quickly with the organization and content of written material *before* beginning to read it. It is an easy method to use and will make a dramatic difference in how you read.

How to Preview

When you preview, try to (1) find only the most important ideas in the material, and (2) notice how they are organized. To do this, look only at the parts that state these important ideas and skip the rest. Previewing is a fairly rapid technique. It should take only a few minutes to preview a fifteen- to twenty-page textbook chapter. The portions to look at in previewing a textbook chapter are listed here.

THE TITLE AND SUBTITLE

The title is a label that tells what the chapter is about. The subtitle, if there is one, suggests how the author approaches the subject. For example, an article titled "Brazil" might be subtitled, "The World's Next Superpower." In this instance, the subtitle tells on what aspects of Brazil the article focuses.

THE FIRST PARAGRAPH

The first paragraph, or introduction, serves as a lead-in to the chapter. It may provide an overview of the chapter and/or offer clues about its organization.

BOLDFACE (DARK PRINT) HEADINGS

Headings, like titles, serve as labels and identify the topic of the material. By reading each heading, you will be reading a list of the important topics the chapter covers. Together, the headings form a mini-outline of the chapter.

THE FIRST SENTENCE UNDER EACH HEADING

The first sentence following the heading often further explains the heading. It may also state the central thought of the entire selection.

TYPOGRAPHICAL AIDS

Typographical aids are those features of a page that make information outstanding or more noticeable. These include italics (slanted print), boldface type, marginal notes, colored ink, underlining, and enumeration (listing). A writer frequently uses typographical aids to call attention to important key words, definitions, and facts.

GRAPHS, CHARTS, AND PICTURES

Graphs, charts, and pictures will point you toward the most important information. Glance at these to determine quickly what information is being emphasized or clarified.

THE LAST PARAGRAPH OR SUMMARY

The last paragraph or summary will give a condensed view of the chapter and help you to identify key ideas. Often, a summary outlines the key points of the chapter.

END-OF-CHAPTER MATERIAL

Glance through any study or discussion questions, vocabulary lists, or outlines that appear at the end of the chapter. These will help you decide what is important in the chapter.

Demonstration of Previewing

The following article is taken from a chapter of a textbook on financial management. It discusses how to purchase an automobile. This article has been included to demonstrate previewing. Everything that you should look at or read has been shaded. Preview this excerpt now, reading only the shaded portions.

PREPURCHASE RESEARCH

Before buying an automobile for the first or fortieth time, money managers should do some basic reading on the product in order to determine what is available. Most individuals can be influenced by more options or something bigger when they get to the car lot or showroom, so it is a good idea to take that list of attributes, update it with information from the prepurchase research, and use it when looking at new or used cars.

Gathering Information

Information can be found at the library in publications such as *Consumer Reports*, *Motor Trend*, *Car and Driver*, and *Changing Times*. The April issue of *Consumer Reports* deals almost entirely with automobiles and certain factors involved when buying a new or used car. It gives recommendations for automobiles as well as suggestions for dealing with dealers, choosing options, and car repair and resale records. If the April issue is unavailable, the *Consumer Reports Annual Buying Guide* is available at most libraries or bookstores and could provide much of the same information. Along with these published sources, car shoppers can get ideas from friends and other car owners, advertisements, product labels, and sales people.

Identifying Desired Automobile Features

In order to save on options, money managers can combine the household's personal preferences with the ideas from the aforementioned publications. With a new car, it may be advantageous to place a special order and avoid the purchase of an overloaded car from the dealer's lot. In the case of a used car, excessive options may raise the price of the car, lower its efficiency, and increase its repair costs.

In deciding on options, it may be of further benefit to look at resale value guides, which indicate how certain options have affected resale values. One commonly used guide is the *National Automobile Dealer Association's (NADA) Official Used Car Guide*. It is available at most depository institutions as well as some libraries.

Checking Product Safety

Details on a new car's acceleration and passing ability, stopping distance, and tire reserve load or safety margin must be made available to all those considering a new car. Along with this information, a consumer can check the repair ratings given in the *Consumer Reports Annual Buying Guide* or in the *Consumer Reports* April issue. These frequency-of-repair records help potential new and used car buyers by giving the incidence of repair on specific models as reported by current car owners.

In considering a used car, the *National Highway Traffic Safety Administration (NHTSA)* can inform consumers whether or not a car has a reported defect or has been recalled. The make, model, and year of the car are needed to obtain the facts from the NHTSA.

Figuring Lifecycle Costs

For some people, the cost of operating an automobile was not a major factor until recently, but as prices continue to rise, the cost of operation is becoming a more influential element in the final selection. Anticipation of these costs is part of the lifecycle cost evaluation.

Although you may not realize it, you have acquired a substantial amount of information from the minute or so that you spent previewing. You have become familiar with the key ideas in this section. To demonstrate, read each of the following statements and mark them T for "True" or F for "False" based on what you learned by previewing.

_____The author suggests several sources of information on buying cars.

_____Only first-time buyers of cars need be concerned with researching before buying.

_____The cost of operating a car should influence your buying decision.

_____Information must be provided on every new car's performance (braking distance, acceleration, and so on).

_____Many individuals are influenced by what they see in the showroom.

This quiz tested your recall of some of the more important ideas in the article. Check your answers by referring back to the article. Did you get most or all of the above items correct? You can see, then, that previewing acquaints you with the major ideas contained in the material before you read it.

EXERCISE 4-4

Directions: *Preview Chapter 6 in this book. After you have previewed it, complete the items below.*

1. What is the subject of Chapter 6?

   _____

2. List the four major topics Chapter 6 covers.

   a. _____

   b. _____

   c. _____

   d. _____

EXERCISE 4-5

Directions: *Preview a chapter from one of your other textbooks. After you have previewed it, complete the items below.*

1. What is the chapter title?

   _____

2. What subject does the chapter cover?

   _____

3. List some of the major topics covered.

   _____

   _____

   _____

ACTIVATE YOUR BACKGROUND KNOWLEDGE

Once you have previewed an assignment, the next step is to discover what you already know about the topic. Regardless of the topic, you probably know *something* about it. We will call this your **background knowledge**. Here is an example.

A student was about to begin reading an article for a sociology class, "Controlling World Terrorism." At first, she thought she knew nothing about controlling terrorism. Then she began thinking of terrorist activities. She recalled several airplane hijackings and situations in which hostages were taken. As she thought about these incidents and how to prevent them, she realized she did have some background knowledge on the topic. This information, once called to mind, will help the student read her assignment and retain its content.

Now, let's take a sample chapter from a business textbook, titled *Small Business Management*. The headings are listed below. Spend a moment thinking about each one; then make a list of things you already know about each:

- Characteristics of Small Businesses

- Small Business Administration

- Advantages and Disadvantages of Small Businesses

- Problems of Small Business

Discovering what you already know, or activating your background knowledge is useful for three important reasons. First, it makes reading easier because you have already thought about the topic. Second, the material is easier to remember because you can connect the new information with what you already know. Third, topics become more interesting if you can connect them to your own experience. You can activate your background knowledge by using one or more of the following techniques:

1. *Ask questions and try to answer them.* For the above business textbook headings, you might ask and try to answer questions such as: Would or wouldn't I want to own a small business? What problems could I expect?

2. *Draw upon your own experience.* For example, if a chapter in your business textbook is titled "Advertising: Its Purpose and Design," then think of several ads you have seen on television, in magazines, and in newspapers and analyze the purpose of each and how each was constructed.

3. *Brainstorm.* On a scrap sheet of paper, jot down everything that comes to mind about the topic. For example, suppose you are about to read a chapter section in your sociology textbook on domestic violence. You might list types of violence—child abuse, rape, and so on. Or, you could write questions such as: "What causes child abuse?" or "How can it be prevented?" Or, you might list incidents of domestic violence you have heard or read about. Any of these approaches will help to make the topic interesting.

EXERCISE 4-6

Directions: *Assume you have just previewed a chapter in your American government text on freedom of speech. Activate your background knowledge using* each *of the techniques suggested above. Then answer the questions below.*

1. Did you discover you knew more about freedom of speech than you initially thought?

2. Which technique worked best? Why?

DEVELOP GUIDE QUESTIONS

Did you ever read an entire page or more and not remember anything you read? Have you found yourself going from paragraph to paragraph without really thinking about what the writer is saying? Most likely you are not looking for anything in particular as you read. As a result, you do not notice or remember anything specific either. The solution is a relatively simple technique that takes just a few seconds: Develop questions that will guide your reading and hold your attention.

How to Ask Guide Questions

Here are a few useful suggestions to help you form questions to guide your reading.

1. Preview before you try to ask questions. Previewing will give you an idea of what is important and indicate what you should ask questions about.

2. Take each major heading and turn it into a question. The question should ask something that you feel is important to know.

3. As you read the section, look for the answer to your question.

4. When you finish reading a section, stop and check to see whether you have found the answer.

5. Avoid asking questions that have one-word answers. Questions that begin with *what, why*, or *how* are more useful.

Here are a few headings and some examples of questions you could ask:

Heading	*Questions*
1. Reducing Prejudice	1. How can prejudice be reduced? What type of prejudice?
2. The Deepening Recession	2. What is a recession? Why is it deepening?
3. Newton's First Law of Motion	3. Who is or was Newton? What is his First Law of Motion?

EXERCISE 4-7

Directions: *Write at least one question for each of the following headings.*

Heading	*Question(s)*
1. World War II and the Growth of Black Protest	1. _____ _____
2. Foreign Policy under Reagan	2. _____ _____
3. The Growth of Single-Parent Families	3. _____ _____
4. Changes in Optical Telescopes	4. _____ _____
5. Causes of Violent Behavior	5. _____ _____

EXERCISE 4-8

Directions: *Preview Chapter 8 of this book. Then write a question for each heading.*

_____

_____

_____

_____

_____

_____

EXERCISE 4-9

Directions: *Turn back to the textbook excerpt on page 59. You have already previewed it. Without reading the article, write three important questions to be answered after reading the article.*

_____

_____

_____

EXERCISE 4-10

Directions: *Select a textbook from one of your other courses. Preview a five-page portion of a chapter that you have not yet read. Then write questions for each heading.*

_____

_____

_____

_____

SUMMARY

This chapter discusses five techniques to use *before* you read that will help you become a more efficient reader:

1. STARTING WITH A POSITIVE ATTITUDE. Ways of thinking of reading that will help you approach difficult reading assignments.

2. CONTROLLING YOUR CONCENTRATION. A two-part task in which you control time, place, and distractions and focus your attention on the assignment.

3. PREVIEWING. A technique that allows you to become familiar with the material before you read it.

4. ACTIVATING YOUR BACKGROUND KNOWLEDGE. A method of bringing to mind what you already know about a topic.

5. USING GUIDE QUESTIONS. A method of forming a series of questions that you expect to answer as you read. The questions guide your reading and increase your recall.

Chapter 5

MONITORING YOUR COMPREHENSION

THIS CHAPTER WILL SHOW YOU HOW TO

1. Recognize comprehension signals

2. Monitor your comprehension

3. Improve your comprehension

For many daily activities you maintain an awareness or "check" on how well you are performing them. You also correct or try to improve your performance whenever possible. In sports such as racquetball, tennis, or bowling, you know if you are playing a poor game; you actually keep score and deliberately try to correct errors and improve your performance. When preparing a favorite food, you often taste it and correct the seasonings, if necessary. You can check to see whether your car is clean after taking it through the car wash and touch-up any spots that were missed.

A similar type of checking should occur as you read. You should be aware of, or *monitor*, your performance. You need to "keep score" of how effectively and efficiently you are understanding what you read. This is called *comprehension monitoring*. As you monitor you also need to take *action* to correct poor comprehension. This chapter will show you how to monitor your comprehension and suggest techniques to use when you are having difficulty understanding what you read.

RECOGNIZING COMPREHENSION SIGNALS

Think for a moment about how you feel when you read material you can understand easily. Now, compare this to what happens when you read something difficult and complicated. When you read easy material, does it seem that everything "clicks?" That is, do ideas seem to fit together and make sense? Is that "click" noticeably absent in difficult reading?

Read each of the following paragraphs. As you read, be alert to your level of understanding of each.

The two most common drugs that are legal and do not require a pre- 1
scription are caffeine and nicotine. Caffeine is the active ingredient in coffee, tea, and many cola drinks. It stimulates the central nervous system and heart and therefore is often used to stay awake. Heavy use—say, seven to ten cups of coffee per day—has toxic effects, that is, acts like a mild poison. Prolonged heavy use appears to be addicting. Nicotine is the active ingredient in tobacco. One of the most addicting of all drugs and one of the most dangerous, at least when obtained by smoking, it has been implicated in lung cancer, emphysema, and heart disease.

In the HOSC experiment, two variables were of sufficient importance 2
to include as stratification (classification) variables prior to the random assignment of class sections to treatments. These two stratification variables were science subject (biology, chemistry, or physics) and teacher's understanding of science (high or low). Inclusion of these two variables in the HOSC design allowed the experimenter to make generalizations about the HOSC treatment in terms of science subject matter and the teacher's understanding of science. Even if the HOSC experiments had selected a completely random sample of American high school science teacher–class sections, generalizations regarding the effectiveness of the HOSC treatment would only be possible in terms of the factors included in the experimental design. . . .[1]

Did you feel comfortable and confident as you read Paragraph 1? Did ideas seem to lead from one to another and make sense? How did you feel while reading Paragraph 2? Most likely you sensed its difficulty and felt confused. You realized that the ideas weren't making sense. Unfamiliar words were used, and you could not follow the flow of ideas.

As you read Paragraph 2, did you know that you were not understanding it? Did you feel lost and confused? Table 5–1 lists and compares some common signals that are useful in monitoring your comprehension. Not all signals must appear at the same time, and not all signals work for everyone. As you study the list, identify those positive signals you sensed as you read Paragraph 1 on common drugs. Then identify those negative signals that you sensed when reading about the HOSC experiment.

Table 5-1   COMPREHENSION SIGNALS

Positive Signals	*Negative Signals*
Everything seems to fit and make sense; ideas flow logically from one to another.	Some pieces do not seem to belong; the ideas do not fit together or make sense.
You are able to understand what the author is saying.	You feel as if you are struggling to stay with the author.
You can see where the author is leading.	You cannot think ahead or predict what will come next.
You are able to make connections among ideas.	You are unable to see how ideas connect.
You read at a regular comfortable pace.	You often slow down or lose your place.
You understand why the material was assigned.	You do not know why the material was assigned and cannot explain why it is important.
You can understand by reading the material once.	You need to reread sentences or paragraphs frequently.
You recognize most words or can figure them out from context.	Many words are unfamiliar.
You can express the key ideas in your own words.	You must reread and use the author's language to explain an idea.
You feel comfortable with the topic; you have some background knowledge.	The topic is unfamiliar; you know nothing about it.

Once you are able to recognize negative signals while reading, the next step is to take action to correct the problem. Specific techniques are given in the last section of this chapter.

EXERCISE 5-1

Directions: *Read the following excerpt from a biology textbook on the theory of continental drift. It is intended to be difficult, so do not get discouraged as you read. As you read it, monitor your comprehension. After reading, answer the following questions:*

In 1912, Alfred Wegener published a paper that was triggered by the common observation of the good fit between South America's east coast and Africa's west coast. Could these great continents ever have been joined? Wegener coordinated this jigsaw-puzzle analysis with other ecological and climatological data and proposed the theory of continental drift. He suggested that about 200 million years ago, all of the earth's continents were joined together into one enormous land mass, which he called Pangaea. In the ensuing millennia, according to Wegener's idea, Pangaea broke apart, and the fragments began to drift northward (by today's compass orientation) to their present location.

Wegener's idea received rough treatment in his lifetime. His geologist contemporaries attacked his naivete as well as his supporting data, and his theory was neglected until about 1960. At that time, a new generation of geologists revived the idea and subjected it to new scrutiny based on recent findings.

The most useful data have been based on magnetism in ancient lava flows. When a lava flow cools, metallic elements in the lava are oriented in a way that provides permanent evidence of the direction of the earth's magnetic field at the time, recording for future geologists both its north-south orientation and its latitude. From such maps, it is possible to determine the ancient positions of today's continents. We now believe that not only has continental drift occurred, as Wegener hypothesized, but that it continues to occur today. . . .

The disruption of Pangaea began some 230 million years ago in the Paleozoic era. By the Mesozoic era, the Eurasian land mass (called Laurasia) had moved away to form the northernmost continent. Gondwanaland, the mass that included India and the southern continents, had just begun to divide. Finally, during the late Mesozoic era, after South America and Africa were well divided, what was to be the last continental separation began, with Australia and Antarctica drifting apart. Both the North and South Atlantic Oceans would continue to widen considerably up to the Cenozoic era, a trend that is continuing today. So we see that although the bumper sticker "Reunite Gondwanaland" has a third-world, trendy ring to it, it's an unlikely proposition.

1. How would you rate your overall comprehension? What positive signals did you sense? Did you feel any negative signals?

2. Test the accuracy of your rating in Question 1 by answering the following questions based on the material you read.

    a. Explain Wegener's theory of continental drift.
    b. Which two continents led Wegener to develop his theory?
    c. What recent findings have supported Wegener's theory?
    d. Describe the way in which Pangaea broke up and drifted to become the continents we know today.

3. In what sections was your comprehension strongest?

4. Did you feel at any time that you had lost, or were about to lose comprehension? If so, go back to that paragraph now. What made that paragraph difficult to read?

5. Would it have been useful to refer to a world map?

6. Underline any difficult words that interfered with your comprehension.

MONITORING TECHNIQUES

At times signals of poor comprehension do not come through clearly or strongly enough. In fact, at times you may think you understood what you read until you are questioned in class or take an exam. Only then do you discover that your comprehension was incomplete. Or you may find that you understand facts, but do not recognize more complicated relationships and implied meanings. Use the following monitoring techniques to determine if you are *really* understanding what you are reading.

Establish Checkpoints

Race car drivers make pit stops during races for quick mechanical checks and repairs; athletes are subject to frequent physical tests and examinations. These activities evaluate or assess performance and correct any problems or malfunctions. Similarly, when reading it is necessary to stop and evaluate.

As you preview a textbook assignment, identify reasonable or logical checkpoints: points at which to stop, check, and, if necessary, correct your performance before continuing. Pencil a checkmark in the margin to designate these points. These checkpoints should be logical breaking points, where one topic ends and another begins or where a topic is broken down into several subtopics. As you reach each of these checkpoints stop and assess your work using the techniques described below.

Use Your Guide Questions

In Chapter 4, you learned how to form guide questions using boldface headings. These same questions can be used to monitor your comprehension. When you finish a boldface headed section, stop and take a moment to recall your guide questions and answer them mentally or on paper. Your ability to answer your questions is a strong indicator of your level of comprehension.

Ask Connection Questions

To be certain that your comprehension is complete and that you are not *only* recalling facts, ask connection questions. *Connection questions* are those that require you to think about content. They force you to draw together ideas and to interpret and evaluate what you are reading. Ask questions such as:

What does this topic have to do with topics discussed earlier in the article or chapter?
Why is this material important?
How can I use this information?

Connection questions help you to determine whether you are simply taking in information or whether you can use and apply the information.

EXERCISE 5–2

Directions: *The following is an excerpt from a business marketing textbook. Preview the excerpt and then write several guide questions. As you read, monitor your comprehension and answer your guide questions. After you have read the material, answer the connection questions listed below.*

PRODUCT LIFE-CYCLE

In 1971, 50,000 smoke detectors were sold in the United States; the market grew to a 10-million-units per-year business by 1978. The rapid growth attracted many competitors who flooded the market. The price of a smoke detector dropped from $50 in 1971 to under $15 in 1984. The market has now started to decline; it was only 8 million units in 1983, and only four of the twenty-five companies previously in the industry are still producing smoke detectors. What has happened in the smoke detector market is an example of product life-cycle. The product life-cycle is the series of stages that a product class goes through from its introduction until it is taken off the market. It is usually divided into four stages: introduction, growth, maturity, and decline.

Introductory Stage

At this stage of the life cycle, the product is launched into the marketplace, typically after a long period of development. Sales are zero at first and are still low even at the end of the introductory stage. Consumers are not aware of the product, its benefits, or potential uses. Thus, there should be an investment in advertising and promotion to educate potential customers. There are typically no important competitors, so this promotional effort is undertaken by only one firm. These high promotion costs and the cost of establishing initial distribution for the product usually mean that the profits will be negative during the introductory stage.

Growth Stage

During the growth stage, sales volume increases rapidly. Profits also increase rapidly, but the growth in profits slows down before the end of this stage. This slowdown in profits occurs because competitors enter the market, which often results in a lowering of prices and creates the need to spend additional promotional dollars to tell consumers why the firm's product is better than the competition's.

Maturity Stage

In the early part of the maturity stage, sales continue to increase, but at a decreasing rate. By the end of the stage, sales have begun to decline. Major home appliances are an example of a product in the maturity stage of the life cycle. As is happening in that industry, profits of both retailers and manufacturers begin to decline in the maturity stage, and many manufacturers cease their marketing efforts. Competition gets very tough, and some competitors cut prices to attract or hold on to business. At this stage, brands have quite similar physical attributes, and it is difficult for marketers to differentiate their products. Sales promotions of all types are used to encourage brand-switching by consumers and to encourage retailers to promote and give shelf space to the company's brands.

Decline Stage

Eventually, sales begin to decline, sometimes even rapidly. The causes of the decline may be market saturation (most households already have smoke detectors), new technology (color television sets replacing black-and-white models), or changes in social values. The decline in volume often results in higher costs. Therefore, it is important for marketers, at this stage, to eliminate those products that are no longer profitable or to find ways of cutting operational and marketing costs by eliminating marginal dealers and distributors, cutting advertising and sales promotion, and minimizing sales costs. These cuts could result in renewed profitability. In effect, the product is "milked"; that is, it is allowed to coast with decreased marketing support as long as it remains profitable. Those products which have developed brand loyalty among their customers will decline less rapidly than those products which have not been differentiated from their competitors.[4]

Guide Questions	*Answers*
_____	_____
_____	_____
_____	_____

Connection Questions	*Answers*
1. How will this information be useful to you as a consumer?	_____ _____
2. Why shouldn't you buy a new product as soon as it is introduced?	_____ _____ _____
3. Why would this information be important if you were a business major? When would you use it?	_____ _____ _____

Use Internal Dialogue

Internal dialogue, or mentally talking to yourself, is another excellent means of monitoring your comprehension. It involves rephrasing to yourself the message the author is expressing. You might think of internal dialogue as explaining what you are reading to someone else who has not read the material. Try to briefly and accurately express each idea. If you are unable to explain ideas in your own words, it is a strong indicator that your understanding is incomplete. Here are a few examples of how internal dialogue can be used.

1. While reading a section in a math textbook, you mentally outline the steps to follow in solving a sample problem.

2. You are reading an essay that argues convincingly that nuclear power plants are unsafe. As you finish reading each stage of the argument, you rephrase it in your own words.

3. As you finish each boldface section in a psychology chapter, you summarize the key points.

EXERCISE 5-3

Directions: *Complete each item as directed.*

1. *Read the following excerpt from a nursing textbook describing how to take a person's pulse. As you read the description use internal dialogue to express each step in your own words.*

TECHNIQUE FOR EVALUATING PULSES

If the pattern of a pulse rate is regular, you can count it for fifteen seconds and multiply by four to determine the person's pulse rate per minute. If it is not regular, you must count the rate for a full minute. Before you begin to take a pulse, be certain that the person is in a comfortable position since you do not know how long you will need to count. If he is lying supine, place his forearm across his chest and his palm downward; if he is sitting, bend his elbow ninety degrees and rest the elbow on the chair armrest. Gently place three of your fingertips on the designated pulse point with very light pressure. If you press on the artery too strongly, you will obscure blood flow and so not be able to feel a pulse any longer. Never palpate for a pulse with your thumb, which has such a strong pulse that it is possible to feel your own pulse when you press with it.[2]

2. *Read the following description of the elasticity of demand taken from an economics textbook. Use internal dialogue to explain to yourself how this principle of economics works.*

ELASTICITY OF DEMAND

We have seen some of the factors that influence consumer response to price changes. Purchases of some goods change much more than purchases of others when their prices rise or fall. For instance, a price change for monogrammed T-shirts is likely to change sales substantially. On the other hand, a price change for calculus textbooks is not likely to have much effect on students' purchases. Economists say that the demand for T-shirts is more elastic than the demand for calculus textbooks. Elasticity measures the response of consumer demand to a change in price. More precisely, demand elasticity is the percentage change in quantity demanded for some good relative to the percentage change in price for that good. This relationship is described by a simple equation:

$$\text{Elasticity} = \frac{\%\ \text{change in quantity demanded}}{\%\ \text{change in price}}$$

Elasticity is a number without units. It doesn't tell us the level of price or quantity but shows how quantity demanded changes when price changes.[3]

IMPROVING YOUR COMPREHENSION

As you monitor your comprehension, you will at times realize that your comprehension is poor or incomplete. When this occurs, take immediate action to improve it. Begin by identifying, as specifically as possible, the cause of the problem. Do this by answering the following question, "Why is this not making sense?" Determine if it is your lack of concentration, difficult words, complex ideas, or organization that is bothering you. Next, make changes in your reading to correct or compensate for it. Table 5-2 lists common problems and offers strategies to correct them.

EXERCISE 5-4

Directions: *Each of the following paragraphs will be difficult to read. Read each and monitor your comprehension as you read. After you have read each, identify and describe problems you experienced in reading. Next, indicate what strategies you would use to correct the problem(s).*

1. A word about food—in the simplest of terms, there are two kinds of organisms: those that make their own food, usually by photosynthesis (autotrophs, "self-feeders") and those that depend upon an outside-the-cell food source (heterotrophs, "other-feeders"). The autotrophs include a few kinds of bacteria, some one-celled eukaryotes (protistans), and all green plants. The heterotrophs encompass most bacteria, many protistans, all fungi, and all animals. Because this chapter is about animal nutrition, attention first will be given to examining the nature of food, then to how food is made available to cells.[4]

   • Problem: _____

   • Strategies: _____

2. There is reason to think that some tranquilizers owe their effects in reducing anxiety to interfering with dopamine. Heavy tranquilizers,

Table 5-2   HOW TO IMPROVE YOUR COMPREHENSION

Problems	*Strategies*
Poor concentration	1. Take frequent breaks. 2. Tackle difficult material when your mind is fresh and alert. 3. Use guide questions (see Chapter 4). 4. Refer to Chapter 4 "Improving Your Concentration."
Words are difficult or unfamiliar	1. Use context and analyze word parts. 2. Skim through material before reading. Mark and look up meanings of difficult words. Jot meanings in the margin.
Sentences are long or confusing	1. Read aloud. 2. Express each sentence in your own words. 3. Refer to Chapter 6 "Reading Difficult Sentences."
Ideas are hard to understand; complicated	1. Rephrase or explain each in your own words. 2. Make notes. 3. Locate a more basic text that explains ideas in simpler form. 4. Study with a classmate; discuss difficult ideas.

Ideas are new and unfamiliar; you have little or no knowledge about the topic and the writer assumes you do	1. Make sure you didn't miss or skip introductory information.
	2. Get background information by
	   a. referring to an earlier section or chapter in the book.
	   b. referring to an encyclopedia.
	   c. referring to a more basic text.

The material seems disorganized or poorly organized or there seems to be no organization	1. Pay more attention to headings. 2. Read the summary, if available. 3. Try to discover organization by writing an outline or drawing a map as you read (Refer to Chapter 11).
You don't know what is important; everything seems important	1. Use previewing. 2. Ask and answer guide questions. 3. Locate and underline topic sentences (See Chapter 7).

such as chlorpromazine (Thorazine) and trifupromazine (Stelazine), used to treat schizophrenics, can lower dopamine levels, which appear to be abnormally high in some types of schizophrenia. Conversely, individuals who have taken heavy tranquilizers to reduce anxiety may develop temporary schizophrenia-like symptoms when they stop using them. Reserpine, the first of the heavy tranquilizers to be put into use in mental hospitals, apparently owes its effectiveness to its ability to reduce the output of norepinephrine in the central nervous system. The effectiveness of milder tranquilizers also is due to interactions with NTs or their receptors. Valium, the most widely prescribed tranquilizer, blocks GABA-receptor sites in postsynaptic membranes of brain neurons. Gamma aminobutyric acid (GABA) is the most abundant NT in the brain.[5]

- Problem: _____

- Strategies: _____

3. The strategic-industry argument. The objective of some tariffs is to protect an industry that produces goods vital to a nation's defense. In the case of a strategic industry, productive efficiency relative to that of other nations may not be an important consideration. The domestic industry—oil, natural gas, shipping, or steel, for example—may require protection because of its importance to national defense. Without protection, such industries might be weakened by foreign competition. Then, in an international crisis, the nation might find itself in short supply of products essential to national defense.[6]

- Problem: _____

- Strategies: _____

SUMMARY

Comprehension monitoring is a means of checking or keeping track of your comprehension as you read. This chapter first describes positive and negative comprehension signals that will help you monitor your comprehension. Four monitoring strategies are presented: establishing checkpoints, using guide questions, asking connection questions, and using internal dialogue. Various problems that cause poor comprehension are described and strategies for overcoming each are presented.

PART TWO REVIEW

MAKING YOUR SKILLS WORK TOGETHER

Part Two focused on techniques to help you read actively—to get involved with what you read, and think about what you are reading. In Chapter 4 you learned five techniques to use before you read to build your comprehension. In Chapter 5 you learned to monitor your comprehension and to take action when it is poor or incomplete. Now let's apply these skills together and see how they affect your comprehension.

EXERCISE 1

Directions: *Read the following article on violence and television. Use the following steps.*

1. Assess your attitude. Are you approaching this assignment as busywork or are you doing it to learn how these skills in Chapters 4 and 5 work together?

2. Assess where you are working. Are your surroundings conducive to concentration? Set a time limit for the completion of this assignment.

3. Preview the article.

4. Activate what you already know about violence in television by asking questions or brainstorming.

5. Develop three to four guide questions and write them below:

   1. _____

   2. _____

   3. _____

   4. _____

6. Read the article. As you read monitor your comprehension.

7. Answer each of your guide questions.

   1. _____

   2. _____

   3. _____

   4. _____

8. Use the following questions to evaluate how well you monitored your comprehension and how well you understood the article.

   1. Without referring to the article, write a list of the major effects of television violence.

   2. Cite three examples in which television led to violent behavior.

TV VIOLENCE: THE SHOCKING NEW EVIDENCE

—Eugene T. Methvin

- San Diego: A high-school honor student watches a lurid ABC-TV   1
fictionalization of the 1890s Lizzie Borden ax murder case; then
chops his own parents and sister to death and leaves his brother a
quadriplegic.

- Denver: *The Deer Hunter* is telecast and a 17-year-old kills himself   2
with a revolver, acting out the movie's climactic game of Russian
roulette. He is the 25th viewer in two years to kill himself that way
after watching the drama on TV.

- Decatur, Ill.: A 12-year-old overdoses on sleeping pills after her   3
mother forbids her to date a 16-year-old boy. "What gave you the
idea of suicide?" an investigating psychiatrist asks. The answer: A
little girl tried it on a TV show, was quickly revived and welcomed
back by her parents with open arms.

Ten years ago, after studying massive research on the subject, the U.S.   4
Surgeon General, Jesse L. Steinfeld, declared, "The causal relationship
between televised violence and antisocial behavior is sufficient to warrant

immediate remedial action." Called before Congress, the presidents of the three networks solemnly agreed.

Yet the University of Pennsylvania's Annenberg School of Com- 5 munications, which for 14 years has charted mayhem in network programming, reports that violent acts continue at about six per prime-time hour and in four out of every five programs. The weekend children's programs are even worse.

Last May the National Institute of Mental Health (NIMH) issued a 6 report summarizing over 2500 studies done in the last decade on television's influence on behavior. Evidence from the studies—with more than 100,000 subjects in dozens of nations—is so "overwhelming," the NIMH found, that there is a consensus in the research community "that violence on television does lead to aggressive behavior."

Television ranks behind only sleep and work as a consumer of our 7 time. In fact, according to the 1982 Nielsen Report on Television, the average American family keeps its set on for 49½ hours each week. The typical youngster graduating from high school will have spent almost twice as much time in front of the tube as he has in the classroom—the staggering equivalent of ten years of 40-hour weeks. He will have witnessed some 150,000 violent episodes, including an estimated 25,000 deaths.

Despite the mayhem, the viewer sees little pain or suffering, a false 8 picture that influences young and old. At a Capitol Hill hearing on TV violence, a dismayed Rep. Billy Tauzin complained to network executives that his three-year-old son had poked his fist through a glass door—in imitation of a TV cartoon character—and almost bled to death. In New Rochelle, N.Y., a killer who re-enacted a TV bludgeon murder told police of his surprise when his victim did not die with the first crunch of his baseball bat, as on the tube, but instead threw up a hand in defense and groaned and cried piteously.

The effect of all this? Research points toward these conclusions: 9

1. TV violence produces lasting and serious harm. University of Il- 10 linois psychology professor Leonard Eron and colleagues compared the television diets and level of aggressive behavior of 184 boys at age eight and again at eighteen. His report: "The more violent the programs watched in childhood, the more combative the young adults became. We found their behavior studded with antisocial acts, from theft and vandalism to assault with a deadly weapon. The children appeared to learn aggressive habits that persisted for at least ten years."

2. Those "action" cartoons on children's programs are decidedly 11 *damaging.* Stanford University psychologist Albert Bandura found cartoon violence as potent as real-life models in increasing violence among youngsters. A University of Kansas researcher reported that Saturday-morning cartoons markedly decreased imaginative play and hiked aggression among

66 preschoolers. In a year-long study of 200 preschoolers, Yale University Drs. Jerome L. and Dorothy Singer found that playground depredations like fighting and kicking were far greater among steady action-cartoon viewers.

Indeed, the Saturday-morning "kid vid" ghetto is the most violent 12 time in TV. It bathes the prime audience of youngsters from three to thirteen years old with 25 violent acts per hour, much of it in a poisonous brew of violent programs and aggressive commercials designed to sell such products as breakfast cereals and action toys. According to one study, these commercials have a rate of violence about three times that of the programs themselves.

3. TV erodes inhibitions. With a $290,000 grant from CBS, British 13 psychologist William A. Belson studied the television diets and subsequent behavior of 1565 London boys ages twelve to seventeen. He found cartoon, slapstick or science-fiction violence less harmful at this age; but realistic fictional violence, violence in close personal relationships, and violence "in a good cause" were deadly poison. Heavy viewers were forty-seven-percent more likely to commit acts such as knifing during a school fight, burning another with a cigarette, slashing car tires, burglary and attempted rape. To Belson's surprise, the TV exposure did not seem to change the boys' opinions toward violence but rather seemed to crumble whatever constraints family, church or school had built up. "It is almost as if the boys then tend to let go whatever violent tendencies are in them. It just seems to explode in spontaneous ways."

4. The sheer quantity of TV watching by youngsters increases 14 *hurtful behavior and poor academic performance.* "When the TV set is on, it freezes everybody," says Cornell University psychologist Urie Bronfen-brenner. "Everything that used to go on between people—the games, the arguments, the emotional scenes out of which personality and ability develop—is stopped. When you turn on the TV, you turn off the process of making human beings human."

Studies in the United States, Canada, Israel, Australia and Europe 15 show that the amount of TV watched, regardless of program content, is a critical variable that contributes heavily to children's later aggressive attitudes and behavior. Dozens of other studies indicate that TV impairs the children's verbal skills and creativeness.

PART THREE

COMPREHENSION SKILLS

Sue was taking a business organization and management course and was finding the textbook difficult to understand. After she got a grade of D on the first exam, she decided to talk with her instructor. She began by explaining that she found the text difficult and felt this was the source of her problem. When the instructor asked why the text was difficult, she said, "It's got a lot of hard words, the sentences and paragraphs are long, and there aren't enough examples." Her instructor sat quietly as Sue mentioned each of these problems.

When she finished, he said, "Sue, I understand all you've told me, but I think you've overlooked one very important problem." Sue was puzzled; she thought for a moment and then asked what she had overlooked. The instructor gave a one-word reply: "YOU!" Then he explained that Sue's reading and study skills also affected how well she was able to understand the textbook. He mentioned such things as her vocabulary level, ability to grasp ideas, and ability to understand the organization of textbook sections, chapters, and paragraphs. He explained all of this is important to understanding a textbook. Sue came to realize that her problem was not that the textbook was too difficult—actually, she lacked the skills to understand it.

The purpose of this part of the book is to develop your reading skills so that you will be able to understand the textbooks you are using.

THIS PART OF THE TEXT WILL HELP YOU IMPROVE YOUR SKILLS SO THAT:

1. You will understand how sentences and paragraphs are structured. (Chapters 6 and 7)

2. You will be familiar with the various organizational patterns that writers commonly use. (Chapter 8)

Chapter 6

UNDERSTANDING SENTENCE PATTERNS

THIS CHAPTER WILL SHOW YOU HOW TO

1. **Identify the parts of a sentence that express its basic meaning**

2. **Recognize sentences that combine ideas**

3. **Read complicated sentences**

Suppose you read the following sentence in a textbook on the United States government:

> The president is his party's leader, not by any authority of the Constitution, whose authors abhorred parties, but by strong tradition and practical necessity.

Try to explain what this sentence means. The real test of whether you understand an idea is whether you can express it in your own words.

Basically, the sentence explains why the president is the leader of his political party. Although less important, the sentence also explains that this is not a rule stated in the Constitution. Finally, the sentence contains the additional information that the authors of the Constitution abhorred, or hated, political parties.

Now, let us look at what was done to arrive at this meaning. Answer each of the following questions:

1. Did you search for the most important information in the sentence?

2. Did you think certain groups of words were more important than others?

3. Did you try to see how the parts of the sentence were connected?

If you answered "yes" to each of these questions, you are well on your way to reading sentences effectively. Together, these questions suggest an approach to sentence reading. This chapter will show you how to find important information in sentences, sort or sift out less-important ideas, and see how ideas are connected.

IDENTIFYING KEY IDEAS

Every sentence expresses at least one key idea, or basic message. This key idea is made up of two parts, a simple subject and a simple predicate. The simple subject, usually a noun, identifies the person or object the sentence is about. The main part of the predicate—the simple predicate—is a verb, which tells what the person or object is doing or has done. Usually a sentence contains additional information about the subject and/or the predicate.

Example:

The average American drank six gallons of beer last year.

The key idea of this sentence is "American drank." It is expressed by the simple subject and predicate. The simple subject of this sentence is *American*; it tells what the sentence is about. The words *the* and *average* give more information about the subject, American, by telling which one. The main part of the predicate is the verb *drank*; this tells what the average American did. The rest of the sentence gives more information about the predicate by telling what and how much was drunk. Here are a few more examples:

George studied for three hours last night.

Kathy lives in Boston near the waterfront.

Food prices have risen drastically in the past four years.

In many long and complicated sentences, the key idea is not as obvious as in the previous examples. To find the key idea, ask:

1. Who or what is the sentence about?

2. What is happening in the sentence?

Here is an example of a complicated sentence that might be found in a psychology textbook:

Intelligence, as measured by IQ, depends on the kind of test given, the skill of the examiner, and the cooperation of the subject.

In this sentence, the answer to the question, "Who or what is the sentence about?" is "intelligence." The verb is *depends*, and the remainder of the sentence explains the factors upon which intelligence depends. Let us look at a few more examples.

William James, often thought of as the father of American psychology, tested whether memory could be improved by exercising it.

Violence in sports, both at amateur and professional levels, has increased dramatically over the past ten years.

Some sentences may have more than one subject and/or more than one verb in the predicate.

Example:

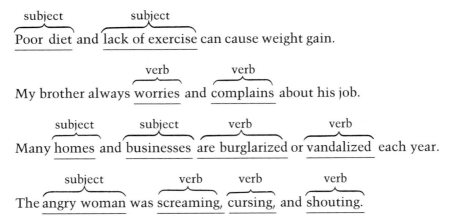

EXERCISE 6-1

Directions: *Find the key idea in each of the following sentences. Draw one line under the simple subject and two lines under the verb.*

Example: The instructor assigned a fifteen-page article to read.

1. Every summer my parents travel to the eastern seacoast.

2. Children learn how to behave by imitating adults.

3. William Faulkner, a popular American author, wrote about life in the South.

4. Psychologists are interested in studying human behavior in many different situations.

5. Mentally ill patients often refuse to take prescribed medication.

6. Elements exist either as compounds or as free elements.

7. Attention may be defined as a focusing of perception.

8. Cocaine, although illegal, is apparently increasing in use.

9. The most accurate method we have of estimating the age of the earth is based on our knowledge of radioactivity.

10. The specific instructions in a computer program are written in a computer language.

LOCATING DETAILS

After you have identified the key idea, the next step in understanding a sentence is to see how the details affect its meaning. Most details either add to or change the meaning of the key idea. Usually they answer such questions about the subject or predicate as what, where, which, when, how, or why. For example:

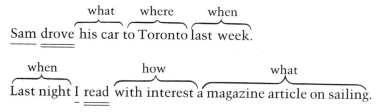

As you read a sentence, be sure to notice how the details change, limit, or add to the meaning of the key idea. Decide, for each of the following examples, how the underlined portion affects the meaning of the key idea.

Chemistry is really a language, <u>a way of describing things we see every day</u>.

The scientists <u>with the most liberal attitudes</u> urged further study of nuclear power.

The film <u>about the death of the basketball star</u> was depressing.

In the first example, the underlined detail explains in what way chemistry is a language. In the second example, the underlined detail tells which scientists (only those with the most liberal attitudes) urged further study. In the third example, the underlined detail describes the film.

EXERCISE 6-2

Directions: *Read each of the following sentences and decide what the underlined part of the sentence tells about the key idea. Write* what, which, when, where, how, *or* why *in the space provided.*

1. You can relieve tension through exercise. _____

2. The English instructor summarized the plot. _____

3. Many students in computer science courses can use the computer terminals only late at night. _____

4. Many shoppers clip coupons to reduce their grocery bill. _____

5. After class I am going to talk to my instructor. _____

6. Astronomers have learned about stars and galaxies by analyzing radiation they emit. _____

7. The world's oil supply is concentrated in only a few places around the globe. _____

8. Light traveling through empty space will move in a straight line. _____

9. Cobalt, essential for the manufacture of jet aircraft engines, is a valuable resource. _____

10. Ebbinghaus, one of psychology's pioneers, studied learning and memory processes. _____

SENTENCES THAT COMBINE IDEAS

Sentences always express one idea. However, some sentences may express *more* than one idea. Two or more complete ideas can be built into or combined into one sentence. Here are two examples:

$$\underbrace{\text{subject}}\quad \underbrace{\text{verb}}\qquad\qquad \underbrace{\text{subject}}\;\underbrace{\text{verb}}$$
Some students decided to take the final, but others chose to write a paper.

$$\underbrace{\text{subject}}\;\underbrace{\text{verb}}\qquad\qquad \underbrace{\text{subject}}\;\underbrace{\text{verb}}$$
I read all the assigned chapters; I wrote an outline of each.

Two ideas within a single sentence are connected in one of two ways:

1. The two ideas may be connected with a **comma and a connecting word**. These are: and, but, or, nor, so, for, yet. Example:

Television is entertaining, and it is educational.

2. Two ideas may also be joined using a **semicolon**.

Example:

Television is entertaining; it is also educational.

Two ideas are often combined to explain and emphasize the relationship between them. The word chosen to connect them often signals the relationship. Here is a list of connecting words and what they tell you about the relationship between the ideas.

Connecting Word	*Meaning Signals*
and	links similar and equally important ideas

Example:

The librarian was knowledgeable about my topic *and* helped me locate several sources.

but, yet	connects opposite ideas or change in thought

Example:

Vanessa expected a high grade, *yet* she received a C.

for, so	indicates reasons or shows that one thing is causing another

Example:

Data processing is my major, *so* I have to take several math courses.

or, nor	suggests choice or options exist

Example:

We will go bowling, *or* we will see a movie.

A semicolon usually signals a close connection between equally important ideas. It functions much the same as the connecting word "and."

Some sentences are made up of one key idea and one less important idea that explains or expands on the key idea. The less important idea has its own subject and verb, but does not make sense by itself. This idea always explains or provides more information about the key idea. It may tell why, when, how, or describe. Here are several examples.

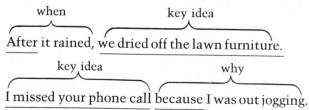

The word that connects the two ideas indicates how the ideas are connected. They are meaning signals. "After" in the first example tells *when* the lawn furniture was dried off. "Because" in the second example indicates a reason will be given. The following list gives common connecting words and tells you the meaning of each.

Connecting words	*Meaning clues*
before, after	indicates time (when)

Example:

Before I left, I said goodbye.

because	gives reasons (why)

Example:

Because I lost my keys, I was late for class.

if, unless	explains conditions or circumstances

Example:

Unless I get my car inspected, I will not be able to drive it.

although, however	qualifies, explains, describes circumstances

Example:

Although I left early, I was late for class.

As you read sentences in which ideas are combined, pay attention to the connecting word used. It should signal the relationship of ideas. You must be sure to pick up the signal. You should know *why* the two ideas have been combined and *what* they have to do with each other.

EXERCISE 6-3

Directions: *For each idea in Column A, find an idea in Column B that could be joined with it to form a sentence. Pay close attention to the connecting words used.*

Column A	*Column B*
1. Because it rained,	a. however, he did not explain why this is true.
2. The dinner at her aunt's house was very nutritional	b. or they will rent a cottage on a lake.
3. The professor taught us that some people have better memories than others,	c. I should get a good grade on it.

4. She recalled the meaning of the word,

    d. for I just wound it a few hours ago.

5. If I study for the exam,

    e. after she took the vocabulary quiz.

6. Roderick's bedroom window was open;

    f. we canceled our annual picnic.

7. My friends will go to California this summer,

    g. he put on his new suit.

8. The grandfather clock ought to run,

    h. however, he enjoyed the films shown in class.

9. Sam disliked the course content, the professor, and the book;

    i. the smell of his neighbor's barbecue blew in and made him hungry.

10. Before Thomas went to the job interview,

    j. and it was absolutely delicious.

EXERCISE 6-4

Directions: *Complete each of the following sentences by supplying a complete thought that makes sense with the first thought. Pay close attention to the connecting word.*

1. Because I ran out of time on my exam. . . _____

2. After I took my psychology exam. . . _____

3. Although the library is open weekends. . . _____

4. Unless I get an "A" on my next paper in English. . . _____

5. After a car runs out of gas. . . _____

6. The poverty rate in the United States is low, but. . . _____

7. Bad eating habits have been found to lead to cancer, so. . . _____

8. Handguns may be made illegal, or. . . _____

9. Russia has agreed to limit
   nuclear weapons, and. . .   _____

10. People have become very health
    conscious, yet   _____

EXERCISE 6-5

Directions: *Read each of the following sentences. In the space provided
describe* how *the underlined idea is related to the rest of the sentence. For
example, does it give a reason, indicate time, explain a condition, present
an opposite idea, or offer choices?*

1. I will probably transfer to a four-year school next year <u>unless I find a
   good job.</u>

2. <u>Although I broke my leg,</u> I am still able to drive a car.

3. She'll become a secretary <u>or she will be forced to go back to school for
   further training.</u>

4. She always picks up her mail <u>after she eats lunch.</u>

5. He would have been drafted to go to Vietnam, <u>but he was a student
   and was exempt.</u>

6. <u>Since the corporation is community-oriented,</u> it donates large amounts
   to local charities.

7. <u>Because violence is regularly shown on television,</u> children accept it as
   an ordinary part of life.

8. <u>As far as scientists can tell from available research,</u> some types of cancer may be caused by a virus.

9. <u>Because a vaccine was developed,</u> polio has practically been elimi-
   nated.

10. <u>Since comparison shopping is a necessary part of the buying process,</u>
    wise consumers look for differences in quality as well as price.

READING COMPLICATED SENTENCES

Many sentences are short, direct, and straightforward, and are easy to
understand. Others are long and complicated. The following example compares a simple sentence with a complicated one. The second sentence is
complicated because some facts were added to explain the key idea (underlined).

Simple Sentence:

> <u>Humans and animals go to sleep</u> once every twenty-four hours.

Complicated Sentence:

> Recent psychological research suggests that due to the operation of a "biological clock," <u>humans and animals go to sleep,</u> on the average, once every 24 hours, even when light, temperature, noise, and humidity are carefully controlled so as not to provide time signals.

In the second sentence you find out *how* we know, *why* sleep occurs every twenty-four hours, and *under what conditions* the clock was tested.

The key to understanding a complicated sentence is to unravel it, identify its key idea, and analyze how each additional piece (fact) modifies the meaning of that idea. Use the following steps:

Step 1. Locate the key idea(s). Establish what the sentence is about and what action is occurring. Be alert for two or more subjects and/or verbs. Many complicated sentences have more than one key idea.

Step 2. Study the modifiers. Identify how each remaining piece of the sentence alters its meaning. Does it describe the subject? Does it tell when, why, how, or where the action occurred?

Step 3. Paraphrase. Express the sentence's basic meaning in your own words without referring to the sentence. Split it into two or more basic sentences, if necessary. This step provides the truest test of whether you actually understand the sentence.

Step 4. Check vocabulary. If Step 3 fails, then difficult or technical vocabulary may be interfering with your comprehension. Check your text's glossary or consult the dictionary.

Here is an example of the above procedure:

Sentence:

> Since various body movements can be interpreted differently by different people and the interpretation may depend on the situation, non-verbal communication, or communication without words, can create confusion, which results in communication failure or distortion.

Step 1. Locate the key idea.

nonverbal communication	can create	confusion
↑	↑	↑
subject	verb	object

Step 2. Study the modifiers. The first part of the sentence gives two reasons why nonverbal communication can create confusion. A brief definition of the term non-verbal communication is included. The end of the sentence tells what happens as a result of the confusion.

Step 3. Paraphrase. The sentence might be paraphrased as follows:

Nonverbal communication, which is communication without words, can create confusion. There are two reasons: (1) differences in interpretation and, (2) meanings may change with the situation. This confusion causes communication to break down or be misunderstood.

Step 4. Check the vocabulary. If necessary, check the meaning of words such as "interpretation" and "distortion."

EXERCISE 6-6

Directions: *Read each of the following sentences, using the procedure suggested above. Underline the key idea of each sentence, and, in the space provided, paraphrase each sentence.*

1. A psychological test is a measuring instrument used to assess an individual's standing, relative to others, on some mental or behavioral characteristic such as intelligence, personality, vocational interest, or scholastic ability.[1]

   _____

   _____

2. One theory of pain control is called the gate-control theory, which assumes that the nervous system is able to handle only a limited amount of information at any one time; if too much information is sent through, certain cells in the spinal cord act as "gates," blocking some signals and sending others.

   _____

   _____

3. Counseling psychologists typically work in community settings— within a business, school, prison, or neighborhood clinic—and use interviews, tests, guidance, and advising to help people solve problems and make decisions.

   _____

   _____

4. Although some students regard listening as a passive process in which they simply monitor what they hear, listening is actually a process that requires both emotional and intellectual involvement.

   _____

   _____

5. Although it requires starting capital and business operational skill, the sole proprietorship, a business owned by one person, is the most common form of business ownership in the United States.

Types of Complicated Sentences

Long or complicated sentences force you to think about how ideas tie together. You must also follow closely the sense and logic of the idea being expressed. The following section describes three types of difficult sentences to watch for as you read. Once you are familiar with each type, you will be able to read them more easily.

REVERSED ORDER OF EVENTS

Most sentences present ideas in chronological order—the order in which they occur—as in the following sentence:

After class, I went to the bookstore.

However, some sentences do not follow this order. Instead, the order is reversed:

I went to the bookstore after class.

To understand this sentence, you easily make a mental switch of events. However, when the ideas are more complex, the sequence is less obvious and sometimes easy to miss:

The industrial workers became union members whereas before they were independent.

Here, you must transform the sentence by thinking: "The workers were independent, then they became union members."

When reading reversed order sentences, stop and establish the correct order of events before continuing to read.

EXERCISE 6-7

Directions: *For each of the following sentences, list the events in correct, chronological order.*

1. American intervention in the Vietnam War followed earlier French involvement.

---

2. Although it has recently been revised and extended, the Omnibus Crime Control and Safe Streets Act, when passed in 1968, was intended to fight lawlessness.

_____

3. In computing federal income tax owed, in order to consult a tax table, you must compute your adjusted gross income and taxable income.

_____

4. In computing net cost, before you subtract cash discount, you must subtract trade discounts from the list price.

_____

5. Prior to a presidential review of the proposed federal budget, the Office of Management and Budget holds hearings and reviews its assessment of the economy.

_____

SPLIT SUBJECT AND VERB

In most sentences the subject and verb immediately follow one another, as in this sentence:

"Effective <u>managers share</u> a number of common characteristics."

However, in some sentences the subject and verb are split. Additional information is placed between them, and the sentence becomes more difficult to read:

<u>Managers,</u> who are powerful and successful in controlling the actions and behavior of others, <u>share</u> a number of common characteristics.

When the subject and verb are split, you are forced to keep the subject in mind while you read the additional information until you reach the action of the sentence. For this type of sentence, deliberately fix the subject in mind. When you reach the verb, be sure to connect it with the subject. Reread if necessary.

EXERCISE 6-8

Directions: *For each of the following sentences underline the subject and verb. Then express each in your own words.*

1. Consumer goods, products purchased for use by households, can be further classified as convenience, substitute, or complementary goods.

_____

2. Israel, with borders easily crossed by hostile tanks and infantry and further limited by its tiny size, has restricted national defense capabilities.

   ———————————————————————————

3. Crimes committed in the course of one's occupation by those who operate inside business, government, or other establishments, in violation of their sense of loyalty to the employer or client, are among the most difficult to identify.

   ———————————————————————————

4. A distinguished panel of educators and lawyers, which recently concluded that the only just system of punishment is one which is severe and strict, proposed a maximum penalty for all crimes but murder of five years imprisonment.[2]

   ———————————————————————————

5. Currency and things that can be changed into currency very easily, such as bank accounts, stocks, bonds, treasury bills, and the like, are termed liquid assets.[3]

   ———————————————————————————

PRONOUN SUBSTITUTIONS

Complicated sentences use pronouns (words such as he, she, they, this, and that) instead of the words they stand for. Pronouns serve as substitutes for other words or phrases in the same sentence or in previous sentences. Here is an example:

Regardless of the problems the two senators faced, <u>they</u> always voted the same way.

Here the pronoun "they" has been substituted for the phrase "the two senators." While this substitution is clearly understood, other substitutions are less obvious, especially if two or more sentences are involved. For example:

Many frustrated minorities blame their problems on past imperialism. Borders violate ethnic lines because <u>they</u> reflect the points at which advancing armies stopped, or where "deals" between big powers were reached.[4]

In these sentences, you must determine to what word the pronoun "they" refers. Does it refer to "minorities," "imperialism," or "borders"? Careful reading reveals it is the "borders" that reflect points . . .

In reading sentences of this type, be certain you clearly identify the word or phrase to which each pronoun refers. For sentences beginning with "this" or "it," look back to previous sentences, if necessary.

EXERCISE 6-9

Directions: *For each of the following sentences, write the word(s) to which the underlined words refer in the margin. Then paraphrase its meaning.*

1. The rate of inflation declined in the early 1980s—from a high of 13 percent in 1980 to 6 percent in 1982, but <u>this</u> was accomplished only by a dramatic slowdown of the economy.

   _____

2. No-name brand products were developed in 1976 in France by the Carrefour supermarket chain. It called these free products, because, it explained, <u>they</u> were free of costly advertising and packaging.

   _____

3. Pregnancy and childrearing once meant long-term interruptions in most women's careers. <u>This</u> helped define women of childbearing age as unpromising employees for jobs that required training or commitment.

   _____

4. According to the Congressional Budget Office, nearly 900,000 workers lost jobs in declining industries by 1983, almost half of them from just four basic industries: auto, primary and fabricated metals, and apparel. <u>These</u> workers are most often (though by no means always) former semiskilled workers in traditional manufacturing.[5]

   _____

5. There are several clues that indicate the ability of a business to adapt and use the skills of <u>its</u> employees.

   _____

SUMMARY

A sentence expresses at least one key idea, which consists of a simple subject and a verb. The remainder of the sentence contains information that explains, clarifies, or limits the key idea. Not all words in a sentence are of equal importance. In reading a sentence, sort through the words to locate the key idea and to determine how the rest of the sentence affects the key idea.

Two or more complete ideas may be combined into a single sentence. This is done to emphasize or clarify the relationship between the ideas. Some sentences contain a key idea and a related but less important idea. Be sure to notice how the two ideas are related. Pay particular attention to the connecting word. Usually the less important idea explains the key idea by describing, expressing cause, stating purpose or reason, describing conditions or circumstances, or expressing time relationships.

The key to reading a complicated sentence is to unravel it. Identify its key idea or ideas and then study how the modifiers alter the meaning. Next, paraphrase, or express the meaning in your own words. Check the meaning of unfamiliar words, if necessary. Three types of difficult sentences are reversed order of events, split subject and verb, and pronoun substitution.

Chapter 7

UNDERSTANDING PARAGRAPHS

THIS CHAPTER WILL SHOW YOU HOW TO

1. **Identify main ideas in paragraphs**

2. **Pick out the key details**

3. **Use transitions to make reading easier**

When you go to see a movie, the first thing you want to know is: "What is it about?" As the movie begins, various characters interact. To understand this interaction, you have to know who the characters are and understand what they are saying. Then you have to note how the characters relate to one another. To grasp the point the film is making, you have to realize what all of the conversation and action, taken together, means.

Understanding a paragraph is similar in ways to understanding a movie. The first thing you need to know is what the paragraph is about. Then you have to understand each of the sentences and what they are saying. Next, you have to see how the sentences relate to one another. Finally, to understand the main point of the paragraph, you have to consider what all the sentences, taken together, mean.

The one thing the whole paragraph is about is called the *topic*. The point that the whole paragraph makes is called the *main idea*. The sentences that explain the main idea are called *details*. To connect their ideas, writers use words and phrases known as *transitions*.

A paragraph, then, is a group of related sentences about a single topic. It has four essential parts: (1) topic, (2) main idea, (3) details, and (4) transitions. To read paragraphs most efficiently, you will need to become familiar with each part of a paragraph and be able to identify and use these parts as you read.

GENERAL AND SPECIFIC IDEAS

To identify topics and main ideas in paragraphs, it will help you to understand the difference between *general* and *specific*. A general idea is a broad idea that applies to a large number of specific items. The term *clothing* is general because it refers to a large collection of specific items— slacks, suits, blouses, shirts, scarves, and so on. A specific idea or term is more detailed or particular. It refers to individual items. The word scarf, for example, is a particular term. The phrase *red plaid scarf* is even more specific.

Examples:

General: pies
Specific: chocolate cream
        apple
        cherry

General: countries
Specific: England
        Finland
        Brazil

General: fruit
Specific: grapes
        lemons
        pineapples

General: types of context clues
Specific: definition
        example
        contrast

General: word parts
Specific: prefix
        root
        suffix

EXERCISE 7-1

Directions: *Read each of the following items and decide what term(s) will complete the group. Write the word(s) in the spaces provided.*

1. General: college courses
   Specific: math

   _____

   _____

2. General: _____

   Specific: roses
   tulips
   narcissus

3. General: musical groups

   Specific: _____

   _____

   _____

4. General: art
   Specific: sculpture

   _____

   _____

5. General: types of movies
   Specific: comedies

   _____

   _____

EXERCISE 7-2

Directions: *Underline the most general term in each group of words.*

1. pounds, ounces, kilograms, weights
2. soda, coffee, beverage, wine
3. soap operas, news, TV programs, sports special
4. home furnishings, carpeting, drapes, wall hangings
5. sociology, social sciences, anthropology, psychology

Now we will apply the idea of general and specific to paragraphs. The main idea is the most general statement the writer makes about the topic. Pick out the most general statement among the following sentences.

1. People differ according to height.

2. Hair color distinguishes some people from others.

3. People differ in a number of different ways.

4. Each person has his or her own personality.

Did you choose item 3 as the most general statement? Now we will change this list into a paragraph, rearranging the list and adding a few facts.

> People differ in numerous ways. They differ according to physical characteristics, such as height, weight, and hair color. They also differ in personality. Some people are friendly and easygoing. Others are more reserved and formal.

In this paragraph, the main idea is expressed in the first sentence. This sentence is the most general statement expressed in the paragraph. All the other statements are specific details that explain this main idea.

IDENTIFYING THE TOPIC

The topic is the one thing a paragraph is about. Every sentence in a paragraph in some way discusses or explains this topic. Think of the topic as the subject of the entire paragraph. If you had to choose a title for a paragraph, the one or two words you would choose are the topic.

To find the topic of a paragraph, ask yourself: What is the one thing the author is discussing throughout the paragraph?

Now, read the following paragraph with this question in mind:

> Flextime, which began in the mid-1960s as an alternative work schedule experiment, will be a fact of life in many industries in the 21st century. We'll work not according to traditional work schedules but according to our biological and emotional rhythms. The night owls among us will be delighted to work the lobster shifts and let the rest of us work during the day. The number of hours worked won't be as significant as what you accomplish when you work. The advantage of flextime is that it permits flexible, cost-effective work arrangements.

In this example, the author is discussing one topic—flextime—throughout the paragraph. Notice that the words *flexible* and *flextime* are used several times. Often the repeated use of a word can serve as a clue to the topic.

EXERCISE 7-3

Directions: *Read each of the following paragraphs. Write the topic of each paragraph in the space provided.*

1. Discrimination doesn't go away: it just aims at whatever group appears to be out of fashion at any given moment. One expert feels that *age* is the major factor in employment discrimination today, although studies have shown older workers may be more reliable than young workers and just as productive. The Age Discrimination in Employment Act gives protection to the worker between forty and sixty-five. If you're in this age range, your employer must prove that you have performed unsatisfactorily before he can legally fire you. This act also prohibits age discrimination in hiring, wages, and benefits. To report age discrimination, call your local office of the Wage and Hours Division of the U.S. Labor Department, or the Human Relations Commission in your state. If local offices are unable to help, try the national Equal Employment Opportunity Commission, Washington, D.C. 20460.[1]

   Topic: _____

2. Traditionally for men, and increasingly for women, one's job or career is tied in intimately with the way one regards oneself. Thus, loss of job becomes in part a loss of identity, and in part a seeming criticism of oneself as a total being, not merely as a worker. Even people who have lost jobs in mass layoffs through no fault of their own often feel guilty, especially if they are in the role of provider and no longer feel competent in fulfilling that role.

   Topic: _____

3. The words "effortless exercise" are a contradiction in terms. Muscles grow in strength only when subjected to overload. Flexibility is developed only by extending the normal range of body motion. Endurance is developed only through exercise that raises the pulse rate enough to achieve a training effect on the heart, lungs, and circulatory system. In all cases, the benefits from exercise come from extending the body beyond its normal activity range. What this requires is, precisely, effort.

   Topic: _____

4. Mental illness is usually diagnosed from abnormal behavior. A woman is asked the time of day, and she begins to rub her arms and recite the Apostles' Creed. A man is so convinced that someone is "out to get him" that he refuses to leave his apartment. Unusual behaviors like these are taken as evidence that the mental apparatus is not working quite right, and mental illness is proclaimed.[2]

   Topic: _____

5. How, exactly, does sleep replenish your body's fund of energy? Despite much interesting recent research on sleep, we still don't know. Certainly the metabolic rate slows during sleep (down to a level of about one met). Respiration, heartbeat, and other body functions slow down; muscular and digestive systems slow or cease their activity, allowing time for tissue repair. But the precise mechanisms by which sleep restores and refreshes us remain a mystery.

Topic: _____

HOW TO FIND THE MAIN IDEA

The main idea of a paragraph is the most important idea; it is the idea that the whole paragraph explains or supports. Usually it is expressed in one sentence called the *topic sentence*. To find the main idea, use the following suggestions.

Locate the Topic

You have learned that the topic is the one thing a paragraph is about. The main idea is the most important thing the author wants you to know about the topic. It is the most important statement about the topic. To find the main idea, ask yourself, "What is the one most important thing to know about the topic?" Now read the following paragraph and answer this question:

Family violence is a widespread problem in the United States. Family disputes account for 30 percent of the aggravated assaults and 33 percent of homicides. More police officers are killed handling domestic disputes than in any other activity. We often assume that such violence is carried on by people who are mentally deranged, but research has found that this is not true. Normal people in all walks of life and at all economic levels fall victim to family violence.

In this example, the topic is family violence. The most important point the author is making is that family violence is a problem in the United States.

Locate the Most General Sentence

The most general sentence in the paragraph expresses the main idea. This sentence is called the topic sentence. This sentence must be general enough to include or cover all the other ideas (details) in the paragraph. In the above paragraph, the first sentence makes a general statement about family violence—that it is a widespread problem in the United States. The rest of the sentences provide specifics about this problem.

Study the Details

The main idea must connect, draw together, and make the rest of the paragraph meaningful. You might think of the main idea as the idea that all the details, when taken together, add up to, explain, or support. In the above paragraph, sentences 2, 3, 4, and 5 each give details about family violence. Sentences 2 and 3 express facts that tell how widespread the problem is. Sentences 4 and 5 explain who the victims are.

Where to Find the Topic Sentence

The topic sentence can be located anywhere in the paragraph. However, there are several positions where it is most likely to be found.

TOPIC SENTENCE FIRST

Most often the topic sentence is placed first in the paragraph. In this type of paragraph, the author first states his or her main point and then explains it.

Example:

> Another important event in the early 1970s was the Watergate scandal, which affected the public on the same level psychologically as the Vietnam War. The Vietnam conflict had ended and we lost face as a result of it. However, Watergate was to drop a great blanket on our trust in government. Everything ugly in American society was reflected in Watergate, which was devastating in its impact. Society had changed, and the result was massive depression. The American people had lost faith in our government; it does not seem as if we got it back during the 1970s.[3]

Here, the writer first states that the Watergate scandal had a psychological effect on the public. The rest of the paragraph explains this effect.

TOPIC SENTENCE LAST

The second most likely place for a topic sentence to appear is last in the paragraph. When using this arrangement, a writer leads up to the main point and then directly states it at the end.

Example:

> At the beginning of this century, only eight percent of marriages ended in divorce. In 1976, just over fifty percent did. The dramatic

change doesn't necessarily mean that people were happy in marriage in the old days and are unhappy today. Expectations have changed, and divorces are now much easier to come by. People who years ago might have suffered along now sever the marriage bond. Yet, however the statistics are interpreted, it is clear that there is a reservoir of dissatisfaction in many marriages.

This paragraph first provides statistics on the increasing rate of divorce. Then possible reasons for the increase are given. The paragraph ends with a general statement of what the statistics do show—that there is much dissatisfaction in many marriages.

TOPIC SENTENCE IN THE MIDDLE

If it is placed neither first nor last, then the topic sentence appears somewhere in the middle of the paragraph. In this arrangement, the sentences before the topic sentence lead up to or introduce the main idea. Those that follow the main idea explain or describe it.

Example:

You could be the greatest mechanical genius since Thomas Edison, but if no one knows about your talent or is in a position to judge it, you're wasting your time. Being in the right field is important. But within that field, it's also a good idea to maintain a high degree of visibility. If you've got the potential to be a brilliant corporate strategist, you may be wasting your time working for a small company employing a dozen or so workers. You'd be better off working for a large corporation where you have the opportunity to take off in any number of directions, learn how the different departments interface, and thus have a larger arena to test your skills.

In this paragraph, the writer begins with an example using Thomas Edison. He then states his main point and continues with examples that illustrate the importance of visibility in career advancement.

TOPIC SENTENCE FIRST AND LAST

Occasionally the main idea will be stated at the beginning of a paragraph and again at the end. Writers may use this organization to emphasize an important idea or to explain an idea that needs clarification.

Example:

Burger King Corporation offers both a service and a product to its customers. Its service is the convenience it offers the consumer—the location of its restaurants and its fast food service—in catering to his or her lifestyle. Its product, in essence, is *the total Burger King expe-*

rience, which starts from the time you drive into the restaurant's parking lot and ends when you drive out. It includes the speed of service, the food you order, the price you pay, the friendliness and courtesy you are shown, the intangible feeling of satisfaction—in short, an experience. Burger King, then, is marketing a positive experience, as promised by its advertising and promotional efforts and delivered by its product.[4]

The first and last sentences both state, in slightly different ways, that Burger King provides a desirable product and service that results in a positive experience.

EXERCISE 7-4

Directions: *Underline the topic sentence in each of the following paragraphs.*

1. The inadequacy of training facilities is not the only reason young people are not pursuing skilled work. Blue collar work has suffered from a poor image, further contributing to the widespread shortage of workers. The reasoning is, why learn a trade when you can go to college or technical school and become either a professional or a technician, career areas which carry a lot more prestige.

2. Dirty words are often used by teenagers in telling off-color stories and this can be considered part of their sex education. As their bodies grow and change, both boys and girls wonder and worry. To keep from being overwhelmed by these fears, they turn them into jokes or dirty-word stories. By telling and retelling off-color stories, they gain a little information, more misinformation and a lot of reassurance. They learn that they aren't the only ones in the group disturbed about their future roles in courtship and marriage. Using dirty words and stories to laugh at sexual doubts and fears, may diminish their importance and make them less frightening.[5]

3. Deciding to buy a product or service takes preparation. Since time has already been spent to gather information and compare what is available, money managers should spend a little more time prior to arriving at a final decision. In this respect it is best if prospective buyers go home before making a selection. At home it is easier to evaluate all of the accumulated information while not under any sales or time pressure to make a purchase. In addition, at home it is possible to take a final look at financial plans to be sure the purchase will mesh with these plans.[6]

4. It is important to realize that the 1950s were to most Americans a time of great security. After World War II, the people prospered in ways they

had never known before. Our involvement in the Korean War was thought to be successful from the point of view of national image. We saw ourselves as *the* world power, who had led the fight for democracy. When Dwight D. Eisenhower was elected president, we entered a period in American history where everything was all right, everyone was getting richer, and tomorrow would always be better than today.

5. The other day a good friend, senior executive of a large company and in his early forties, dropped by for a visit. He told me he had been thinking of divorce after sixteen years of marriage. The couple have a boy, twelve, and two girls, one of whom is ten, the other eight. "We've grown apart over the years, and we have nothing in common left anymore other than the children. There are at least twenty years of enjoying life still ahead of me. I was worried about the children until we discussed it with them. So many of their schoolmates have had divorced parents or parents who had remarried, they are accustomed to the idea. It's part of life. Of course, if the older ones need help, I want them to see a good psychiatrist while we go through with this. My wife is still a good-looking woman, younger than I, and probably will remarry. I'm not thinking of it now, but I'll probably remarry someday." This situation illustrates an attitude and the climate of the times. Divorce has become as much an institution as marriage.[7]

INFERRING UNSTATED MAIN IDEAS

Although most paragraphs do have a topic sentence, some do not. This type of paragraph contains only details or specifics that, taken together, point to the main idea. In paragraphs in which no one sentence clearly expresses the main idea, you must figure it out.

Reading a paragraph in which the main idea is unstated is similar to doing a math problem. It is a process of adding up the facts and deciding what they mean together. To solve this math problem you add the numbers and come up with a total sum.

46	fact
74	fact
89	fact
22	fact
+ 10	+ fact
241	main idea

Think of a paragraph without a topic sentence in a similar way. It is a list of facts or details that you add up or put together to determine the meaning of the paragraph as a whole.

Use the following steps as a guide to finding unstated main ideas:

1. Find the topic. Ask yourself: "What is the one thing the author is discussing throughout the paragraph?"

2. Decide what the writer wants you to know about the topic. Look at each detail and decide what larger idea each explains.

3. Express this idea in your own words.

Read the following paragraph; then follow the three steps listed above.

> In the past, most individuals were educated during a specific period of their lives. By the time they reached their mid-20s, they could retire their notebooks, textbooks, carbon paper, scratch pads, and pencils and pens and concentrate on building their careers. Tomorrow's workers will have to hold on to their training paraphernalia because they can expect to be retrained throughout their working lives. It may mean taking company-sponsored courses every few months, after-work seminars, or spending a number of days or weeks in a nearby university attending lectures at different points during the year.

The topic of this paragraph is education. The writer begins by explaining that in the past, education took place during a certain time period in our lives. Then the writer predicts that in the future, education will continue throughout a person's life. The main point the writer makes is that the idea of education is changing. Notice, however, that no single sentence states this idea clearly. The reader had to infer this idea from the way all the sentences in the paragraph worked together.

EXERCISE 7-5

Directions: *None of the following paragraphs has a topic sentence. Read each paragraph and, in the space provided, write a sentence that expresses the main idea.*

1. Today in America, $2 out of every $5 spent for food is spent eating away from home. In 1954 it was nearer $1 out of every $10. Based on these facts it is not difficult to see the tremendous opportunity that has existed in the foodservice industry during the past 20 years. Yet, from my vantage point as a keen observer of industry trends and events, I've seen hundreds of people and thousands of restaurants go broke. At the same time, I am personally aware of over 100 different people who have become millionaires in their endeavors in the foodservice field.[8]

Main idea: _____

_____

2. Jack Schultz and Ian Baldwin found last summer that trees under attack by insects or animals will release an unidentified chemical into the air as a distress signal. Upon receiving the signal, nearby trees step up their production of tannin—a poison in the leaves that gives insects indigestion. The team learned, too, that production of the poison is in proportion to the duration and intensity of the attack.[9]

Main idea: _____

_____

3. When President Lincoln was shot, the word was communicated by telegraph to most parts of the United States, but because we had no links to England, it was five days before London heard of the event. When President Reagan was shot, journalist Henry Fairlie, working at his typewriter within a block of the shooting, got word of it by telephone from his editor at the *Spectator* in London, who had seen a rerun of the assassination attempt on television shortly after it occurred.[10]

Main idea: _____

_____

4. Suppose you wanted to teach your pet chimpanzee the English language. How would you go about it? Two psychologists raised Gua, a female chimpanzee, at home with their son, Donald. Both boy and chimp were encouraged to speak, but only Donald did. Gua indicated she could comprehend some language, for she could respond appropriately to about 70 different utterances, but she never *produced* a single word. A second attempt involved more intensive training in speech, and Viki, another chimpanzee, was eventually able to pronounce three recognizable words: "Mama," "Papa," and "cup."

Main idea: _____

_____

5. Traffic is directed by color. Pilot instrument panels, landing strips, road and water crossings are regulated by many colored lights and signs. Factories use colors to distinguish between thoroughfares and work areas. Danger zones are painted in special colors. Lubrication points and removable parts are accentuated by color. Pipes for transporting water, steam, oil, chemicals, and compressed air, are designated by different colors. Electrical wires and resistances are color coded.[11]

Main idea: _____

_____

RECOGNIZING SUPPORTING DETAILS

Supporting details are those facts and ideas that prove or explain the main idea of a paragraph. While all the details in a paragraph do support the main idea, not all details are equally important. As you read, try to identify and pay attention to the most-important details. Pay less attention to details of lesser importance. The key details directly explain the main idea. Other details may provide additional information, offer an example, or further explain one of the key details.

The following diagram shows how details relate to the main idea and how details range in degree of importance. In the diagram, more-important details are placed toward the left; less-important details are closer to the right.

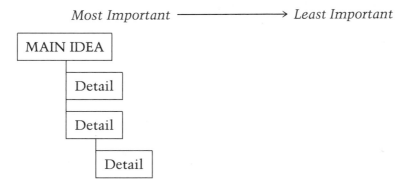

Read the following paragraph and study the corresponding diagram (page 114).

> The skin of the human body has several functions. First, it serves as a protective covering. In doing so, it accounts for 17 percent of the body weight. Skin also protects the organs within the body from damage or harm. The skin serves as a regulator of body functions. It controls body temperature and water loss. Finally, the skin serves as a receiver. It is sensitive to touch and temperature.

From this diagram you can see that the details that state the three functions of skin are the key details. Other details, such as "protects organs," provide further information and are at a lower level of importance.

Read this paragraph and try to pick out the more-important details.

> Women and racial minorities have legal protection against job discrimination. Two laws protect them: the Title VII Civil Rights Act and the Equal Pay Act. Title VII prohibits discrimination based on

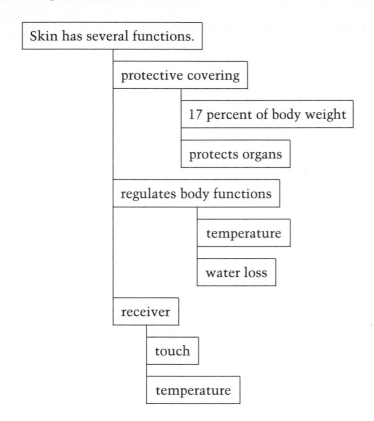

race, color, religion, sex, or national origin. Employers are not allowed to question job applicants about these topics. The Equal Pay Act basically says, "Equal pay for equal work." It guarantees that regardless of sex or race, employees doing the same job must receive the same pay. If you encounter racial or sexual discrimination, you can report it as a violation of federal law. The Equal Opportunity Commission will handle your complaint and offer advice.

This paragraph could be diagrammed as follows (key details only):

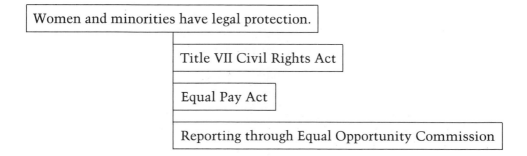

EXERCISE 7-6

Directions: *Read each of the following paragraphs and underline only the most important details.*

1. *Physical dependence* is what was formerly called addiction. It is characterized by *tolerance* and *withdrawal. Tolerance* means that more and more of the drug must be taken to achieve the same effect, as use continues. *Withdrawal* means that if use is discontinued, the person experiences unpleasant symptoms. When I quit smoking cigarettes, for example, I went through about five days of irritability, depression, and restlessness. Withdrawal from heroin and other narcotics is much more painful, involving violent cramps, vomiting, diarrhea, and other symptoms that continue for at least two or three days. With some drugs, especially barbiturates, cold-turkey (sudden and total) quitting can result in death, so severe is the withdrawal.

2. The two most common drugs that are legal and do not require a prescription are caffeine and nicotine. *Caffeine* is the active ingredient in coffee, tea, and many cola drinks. It stimulates the central nervous system and heart and therefore is often used to stay awake. Heavy use— say, seven to ten cups of coffee per day—has toxic effects, that is, acts like a mild poison. Prolonged heavy use appears to be addicting. *Nicotine* is the active ingredient in tobacco. One of the most addicting of all drugs and one of the most dangerous, at least when obtained by smoking, it has been implicated in lung cancer, emphysema, and heart disease.

3. Hypnosis today is used for a number of purposes, primarily in psychotherapy or to reduce pain, and it is an acceptable technique in both medicine and psychology. In psychotherapy, it is most often used to eliminate bad habits and annoying symptoms. Cigarette smoking can be treated, for example, by the suggestion that the person will feel nauseated whenever he or she thinks of smoking. Sufferers of migraine headaches treated with hypnotic suggestions to relax showed a much greater tendency to improve than sufferers treated with drugs; 44 percent were headache-free after 12 months of treatment, compared to 12 percent of their drug-treated counterparts.

4. There are four main types of sunglasses. The traditional *absorptive* glasses soak up all the harmful sun rays. *Polarizing* sunglasses account for half the market. They're the best buy for knocking out glare, and reflections from snow and water, but they may admit more light rays than other sunglasses. *Coated* sunglasses usually have a metallic covering that itself reflects light. They are often quite absorptive, but a cheap pair of coated glasses may have an uneven or nondurable coating that

could rub off after a short period of time. New on the market are the somewhat more expensive *photochromatic* sunglasses. Their chemical composition causes them to change color according to the brightness of the light: in the sun, they darken; in the shade, they lighten. This type of sunglasses responds to ultraviolet light only, and will not screen out infrared rays, so they're not the best bet for continual exposure to bright sun.[12]

5. In simplest outline, how is a President chosen? First, a candidate campaigns within his party for nomination at a national convention. After the convention comes a period of competition with the nominee of the other major party and perhaps the nominees of minor parties. The showdown arrives on Election Day. The candidate must win more votes than any other nominee in enough states and the District of Columbia to give him a majority of the electoral votes. If he does all these things, he has won the right to the office of President of the United States.[13]

TYPES OF SUPPORTING DETAILS

There are many types of details that a writer can use to explain or support a main idea. As you read, it is important to know *how* or what types of detail a writer used to support his or her main idea. As you will see in later chapters, the manner in which a writer explains and supports an idea may influence how readily you will accept or agree with an idea. The most common types of supporting details are (1) examples, (2) facts or statistics, (3) reasons, (4) descriptions, and (5) steps or procedures. Each will be discussed briefly.

Examples

One way a writer may support an idea is by using examples. Examples make ideas and concepts real and understandable. For instance, a writer may explain stress by giving examples of it. It the following paragraph, an example is used to explain instantaneous speed.

The speed that a body has at any one instant is called instantaneous speed. It is the speed registered by the speedometer of a car. When we say that the speed of a car at some particular instant is 60 kilometers per hour, we are specifying its instantaneous speed, and we mean that if the car continued moving as fast for an hour, it would travel 60 kilometers. So the instantaneous speed, or speed at a particular instant, is often quite different from average speed.[14]

In this paragraph the author uses the speed of a car to explain instantaneous speed. As you read illustrations and examples, try to see the relationship between the example and the concept or idea it illustrates.

Facts and Statistics

Another way a writer supports an idea is by including facts and/or statistics. The facts and statistics may provide evidence that the main idea is correct. Or the facts may further explain the main idea. For example, to prove that the divorce rate is high, the author may give statistics about the divorce rate and percentage of the population that is divorced. Notice how, in the following paragraph, the main idea stated in the first sentence is explained using statistics.

Elderly men and women differ sharply in their marital status. More than three-fourths of all older men are married and living with their spouse, compared with less than half of the women. The most dramatic difference in marital status between the sexes is shown under the category "Widowed." In 1982, of those age sixty-five to seventy-four, 7.5 percent of the men and 38.3 percent of the women were widowed. Of those age seventy-five and over, 21.7 percent of the men and 68.5 percent of women were widowed.

In this paragraph, the main idea that elderly men and women differ in marital status is supported using statistics.

Reasons

A writer may support an idea by giving reasons *why* a main idea is correct. A writer might explain *why* nuclear power is dangerous or give reasons *why* a new speed limit law should be passed by Congress. In the following paragraph, the author explains why warm air rises.

We all know that warm air rises. From our study of buoyancy we can understand why this is so. Warm air expands and becomes less dense than the surrounding air and is buoyed upward like a balloon. The buoyancy is in an upward direction because the air pressure below a region of warmed air is greater than the air pressure above. And the warmed air rises because the buoyant force is greater than its weight.[15]

Description

When the topic of a paragraph is a person, object, place or process, the writer may develop the paragraph by describing the object. Descriptions are details that help you create a mental picture of the object. In the following paragraph, the author describes a sacred book of the Islamic religion, by telling what it contains.

The *Koran* is the sacred book of the Islamic religion. It was written during the lifetime of Mohammed (570–630) during the years in which he recorded divine revelations. The *Koran* includes rules for family relationships, including marriage and divorce. Rules for inheritance of wealth and property are specified. The status of women as subordinate to men is well-defined.

Steps or Procedures

When a paragraph is written to explain how to do something, the paragraph details are often lists of steps or procedures to be followed. For example, if the main idea of a paragraph is how to prepare an outline for a speech, then the details would list or explain the steps in preparing an outline. In the following paragraph the author explains how fog is produced.

Warm breezes blow over the ocean. When the moist air moves from warmer to cooler waters or from warm water to cool land, it chills. As it chills, water vapor molecules begin coalescing rather than bouncing off one another upon glancing collisions. Condensation takes place, and we have fog.[16]

EXERCISE 7-7

Directions: *For each paragraph listed in Exercise 7-6, identify the type or types of details used to support the main idea.*

TRANSITIONS

Transitions are linking words or phrases that a writer uses to lead the reader from one idea to another. If you get in the habit of recognizing transitions, you will see that they often guide you through a paragraph, enabling you to read it more easily.

In the following paragraph, notice how the underlined transitions lead you from one important detail to the next.

The principle of rhythm and line also contributes to the overall unity of the landscape design. This principle is responsible for the sense of continuity between different areas of the landscape. <u>One</u> way in which this continuity can be developed is by extending planting beds from one area to another. <u>For example,</u> shrub beds developed around the entrance to the house can be continued around the sides and into the backyard. Such an arrangement helps to tie the front and rear areas of the property together. <u>Another</u> means by which rhythm

Table 7-1 COMMON TRANSITIONS

Type of Transition	Example	What They Tell the Reader
Time—Sequence	first, later, next, finally	The author is arranging ideas in the order in which they happened.
Example	for example, for instance, to illustrate, such as	An example will follow.
Enumeration	first, second, third, last, another, next	The author is marking or identifying each major point (sometimes these may be used to suggest order of importance).
Continuation	also, in addition, and, further, another	The author is continuing with the same idea and is going to provide additional information.
Contrast	on the other hand, in contrast, however	The author is switching to a different, opposite, or contrasting idea than previously discussed.
Comparison	like, likewise, similarly	The writer will show how the previous idea is similar to what follows.
Cause—Effect	because, thus, therefore, since, consequently	The writer will show a connection between two or more things, how one thing caused another, or how something happened as a result of something else.

is given to a design is to repeat shapes, angles, or lines between various areas and elements of the design.[17]

Not all paragraphs contain such obvious transitions, and not all transitions serve as such clear markers of major details. Transitions may be used to alert you to what will come next in the paragraph. If you see the phrase *for instance* at the beginning of a sentence, then you know that an example will follow. When you see the phrase *On the other hand*, you can predict that a different, opposing idea will follow. Table 7-1 lists some of the most common transitions used within a paragraph and indicates what they tell you.

EXERCISE 7-8

Directions: *Turn back to Exercise 7-6 on pages 115–116. Reread each paragraph and underline any transitions that you find.*

EXERCISE 7-9

Directions: *Each of the following excerpts uses a transitional word or phrase to tell the reader what will follow in the paragraph. Read each excerpt, paying particular attention to the underlined word or phrase. Then, in the space provided, describe as specifically as you can what you would expect to find next in the paragraph.*

1. Price is not the only factor to consider in choosing a pharmacy. Many provide valuable services that should be considered. For instance. . . .

   _____

2. There are a number of things you can do to prevent a home burglary. First, . . .

   _____

3. Most mail order businesses are reliable and honest. However, . . .

   _____

4. One advantage of a compact stereo system is that all the components are built into the unit. Another. . . .

   _____

5. Taking medication can have an affect on your hormonal balance. Consequently, . . .

   _____

6. To select the presidential candidate you will vote for, you should examine his or her philosophy of government. Next. . . .

   _____

7. Eating solely vegetables drastically reduces caloric and fat intake, two things on which most people overindulge. On the other hand. . . .

   _____

8. Asbestos, a common material found in many older buildings in which people have worked for decades, has been shown to cause cancer. Consequently, . . .

   _____

9. Cars and trucks are not designed randomly. They are designed individually for specific purposes. <u>For instance.</u> . . .

_____

10. Jupiter is a planet surrounded by several moons. <u>Likewise.</u> . . .

_____

EXERCISE 7-10

Directions: *Read each of the following sentences. In each blank, supply a transitional word or phrase that makes sense in the sentence.*

1. As a young poet, ee cummings was traditional in his use of punctuation and capitalization. _____, he became much more experimental and began to create his own grammatical rules.

2. Some metals, _____ gold and silver, are represented by symbols derived from their Latin names.

3. In order to sight read music, you should begin by scanning it. _____, you should identify the key and tempo.

4. The *Oxford English Dictionary*, by giving all present and past definitions of words, shows how word definitions have changed with time. _____, it gives the date and written source where each word appears to have first been used.

5. Some scientists believe intelligence to be determined equally by heredity and environment. _____, other scientists believe heredity to account for about sixty percent of it and environment for the other forty percent.

6. Tigers tend to grow listless and unhappy in captivity. _____, pandas grow listless and have a difficult time reproducing in captivity.

7. Touching the grooves on a record is not advisable _____ oils and minerals in the skin get into the grooves and reduce the quality of sound.

8. Many rock stars have met with tragic ends. _____, John Lennon was gunned down, Buddy Holly and Ritchie Valens were killed in a plane crash, and Janis Joplin died of a drug overdose.

9. American voters tend to vote according to the state of the economy. _____, if the economy is good, they tend to vote for the party in power and if the economy is poor, they tend to vote for the party not in power.

10. Buying smaller sized clothing generally will not give an overweight person the incentive to lose weight. People with weight problems tend to eat when they're upset or disturbed, and _____ wearing smaller clothing is frustrating and upsetting, overweight people will generally gain weight by doing so.

SUMMARY

A paragraph is a group of related sentences about a single topic. It has four essential parts:

1. TOPIC   The one thing the entire paragraph is about

2. MAIN IDEA   The most important idea the writer wants the reader to know about the topic

3. DETAILS   Facts and ideas that prove or explain the main idea

4. TRANSITIONS   Words and phrases that lead the reader from one idea to another

A paragraph, then, provides explanation and support for a main idea about a particular topic. The sentence that expresses this main idea is called the topic sentence. A topic sentence may be located anywhere in a paragraph, but the most common positions are first, last, in the middle, or both first and last.

While most paragraphs contain a topic sentence, occasionally a writer will write a paragraph in which the main idea is not stated in a single sentence. Instead, it is left up to the reader to infer, or reason out, the main idea.

There are five types of details that are commonly used to support the main idea: examples, facts and statistics, reasons, description, and steps and procedures.

Chapter 8

FOLLOWING THE AUTHOR'S THOUGHT PATTERNS

THIS CHAPTER WILL SHOW YOU HOW TO

1. **Improve your understanding and recall by recognizing thought patterns**

2. **Identify five commonly used thought patterns**

As a way of beginning to think about authors' thought patterns, complete each of the following steps:

1. Study each of these drawings for a few seconds (count to ten as you look at each one):

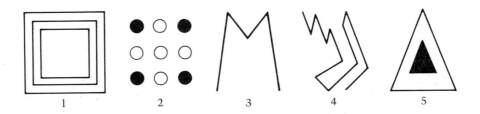

2. Cover up the drawings and try to draw each from memory.

3. Check to see how many you had exactly correct.

Most likely you drew all but the fourth correctly. Why did you get that one wrong? How does it differ from the others?

Drawings 1, 2, 3, and 5 have patterns. Drawing 4, however, has no pattern; it is just a group of randomly arranged lines.

From this experiment you can see that it is easier to remember drawings that have a pattern, some understandable form of organization. The same is true of written material. If you can see how a paragraph is organized, it will be easier to understand and remember. Writers often present their ideas in a recognizable order. Once you can recognize the organizational pattern, you will remember more of what you read.

This chapter briefly reviews some of the more common patterns that writers use and shows how to recognize them: (1) illustration–example, (2) definition, (3) comparison–contrast, (4) cause–effect, (5) classification, and (6) chronological order–process.

ILLUSTRATION–EXAMPLE

One of the clearest, most practical, and most obvious ways to explain something is to give an example. Suppose you had to explain what anthropology is. You might give examples of the topics you study. By using examples, such as the study of apes, early man, and the development of modern man, you would give a fairly good idea of what anthropology is all about. When a subject is unfamiliar, an example often makes it easier to understand.

Usually a writer will state the idea first and then follow with examples. Several examples may be given in one paragraph, or a separate paragraph may be used for each example. It may help to visualize the illustration–example pattern this way:

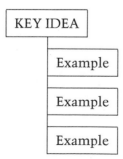

Notice how this thought pattern is developed in the following passage.

> Electricity is all around us. We see it in lightning. We receive electric shocks when we walk on a nylon rug on a dry day and then touch something (or someone). We can see sparks fly from a cat's fur when we pet it in the dark. We can rub a balloon on a sweater and make the balloon stick to the wall or the ceiling. Our clothes cling together when we take them from the dryer.
>
> These are all examples of *static electricity*. They happen because there is a buildup of one of the two kinds of electrical charge, either positive or negative. . . .

In the preceding passage, the concept of static electricity was explained through the use of everyday examples. You could visualize the selection as follows:

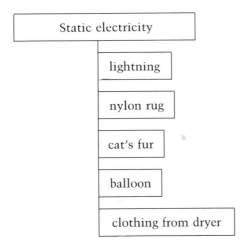

Here is another passage in which the main idea is explained through example:

> It is a common observation that all bodies do not fall with equal accelerations. A leaf, a feather, or a sheet of paper, for example, may flutter to the ground slowly. That the air is the factor responsible for these different accelerations can be shown very nicely with a closed glass tube containing a light and heavy object, a feather and a coin, for example. In the presence of air, the feather and coin fall with quite unequal accelerations. But if the air in the tube is evacuated by means of a vacuum pump, and the tube is quickly inverted, the feather and coin fall with the same acceleration. . . . Although air resistance appreciably alters the motion of falling feathers and the like, the motion of heavier objects like stones and baseballs is not appreci-

ably affected by the air. The relationships $v = gt$ and $d = \frac{1}{2}gt^2$ can be used to a very good approximation for most objects falling in air.[1]

The author explains that objects do not fall at equal rates by using the examples of a leaf, a feather, and a sheet of paper.

EXERCISE 8-1

Directions: *For each of the following paragraphs, underline the topic sentence and list the examples used to explain it.*

1. Perception is the process of gathering information and giving it meaning. You see a movie and you give meaning to it: "It's one of the best I've seen." You come away from class after the third week and you give meaning to it: "It finally makes sense." We gather information from what our senses see, hear, touch, taste, and smell, and we give meaning to that information. Although the information may come to us in a variety of forms, it is all processed, or *perceived*, in the mind.

   Examples: _____

2. The action and reaction forces make up a *pair* of forces. Forces always occur in pairs. There is never a single force in any situation. For example, in walking across the floor, we push against the floor, and the floor in turn pushes against us. Likewise, the tires of a car push against the pavement, and the pavement pushes back on the tires. When we swim, we push the water backward, and the water pushes us forward. The reaction forces, those acting in the direction of our resulting accelerations, are what account for our motion in these cases. These forces depend on friction; a person or car on ice, for example, may not be able to exert the action force to produce the needed reaction force by the ice.[2]

   Examples: _____

3. Have you ever noticed that some foods remain hotter much longer than others? Boiled onions and squash on a hot dish, for example, are often too hot to eat when mashed potatoes may be eaten comfortably. The filling of hot apple pie can burn your tongue while the crust will not, even when the pie has just been taken out of the oven. And the aluminum covering on a frozen dinner can be peeled off with your bare fingers as soon as it is removed from the oven. A piece of toast may be comfortably eaten a few seconds after coming from the hot toaster, but we must wait several minutes before eating soup from a stove no hotter than the toaster. Evidently, different substances have different capacities for storing internal energy.[3]

   Examples: _____

EXERCISE 8-2

Directions: *Choose one of the topics listed below. On a separate sheet, write a paragraph in which you use illustration—example to organize and express your ideas on the topic. Then draw a diagram showing the organization of your paragraph.*

1. Parents or friends are helpful (or not helpful) in making decisions.

2. Attending college has (has not) made a major change in my life.

DEFINITION

Another way to provide an explanation is to offer a definition. Let's say that you see an opossum while driving in the country. You mention this to a friend. Since your friend does not know what an opossum is, you have to give a definition. Your definition should describe an opossum's characteristics or features. The definition should have two parts: (1) Tell what general group or class an opossum belongs to—in this case, animals. (2) Explain how an opossum is different or distinguishable from other items in the group. For the term *opossum*, you would need to describe features of an opossum that would help someone tell the difference between it and other animals, such as dogs, raccoons, and squirrels. Thus, you could define an opossum as follows:

> An opossum is an animal with a ratlike tail that lives in trees. It carries its young in a pouch. It is active at night and pretends to be dead when trapped.

This definition can be diagrammed as follows:

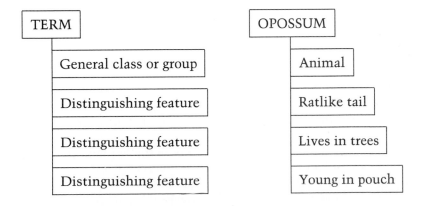

The following passage was written to define the term *ragtime music.*

Ragtime music is a piano style that developed at the turn of the twentieth century. Ragtime music usually has four themes. The themes are divided into four musical sections of equal length. In playing ragtime music, the left hand plays chords and the right hand plays the melody. There is an uneven accenting between the two hands.

The thought pattern of this passage might be diagrammed as follows:

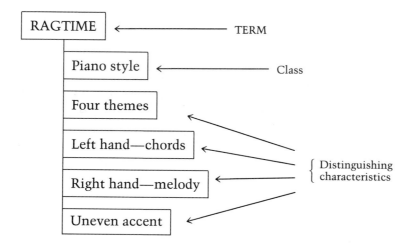

As you read passages that use the definition pattern, keep these questions in mind:

1. What is being defined?

2. What general group or class does it belong to?

3. What makes it different from others in the group?

Read the following passage and apply the above questions.

Nez Percé Indians are a tribe that lives in north-central Idaho. The rich farmlands and forests in the area form the basis for the tribe's chief industries, agriculture and lumber.

The name *Nez Percé* means *pierced nose,* but few of the Indians ever pierced their noses. In 1805, a French interpreter gave the name to the tribe after seeing some members wearing shells in their noses as decorations.

The Nez Percé originally lived in the region where the borders of Idaho, Oregon, and Washington meet. Prospectors overran the Nez Percé reservation after discovering gold there in the 1860's.

The Nez Percé resisted the efforts of the government to move them to a smaller reservation. In 1877, fighting broke out between the Nez Percé and U.S. troops. Joseph, a Nez Percé chief, tried to lead a band of the Indians into Canada. But he surrendered near the United States-Canadian border.

This passage was written to define the Nez Percé. The general group or category is "Indian tribe." The distinguishing characteristics include their original location, their fight against relocation, and the source of their name.

EXERCISE 8-3

Directions: *Read each of the following paragraphs. Then identify the term being defined, its general class, and its distinguishing features.*

1. The partnership, like the sole proprietorship, is a form of ownership used primarily in small business firms. Two or more owners comprise a partnership. The structure of a partnership may be established with an almost endless variation of features. The partners establish the conditions of the partnership, contribution of each partner to the business, and division of profits. They also decide on the amount of authority, duties, and liability each will have.

   Term: _____

   General class: _____

   Distinguishing features: _____

2. The consumer price index (CPI) is a broad measure of the cost of living for consumers and is published monthly by the U.S. Bureau of Labor Statistics. More than 400 prices of various goods and services sold across the country are tracked, recorded, weighted for importance in a hypothetical budget, and totaled. The index has a base time period from which to make comparisons. If 1977 is the base year of 100 and the CPI is 210.6 in 1987, the cost of living will have risen 110.6 percent since the base period. Similarly, if in 1988 the index should rise to 224.8 from 210.6 the previous year, the cost of living would have gone up. This time the increase would have been 6.7 percent over one year $(224.8 - 210.6 = 14.2 \div 210.6)$.[4]

   Term: _____

   General class: _____

   Distinguishing features: _____

3. The Small Business Administration (SBA) is an independent agency of the federal government that was created by Congress when it passed the Small Business Act in 1953. Its administrator is appointed by and reports to the President. Purposes of the SBA are to assist people in getting into business, to help them stay in business, to help small firms

win federal procurement contracts, and to act as a strong advocate for small business.

Term: _____

General class: _____

Distinguishing features: _____

EXERCISE 8-4

Directions: *Choose one of the topics listed below. On a separate sheet, write a paragraph in which you define the topic. Be sure to include both the general group and what makes the item different from other items in the same group. Then draw a diagram showing the organization of your paragraph.*

1. A type of music

2. Soap operas

3. Junk food

COMPARISON—CONTRAST

Often a writer will explain something by using comparison or contrast—that is, by showing how it is similar to or different from a familiar object or idea. Comparison treats similarities, while contrast emphasizes differences. For example, an article comparing two car models might mention these common, overlapping features: radial tires, clock, radio, power steering, power brakes. The cars may differ in gas mileage, body shape, engine power, braking distance, and so forth. When comparing the two models, the writer would focus on shared features. When contrasting the two cars the writer would focus on individual differences. Such an article might be diagrammed as follows:

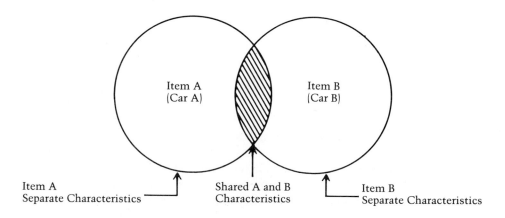

In this diagram, Items A and B are different except where they overlap and share the same characteristics.

In most articles that use the comparison–contrast method, you will find some passages that only compare, some that only contrast, and others that both compare and contrast. To read each type of passage effectively, you must follow the pattern of ideas. Passages that show comparison and/or contrast can be organized in a number of different ways. The organization depends on the author's purpose.

Comparison

If a writer is concerned only with similarities, he or she may identify the items to be compared and then list the ways in which they are alike. The following paragraph shows how chemistry and physics are similar.

> Although physics and chemistry are considered separate fields of study, they have much in common. First, both are physical sciences and are concerned with studying and explaining physical occurrences. To study and record these occurrences, each field has developed a precise set of signs and symbols. These might be considered a specialized language. Finally, both fields are closely tied to the field of mathematics and use mathematics in predicting and explaining physical occurrences.[5]

Such a pattern can be diagrammed as follows:

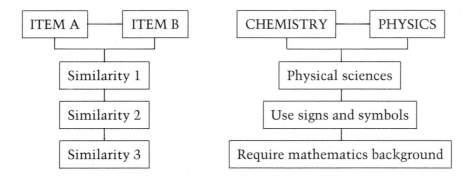

Contrast

A writer concerned only with the differences between sociology and psychology might write the following paragraph.

> Sociology and psychology, although both social sciences, are very different fields of study. Sociology is concerned with the structure, organization, and behavior of groups. Psychology, on the other hand, focuses on individual behavior. While a sociologist would study characteristics of groups of people, a psychologist would study the in-

dividual motivation and behavior of each group member. Psychology and sociology also differ in the manner in which research is conducted. Sociologists obtain data and information through observation and survey. Psychologists obtain data through carefully designed experimentation.

Such a pattern can be diagrammed as follows:

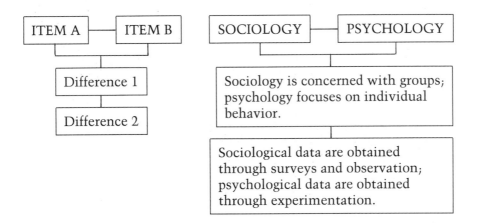

Comparison and Contrast

In many passages, writers discuss both similarities and differences. Suppose you wanted to write a paragraph discussing the similarities and differences between sociology and psychology. You could organize the paragraph in several different ways.

1. You could list all the similarities and then all the differences, as shown in this diagram:

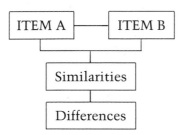

2. You could discuss Item A first, presenting both similarities and differences, and then do the same for Item B. Such a pattern would look like this:

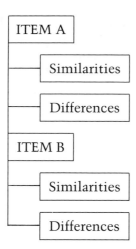

The following paragraph discusses housing in New York City. As you read it, try to visualize its pattern.

> Housing in New York City differs in several ways from that in most other cities of the United States. About 60 per cent of New York's families live in apartment buildings or hotels. In other cities, most people live in one- or two-family houses. About 75 per cent of the families in New York rent their homes. In other U.S. cities, most families own their homes. About 70 per cent of the housing in New York City is more than 30 years old, and over 300,000 families live in buildings that are more than 70 years old. Most other cities have a far larger percentage of newer housing.

Did you visualize the pattern like this?

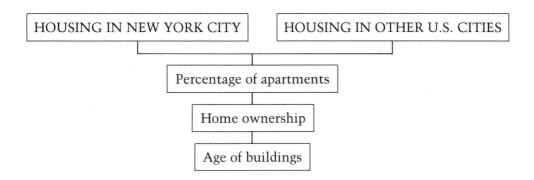

Now read the following passage and decide whether it discusses similarities, differences, or both.

A program must be written in a form that a computer can understand. Every instruction must be prepared according to specific rules. The rules form a language that we use to instruct the computer. Humans use *natural languages* such as English and Spanish to communicate with each other. When we communicate with a computer we use a *computer programming language.*

To write a sentence in a natural human language, we form words and phrases from letters and other symbols. The construction of the sentence is determined by the grammar rules of the language. The meaning of the sentence depends on what words are used and how they are organized. A computer programming language also has rules that describe how to form valid instructions. These rules are called the *syntax* of the language. The meanings or effects of the instructions are called the *semantics* of the language.

This passage *compares* natural language with computer programming language. Both are means of communication and both are based on sets of rules.

EXERCISE 8-5

Directions: *Read each of the following passages and identify the items being compared or contrasted. Then describe the author's approach to the items. Are they compared, contrasted, or both compared and contrasted?*

1. Perhaps it will be easier to understand the nature and function of empathic listening if we contrast it to deliberative listening. When we make a definite, "deliberate" attempt to hear information, analyze it, recall it at a later time, and draw conclusions from it, we are listening deliberatively. This is the way most of us listen because this is the way we have been trained. This type of listening is appropriate in a lecture-based education system where the first priority is to critically analyze the speaker's content.

   In empathic listening the objective is also understanding, but the first priority is different. Because empathic listening is transactional, the listener's first priority is to understand the communicator. We listen to what is being communicated not just by the words but by the other person's facial expressions, tone of voice, gestures, posture, and body motion.

   Items Compared or Contrasted: _____

   Approach: _____

2. The term primary group, coined by Charles H. Cooley (1909) is used to refer to small, informal groups who interact in a personal, direct and intimate way . . . A secondary group is a group whose members interact in an impersonal manner, have few emotional ties, and come together for a specific purpose. Like primary groups, they are usually small and involve face to face contacts. Although the interactions may be cordial or friendly, they are more formal than primary group interactions. Sociologically, however, they are just as important. Most of our time is spent in secondary groups—committees, professional groups, sales-related groups, classroom groups, or neighborhood groups. The key difference between primary and secondary groups is in the quality of the relationships and the extent of personal intimacy and involvement. Primary groups are person-oriented, whereas secondary groups tend to be goal-oriented.

   Items Compared or Contrasted: _____ _____

   Approach: _____

3. The differences in the lifestyles of the city and the suburbs should be thought of as differences of degree, not kind. Suburban residents tend to be more family-oriented and more concerned about the quality of education their children receive than city dwellers. On the other hand, because the suburbs consist largely of single-family homes, most young and single people prefer city life. Suburbanites are usually more affluent than city residents and more apt to have stable career or occupational patterns. As a result, they seem to be more hardworking and achievement oriented than city residents. They may also seem to be unduly concerned with consumption, since they often buy goods and services that offer visible evidence of their financial success.

   Items Compared or Contrasted: _____

   Approach: _____

EXERCISE 8-6

Directions: *Choose one of the topics listed below. On a separate sheet, write a paragraph in which you compare and/or contrast the two items. Then draw a diagram showing the organization of your paragraph.*

1. Two restaurants

2. Two friends

3. Two musical groups

CAUSE–EFFECT

The cause–effect pattern is used to describe an event or action that is caused by another event or action. A cause–effect passage explains why or how something happened. For example, a description of an automobile accident would probably follow a cause–effect pattern. You would tell what caused the accident and what happened as a result.

Basically, this pattern describes four types of relationships:

1. Single cause–single effect

    Example:

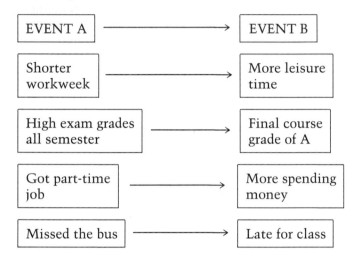

2. Single cause–multiple effects

   Examples:

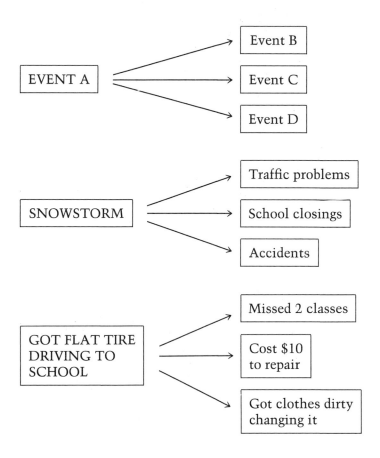

3. Multiple cause–single effect

    Examples:

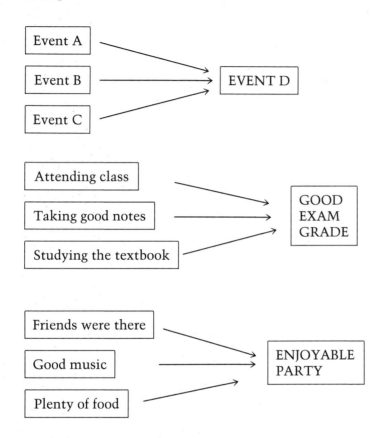

4. Multiple causes–multiple effects

    Example:

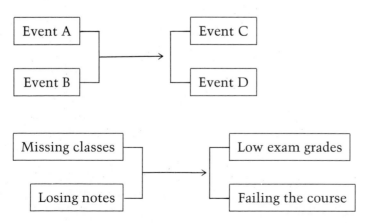

Read the following paragraph and determine which of the previous four relationships it describes.

Research has shown that mental illnesses have various causes, but the causes are not fully understood. Some mental disorders are due to physical changes in the brain resulting from illness or injury. Chemical imbalances in the brain may cause other mental illnesses. Still other disorders are mainly due to conditions in the environment that affect a person's mental state. These conditions include unpleasant childhood experiences and severe emotional stress. In addition, many cases of mental illness probably result from a combination of two or more of these causes.

In this paragraph a single effect (mental illness) is stated as having multiple causes (chemical and metabolic changes, psychological problems).

To read paragraphs that explain cause–effect relationships, pay close attention to the topic sentence. It usually states the cause–effect relationship that is detailed in the remainder of the paragraph. Then look for connections between causes and effects. What event happened as the result of a previous action? How did one event cause the other to happen?

Look for the development of the cause–effect relationship in the following paragraph about racial conflict.

Racial conflicts in New York City have had many causes. A major cause has been discrimination against blacks, Puerto Ricans, and other minority groups in jobs and housing. Many minority group members have had trouble obtaining well-paying jobs. Many also have had difficulty moving out of segregated neighborhoods and into neighborhoods where most of the people are white and of European ancestry. When members of a minority group have begun moving into such a neighborhood, the white residents often have begun moving out. In this way, segregated housing patterns have continued, and the chances for conflicts between the groups have increased.

This paragraph explains why conflicts occur. It can be diagrammed as follows:

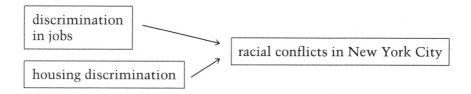

Within this paragraph, a second cause–effect relationship is introduced:

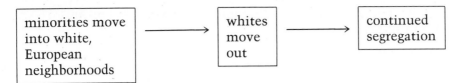

EXERCISE 8-7

Directions: *Read each of the following paragraphs, then describe the cause–effect relationship in each.*

1. By far the major cause of all business failure is inadequate management. As the Dun & Bradstreet data show, nearly 92 percent of all business failures are attributed to this one cause. What contributes to inadequate management? We see that causes of inadequate management include a lack of experience, unbalanced business experience, and incompetence.

   Cause–Effect _____

2. If a light is directed into one eye, the pupils of both eyes normally constrict. The decrease in pupil size is caused by contraction of the sphincter muscles of the iris. Constriction of the pupil in the eye in which the light was directed is known as the direct light reflex. Whereas, constriction of the pupil in the other eye is called the consensual light reflex. Both light reflexes have the typical reflex components: a sensory pathway, a motor pathway, and a central nervous system integration center.[6]

   Cause–Effect _____

3. Snow is a poor conductor and hence is popularly said to keep the earth warm. Its flakes are formed of crystals, which collect feathery masses, imprisoning air and thereby interfering with the escape of heat from the earth's surface. The winter dwellings of the Eskimos are shielded from the cold by their snow covering. Animals in the forest find shelter from the cold in snowbanks and in holes in the snow. The snow doesn't provide them with heat; it simply prevents the heat they generate from escaping.[7]

   Cause–Effect _____

EXERCISE 8-8

Directions: *Choose one of the topics listed below. On a separate sheet, write a paragraph using one of the four cause–effect patterns described above to explain the topic. Then draw a diagram showing the organization of your paragraph.*

1. Why you are attending college

2. Why you chose the college you are attending

3. How a particularly frightening or tragic event happened

CLASSIFICATION

A common way to explain something is to divide the topic into parts and explain each part. For example, you might explain how a home computer works by describing what each major component does. You would explain the functions of the monitor (screen), the disc drives, and the central processing unit. Or you might explain the kinds of courses taken in college by dividing the courses into such categories as electives, required basic courses, courses required for a specific major, and so on and then describing each category.

Textbook writers use the classification pattern to explain a topic that can easily be divided into parts. These parts are selected on the basis of common characteristics. For example, a psychology textbook writer might explain human needs by classifying them into two categories, primary and secondary. Or in a chemistry textbook, various compounds may be grouped or classified according to common characteristics, such as the presence of hydrogen or oxygen.

The following paragraph explains horticulture. As you read, try to identify the categories into which the topic of horticulture is divided.

Horticulture, the study and cultivation of garden plants, is a large industry. Recently it has become a popular area of study. The horticulture field consists of four major divisions. First, there is pomology, the science and practice of growing and handling fruit trees. Then there is olericulture, which is concerned with growing and storing vegetables. A third field, floriculture, is the science of growing, storing, and designing flowering plants. The last category, ornamental and landscape horticulture, is concerned with using grasses, plants, and shrubs in landscaping.

This paragraph approached the topic of horticulture by describing its four areas or fields of study. You could diagram the paragraph as follows:

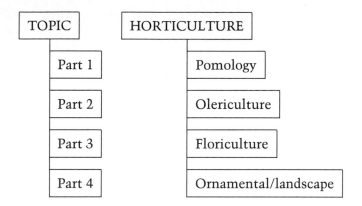

When reading textbook material that uses the classification pattern, be sure you understand *how* and *why* the topic was divided as it was. This technique will help you remember the most important parts of the topic.

Here is another example of the classification pattern:

> A newspaper is published primarily to present current news and information. For large city newspapers, more than 2000 people may be involved in the distribution of this information. The staff of large city papers, headed by a publisher, is organized into departments: editorial, business, and mechanical. The editorial department, headed by an editor-in-chief, is responsible for the collection of news and preparation of written copy. The business department, headed by a business manager, handles circulation, sales, and advertising. The mechanical department is run by a production manager. This department deals with the actual production of the paper, including typesetting, layout, and printing.

You could diagram this paragraph as follows:

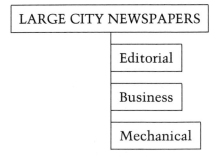

EXERCISE 8-9

Directions: *Read each of the following passages. Then identify the topic and the parts into which it is divided.*

1. There are four basic types of shopping centers. The convenience centers are located along heavily traveled streets and may consist of from 5 to 10 convenience goods and personal services outlets, such as a convenience store and a laundromat. The neighborhood shopping center usually has from 10 to 25 stores. This center might consist of a barber shop, drug store, beauty shop, bakery, dry cleaner, and appliance store, with a supermarket as the main store. Community centers are larger, with from 25 to 50 stores. These centers usually have major stores, such as a supermarket, variety store, or small department store, and smaller stores similar to those in neighborhood centers. Regional shopping centers consist of from 50 to 200 or more stores. They ordinarily have several department stores, many kinds of single-line and specialty stores and perhaps a variety store and a supermarket. Many modern shopping centers are enclosed malls for added customer convenience when shopping.

    Topic: _____

    Parts: _____

2. When we communicate with others we use either verbal messages, nonverbal messages, or a combination of the two. Verbal messages are either sent or not sent, just as a light switch is either on or off. They have an all or nothing feature built in. Nonverbal cues are not as clear-cut.

    Nonverbal communication includes such behaviors as facial expressions, posture, gestures, voice inflection, and the sequence and rhythm of the words themselves. Just as a dimmer switch on the light can be used to adjust, nonverbal cues often reveal shades or degrees of meaning. You may say, for example, "I am very upset" but *how* upset you are will be conveyed more by your facial expressions and gestures than by the actual words.

    Topic: _____

    Parts: _____

3. The word script is used in this concept to mean a habitual pattern of behavior. Thomas Harris defines scripts as decisions about how life should be lived. Muriel James and Dorothy Jongeward suggest that there are various levels of scripts: (1) cultural which are dictated by society; (2) subcultural defined by geographical location, ethnic back-

ground, religious beliefs, sex, education, age and other common bonds; (3) family, the identifiable traditions and expectations for family members; and (4) psychological, people's compulsion to perform in a certain way, to live up to a specific identity, or to fulfill a destiny.

Topic: _____

Parts: _____

EXERCISE 8-10

Directions: *Choose one of the topics listed below. On a separate sheet, write a paragraph explaining the topic, using the classification pattern. Then draw a diagram showing the organization of your paragraph.*

1. Advertising

2. Colleges

3. Entertainment

CHRONOLOGICAL ORDER–PROCESS

The terms *chronological order* and *process* both refer to the order in which something is done. Chronological order, also called sequence of events, is one of the most obvious patterns. In a paragraph organized by chronology, the details are presented in the order in which they occur in time. That is, the event that happened first, or earliest in time, appears first in the paragraph, and so on. Process refers to the steps or stages in which something is done.

You might expect to read a description of the events in a World War II battle presented in the order in which they happened—in chronological order. Similarly, in a computer programming manual, the steps to follow to locate an error in a computer program would be described in the order in which you should do them.

Both chronological order and process patterns can be diagrammed as follows:

```
┌─────────────────────┐
│ EVENT OR PROCESS    │
└──┬──────────────────┘
   │   ┌──────────────────────┐
   ├───│ 1. Action or step    │
   │   └──────────────────────┘
   │   ┌──────────────────────┐
   ├───│ 2. Action or step    │
   │   └──────────────────────┘
   │   ┌──────────────────────┐
   └───│ 3. Action or step    │
       └──────────────────────┘
```

Read the following paragraph, paying particular attention to the order of the actions or steps.

> In the early 1930s, the newly established Federal Bureau of Narcotics took on a crucial role in the fight against marijuana. Under the directorship of Harry J. Anslinger, a rigorous campaign was waged against the drug and those using it. By 1937 many states had adopted a standard bill making marihuana illegal. In that same year, the federal government stepped in with the Marihuana Tax Act, a bill modeled after the Harrison "Narcotics" Act. Repressive legislation continued, and by the 1950s severe penalties were imposed on those convicted of possessing, buying, selling, or cultivating the drug.[8]

This paragraph traces the history of actions taken to limit the use of marijuana. These actions are described in chronological order, beginning with the earliest event and concluding with the most recent.

When reading text material that uses the chronological order–process pattern, pay particular attention to the order of the information presented. Both chronological order and process are concerned with the sequence of events in time.

EXERCISE 8-11

Directions: *Read each of the following paragraphs. Identify the topic and write a list of the actions, steps, or events described in each period.*

1. These benefits of good listening occur only when the cues we give back to a speaker allow that person to know how we receive the message, permitting the speaker to adjust the message as needed. This important process is known as *feedback*. Feedback is not a simple, one-step process. First, it involves monitoring the impact or the influence of our messages on the other person. Second, it involves evaluating why the reaction or response occurred as it did. Third and finally, it involves adjustment or modification. The adjustment of our future messages reveal the process-oriented nature of communication, and, too, the impact the receiver has on the communication cycle. Feedback can provide reinforcement for the speaker if it shows if he or she is being clear, accepted, or understood.

   _____

   _____

   _____

2. A geyser is a periodically erupting pressure cooker. It consists of a long, narrow, vertical hole into which underground streams seep. The col-

umn of water is heated by volcanic heat below to temperatures exceeding 100° C. This is because the vertical column of water exerts pressure on the deeper water, thereby increasing the boiling point. The narrowness of the shaft shuts off convection currents, which allows the deeper portions to become considerably hotter than the water surface. Water at the surface, of course, will boil at 100°C. The water is heated from below, so a temperature high enough to permit boiling is reached near the bottom before it is at the top. Boiling therefore begins near the bottom, the rising bubbles push out the column of water above, and the eruption starts. As the water gushes out, pressure and the remaining water is reduced. It then rapidly boils and erupts with great force.[9]

_____

_____

_____

3. Following Nehru's death in 1964 his daughter, Indira Gandhi, became prominent in politics, and was named prime minister (of India) in 1966. Her popularity reached a peak with the defeat of Pakistan in 1971. Within two years, however, India's mildly Socialist economy was battered by serious harvest shortages, food riots, strikes, and student unrest. In June 1975 Gandhi announced a state of emergency and the government's assumption of dictatorial powers. At least 10,000 of her critics were jailed, a rigid press censorship imposed, and fundamental civil rights were suspended.[10]

_____

_____

_____

EXERCISE 8-12

Directions: *On a separate sheet, write a paragraph explaining how to do something that you do well or often, such as cross-country ski, change a tire, or use a VCR to tape a TV show. Use the chronological order—process pattern. Then draw a diagram showing the organization of your paragraph.*

Diagram:

EXERCISE 8-13

Directions: Read each of the following selections and identify the thought pattern used. Write the name of the pattern in the space provided. Choose from among these patterns: illustration–example, definition, comparison–contrast, cause–effect, classification, chronological order–process. Next, write a sentence explaining your choice. Then draw a diagram that shows the organization of each selection.

1. Many wedding customs have been popular since ancient times. For example, Roman brides probably wore veils more than 2,000 years ago. Bridal veils became popular in Great Britain and the New World during the late 1700's. The custom of giving a wedding ring may also date back to the ancient Romans. The roundness of the ring probably represents eternity, and the presentation of wedding rings symbolizes that the man and woman are united forever. Wearing the wedding ring on the ring finger of the left hand is another old custom. People once thought that a vein or nerve ran directly from this finger to the heart. An old superstition says that a bride can ensure good luck by wearing "something old, something new, something borrowed, and something blue." Another superstition is that it is bad luck for a bride and groom to see each other before the ceremony on their wedding day.

   Pattern: _____

   _____

   Diagram:

2. Muscle is the tough, elastic tissue that makes body parts move. All animals except the simplest kinds have some type of muscle.

   People use muscles to make various movements, such as walking, jumping, or throwing. Muscles also help in performing activities necessary for growth and for maintaining a strong, healthy body. For example, people use muscles in the jaw to chew food. Other muscles help move food through the stomach and intestines, and aid in digestion. Muscles in the heart and blood vessels force the blood to circulate. Muscles in the chest make breathing possible.

   Muscles are found throughout the body. As a person grows, the muscles also get bigger. Muscle makes up nearly half the body weight of an adult.

Pattern: _____

_____

Diagram:

3. Since the late 1960's, musicals have been noted for their enormous range of subjects and styles. *Hair* (1967) dealt with American young people in the 1960's who rebelled against society during the Vietnam War. *Grease* (1972) was a rock 'n' roll musical about high school life during the 1950's. A number of revivals of earlier musicals proved popular during the 1970's. These revivals included a 1971 restaging of Vincent Youmans' 1925 musical *No, No, Nanette* and the burlesque-style *Sugar Babies* (1979).

Many critics consider Stephen Sondheim as the most creative figure in musical comedy today. Sondheim began his career as a lyricist but soon began to write both words and music for his shows. Sondheim gained praise for the wit and sophistication of his lyrics and for the originality of his subject matter. His best-known shows include *Company* (1970), *A Little Night Music* (1973), and *Sweeney Todd* (1979).

Choreographer Michael Bennett created *A Chorus Line* (1975) with music by Marvin Hamlisch. The show explores the personal and professional lives of a number of dancers trying out for a new musical. *A Chorus Line* became one of the greatest successes in theater history.

The greatest problem facing the musical theater in the 1970's and 1980's is the constantly increasing costs of staging a show. Some musicals cost more than $1 million to produce. As a result, fewer musicals are being presented. Many musical comedies today also have small casts and few changes of scenery to keep expenses low.

Pattern: _____

_____

Diagram:

4. Mimosa is the name of a group of trees, shrubs, and herbs which have featherlike leaves. The mimosa grows chiefly in warm and tropical lands. The tree is similar to the acacia. The seed, or fruit, grows in flat pods. The small flowers may be white, pink, lavender, or purple. Mimosa grows throughout Asia, Africa, Mexico, and Australia. In the United States, it grows along the valley of the Rio Grande and in many states, including West Virginia, Virginia, Alabama, Kentucky, Louisiana, and Indiana.

Pattern: _____

_____

Diagram:

5. Morphine makes severe pain bearable and moderate pain disappear. The drug also stops coughing and diarrhea, checks bleeding, and may help bring sleep. Doctors give patients morphine only if other medicines would fail. Besides being addictive, it interferes with breathing and heart action and may cause vomiting. Small doses of morphine leave the mind fairly clear. Larger doses cloud the mind and make the user feel extremely lazy. Most morphine users feel little hunger, anger, sadness, or worry, and their sex drive is greatly reduced. Most people with mental or social problems feel happy after using morphine, even though their problems have not really been solved.

Pattern: _____

_____

Diagram:

6. Personality disorders are character traits that create difficulties in personal relationships. For example, *antisocial personality disorder* is characterized by aggressive and harmful behavior that first occurs before the age of 15. Such behavior includes lying, stealing, fighting, and resisting authority. During adulthood, people with this disorder often have difficulty keeping a job or accepting other responsibilities.

Individuals with *paranoid personality disorder* are overly suspicious, cautious, and secretive. They may have delusions that people are watching them or talking about them. They often criticize others but have difficulty accepting criticism.

People who suffer from *compulsive personality disorder* attach great importance to organization. They strive for efficiency and may spend a great deal of time making lists and schedules. But they are also indecisive and seldom accomplish anything they set out to do. They often make unreasonable demands on other people and have difficulty expressing emotions.

Pattern: _____

_____

Diagram:

7. Only female mosquitoes "bite," and only the females of a few species attack man and animals. They sip the victim's blood, which they need for the development of the eggs inside their bodies. Mosquitoes do not really bite because they cannot open their jaws. When a mosquito "bites," it stabs through the victim's skin with six needlelike parts called *stylets*, which form the center of the proboscis. The stylets are covered and protected by the insect's lower lip, called the *labium*. As the stylets enter the skin, the labium bends and slides upward out of the way. Then saliva flows into the wound through channels formed by the stylets. The mosquito can easily sip the blood because the saliva keeps it from clotting. Most persons are allergic to the saliva, and an itchy welt called a "mosquito bite" forms on the skin. After the mosquito has sipped enough blood, it slowly pulls the stylets out of the wound, and the labium slips into place over them. Then the insect flies away.

Pattern: _____

_____

Diagram:

8. Since 1950, scientists have developed a number of medications that have proved extremely successful in the treatment of certain mental disorders. Psychiatrists use *tricyclic antidepressants* to treat patients with severe depression. In most cases, these drugs restore the depressed patient to normal. *Lithium carbonate* is the most effective drug for patients who suffer from manic-depressive disorder. It reduces the frequency and severity of both the manic and the depressive periods and, in many cases, eliminates them entirely. Medications called *anti-anxiety drugs* or *tranquilizers* help relieve the tension caused by anxiety disorders. Psychiatrists often use *antipsychotic drugs* to treat schizophrenia. These drugs help relieve hallucinations, delusions, and other symptoms of schizophrenia.

   Pattern: _____

   _____

   Diagram:

9. People turn to magic chiefly as a form of insurance—that is, they use it along with actions that actually bring results. For example, hunters may use a hunting charm. But they also use their hunting skills and knowledge of animals. The charm may give hunters the extra confidence they need to hunt even more successfully than they would without it. If they shoot a lot of game, they credit the charm for their success. Many events occur naturally without magic. Crops grow without it, and sick people get well without it. But if people use magic to bring a good harvest or to cure a patient, they may believe the magic was responsible.

   People also tend to forget magic's failures and to be impressed by its apparent successes. They may consider magic successful if it appears to work only 10 per cent of the time. Even when magic fails, people often explain the failure without doubting the power of the magic. They may say that the magician made a mistake in reciting the spell or that another magician cast a more powerful spell against the magician.

   Many anthropologists believe that people have faith in magic because they feel a need to believe in it. People may turn to magic to reduce their fear and uncertainty if they feel they have no control over the outcome of a situation. For example, farmers use knowledge and skill when they plant their fields. But they know that weather, insects, or diseases might ruin the crops. So farmers in some societies may also plant a charm or perform a magic rite to ensure a good harvest.

Pattern: _____

_____

Diagram:

10. Almost all companies realize the tremendous value of mathematics in research and planning. Many major industrial firms employ trained mathematicians. Mathematics has great importance in all engineering projects. For example, the design of a superhighway requires extensive use of mathematics. The construction of a giant dam would be impossible without first filling reams of paper with mathematical formulas and calculations. The large number of courses an engineering student must take in mathematics shows the importance of mathematics in this field.

Pattern: _____

_____

Diagram:

SUMMARY

Recognition of an author's thought, or organizational, pattern is an aid to comprehension and recall. This chapter focused on six of the most common ways paragraphs are organized:

1. ILLUSTRATION–EXAMPLE   An idea is explained by providing specific instances or experiences that illustrate it.

2. DEFINITION   An object or idea is explained by describing the general class or group to which it belongs and how the item differs from others in the same group (distinguishing features).

3. COMPARISON–CONTRAST A new or unfamiliar idea is explained by showing how it is similar to or different from a more familiar idea.

4. CAUSE–EFFECT Connections between events are explained by showing what caused an event or what happened as a result of a particular event.

5. CLASSIFICATION An object or idea is explained by dividing it into parts and describing or explaining each.

6. CHRONOLOGICAL ORDER–PROCESS Events or procedures are described in the order in which they occur in time.

PART THREE REVIEW

MAKING YOUR SKILLS WORK TOGETHER

UNDERSTANDING SENTENCES AND PARAGRAPHS

Part Two focused on two units of meaning: the sentence and the paragraph. Used together with the vocabulary skills presented in Part One, these provide the skills necessary to understand written materials. The following summary suggestions will help you understand sentences and paragraphs more easily:

1. Search for information. Try to sort the more-important ideas from the less-important ones. In sentences, sort key ideas from the information that explains them. In paragraphs, search for the main ideas and sift through the details to find the most-important ones to remember.

2. Look for relationships. In reading sentences, try to see how parts of the sentence are connected. In reading paragraphs, discover how the details explain the main idea.

3. Look for patterns in the way ideas are organized or put together. In sentences, try to see whether there is one basic idea, two combined ideas, or two or more related ideas. In paragraphs, look for the thought pattern that is used to tie details together.

4. Keep this question constantly in mind: Do I understand this? The moment you feel the answer might be "no," stop and go back. Find out what is wrong. The problem may be an unknown word or words. If so, use the vocabulary skills you learned in Part One. The problem may be a long, complicated sentence or a confusing paragraph. If so, analyze it using the techniques suggested in Part Two.

EXERCISE 1

Directions: *The following selection, taken from a business communications textbook, has been specially marked and includes marginal notes. They call your attention to the clues that help you to find what is important and to notice patterns and relationships. Read the selection, paying attention to the special markings and notes. Then answer the questions that follow.*

Purpose for reading: What are the barriers to effective listening?

BARRIERS TO EFFECTIVE LISTENING

—Norman B. Sigband

First barrier

Perhaps the ⟦most important barrier⟧ to effective listening results from the fact that most of us talk at about 125–150 words per minute while we can listen and comprehend some 600–800 words per minute. Quite obviously if the sender talks at 125 words and the receiver listens at 600, the latter is left with a good deal of time to think about matters other than the message; and he does: illness, bills, cars, the baseball results, what's for dinner tonight, and so on. This is the ⟦internal⟧ competition for attention.   1

Signals contrast, new barrier

⟦However,⟧ there is also the ⟦external⟧ competition to effective listening. These are the distractions caused by clattering typewriters, ringing telephones, noisy production lines, heated arguments, intriguing smells, captivating sights, and dozens of other factors we all encounter in a busy, complex society.   2

New barrier introduced

Time, or more accurately, the lack of it, ⟦also contributes⟧ to inefficient listening. Effective listening requires that we give others a block of time so they may express their ideas as well as their feelings. Some individuals require more time than others to do this. If we are, or we appear to be, impatient they will either not express themselves fully or will require more time than usual. And yet the listener possesses a limited amount of time also. In addition, there are some individuals who will monopolize *all* your listening time. As a matter of fact, if you begin to listen to such a person at noon, you will probably still be listening at 10:00 P.M..   3

That person you must turn off as tactfully as possible. However,   4 there are others with whom you work or live that you should give time to so you may listen with undivided attention. Remember, if *you* don't listen to "them," they will always find someone who *will*.

If an employee feels her supervisor won't listen to her, she will find another employee or the union representative who will; if a youngster feels his parents won't or don't listen to him, he may find a friend, gang member, or someone whose influence might be detrimental. And if customers feel a supplier really isn't listening, they will find a competitor to the supplier who will. 5

There is no such thing as a vacuum in communication. 6

New barrier
Use context
to define
conditioning

Conditioning is still another factor that contributes to poor listening. Many of us have conditioned ourselves not to listen to messages that do not agree with our philosophy or that irritate, upset, or anger us. TV and radio play a role in this conditioning. If the program we see or hear doesn't entertain or intrigue us, we have been conditioned to reach over and simply change channels or stations. And this habit of changing the channel to tune a message out, we carry into our daily listening activities. 7

New barrier

Our tendency to evaluate what we hear may constitute still another barrier. So often we listen and almost immediately evaluate and reject the idea before it is completely voiced. Or we listen and then detour mentally while the individual is still talking. Of course, it is not possible *not* to evaluate, but one should continue to listen *after* evaluating. The problem is that most of us tune out as soon as we hear an idea or point of view that does not agree with ours. 8

New barrier

Emotions, if colored or at a high level, may also get in the way of effective listening. Surely if an individual hears ideas which are counter to his, or is involved in a confrontation, or is emotionally upset because of fear, anger, or happiness, effective listening becomes very difficult. 9

New barrier

Lack of training on how to listen is still another barrier. Most of us have received much instruction on how to write more concisely and clearly, read more efficiently and rapidly, and speak more forcefully and effectively. But few of us have ever received any instruction on how to listen. Perhaps this flaw in our educational system is due to the belief on the part of many educators that if one hears, that individual is also listening. The fact remains that more effective listening *can* be taught. Fortunately more and more schools today are teaching youngsters how to listen more effectively, and there are even programs available in many universities. 10

New barrier

Our failure to concentrate is another barrier to effective listening. That may be due to the fact that many of us have not been taught how to listen or to the simple fact that we don't *work* at listening. 11

All you need do is look around the room at the next meeting you attend. Note how many people are sitting in a completely sprawled posture; some even have their feet stretched out on the chair next to them or on top of the meeting table or desk. How can anyone really work at lis- 12 tening while in a completely relaxed posture? And even if the individual does listen well in that position, think of what that posture conveys non-verbally to the speaker!

It does little good, except as items of information, to name (as   13 we have) eight reasons why many of us don't listen well. What is really of concern to us, is how we can become better listeners . . . and most of us *can* become better.

1. Review the article and locate any difficult words that you don't know the meaning of. List them below. Study the context for clues. If there are no clues, analyze each word's parts and/or check the meaning in the dictionary. Write a brief definition of each.

   _____

   _____

   _____

2. Underline the sentence in the first paragraph that best explains why our mind wanders while listening.

3. Underline the main idea of each of the remaining paragraphs in the selection.

4. What thought pattern is used throughout the selection? Give a reason for your answer.

   _____

   _____

5. Do paragraphs 4 and 5 introduce new barriers to listening? If so, list them below. If not, explain the function of these paragraphs.

   _____

   _____

6. In the last paragraph the author indicates that eight barriers to listening have been discussed. Without looking back to the article, list as many barriers as you can recall. Then, check to find any you missed.

   _____   _____

   _____   _____

   _____   _____

   _____   _____

   _____   _____

PART FOUR

COMPREHENSION AND RETENTION: Articles, Essays, and Chapters

Let us take the case of a typical college student, Sam Sample, and look at how he prepared for an exam in sociology. The exam was to cover five chapters in Sam's textbook as well as several articles assigned by the instructor. To prepare for the exam, Sam reread each of the textbook chapters. The articles were on reserve in the library, so Sam read but did not reread or review them. He spent a total of six hours studying, mostly on the day before the exam. A week later, when he got his graded exam paper back, he learned he had failed. Sam was angry and disappointed; he was overheard saying to a friend, "I don't know what the instructor expects. I spent six hours studying and I still failed!" Why do you think Sam failed?

The main reason Sam failed is that, although he spent time studying, he did not study *in the right way*. In fact, he used one of the *least effective* ways to study—reading and rereading. Sam's failure to review the assigned articles may also explain his poor grade. Although he could not take the articles from the library, he could have written an outline or a summary of each for review purposes. Finally, Sam limited his study to the day before the exam and did not allow himself time to think about and organize the material mentally.

**THIS PART OF THE TEXT WILL HELP YOU
IMPROVE YOUR ABILITY TO UNDERSTAND
AND REMEMBER WHAT YOU READ SO THAT**

1. **You will be familiar with various types of articles and essays and how they are organized. (Chapter 9)**

2. **You will be able to recognize the organization of textbook chapters and the learning aids they contain. (Chapter 10)**

3. **You will know three ways to review, each of which is much more effective than rereading. (Chapter 11)**

Chapter 9

READING ARTICLES AND ESSAYS

THIS CHAPTER WILL SHOW YOU HOW TO

1. **Use organizational features of articles and essays**

2. **Recognize various types of articles and essays and read them more effectively**

Most college students expect to be given textbook reading assignments. However, many are surprised when their instructors assign other types of reading as well. Many instructors assign supplementary (additional) readings in books or magazines. Others distribute reading lists or place material on reserve in the library. These assignments add to the information the textbook provides. Some may present a particular viewpoint on a controversial issue. Others may update information in the text. Still others may show a particular application of concepts and theories learned in the course.

When reading assigned articles and essays, you must first comprehend the material. Becoming familiar with organizational features will make comprehension easier. Reading will also be easier if you know what type of article or essay you are reading and how to approach it.

ORGANIZATIONAL FEATURES

Most articles and essays follow a basic organizational pattern. Once you are familiar with this pattern, reading articles and essays will be an easier task. With few exceptions, articles and essays have five basic parts:

1. Title

2. Introduction

3. Thesis statement

4. Supporting information

5. Conclusion or summary

Title

There are two basic kinds of titles, descriptive and interest-catching. The title of the article on page 163, "How Muzak Manipulates You," is descriptive. It announces what the article will be about. From this title you know the article is about Muzak (a type of background music). From the word *manipulate*, you can also tell that the article will discuss how Muzak is used to control people. This article might have been titled "Are You Being Controlled?" but although such a title might catch your interest, it does not tell the subject of the article. Here are a few examples of interest-catching titles along with the actual subjects of the articles.

Title	*Subject*
1. Paradise or Dull Routine?	1. Different models of marriage
2. Rolling Along	2. Roller derbies
3. Man at the Top	3. Flagpole-sitting contests

EXERCISE 9-1

Directions: *Read each title and, when possible, describe what you expect the article to be about.*

1. "Ancient Sports Revisited"

_____

2. "Changing Times, Changing Morals"

_____

3. "The Woman Question"

_____

4. "The Graying of the American Family"

   _____

5. "Roots of Rock"

   _____

6. "City That Finds Its Children"

   _____

7. "How to Fight the Hungries"

   _____

8. "Saving the Third World's Children"

   _____

9. "A Cop to the Core"

   _____

10. "In Pursuit of the Perfect Hamburger"

   _____

Introduction

When reading an article, it is tempting to rush through the first paragraph in order to get right into the main part of the article. Actually, the introduction is one of the most important parts of an article because it usually:

- Announces the subject
- Provides a focus and context for the subject
- Gives pertinent background information
- Builds interest in the subject

Read the first paragraph of the following article "How Muzak Manipulates You." Did you notice how it introduces the subject and provides a context by establishing where and how Muzak is commonly heard?

HOW MUZAK MANIPULATES YOU

—Andrea Dorfman

Every day, millions of people in offices and supermarkets and on assembly lines worldwide hear the bland strains of Muzak. That soundtrack is more than just the homogenization of good music. <u>It</u>

has been painstakingly engineered to direct behavior—to improve employee performance by reducing on-the-job stress, boredom and fatigue or to control consumers' shopping habits.

Background music can, indeed, enhance or interfere with busi- 2 ness, concludes Ronald Milliman, a marketing professor at Loyola University in New Orleans. "Very few stores that play music play it for any particular purpose," he says. "But walking into an environment where music is playing apparently makes a difference."

Milliman measured the effects of fast- and slow-tempo music 3 on a supermarket's traffic flow and sales. Fast music hardly affected sales when compared with no music, he reported in the *Journal of Marketing*, but pieces played lento slowed shoppers and boosted receipts 38 percent above what they had been when fast music was playing.

Increases Patience

Restaurants can also use music advantageously, he found. In the 4 evening, slow-paced music lengthens meals and increases the patience of waiting customers. When quick turnover is important— lunch, for example—lively music does the trick.

The best-known supplier of background music is a company 5 called Muzak. But it's not the only one. In Chicago, there is Musi-Call. In California, Musicast. And in the New York area, General Background Music (GBM).

Muzak calls its product "environmental music" and has done 6 over 100 studies—from simple surveys of employee responses to comparison of production output before and after Muzak installation—to prove its effectiveness. A recent test involved workers preparing precision parts according to exacting specifications. Overall improvement generally ranges from 5 to 10 percent to as much as 30 percent. Results are easier to obtain when routine tasks are involved; people with relatively interesting jobs, however, are also affected.

The key to Muzak's programs is something called stimulus pro- 7 gression. Each tune is given a stimulus code based on its tempo, instrumentation, feel and the date it was added to the firm's library. "We punch these codes into our computer, and it slots the material into fifteen-minute segments of five tunes each," music director Ralph Smith explains. "We start with a tune that has a low stimulus value—one that's slow in tempo and string-dominated—and gradually build to an up-tempo, pop sound."

After a two-minute pause, a new segment begins on a stimulus 8 level that's higher overall than the preceding ones. In this fashion, the day's program builds to mid-morning and mid-afternoon "crescendos" designed to give workers a needed boost.

"Since Muzak's main function is in the workplace, we naturally 9 have to program against people's normal slumps," Smith notes. "Around ten-thirty, you're running down a little, but lunch is still a distance away. So, about ten-fifteen, the stimulus value for the entire segment jumps an extra notch to bring you out of the doldrums."

"Changing the order of things produces a different effect," says   10
psychologist William Wokoun, chairman of Muzak's scientific advisory board. "When this so-called ascending program is played in reverse, it seems to lull people to sleep. Reaction times become slower and more variable."

Like Muzak, GBM focuses on the mind of the nine-to-five em-   11
ployee. "All day long, you have ups and downs, peaks and valleys," vice-president Mel Bernstein explains. "During key periods, psychological programmers change the tempo to increase workers' adrenaline flow, which in turn increases their efficiency. The music becomes part of the surroundings. Workers no longer notice its effects on their behavior."

The difference between GBM and Muzak, says Bernstein, is that   12
Muzak isn't regional; it has only one product. "But there is a very definite New York sound," he asserts, "just as there is a Midwest sound and a Los Angeles sound. And we even have rainy-day music."

Bernstein also says that Muzak, with its two-minute pauses   13
every quarter hour, may help workers keep time subconsciously.

Thesis Statement

The thesis statement is the one important idea the article presents. It may also suggest the organization, purpose, and focus of the article. Just as a paragraph develops one main idea, so an article or essay also develops a single idea throughout. Writers usually express their thesis in one sentence near the beginning of the article. Often it is included as part of the introduction.

Now turn to the article on page 163 and reread the underlined thesis statement in the first paragraph. This sentence first states the main point of the article—that Muzak is used to direct behavior. Then, in the same sentence, the write provides several examples of the behavior Muzak controls.

Supporting Information

You know that a paragraph contains details that explain the main idea (see Chapter 6). Similarly, an article or essay contains supporting ideas that explain the thesis statement. Again, as is true in paragraphs, not all supporting ideas are of equal importance (see Chapter 6). A quick rule of thumb is that you can expect at least one major supporting idea per paragraph. As you read supporting ideas, keep one question in mind: How does this information support the thesis of the selection?

Most writers use various types of supporting information. Often this information is organized by means of one or more of the patterns described in Chapter 8. In addition to these common patterns, writers may support their ideas by giving descriptions (see page 173 of this chapter) or by citing facts, statistics, or research.

Turn again to page 164 and read the remainder of the article. Decide how the writer supports the thesis.

The author begins by referring to research conducted by Milliman that suggests some of the effects of Muzak (see paragraphs 2–4). Then she reviews the type, use, and purpose of background music supplied by two major companies, Muzak and GBM (see paragraphs 5–12). This writer, then, uses facts, statistics, and examples to support her main points.

Conclusion or Summary

An article or essay is usually brought to a close with a summary or conclusion. Each in its own way brings together the ideas expressed in the article.

A summary provides a review of important ideas. It can be thought of as an outline in paragraph form. The order in which the information appears in the summary reflects the organization of the article itself.

A conclusion is a final statement about the subject of the article. A conclusion does not review content as a summary does. Instead, a conclusion usually suggests a new or further direction of thought. It most always introduces an idea that has not been stated previously or a new way of looking at what has been stated.

Turn back to the Muzak article and reread the last paragraph, on page 165. Is it a summary or a conclusion? Since this one-sentence paragraph does not review all the major points of the article, it is not a summary. It does suggest a new, not previously mentioned, value of Muzak, so it is a conclusion.

EXERCISE 9-2

Directions: *Read the following selection and answer the questions that follow.*

TECHNO-STRESS INVADES THE HOME

Danny, a 36-year-old computer programmer, has been married   1
and divorced twice. His marriages fell apart because of his computers.

Danny owns $14,000 worth of equipment, and he's addicted to it. After an 8-hour day at his terminal at work, he'll spend another 8 to 10 hours at home communing with his chips. His first wife left, he mumbles, because "she just didn't understand me." His second tried to resolve an argument by throwing two of his five computers out on the front lawn.

Danny may be an extreme case, but he is part of a growing problem: People who interact with computers full-time have trouble interacting with people. 2

"Thousands of people are experiencing stresses in their relationships because of computers," says psychologist Thomas McDonald, of Transition Associates in La Jolla, California, "and there'll be many more as the computer becomes a part of our lives." Computers are consistently, satisfyingly logical, McDonald notes, and for many people they become a refuge from the messy complexities of interpersonal relationships. 3

According to psychologist Alex Randall, a member of the Boston Computer Society's Social Impact Group, a dialogue with a computer is warped because it is always based on the machine's rational terms. "Linear logic," he says, "is not what personal relationships require." 4

Computer users also enjoy the intoxication of always being in control. Says Joseph Weizenbaum, professor of computer science at MIT, "The sense one gets is that one is in a world of one's own making. It's not often that you have the opportunity to set the stage, write the play and control the actors." 5

Obsessed Hackers

Thomas McDonald reports that he first began counseling computer-plagued couples about two years ago. Since then, through his practice, discussion groups and surveys, he has seen perhaps 1,000 people with the problem. The victims, he says, are nearly always males who deal with computers at work: "This isn't the little guy who buys a VIC-20 and piddles around with it." He adds that truly obsessed hackers, who hardly pause to eat or sleep, have no problems with intimate relationships because "they don't have any." 6

Joseph Weizenbaum notes, "The computer acts as a selector. It attracts people who have trouble with personal relationships anyway. Then it's like creeping alcoholism. There are a lot of people who have two to three martinis at lunch and are looped all the time." 7

Blinking Negligee

Thomas McDonald quotes a counseling session with a representative couple: 8

The Wife: What can I say? Maybe if I put on a negligee with blinking lights and a picture of a computer, he'd notice me. 9

The Husband: Maybe if you'd be interested in what I do, I'd be   10
able to talk to you.
(Silence)

1. Which type of title is used for this selection, descriptive or interest catching? What does the title tell you about the selection?

   _____

   _____

2. Does the first paragraph function as an introduction? If so, what information does it provide?

   _____

3. What is the thesis of this selection?

   _____

4. How does the writer support his or her ideas?

   _____

5. Is the last paragraph a conclusion or a summary? Why?

   _____

TYPES OF ARTICLES AND ESSAYS

Throughout college you will be required to read numerous articles and essays. This section presents a brief review of the various types of articles and essays and suggestions for understanding each.

Narrative

Narrative articles and essays tell a story. They review events that have happened. Usually the events are presented in the order in which they occurred. The story is told, however, to make a point or to explain an idea. If you wrote an essay describing an important event or telling how someone influenced your life, you would use the narrative form. You would describe events as they happened, showing how or why they were important.

In addition to essays, many types of material use the narrative style —biographies, autobiographies, historical accounts, travel books. Follow these steps when reading narratives:

1. Determine when and where the events are taking place.

2. Notice the sequence of events.

3. Notice how the story is told and who is telling it.

4. Look beyond the specific events to the overall meaning. Ask yourself why the writer is telling the story. What is the point the author is trying to make?

5. Watch for the writer's commentary as he or she tells the story.

The following selection is taken from a book titled *Mortal Lessons,*[1] written by a medical doctor. This selection tells the story of a patient who is recovering from surgery that left her face deformed.

I stand by the bed where a woman lies, her face postoperative, her mouth twisted in palsy, clownish. A tiny twig of the facial nerve, the one to the muscles of her mouth, has been severed. She will be thus from now on. The surgeon had followed with religious fervor the curve of her flesh; I promise you that. Nevertheless, to remove the tumor in her cheek, I had cut the little nerve.

Her young husband is in the room. He stands on the opposite side of the bed, and together they seem to dwell in the evening lamplight, isolated from me, private. Who are they, I ask myself, he and this wry-mouth I have made, who gaze at and touch each other so generously, greedily? The young woman speaks.

"Will my mouth always be like this?" she asks.

"Yes," I say, "it will. It is because the nerve was cut."

She nods, and is silent. But the young man smiles.

"I like it," he says. "It is kind of cute."

All at once I *know* who he is. I understand, and I lower my gaze. One is not bold in an encounter with a god. Unmindful, he bends to kiss her crooked mouth, and I so close I can see how he twists his own lips to accommodate to hers, to show her that their kiss still works. I remember that the gods appeared in ancient Greece as mortals, and I hold my breath and let the wonder in.

The incident takes place in a hospital where a woman is recovering from surgery to remove a tumor on her cheek. The author, who is the surgeon, describes the occasion when the woman learns her mouth will be permanently twisted. The surgeon's purpose in writing becomes clear in the last paragraph. His main point is that the husband's kiss is godlike—it determines the woman's response to and acceptance of her deformity.

EXERCISE 9-3

Directions: *Read the following narrative essay and answer the questions that follow.*

WHY GRANNIE SET A BOUNTIFUL THANKSGIVING TABLE

—Patrice Gaines-Carter

One of my biggest moves in life was when I was whisked 1 from the "children's table" to the "adult table" on Thanksgiving Day, 1965.

In one swift move my mother picked up my plate and sil- 2 verware and moved it from one table to another, thus announcing silently that I was no longer a 12-year-old girl, but had become a 12-year-old woman.

In all of my recollections of Thanksgiving at Grannie's, 3 there is the memory of two tables: one for the children and one for the adults.

The children's table was smaller. It was a card table, usu- 4 ally pushed against one end of the large dining-room table. But it was shorter than the dining-room table, and we children always felt like dwarfs sitting there.

Although my mother covered it with a white lace cloth, 5 none of us was fooled: It was still the card table on which the grown-ups played Pokeno, and countless glasses of bourbon had been spilled on its top.

So when I, the oldest of the children, finally moved to the 6 big table, my sisters cut their eyes to me and sighed with envy. They were also relieved, though.

Before that day it never occurred to any of us that we 7 would be able to sit at that table, at least not before we married and bore children. There had been no precedent. My move gave hope to everyone at the "children's" table.

For me, it meant I was nearly grown and didn't even know 8 it. I wondered: If being grown could sneak up on you, could being old creep up on you, also?

My sister Sheila was definitely still young—five years 9 younger than I to be exact. She looked to me for wisdom, and every Thanksgiving she asked me the same question. "Why does Grannie cook so much food?" she'd whisper.

She wasn't being ungrateful. It was true. There was food 10 everywhere we looked: down the table to the left, down the table to the right.

To a child, it looked like an airport runway laden with turkey, 11
ham, rabbit in gravy, collards, string beans, potato salad, candied
yams, rice, macaroni and cheese, cranberry sauce and breads, cakes,
pies and beverages.

We would leave for home with bags of food tucked under our 12
arms. We would be eating turkey salad, turkey sandwiches, turkey
and gravy, turkey and anything my mother could come up with for
the next couple of weeks.

Before I was grown I did not take Sheila's question seriously. But 13
after my move to the adult table I felt I owed her an answer. I
repeated the question to my mother, and she shared with me a little
story.

"Your grandmother has not forgotten her poor times," she said. 14
"She has to always have too much, just so she'll feel that she has
enough. Understand?"

Sounded like adult gibberish to me. But I nodded yes and 15
encouraged her to continue.

"We were poor when I was little," she said. "But your 16
grandmother always made sure I ate and had clean clothes. Then one
Christmas she was sick and couldn't work.

"There wasn't any money, but I didn't know it. I woke up and 17
ran to see what Santa Claus had brought. All I found was some fruit.

"I didn't believe that was all I had gotten, so I kept searching the 18
house. I figured your grandmother had hidden the toys, and I had to
find them.

"All the time your grandmother was crying and crying, trying to 19
tell me that there was nothing else. I searched until I started crying,
too. Then I stopped, and we cried together."

That story made me older. It marked the first time I realized that 20
people did things for reasons—that they didn't behave a certain way
simply because they wanted to.

I put this knowledge in my walk and my talk and wore it as 21
proof of my maturity. I am the oldest child and therefore, I reasoned, I
should be the smartest.

The next time Sheila asked, "Why does Grannie fix so much 22
food?" I told her the story. But she was not grown yet, and she did not
understand what Christmas had to do with Thanksgiving, or toys had
to do with food.

She agreed, though, that it was a sad story, and I noticed the next 23
year that she didn't ask the question.

By 1981 I was used to looking through what people did, to search 24
for the "why." When my grandmother did not cook Thanksgiving dinner that year, I was not surprised. I had recognized an omen
a month earlier. It was an omen that had to do with biscuits.

I had been living in Miami, and whenever I came home to   25
Washington, Grannie would fix me long pans of perfect, flaky biscuits
that melted in my mouth. I ate them with molasses, with homemade
crabapple jelly, with butter or right out of the pan. She loved to watch
me, and I gave her a good show.

I once got out my pad and pencil and asked her how to make the   26
biscuits. She couldn't tell me. I led her into the kitchen so she could
show me. She started pouring the flour into a bowl without
measuring it.

"How can you tell when you have the right amount?" I asked.   27

She picked up the bowl in her hands and shook the flour around   28
so she could feel its weight in the bowl. I gave up.

In 1981 I moved back to Washington a month before   29
Thanksgiving. I asked Grannie for two things: "a pan of biscuits and a
lemon cake."

"I'm too old to fix biscuits," she said, looking me straight in the   30
eyes, daring me to disagree.

"I never heard of anything so ridiculous," I said. I have her   31
spunk.

But she didn't fix the biscuits, and she didn't fix the cake either.
I was devastated, not for myself but for her. It was the omen.

"Any woman too old to fix biscuits," I reasoned, "is ready to   32
die."

There was no Thanksgiving dinner at Grannie's that year. We all   33
had Thanksgiving at my parents' house, where there was no
"children's" table.

We have had dinner at my parents' every Thanksgiving since   34
then. There are only a few children now, and they are my grandmother's great-grandchildren.

At my parents' house these new children, including my   35
daughter, sit at the breakfast bar that faces the dining room table.
(They actually sit higher than the adults.)

In May 1982 my grandmother had a stroke. She has had two   36
more strokes since then. She is confined to a wheelchair and partially
paralyzed.

When I visit her, it seems absurd to think of such small things,   37
but I look at her hands, and I think about those biscuits.

Age has crept up on us both. I am old enough to have my own   38
recipes, and I do have a good recipe for yeast rolls.

On every Thanksgiving since 1981 my family has eaten my   39
yeast rolls. We will eat them this Thanksgiving. They are good rolls.

My grandmother comes to most of the dinners and she even eats   40
my rolls. But as I chew them, I think: These are not biscuits; the
biscuits are gone.

1. Trace the major events in the essay, beginning with 1965 up to the present. Write a list of these events.

   _____

   _____

   _____

2. Who is telling the story? _____

3. At various points in the narrative, the writer makes statements that comment on life or the importance of certain events. Review the essay and underline these statements. Use these to help you answer question 4.

4. What is the writer's purpose in telling the story?

   _____

5. How does the writer feel toward her grandmother? Support your answer with reference to events or statements in the essay.

   _____

   _____

6. Why do you think the author bakes yeast rolls instead of biscuits for Thanksgiving dinner at her parents' home?

   _____

   _____

EXERCISE 9-4

Directions: *Choose one of the topics listed below. On a separate sheet, write a paragraph that uses the narrative style to explain the topics.*

1. An important event in your life

2. Your first day at college

3. One of those days when everything goes wrong

Descriptive

Descriptive articles and essays present ideas by providing details about characteristics of people, places, and things. The details are intended to appeal to your senses, to help you create a mental picture, or to make you feel a certain way. For example, descriptive writing is used frequently in advertising. Notice, in the following travel ad, how the writer helps you imagine what Bermuda is like.

> For more than a century, people who value relaxation have been returning to Bermuda year after year. They appreciate the pink-tinted beaches, the flower-laden garden paths, the cozy pubs, and the clear, turquoise waters.

Now can you picture a beach in Bermuda?

In reading descriptive writing, be sure to follow these steps:

1. Identify the subject of the essay (ask yourself who or what is being described).

2. Pay close attention to the writer's choice of words. The writer often paints a picture with words. Through word choice, a writer tries to create an attitude or feeling (see the section on connotation in Chapter 12). Try to identify that feeling.

3. Look for the overall impression the writer is trying to create. Ask yourself: What do all these details, taken together, suggest about the subject? What is the writer trying to say? How am I supposed to feel about the subject?

4. Pay particular attention to the first and last paragraphs. There you are likely to find the most clues about the writer's main points and purpose for writing.

Read the following descriptive passage. It describes the first use of chemical warfare by the German army during World War I. Try to create a mental picture of the event.

> At five o'clock, three red rockets streaked into the sky, 1 signalling the start of a deafening artillery barrage. High explosive shells pounded into the deserted town of Ypres and the villages around it. At the same time the troops sheltering near Langemarck saw two greenish-yellow clouds rise from the enemy's lines, catch the wind, and billow forwards, gradually merging to form a single bank of blue-white mist: out of sight, in special emplacements protected by sandbags and concrete, German pioneers were opening the valves of 6,000 cylinders spread out along a four mile front. The cylinders contained liquid chlorine—the instant the pressure was released and it came into contact with the air it vaporized and hissed out to form a dense cloud. At thirty parts per million of air chlorine gas produces a rasping cough. At concentrations of one part per thousand it is fatal. The breeze stirred again, and one hundred and sixty

tons of it, five feet high and hugging the ground, began to roll towards the Allied trenches.

Chemical warfare had begun.   2

The wave broke over the first line within a minute, enveloping   3
tens of thousands of troops in an acrid green cloud so thick they could no longer see their neighbours in the trench. Seconds later they were clutching at the air and at their throats, fighting for breath.

Chlorine does not suffocate: it poisons, stripping the lining of   4
the bronchial tubes and lungs. The inflammation produces a massive amount of fluid that blocks the windpipe, froths from the mouth and fills the lungs. In an attempt to escape the effects, some men tried to bury their mouths and nostrils in the earth; others panicked and ran. But any exertion or effort to outdistance the cloud only resulted in deeper breaths and more acute poisoning. As the tide of gas washed over the struggling men their faces turned blue from the strain of trying to breathe; some coughed so violently they ruptured their lungs. Each man, as the British casualty report was later to put it, was 'being drowned in his own exudation.'

Do you have a picture in your mind? Can you imagine the gas rising and moving toward the trenches? Can you picture the reaction of the troops to the chlorine? Underline words in the selection that you felt were particularly helpful to you in imagining this event. Did you underline such words and phrases as *greenish-yellow clouds, billow, blue-white mist, hugging the ground, clutching at the air, turned blue*? Together these words suggest the appearance and severe effects of the chlorine gas.

Look at the selection once again and try to answer this question: How is the writer trying to make you feel about chemical warfare?

From the choice of words, you can see that the writer thinks chemical warfare is a violent form of poisoning. Also, since the writer described in detail the troops' physical reaction to the gas, you can tell that the writer wanted you to be shocked or horrified.

EXERCISE 9-5

Directions: *Read the following descriptive article and answer the questions that follow.*

IN IDAHO: LIVING OUTSIDE OF TIME

—Gregory Jaynes

Twice a week in the warm months, twice a month in the cold, a   1
pilot named Ray Arnold ferries mail and sundries to people who live so far back in the mountains of Idaho that it sometimes seems the

sun sets between them and the nearest town. To many of the people along this route, that nearest town is Cascade, where Arnold Aviation is based. There, in a cheerful office off to one side of a hangar, Arnold's wife Carol receives shopping lists from the backwoodsmen on her short-wave radio; then she does all their marketing. These goods are flown to a breed of Americans who choose to live outside of time.

"Now, how many was that on the pitted black olives?" Carol   2
was saying into her radio one morning when the temperature was 10 below.

"Two jars. And a fifth of Christian Brothers brandy and a fifth of   3
Dark Myers's rum. A small container of nutmeg and two quarts of eggnog."

"O.K., got it." Taped to the wall above Carol's desk was a   4
marching line of signed blank checks collected the last time Ray made the rounds. The customers trust the Arnolds, with good reason. The Arnolds are their contact, their cablehead to civilization. So intimate is this bush network, Carol can calculate the state of marital relations in the mountains by the quantity of condom orders, though she chooses to push this intelligence out of mind.

In the hangar Ray was loading the plane. Four dozen eggs. A case   5
of Old Milwaukee. A case of Budweiser. A roll of roofing tar paper. Cat Chow. Meow Mix. Grape-Nuts flakes. Bread. A broom. "Some of them out there are brand conscious," Carol said. "Some are quality conscious. Some you just know what to get. One cat at the Allison ranch, for instance, won't eat anything but Purina."

Ray had a passenger, a young bearded fellow named Hal who was   6
going to be caretaker of a University of Idaho research station where wildlife patterns are studied. "Might as well put in another sleeping bag," Ray said. "If something happens, I sure don't want to sleep in the same bag with you."

The pilot had one last cup of coffee in the office. It is one of   7
those offices adorned with chummy signs: DO YOU WANT TO TALK TO THE ONE IN CHARGE OR THE ONE WHO KNOWS WHAT'S GOING ON? The people of Cascade (pop. 1,000) hang around here as the people in small towns in warmer climes do around certain gas pumps. They waved Ray Arnold off as he taxied away on skis.

There have been times when the weather socked the pilot in and   8
the mail run had to be postponed for up to five days. But this day was so clear you could almost see tomorrow. The Salmon River Mountains were below. The way the snow caught the sun, the snow looked like diamond dust. Off the starboard wing the Sawtooth Mountain Range made a ragged platinum horizon. Down canyons, through passes, over peaks, the Cessna with the skis affixed to its

wheels threw a shadow that caused elk, long-horned sheep and mountain goats to bolt. On the control panel Arnold has tacked a sign: IF YOU WISH TO SMOKE, PLEASE STEP OUTSIDE.

In Idaho, skis and risk have always been a part of mail delivery. 9 In the 1880s, carriers used 11-ft. skis to get over the high passes to reach the miners' camps. Three carriers died in avalanches. A fourth froze to death, his bag jammed with Christmas mail. Arnold has crashed twice, once when the wind shifted wildly over a jury-rigged runway and put him into the trees. The second time, a crack developed in the exhaust system, carbon monoxide leaked into the cabin, and the pilot passed out. The plane's premature landing, fortunately, was again cushioned by the trees.

Both aircraft were total losses. The pilot walked away from the 10 first, cracked a vertebra in the second. What is more, the Federal Aviation Administration cited him 13 times for the second crash. Among his wrongdoings, said the FAA, was flying too low. That was a hard charge to dodge, since it is difficult to keep your nose up when you are unconscious and going down. In the end he enriched the FAA by $400.

When it is not possible to land, Arnold drops the mail, 11 employing passengers, if he has any, as bombardiers. He orders them to open a window, makes a pass at the lowest FAA-permitted altitude of 500 ft., yells, "Get ready . . ." and then explodes with "Now!" When the drop is dead on the money, as it often is, the involuntary first-time mail bomber gets a rush not unlike the sensation one associates with having just saved the Republic.

Arnold's own personal rush comes from the warmth of his 12 customers. They need him desperately, after all, and when they hear his plane they are out on their makeshift runways, pulling sleds, flashing blinding smiles. On this route the mailman is always invited inside. A couple who wish to be known only as Newt and Sharon baked him a cherry pie on this particular visit. Sharon makes her pastries with bear fat. They talked of the six otters they had seen outside in the Salmon River that morning. Newt tore through his mail, furiously writing checks as he went. "This is one of the few places where the bills are late before they get here," he explained. "Computers don't understand that."

At the University of Idaho research station, Ray had dropped off 13 his first passenger and picked up Jim Akenson, who had been studying cougars and elk but was now "coming out" to visit family. People along the Salmon River, the River of No Return the pioneers called it, speak of leaving or returning as "going out" and "coming in," or "leaving the river" and "coming to the river." Jim had known Newt and Sharon by radio for 30 months but had never met them. They live 65 miles apart. "You don't look the way I pictured you," said Jim.

"Neither do you," said Sharon.   14

They spoke of "going out." Sharon said that this "has been a bad   15
year. Everybody on the river has had to go to town." She said that she
had had to have her teeth attended to and that Newt had got sick.
"Newt hadn't been to town since December 1980. We hate to go to
town."

The mailman left with two steelhead filets Newt wanted him to   16
pass on to a neighbor miles away through the wilderness. He would
be back that afternoon to drop off a fresh-killed elk another neighbor
wanted Newt and Sharon to have. All along the route this day, he
would be transferring gifts, books, food, goods and good wishes
between these isolationists. It is a service not set down in his $20,000-
a-year contract with the postal service."Oh, I take it out in trade,"
Ray said. "The weather could ground me, and then I'd have to stay
overnight with them, so I stay on their good side."

At the next stop, a woman named Frances Wisner, a south Texas   17
telephone operator who settled on the river in 1940, sat waiting with
her German shepherd under a lean-to. She wore more layers than a
high-society wedding cake. She gave Ray Arnold a meat-loaf sand-
wich, a cup of steaming coffee and a piece of her mind. She said it
might help the federal deficit if they placed higher taxes on every soft
drink but Coca-Cola, which she drinks, and every candy bar but
Milky Way, which she favors. Around them, gathering dusk turned
the day and the canyon blue, the way it does on snowy landscapes.

Ray Arnold flew home with a full moon rising. He had covered   18
550 miles. The people he had seen are not hermits in the real sense,
not even xenophobic (they chatter all day on their radios; they wel-
come strangers who accompany Ray), so much as they are shot
through with old-time ornery independence, misfits with a thing
against clocks. To understand what drew them here, one need only
remember those maps where population density is shown by clusters
of black dots—each dot representing 100,000 people, say—on a white
background.

On a map like that, the corridor between Washington and   19
Boston looks like a great oil spill at sea. By contrast, Idaho, because of
its configuration and lack of residents, looks like an alabaster chim-
ney with only a few smudges. Idaho, the popular saying goes, "is
what America was."

1. Underline the information in the article that you feel best describes Ray
   Arnold.

2. What type of person is Ray Arnold? Write your own description of him. Support your description with information from the article.

_____

_____

_____

3. What facts about the people who live along the Salmon River were most useful in helping you imagine what they are like? Underline them.

4. Write your own description of the backwoods people of the Salmon River area. Support your answer with references to the article.

_____

_____

_____

EXERCISE 9-6

Directions: *Think of a topic that you could describe in as much detail as in the article about chlorine gas or the one about life along the Salmon River. On a separate sheet, write a paragraph describing your topic.*

Expository

Expository articles and essays are written to explain. They are intended to present information about a topic or to explain an idea. Most textbooks, magazine articles, and nonfiction books use the expository style. Writers use various methods to develop their subjects and present their ideas. The most common approaches include the following:

1. Illustration/example—giving examples

2. Definition—describing characteristics

3. Comparison—showing similarities

4. Contrast—showing differences

5. Cause–effect—showing relationships or connections

6. Classification—grouping ideas based on similar characteristics

7. Process—describing a procedure or giving a step-by-step list

You may have noticed that these approaches are similar to the thought patterns described in Chapter 8.

Entire articles or essays may follow one of these approaches. Often, however, you may find that a writer uses several patterns at once or moves from one to another in mid-essay. For example, a writer may use classification and then further explain the classification by giving examples. Or a narrative essay may also be descriptive.

In general, reading expository writing involves the sifting and sorting out of information. Most expository writing contains many facts and details. The reader's task is to identify and remember those that are important. Much of what you have already learned about the relationship of ideas in both sentences and paragraphs will guide you in locating these important ideas (see Chapters 6 and 7). Your purpose for reading will determine the type of information you need to recall. Later, in Chapter 11, you will learn how to organize and remember the information that you have identified as important.

The following questions may be used as a guide in reading expository writing:

1. What is this material about?

2. What main points is the writer making?

3. How is this material organized? How are the main points connected together?

4. How much detail do I need to recall?

The following excerpt from a newspaper article is a good example of expository writing. It tells what the job market will be like in the twenty-first century.

THE WORKPLACE IS IN FOR A REVOLUTION

—Barbara S. Moffet

"And what do you do?" may still be the favorite question at 21st century cocktail parties, but the answers will add up to something new.   1

Most Americans will be working in information-related fields, futurists say. Hardly anyone will work in factories, and even fewer on farms.   2

There will be more biologists than there are today, and, because of the older population, more paramedics and geriatric social workers. The number of restaurateurs and travel agents will increase to help us fill our expanding leisure time.   3

The cocktail party may include a genetic-engineering specialist   4 or a robot technician. And sometime in the next century, we may travel in social circles with a space-flight attendant or a space pharmacist.

But telephone operators, postal clerks, meter readers and aircraft 5 structure assemblers may be hard to find. New technologies could make many of their jobs unnecessary.

The view of the 21st century remains a bit murky in 1984, but 6 technological breakthroughs occurring today—especially the development of industrial robots, telecommunications and biotechnology— guarantee that the worker of 2000 and beyond will face a choice of occupations different from today's.

There will still be doctors, lawyers and merchants, but 7 automation will send the bank teller, the supermarket checkout clerk, the metal worker and the machinist the way of the elevator operator, the milkman and the bowling pinsetter.

A bulletin board of job openings might contain these de- 8 scriptions:

• Biomedical engineer—Makes bionic arms, legs, hands and feet, as well as instruments to let the blind see and the deaf hear.

• Laser inspection technician—Installs and maintains laser devices used everywhere from grocery checkouts to factories.

• Hazardous-waste technician—Monitors, collects, transports and disposes of hazardous wastes.

• High-skilled paramedic—Under the eye of a portable TV camera, performs emergency procedures on accident victims, supervised by doctors watching monitors at a hospital.

The century will see more women and older people on the job, 9 futurists say. More people will work at home, especially the handicapped, who will be able to "telecommute" to an all-electronic office by computer.

Whatever we do, we'll probably do less of it. 10

"In the last 100 years, we cut our number of working hours in 11 half, and I think we'll do that again in half the time," says John Naisbitt, author of the book "Megatrends." But few workers will hold one job for life; changing technologies will force a series of career changes and mid-career training sabbaticals.

W. Clyde Helms of Occupational Forecasting Inc. in Fairfax, Va., 12 is convinced that Americans are not ready for the jobs of the future. "The future doesn't begin at 12:01 a.m. Jan. 1, 2000; it's happening today," he asserts. "The youths entering school today are the work force of the 21st century."

Technology has led in the evolution of the typical American 13 worker from farmer to factory laborer to information specialist. Today more than half of all Americans work in creating, processing and disseminating information—programmers, teachers, secretaries, accountants, insurance people, engineers, librarians, television and newspaper reporters—and the percentage is increasing.

When President Reagan was born in 1911, almost a third of   14 Americans worked on farms. Now barely one in 30 works the land, and most analysts expect even fewer farmers in the 21st century.

Manufacturing is shrinking, too. In 1980, 28 percent of the work   15 force was in manufacturing. The percentage is expected to drop, possibly to only 3 percent by 2030, says S. Norman Feingold, president of National Career and Counseling Services in Washington.

Increasing numbers of blue-collar workers are in service jobs   16 rather than manufacturing. Already, far more people work for McDonald's, for example, than for U.S. Steel.

Notice that the writer uses a number of different methods to explain the topic. She offers facts and statistics about the changing market. She makes comparisons with current and past job markets. She provides examples of the types of jobs there will be in the future by imagining a bulletin board. She offers reasons for the predicted changes (technology, shrinking manufacturing, and so on).

EXERCISE 9-7

Directions: *Answer the following questions after reading the expository essay "The Workplace Is In for a Revolution."*

1. Part of the task in reading expository essays is to sort out what is important from what is less so. Review the essay and underline the information that you feel is most important.

2. What does the writer think jobs will be like in the 21st century?

   _____

   _____

3. What thought patterns are most commonly used in the essay? Justify your answer.

   _____

   _____

4. Is the title of the essay descriptive or interest-catching? Give a reason for your answer.

   _____

   _____

5. What is the function of the first introductory paragraph of the essay?

_____

Persuasive

Persuasive articles and essays are written to convince the reader of something. They are usually concerned with controversial issues or those for which there is no clear-cut right and wrong. This type of writing encourages you to change your beliefs or attitudes. The two principal methods authors use to accomplish this are logical argument and appeal to the reader's emotions.

Reading a persuasive article or essay involves skills of interpretation as well as basic comprehension skills. You will find many of the skills presented in Part Five of this book useful in critically reading and evaluating persuasive writing. The following suggestions provide an overview of, or brief introduction to, critical reading and evaluation:

1. Approach the article or essay with two major questions in mind:
   a. Of what is the writer trying to convince me?
   b. Does the writer provide sufficient evidence for me to accept his or her argument?

2. Pay particular attention to _how_ the writer tries to persuade you. What persuasive techniques are used?

3. Does the writer present an objective view of the subject or does he or she look at only one side of an issue?

4. What are the qualifications of the author to write on the subject?

Now read the following paragraph of a persuasive essay. Decide whether the writer will use a logical argument or make an emotional appeal.

My point of view is that of a cancer researcher who has been working for the last 20 years with RNA viruses that cause cancer in chickens. Since the early years of this century, it has been known that viruses cause cancer in chickens. In more recent years viruses have been shown to cause cancer not only in chickens, but also in mice, cats, and even in some primates. Therefore, it was a reasonable hypothesis that viruses might cause cancer in humans and that, if a human cancer virus existed, it could be prevented by a vaccine as so many other virus diseases have been prevented.[2]

In the first paragraph, the author tells you that he is a researcher. This is your first clue that a logical argument will be presented. In the second

paragraph, the words *reasonable hypothesis* and *therefore* also suggest a
logical presentation.

EXERCISE 9-8

Directions: *Read the following persuasive essay and answer the questions that follow.*

I WANT A WIFE

—*Judy Syfers*

I belong to that classification of people known as wives. I am A 1
Wife. And, not altogether incidentally, I am a mother.

Not too long ago a male friend of mine appeared on the scene 2
fresh from a recent divorce. He had one child, who is, of course, with
his ex-wife. He is obviously looking for another wife. As I thought
about him while I was ironing one evening, it suddenly occurred to
me that I, too, would like to have a wife. Why do I want a wife?

I would like to go back to school so that I can become 3
economically independent, support myself, and, if need be, support
those dependent upon me. I want a wife who will work and send me
to school. And while I am going to school I want a wife to take care
of my children. I want a wife to keep track of the children's doctor
and dentist appointments. And to keep track of mine, too. I want a
wife to make sure my children eat properly and are kept clean. I want
a wife who will wash the children's clothes and keep them mended. I
want a wife who is a good nurturant attendant to my children, who
arranges for their schooling, makes sure that they have an adequate
social life with their peers, takes them to the park, the zoo, etc. I
want a wife who takes care of the children when they are sick, a wife
who arranges to be around when the children need special care, because, of course, I cannot miss classes at school. My wife must arrange to lose time at work and not lose the job. It may mean a small
cut in my wife's income from time to time, but I guess I can tolerate
that. Needless to say, my wife will arrange and pay for the care of the
children while my wife is working.

I want a wife who will take care of *my* physical needs. I want a 4
wife who will keep my house clean. A wife who will pick up after
me. I want a wife who will keep my clothes clean, ironed, mended,
replaced when need be, and who will see to it that my personal things
are kept in their proper place so that I can find what I need the minute I need it. I want a wife who cooks the meals, a wife who is a *good*

cook. I want a wife who will plan the menus, do the necessary grocery shopping, prepare the meals, serve them pleasantly, and then do the cleaning up while I do my studying. I want a wife who will care for me when I am sick and sympathize with my pain and loss of time from school. I want a wife to go along when our family takes a vacation so that someone can continue to care for me and my children when I need a rest and change of scene.

I want a wife who will not bother me with rambling complaints 5 about a wife's duties. But I want a wife who will listen to me when I feel the need to explain a rather difficult point I have come across in my course of studies. And I want a wife who will type my papers for me when I have written them.

I want a wife who will take care of the details of my social life. 6 When my wife and I are invited out by my friends, I want a wife who will take care of the babysitting arrangements. When I meet people at school that I like and want to entertain, I want a wife who will have the house clean, will prepare a special meal, serve it to me and my friends, and not interrupt when I talk about the things that interest me and my friends. I want a wife who will have arranged that the children are fed and ready for bed before my guests arrive so that the children do not bother us. I want a wife who takes care of the needs of my guests so that they feel comfortable, who makes sure that they have an ashtray, that they are passed the hors d'oeuvres, that they are offered a second helping of the food, that their wine glasses are replenished when necessary, that their coffee is served to them as they like it. And I want a wife who knows that sometimes I need a night out by myself.

I want a wife who is sensitive to my sexual needs, a wife who 7 makes love passionately and eagerly when I feel like it, a wife who makes sure that I am satisfied. And, of course, I want a wife who will not demand sexual attention when I am not in the mood for it. I want a wife who assumes the complete responsibility for birth control, because I do not want more children. I want a wife who will remain sexually faithful to me so that I do not have to clutter up my intellectual life with jealousies. And I want a wife who understands that *my* sexual needs may entail more than strict adherence to monogamy. I must, after all, be able to relate to people as fully as possible.

If, by chance, I find another person more suitable as a wife than 8 the wife I already have, I want the liberty to replace my present wife with another one. Naturally, I will expect a fresh, new life; my wife will take the children and be solely responsible for them so that I am left free.

When I am through with school and have a job, I want my wife 9 to quit working and remain at home so that my wife can more fully and completely take care of a wife's duties.

My God, who *wouldn't* want a wife? 10

1. In the first paragraph, Judy Syfers identifies herself as a wife and mother. In the second paragraph and throughout the essay, she says she wants a wife. Does she really mean what she says? Explain your answer.

    _____

    _____

    _____

2. Syfers says she wants a wife, but she is saying so only to make a point. What main point is she making throughout the essay?

    _____

3. What types of evidence does Syfers give to support her argument that the role of a wife is ideal for everyone but the wife?

    _____

    _____

4. Is Syfers's argument convincing? Explain your answer by referring to the article.

    _____

    _____

5. Does the writer present an objective or subjective view of the role of a wife? Explain your answer by referring to the article.

    _____

    _____

6. Syfers takes a critical view of the role of a wife. Are there advantages that she does not discuss? On a separate sheet, write a paragraph that explains the benefits of being a wife.

EXERCISE 9-9

Directions: *Choose one of the topics listed below. On a separate sheet, write a paragraph to persuade the reader to accept your point of view on the topic.*

1. Legal drinking age

2. Gun control

3. Abortion

4. Terrorism

EXERCISE 9-10

Directions: *Read each of the following selections and answer the questions that follow.*

A BLACK ATHLETE LOOKS AT EDUCATION

—*Arthur Ashe*

Since my sophomore year at UCLA, I have become convinced 1
that we blacks spend too much time on the playing fields and too little time in the libraries. Consider these facts: for the major professional sports of hockey, football, basketball, baseball, golf, tennis
and boxing, there are roughly only 3170 major league positions available (attributing 200 positions to golf, 200 to tennis and 100 to boxing). And the annual turnover is small.

There must be some way to assure that those who try but don't 2
make it to pro sports don't wind up on street corners or in unem-
ployment lines. Unfortunately, our most widely recognized role
models are athletes and entertainers—"runnin'" and "jumpin'" and
"singin'" and "dancin'."

Our greatest heroes of the century have been athletes—Jack 3
Johnson, Joe Louis, and Muhammad Ali. Racial and economic discrimination forced us to channel our energies into athletics and entertainment. These were the ways out of the ghetto, the ways to get
that Cadillac, those regular shoes, that cashmere sport coat.

Somehow, parents must instill a desire for learning alongside the 4
desire to be Walt Frazier. Why not start by sending black professional
athletes into high schools to explain the facts of life?

I have often addressed high school audiences and my message is 5
always the same: "For every hour you spend on the athletic field,
spend two in the library. Even if you make it as a pro athlete, your career will be over by the time you are 35. You will need that diploma."

Have these pro athletes explain what happens if you break a leg, 6
get a sore arm, have one bad year or don't make the cut for five or six
tournaments. Explain to them the star system, wherein for every star
earning millions there are six or seven others making $15,000 or
$20,000 or $30,000. Invite a bench-warmer or a guy who didn't make
it. Ask him if he sleeps every night. Ask him whether he was graduated. Ask him what he would do if he became disabled tomorrow.
Ask him where his old high school athletic buddies are.

We have been on the same roads—sports and entertain- 7
ment—too long. We need to pull over, fill up at the library and speed

away to Congress and the Supreme Court, the unions and the business world.

I'll never forget how proud my grandmother was when I 8 graduated from UCLA. Never mind the Davis Cup. Never mind the Wimbledon title. To this day, she still doesn't know what those names mean. What mattered to her was that of her more than thirty children and grandchildren, I was the first to be graduated from college, and a famous college at that. Somehow, that made up for all those floors she scrubbed all those years.

1. What type of essay is this—narrative, descriptive, or persuasive? Give reasons for your choice.

_____

_____

2. What is the author's main point?

_____

3. What type of evidence does Ashe offer to support his ideas?

_____

_____

SALVATION

—Langston Hughes

I was saved from sin when I was going on thirteen. But not really 1 saved. It happened like this. There was a big revival at my Auntie Reed's church. Every night for weeks there had been much preaching, singing, praying, and shouting, and some very hardened sinners had been brought to Christ, and the membership of the church had grown by leaps and bounds. Then just before the revival ended, they held a special meeting for children, "to bring the young lambs to the fold." My aunt spoke of it for days ahead. That night I was escorted to the front row and placed on the mourners' bench with all the other young sinners, who had not yet been brought to Jesus.

My aunt told me that when you were saved you saw a light, and 2 something happened to you inside! And Jesus came into your life! And God was with you from then on! She said you could see and hear and feel Jesus in your soul. I believed her. I had heard a great many old people say the same thing and it seemed to me they ought to know. So I sat there calmly in the hot, crowded church, waiting for Jesus to come to me.

The preacher preached a wonderful rhythmical sermon, all   3
moans and shouts and lonely cries and dire pictures of hell, and then
he sang a song about the ninety and nine safe in the fold, but one little lamb was left out in the cold. Then he said: "Won't you come?
Won't you come to Jesus? Young lambs, won't you come?" And he
held out his arms to all us young sinners there on the mourners'
bench. And the little girls cried. And some of them jumped up and
went to Jesus right away. But most of us just sat there.

A great many old people came and knelt around us and prayed,   4
old women with jet-black faces and braided hair, old men with work-
gnarled hands. And the church sang a song about the lower lights are
burning, some poor sinners to be saved. And the whole building
rocked with prayer and song.

Still I kept waiting to *see* Jesus.   5

Finally all the young people had gone to the altar and were   6
saved, but one boy and me. He was a rounder's son named Westley.
Westley and I were surrounded by sisters and deacons praying. It was
very hot in the church, and getting late now. Finally Westley said to
me in a whisper: "God damn! I'm tired o' sitting here. Let's get up
and be saved." So he got up and was saved.

Then I was left all alone on the mourners' bench. My aunt came   7
and knelt at my knees and cried, while prayers and songs swirled all
around me in the little church. The whole congregation prayed for
me alone, in a mighty wail of moans and voices. And I kept waiting
serenely for Jesus, waiting, waiting—but he didn't come. I wanted to
see him, but nothing happened to me. Nothing! I wanted something
to happen to me, but nothing happened.

I heard the songs and the minister saying: "Why don't you   8
come? My dear child, why don't you come to Jesus? Jesus is waiting
for you. He wants you. Why don't you come? Sister Reed, what is this
child's name?"

"Langston," my aunt sobbed.   9

"Langston, why don't you come? Why don't you come and be   10
saved? Oh, Lamb of God! Why don't you come?"

Now it was really getting late. I began to be ashamed of myself,   11
holding everything up so long. I began to wonder what God thought
about Westley, who certainly hadn't seen Jesus either, but who was
now sitting proudly on the platform, swinging his knickerbockered
legs and grinning down at me, surrounded by deacons and old women
on their knees praying. God had not struck Westley dead for taking
his name in vain or for lying in the temple. So I decided that maybe
to save further trouble, I'd better lie, too, and say that Jesus had come,
and get up and be saved.

So I got up.   12

Suddenly the whole room broke into a sea of shouting, as they   13 saw me rise. Waves of rejoicing swept the place. Women leaped in the air. My aunt threw her arms around me. The minister took me by the hand and led me to the platform.

When things quieted down, in a hushed silence, punctuated by a few ecstatic "Amens," all the new young lambs were blessed in the name of God. Then joyous singing filled the room.   14

That night, for the last time in my life but one—for I was a big boy twelve years old—I cried. I cried, in bed alone, and couldn't stop. I buried my head under the quilts, but my aunt heard me. She woke up and told my uncle I was crying because the Holy Ghost had come into my life, and because I had seen Jesus. But I was really crying because I couldn't bear to tell her that I had lied, that I had deceived everybody in the church, and that I hadn't seen Jesus, and that now I didn't believe there was a Jesus any more, since he didn't come to help me.   15

1. What type of essay is this—narrative, descriptive, or persuasive? Give reasons for your choice.

   _____

   _____

2. Summarize the events this selection described.

   _____

   _____

   _____

3. Why do you think the author told this story? What point is he trying to make?

   _____

   _____

4. Underline portions of the selection in which the author shows how he feels about the events he relates.

SUMMARY

Many college instructors require students to read articles and essays to supplement the textbook assignments. Articles and essays differ from textbooks in format, content, and structure. This chapter first focused on the organizational features of articles and essays. The purpose and use of the title, introduction, thesis statement, supporting information, and conclusion or summary were discussed. Then the various types of essays —narrative, descriptive, expository, and persuasive—were described and their style and organization discussed.

Chapter 10

READING TEXTBOOK CHAPTERS

THIS CHAPTER WILL SHOW YOU HOW TO

1. **Use textbook learning aids**
2. **Follow the organization of textbook chapters**
3. **Read technical material**

Do you ever wonder how you will be able to learn the vast amounts of information contained in each of your textbooks? Fortunately, nearly all textbook authors are college instructors. They work with students daily and understand students' difficulties. Therefore, they include in their textbooks numerous features or aids to make learning easier. They also organize chapters in ways that express their ideas as clearly as possible. This chapter will discuss textbook learning aids and the organization of textbook chapters. It will also suggest special approaches to use when reading technical material.

TEXTBOOK LEARNING AIDS

While textbooks may seem long, difficult, and impersonal, they do contain numerous features that are intended to help you learn. By taking advantage of these features, you can make textbook reading easier.

The Preface

The preface is the author's introduction to the text. In some books this section may be labeled "Introduction" or "To the Student." The preface presents basic information about the text you should know before you begin reading. The preface may contain such information as this:

- Why the author wrote the text and for whom

- How the text is organized

- Limitations of the text (topics not covered)

- References and authorities consulted

- Major points of emphasis

- Learning aids included and how to use them

The following is an excerpt from the preface of a computer programming text. Read the excerpt, noting the type of information it provides.

PREFACE

The Unique Approaches in This Text

The purpose of this text is to teach FORTRAN in the most efficient manner possible. The approach has been designed specifically for readers who have had no previous instruction in programming. The method is inductive; the reader learns a computer language by examples. Each example has been carefully designed to introduce the reader to the most important underlying concepts. After spending a few minutes on an example, the reader should be able to. . . .

Purpose of the text

Intended audience

Approach

The Organization of the Text

Each section starts with an example, followed by several important points which illustrate the learning objective for that example. The examples are designed to help the reader understand the progression of a program's logic, structure and techniques. Next, the reader is presented with solved problems to help reinforce the learning process. The solved problems illustrate some of the common mistakes a novice programmer might make. Finally, exercises provide practice to help master the fundamentals presented within each section. For most of the text, no knowledge of mathematics beyond basic algebra is required. Only Chapter 10 discusses the application of programs in mathematics.

Purpose of examples

Purpose of solved problems

Level of math needed

Language syntax, techniques of problem solving, structured programming, modular approach, planning, and good programming practices are introduced gradually for ease of learning. Abundant exercises at the end of each chapter with a variety of applications challenge the student to practice what has been learned. They are arranged from simple to complex.

Arrangement of exercises

EXERCISE 10-1

Directions: *Read or reread the "To the Student" Section on page ix of this book. Then answer the following questions.*

1. For what purpose was this book written?

   _____

2. For whom is this book written?

   _____

3. Underline the portions of the introduction that indicate the topics the text covers.

4. Underline the part(s) of the introduction that tell how the text is organized.

5. What features (learning aids) does this text contain to help you learn?

   _____

   _____

Table of Contents

The table of contents is an outline of the text. It lists all the important topics and subtopics covered. Glancing through a table of contents will give you an overview of the text and suggest its organization.

Before beginning to read a particular chapter in a textbook, refer to the table of contents again. Although chapters are intended to be separate parts of a book, it is important to see how they fit together as parts of the whole—the textbook itself.

The Opening Chapter

The first chapter of a textbook is one of the most important. Here the author sets the stage for what is to follow. At first glance, the first chapter may not seem to say much, and you may be tempted to skip it. Actually the opening chapter deserves close attention. It presents the framework for the text. More important, it introduces the important terminology used throughout the text.

Typically you can expect to find as many as forty to sixty new words introduced and defined in the first chapter. These words are the language of the course, so to speak. To be successful in any new subject area, it is essential to learn to read and speak its language.

Typographical Aids

Textbooks contain various typographical aids (arrangements or types of print) that make it easy to pick out what is important to learn and remember. These include the following:

1. *Italic type* (slanted print) is often used to call attention to a particular word or phrase. Often new terms are printed in italics in the sentence in which they are defined.

   Example: The term *drive* is used to refer to internal conditions that force an individual to work toward some goal.

2. *Enumeration* refers to the numbering or lettering of facts and ideas within a paragraph. It is used to emphasize key ideas and to make them easy to locate.

   Example: Consumer behavior and the buying process involve five mental states: (1) awareness of the product, (2) interest in acquiring it, (3) desire or perceived need, (4) action, and (5) reaction or evaluation of the product.

3. *Headings and subheadings* divide the chapters into sections and label the major topic of each section. Basically, they tell in advance what each section will be about. When read in order, the headings and subheadings form a brief outline of the chapter.

4. *Colored print* is used in some texts to emphasize important ideas or definitions.

Graphic Aids

Graphic aids refer to all material other than words. Their general purposes are to clarify and emphasize. Again, students often make the mistake of skipping over these important aids to learning. Graphic aids include the following:

1. *Photographs* are used to add interest and to help you visualize an event, concept, or feeling. Often they are intended to create some type of emotional response or reaction. (A photograph of an extremely malnourished child, for instance, creates a feeling of shock and sympathy as well as an understanding of the problems of poverty.) At other times photographs illustrate a point, as shown in Figure 10-1.[1]

   The thousands of wires and connections in the photograph, along with its caption, clearly suggest how complicated memory can be. Would the same information have been expressed as effectively with words alone?

Figure 5.3   *Does human memory work with information in the same way as a computer does?*

Ellis Herwig/Stock Boston

Figure 10-1   Sample photograph that makes a point.

2. *Maps* provide a visual picture of a geographic area. They enable you to grasp quickly the relationship among places.

3. *Charts and tables* present facts, figures, or statistics in an orderly sequence for convenient, quick reference. Be sure to read the title and note the heading and arrangement of each column. As you read a chart or table, look for trends or patterns in the data. For example, the table in Figure 10-2[2] compares years of education with weekly income for males and females. You should see that the general trends are as follows: (1) those with more education have higher salaries and (2) women's salaries are not as high as men's for the same educational level.

4. *Diagrams* explain by outlining information that is too complicated to explain in words. Their purpose is to simplify or clarify. For example, the diagram of the human ear in Figure 10-3[3] gives a clear picture of the main parts of the ear and their locations without lengthy description.

Table 6-4
Schooling and earnings, full-time workers, 1981

Years of schooling completed	Median weekly earnings	
	Males	*Females*
Total, 25 years old and over	$378	$237
8 years of school or less	259	169
Less than 4 years of high school	290	180
4 years of high school	363	222
4 years of college	459	299
5 years of college or more	507	362

Source: Adapted from Earl F. Mellor and George D. Stanas, "Usual Weekly Earnings: Another Look at Intergroup Differences and Basic Trends," *Monthly Labor Review*, April 1982, p. 16. Reprinted with permission.

Figure 10-2 Sample table.

Main Parts of the Human Ear
The pinna funnels sound through the auditory canal to the tympanic membrane (eardrum), which vibrates. These vibrations are carried and amplified by the three small bones of the middle ear to the cochlea of the inner ear. The pattern of vibration sets fluid in the cochlea in motion, and this motion activates hair cells that send nerve impulses to the brain via the auditory nerve. The semicircular canals of the inner ear are not involved in hearing, but they play a large role in the vestibular system that is responsible for balance.

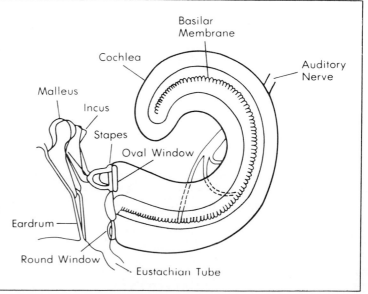

Figure 10-3 Sample diagram.

5. *Graphs* describe the relationship between two or more items. They compare one set of facts with another. When studying a graph, first read the title and determine what items are being compared. Then look for a general trend or pattern. Study the graph in Figure 10-4.[4] The graph compares three things: types of federal spending, amounts, and years. The general trend is that the total amount of spending has gradually increased, and the largest area of increase has been payments for individuals.

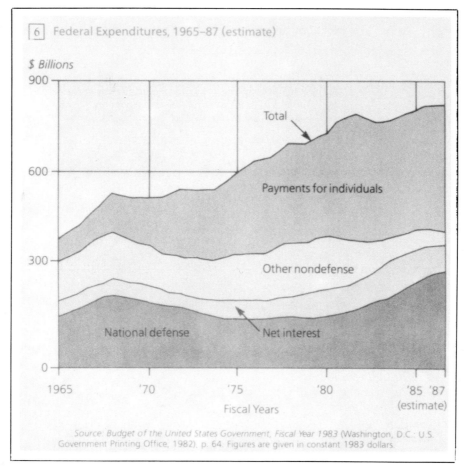

6 Federal Expenditures, 1965–87 (estimate)

$ Billions

Total

Payments for individuals

Other nondefense

National defense   Net interest

1965   '70   '75   '80   '85 '87 (estimate)

Fiscal Years

Source: Budget of the United States Government, Fiscal Year 1983 (Washington, D.C.: U.S. Government Printing Office, 1982). p. 64. Figures are given in constant 1983 dollars.

Figure 10-4 Sample graph.

EXERCISE 10-2

Directions: *Study each of the following graphic aids[5] and answer the questions that follow.*

1.

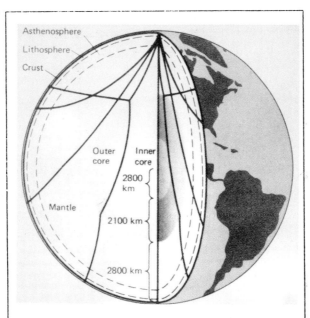

The earth's internal structure as revealed by seismic waves. The principal layers are labeled. Information about these layers is obtained by analyzing data from seismic recordings of earthquake vibrations passing through the earth. The velocities of the waves and their paths change abruptly at the interfaces between adjoining layers, as shown in the diagram.

a. What does this diagram show?

_____

_____

b. List the principal layers of the earth.

_____

_____

_____

2.

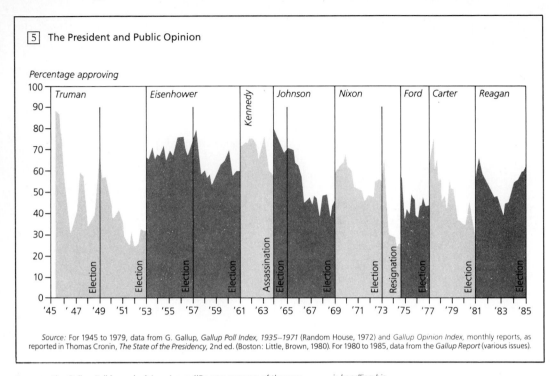

5 The President and Public Opinion

Percentage approving

Source: For 1945 to 1979, data from G. Gallup, *Gallup Poll Index, 1935–1971* (Random House, 1972) and *Gallup Opinion Index,* monthly reports, as reported in Thomas Cronin, *The State of the Presidency,* 2nd ed. (Boston: Little, Brown, 1980). For 1980 to 1985, data from the *Gallup Report* (various issues).

For years the Gallup Poll has asked Americans, "Do you approve of the way _____ is handling his job as president?" Here you can track the percentage approving presidential performance from Truman to Reagan. Notice that all presidents seem to be most popular when they first enter office; later on, their popularity eroded.

    a. What does this graph compare?

    _____

    _____

    b. What general trend or pattern does the graph show?

    _____

    _____

    c. Which president experienced the largest variation in his popularity?

    _____

    d. Which president was consistently most popular?

    _____

3.

	Probability
U.S. total	1 out of 153
Male	1 out of 100
Female	1 out of 323
White total	1 out of 240
Male	1 out of 164
Female	1 out of 450
Nonwhite total	1 out of 47
Male	1 out of 28
Female	1 out of 117

Source: Federal Bureau of Investigation, *Uniform Crime Reports, 1981* (Washington, D.C.: Government Printing Office, August 1982), p. 339.

Table 11-5
Probability of lifetime risk of murder, by race and sex

a. What information does this table summarize?

_____

_____

b. What general trend or pattern does the table show?

_____

_____

Chapter Questions

Many textbooks include discussion and/or review questions at the end of each chapter. Try to read these through when you preread the chapter (see Chapter 4). Then, after you have read the chapter, use the questions to review and test yourself. Since the review questions cover the factual content of the chapter, they can help you prepare for objective exams. Discussion questions often deal with interpretations or applications of the content. Use these in preparing for essay exams. Math, science, or technical courses may have problems instead of questions (see page 214 of this chapter). Here are a few sample review and discussion questions taken from a business marketing textbook.

REVIEW QUESTIONS

1. List some product characteristics that are of concern to marketers.
2. Distinguish between a trademark and a brand name.
3. What are some characteristics of good brand names?
4. Describe the three kinds of labels.

DISCUSSION QUESTIONS

1. What do you think is the future of generic products?
2. Go to your local food store and look at the ways the products are packaged. Find three examples of packages that have value in themselves. Find three examples of packages that promote the products' effectiveness.
3. There is much controversy about the use of warning labels on products. Outline the pros and cons of this issue.
4. How would you go about developing a brand name for a new type of bread?

Did you notice that the review questions check your knowledge of factual information? These questions ask you to list, describe, or explain. To answer these, you have to recall the information contained in the chapter. The discussion questions, on the other hand, cannot be answered simply by looking up information in the text. Instead, you have to apply the information in the text to a practical situation or pull together and organize information.

Vocabulary List

Textbooks often contain a list of new terms introduced in the book. This list may appear at the beginning or end of individual chapters or at the back of the book. In some texts new terms are printed in the margin next to the portion of the text in which the term is introduced. Regardless of where they appear, vocabulary lists are a valuable study and review aid. Many instructors include on exams items that test mastery of new terms. Here is a sample vocabulary list taken from a financial management textbook.

KEY TERMS

assets
budget
cash flow statement
fixed disbursements
liabilities
money market fund

net worth
net worth statement
occasional disbursements

Notice that the author identifies the terms but does not define them. In such cases, mark new terms as you come across them in a chapter. After you have finished the chapter, review each marked term and its definition. To learn the terms, use the index card system suggested in Chapter 3.

Glossary

A glossary is a mini-dictionary that lists alphabetically the important vocabulary used in a book. A glossary is faster and more convenient to use than a dictionary. It does not list all the common meanings of a word as a dictionary does but instead gives only the meaning used in the text. Here is an excerpt from the glossary of an American government textbook.

> **pork barrel.**   The list of federal projects, grants, and contracts available to cities, businesses, colleges, and institutions in a district. For members of Congress these provide a means of "servicing the constituency." See also **casework.** (11)
>
> **potential group.**   Composed of all people who might be group members because they share some common interest. Potential groups are almost always larger than **actual groups.** (9)
>
> **poverty line.**   According to the Bureau of the Census, this line is drawn at a sum of money that takes into account what a family would need to spend for "austere" but minimally adequate amounts of nutrition, housing, and other needs. (17)
>
> **power.**   According to Robert Dahl, the capacity to get others to do something they would not otherwise do. The desire for power is one reason why people play the **politics** game. (1)
>
> **precedent.**   The way similar **cases** were settled in the past that proves to be important in later decisions. (14)
>
> **presidential primary.**   An election in which party voters in a state vote for a candidate (or a slate of delegates committed to the candidate) as their choice for the party's **nomination.** (8)

The numbers in parentheses indicate the chapter in which the term is discussed. Look at the entry for the word *power*. First, you can see that *power* is defined only as the term is used in the field of government. The word *power* has many other meanings (see the section on multiple-meaning words in Chapter 3). Compare the glossary definition with the collegiate dictionary definition of the same word shown at the top of page 204. Try to pick out the definition of *power* that is closest to the one given in the glossary. Did it take time to find the right definition? You can see that a glossary is a time-saving device.

At the end of a course, a glossary can serve as a useful study aid, since it lists the important terminology introduced throughout the text. Review the glossary and test your recall of the meaning of each entry.

pow·er (pou′ər) *n. Abbr.* **pwr. 1.** The ability or capacity to act or perform effectively. **2.** *Often plural.* A specific capacity, faculty, or aptitude: *his powers of concentration.* **3.** Strength or force exerted or capable of being exerted; might. **4.** The ability or official capacity to exercise control; authority. **5.** A person, group, or nation having great influence or control over others. **6.** The might of a nation, political organization, or similar group. **7.** Forcefulness; effectiveness. **8.** *Regional.* A large number or amount. **9.** *Physics.* The rate at which work is done, mathematically expressed as the first derivative of work with respect to time and commonly measured in units such as the watt and horsepower. **10.** *Electricity.* **a.** The product of applied potential difference and current in a direct-current circuit. **b.** The product of the effective values of the voltage and current with the cosine of the phase angle between current and voltage in an alternating-current circuit. **11.** *Mathematics.* **a.** An **exponent** *(see).* **b.** The number of elements in a finite set. **12.** *Optics.* A measure of the **magnification** *(see)* of an optical instrument, as a microscope or telescope. **13.** *Plural. Theology.* The sixth group of angels in the hierarchical order of nine. See **angel. 14.** *Archaic.* An armed force. —See Synonyms at **strength.** —*tr.v.* **powered, -ering, -ers.** To supply with power, especially mechanical power. [Middle English *poer, povoir,* from Old French *poeir, povoir,* from *poeir,* to be able, from Old Latin *potēre* (unattested) (superseded by *posse*). See **poti-** in Appendix.*]

EXERCISE 10-3

Directions: *Choose a textbook from one of your other courses. (Do not choose a workbook or book of readings.) If you do not have a textbook, use a friend's or borrow one from the library. Answer each of the following questions by referring to the textbook.*

Textbook title: _____

1. What learning aids does the book contain?

_____

_____

_____

2. Of what importance is the information given in the preface?

_____

_____

3. Preread the opening chapter. What is its function?

_____

_____

4. Review the table of contents. How is the subject divided?

_____

_____

HOW TEXTBOOK CHAPTERS ARE ORGANIZED

Have you ever walked into an unfamiliar supermarket and felt lost and confused? You did not know where anything was located and thought you would never find the items you needed. How did you finally locate what you needed? You probably found that signs hanging over the aisles indicated the types of products shelved in each section, which enabled you to find the right aisle. Then you no doubt found that similar products were grouped together, for example, all the cereal was in one place, all the meat was in another, and so forth.

It is easy to feel lost and confused when reading textbook chapters, too. A chapter can seem like a huge, disorganized collection of facts, ideas, numbers, dates, and events to be memorized. Actually, a textbook chapter is, in one respect, much like a large supermarket. It, too, has signs that

READING TEXTBOOK CHAPTERS	CHAPTER TITLE
Textbook Learning Aids	Major Heading
The Preface	Subheading
Table of Contents	Subheading
The Opening Chapter	Subheading
Typographical Aids	Subheading
Graphic Aids	Subheading
Chapter Questions	Subheading
Vocabulary List	Subheading
Glossary	Subheading
How Textbook Chapters Are Organized	Major Heading
Reading Technical Material	Major Heading

identify what is located in each section. These signs are the headings that divide the chapter into topics. Underneath each heading, similar ideas are grouped together, just as similar products are grouped together in a super-market. Sometimes a group of similar or related ideas is labeled by a sub-heading (print that is not as noticeable as that used for a heading). In most cases, several paragraphs come under one heading. In this way chapters take a major idea, break it into its important parts, and then break those parts into smaller parts.

You could picture the organization of the present chapter as shown in the diagram on page 205.

Notice that this chapter has three major headings and that the first major heading is divided into eight subheadings. Since the chapter is divided into three major headings, you know that it covers three major topics. You can also tell that the first major heading discusses eight types of textbook aids. Of course, the number of major headings, subheadings, and paragraphs under each will vary from chapter to chapter in a book.

When you know how a chapter is organized, you can use this knowledge to guide your reading. Once you are familiar with the structure, you will also begin to see how ideas are connected. The chapter will then seem orderly, moving from one idea to the next in a logical fashion.

Look at the following partial listing of headings and subheadings from a chapter of an anthropology textbook.

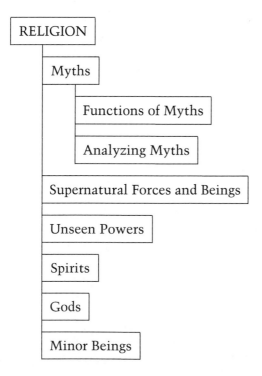

In this chapter on religion, "Myths" and "Supernatural Forces and Beings" are the first two major topics. The topic "Myths" is broken into two parts: functions and analysis. Although not shown on the diagram, each subtopic is further divided into paragraphs that list and describe particular functions and, for the second topic, present methods of analysis. If there were four paragraphs under the subheading "Functions of Myths," it would be reasonable to expect that four main points will be presented about the functions of myths.

You are probably beginning to see that titles and headings, taken together, form a brief outline of a chapter. Later, in Chapter 11, you will see how these headings can help you make a more complete outline of a chapter. For now, think of headings as a guide to reading that directs you through a chapter point by point.

EXERCISE 10-4

Directions: *On a separate sheet, draw a diagram that shows the organization of Chapter 4 of this book.*

EXERCISE 10-5

Directions: *Choose one of the textbooks that you are using for another course. Select a chapter that you have already read and, on a separate sheet, draw an organizational diagram of its contents. Use the diagram on page 206 as a guide.*

READING TECHNICAL MATERIAL

If you are taking courses in the sciences, technologies, engineering, data processing, or health-related fields, you are working with a specialized type of textbook. This type of textbook is also used in courses that prepare students for specialized careers, such as food service, air conditioning and refrigeration repair, lab technology, and so forth.

In this section you will see how technical textbooks differ from those used in other classes. You will also learn several specific approaches to reading technical material.

Each of the following paragraphs describes a spice called nutmeg. Read each and decide how they differ.

Example 1:

Nutmeg is a spice derived by grating the kernel of the fruit produced by the nutmeg tree. This tree belongs to the nutmeg family,

Myristicacae, genus *Myristica*, species *M. fragrans*. The tree grows to a height of seventy feet and is an evergreen. As the fruit of the tree ripens, it hardens and splits open at the top, showing a bright scarlet membrane. The spice called mace is made from this membrane.

Example 2:

> Nutmeg is a pungent, aromatic spice often added to foods to give them a delicious tang and perfume. It adds a subtle spiciness to desserts and perks up the flavor of such bland dishes as potatoes. Nutmeg comes from a tree grown in warm climates. The nutmeg tree is tall and gracious, with long, pale leaves and beautiful yellow flowers.

Did you notice that the first paragraph presented only precise, factual information? The words used have exact meanings. Some words have technical meanings (*genus, species, Myristica*). Others are everyday words used in a special way (*evergreen, membrane*). An abbreviation, *M.*, was also used. Because of its language, the paragraph does not allow for interpretation or expression of opinion. In fact, you cannot tell whether the writer likes or has ever tasted nutmeg. The purpose of the paragraph is to give clear, detailed information about nutmeg.

The second paragraph is written quite differently. It presents fewer facts and more description. Many words—such as *delicious, beautiful, gracious*, and *subtle*—do not have a precise meaning. They allow room for interpretation and judgment. This paragraph is written to help you imagine how nutmeg tastes as well as to tell where it comes from.

Paragraph 1 is an example of technical writing. You can see, then, that technical writing is a precise, exact, factual type of writing. This section will discuss particular features of technical writing and suggest approaches to reading technical material.

Fact Density

Technical writing is highly factual and dense (packed with ideas). A large number of facts are closely fitted together in each paragraph. Compared to other types of writing, technical writing may seem crowded with information and difficult to read. Here are a few suggestions on how to handle densely written material:

1. Read technical material more slowly and carefully than other textbooks. Allow more time for a technical reading assignment than for other assignments.

2. Plan on rereading various sections several times. Sometimes it is useful to read a section once rather quickly to learn what key ideas it contains. Then read it a second time carefully, fitting together all the facts that explain the key ideas.

3. Keep a notebook of important information. In some textbooks, you can underline what is important to remember. (This method is discussed in Chapter 10.) However, since technical books are so highly factual, underlining may not work well—it may seem that everything is important, and you will end up with most of a page underlined. Instead, try using a notebook to record information you need to remember. Writing information in your own words is a good way to check whether you really understand it.

EXERCISE 10-6

Directions: *Refer to the two paragraphs about nutmeg on pages 206–207. Count how many facts (separate pieces of information) each paragraph contains. Write the number in the space provided. Then list several facts as examples.*

	Paragraph 1	*Paragraph 2*
Number of facts:	_____	_____
Examples:	1. _____	1. _____
	2. _____	2. _____
	3. _____	3. _____

The Vocabulary of Technical Writing

Reading a technical book is in some ways like visiting a foreign country where an unfamiliar language is spoken. You hear an occasional word you know, but for the most part, the people are communicating in a way you cannot understand.

Technical writing is built upon a set of precise, exact word meanings in each subject area. Since each field has its own language, you must learn the language in order to understand the material. Here are a few sentences taken from several technical textbooks. As you read each sentence, note the large number of technical words used.

Engineering Materials

If the polymer is a mixture of polymers, the component homopolymers (polymers of a single monomer species) and their percentages should be stated.[6]

Auto Mechanics

Each free end of the three stator windings is connected to the leads of one negative diode and one positive diode.[7]

Table 10-1   EXAMPLES OF SPECIALIZED VOCABULARY IN TECHNICAL WRITING

Field	Word	Technical Meaning
Familiar words		
chemistry	base	a chemical compound that reacts with an acid to form a salt
electrical engineering	ground	a conductor that makes an electrical connection with the earth
nursing	murmur	an abnormal sound heard from a body organ (especially the heart)
Specialized terms		
computer science	modem	an interface (connector) that allows the computer to send and receive digital signals over telephone lines or through satellites
astronomy	magnetosphere	the magnetic field that surrounds the earth or other magnetized planet
biology	cocci	spherically shaped bacteria

Data Processing

> Another advantage of the PERFORM/VARYING statement is that the FROM value and the BY value may be any numeric value (except that the BY value may not be zero).

In the above examples, some words are familiar ones with new, unfamiliar meanings *(FROM, BY)*. Others are words you may never have seen before *(monomer, stator)*.

In technical writing, there are two types of specialized vocabulary, familiar words with new technical meanings and specialized terms. Examples of each are given in Table 10-1.

Tips for Learning Technical Vocabulary

Many of the techniques you have already learned for developing your general vocabulary also work with technical vocabulary. Here are some ways to apply these techniques:

1. Context clues (see Chapter 1) are commonly included in technical writing. A definition clue is most frequently used when a word is introduced for the first time. As each new word is introduced, mark it in your text and later transfer it to your notebook. Organize this section of your notebook by chapter. Use the card system described in Chapter 3 to learn words you are having trouble remembering.

2. Analyzing parts (see Chapter 2) is a particularly useful approach for developing technical vocabulary. The technical words in many fields are created from particular sets of prefixes, roots, and suffixes. Here are several examples from the field of medicine.

Prefix	*Meaning*	*Example*	*Definition*
cardi	heart	cardiogram	test that measures contractions of the heart
		cardiology	medical study of diseases and functioning of the heart
		cardiologist	physician who specializes in heart problems
hem/hema/hemo	blood	hematology	study of the blood
		hemophilia	disease in which blood fails to clot properly
		hemoglobin	protein contained in the red blood cells

    Most technical fields have a core of commonly used prefixes, roots, and suffixes. As you read technical material, keep a list of common word parts in your notebook. Add to the list throughout the course. For those you have difficulty remembering, use a variation of the word card system suggested in Chapter 3. Write the word on the front and its meaning, its pronunciation, and a sample sentence on the back.

3. Learn to pronounce each new term you come across. Pronouncing a word is a good way to fix it in your memory and will also help you remember its spelling.

4. Make use of the glossary in the back of the textbook, if it has one. (See page 203 in this chapter for further information on using a glossary.)

5. If you are majoring in a technical field, it may be worthwhile to buy a subject area dictionary (see Chapter 3). Nursing students, for example, often buy a copy of Taber's *Cyclopedic Medical Dictionary.*

Abbreviations and Notations

In many technical fields, sets of abbreviations and notations (signs and symbols) provide shortcuts to writing out complete words or meanings.

Examples:

Field	Symbol	Meaning
Chemistry	Al	aluminum
	F	fluorine
	Fe	iron
Biology	X	crossed with
	♀	female organism
	♂	male organism
Physics	M	mass
Astronomy	D	diameter
	Δ	distance

To understand technical material, you must learn the abbreviations and notation systems that are used in a specific field. Check to see whether lists of abbreviations and symbols are included in the appendix (reference section) in the back of the textbook. Make a list in your notebook of those you need to learn. Make a point of using these symbols in your class notes whenever possible. Putting them to use regularly is an excellent way to learn them.

Graphic Aids

Most technical books contain numerous drawings, charts, tables, and diagrams. These may make the text look difficult and complicated, but actually, such graphic aids help explain and make the text easier to understand. Illustrations, for example, give a visual picture of the idea or process being explained. Here is an example of a diagram taken from a computer programming text. The text to which the diagram refers is also included. Would you find the text easy to understand without the diagram?

An *input device* is a mechanism that accepts data from outside the computer and converts it into an electronic form understandable to the computer. The data that is accepted is called *input data*, or simply *input*. For example, one common way of entering input into a computer is to type it with a typewriter-like *keyboard*.

An *output device* performs the opposite function of an input device. An output device converts data from its electronic form inside the computer to a form that can be used outside. The converted data is called *output data*, or simply *output*. . . .

Between the input devices and the output devices is the component of the computer that does the actual computing or processing. This is the *central processing unit*, or CPU. Input data is converted into an electronic form by an input device and sent to the central processing unit where the data is stored. In the CPU the data is used in calculations or other types of processing to produce the solution to the desired problem. The central processing unit contains two basic

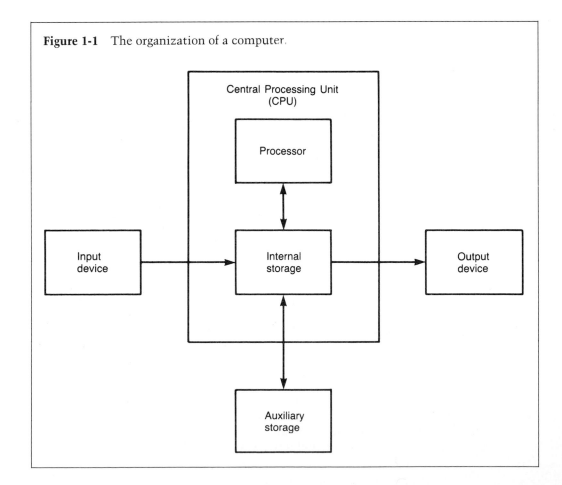

Figure 1-1   The organization of a computer.

units: the internal storage and the processor. The *internal storage* is the "memory" of the computer. The *processor* is the unit that executes instructions to the program. Among other things, the processor contains electronic circuits that do arithmetic and perform logical operations. The final component of a computer is the *auxiliary storage*. This component stores data that is not currently being processed by the computer and programs that are not currently in use.

Here are a few suggestions on how to use illustrations:

1. Go back and forth between the text and the illustrations. Illustrations are intended to be used together with the paragraphs that refer to them. You may have to stop reading several times to refer to an illustration. For example, when *input device* is mentioned in the preceding example, stop reading and find where the input device is located on the diagram. You may also have to reread parts of the explanation several times.

2. Study each illustration carefully. Read the title or caption. These tell what the illustration is intended to show. Then look at each part of the illustration and try to see how they are connected. Notice any abbreviations, symbols, arrows, or labels. In the example given, the arrows are important. They suggest the direction or order in which the parts of the computer operate.

3. Test your understanding of illustrations by drawing and labeling an illustration of your own without looking at the one in the text. Then compare your drawing with the text. Notice whether anything is left out. If so, continue drawing and checking until your drawing is complete and correct. Include these drawings in your notebook and use them for review and study.

Examples and Sample Problems

Technical books include numerous examples and sample problems. Use the following suggestions when working with these:

1. Pay more attention to examples than you normally do in other textbooks. Examples and sample problems will often help you understand how rules, principles, theories, or formulas are actually used. Think of examples as connections between ideas on paper and practical, everyday use of those ideas.

2. Be sure to work through sample problems. Make sure you understand what was done in each step and why. For particularly difficult problems, try writing in your notebook a step-by-step list of how to solve that type of problem. Refer to sample problems as

guides or models when doing problems at the end of the chapter or others assigned by the instructor.

3. Use the problems at the end of the chapter as a self-test. As you work through each problem, keep track of rules and formulas that you did not know and had to look up. Make note of the types of problems you could not solve without referring to the sample problems. You will need to do more work with each of these types.

EXERCISE 10-7

Directions: *Read the following excerpt from a textbook chapter titled "Mechanics"*[9] *and answer the questions that follow.*

MECHANICS

Potential Energy

An object may store energy by virtue of its position. Such stored energy is called *potential energy*, for in the stored state an object has the potential for doing work. A stretched or compressed spring, for example, has potential energy. When a BB gun is cocked, energy is stored in the spring. A stretched rubber band has potential energy because of its position, for if it is part of a slingshot it is capable of doing work.

The chemical energy in fuels is potential energy, for it is actually energy of position when looked at from a microscopic point of view. This energy is available when the positions of electrical charges within and between molecules are altered, that is, when a chemical change takes place. Potential energy is possessed by any substance that can do work through chemical action. The energy of coal, gas, electric batteries, and foods is potential energy.

Potential energy may be due to an elevated position of a body. Water in an elevated reservoir and the heavy ram of a pile driver when lifted have energy because of position. The energy of elevated positions is usually called *gravitational potential energy*.

The measure of the gravitational potential energy that an elevated body has is the work done against gravity in lifting it. The upward force required is equal to the weight of the body W, and the work done in lifting it through a height h is given by the product Wh; so we say

$$\text{Gravitational potential energy} = Wh$$

The potential energy of an elevated body depends only on its weight and vertical displacement h and is independent of the path taken to raise it (Figure 4.3).

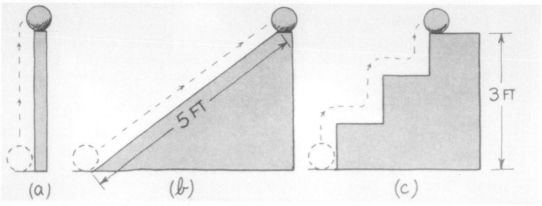

Fig. 4.3 *The potential energy of the 10-lb ball is the same in each case because the work done in elevating it 3 feet is the same whether it is (a) lifted with 10 lb of force, of (b) pushed with 6 lb of force up the 5-foot incline, or (c) lifted with 10 lb up each 1-foot stair—no work is done in moving it horizontally (neglecting friction).*

Kinetic Energy

If we push on an object, we can set it in motion. More specifically, if we do work on an object, we can change the energy of motion of that object. If an object is in motion, by virtue of that motion it is capable of doing work. We call energy of motion *kinetic energy*. The kinetic energy of an object is equal to half its mass multiplied by its velocity squared.

$$\text{Kinetic energy} = \tfrac{1}{2}\,mv^2$$

It can be shown that the kinetic energy of a moving body is equal to the work it can do in being brought to rest.*

$$\text{Net force} \times \text{distance} = \text{kinetic energy}$$

or, in shorthand notation,

$$Fd = \tfrac{1}{2}\,mv^2$$

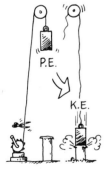

Accident investigators are well aware that an automobile traveling at 60 miles per hour has four times as much kinetic energy as an automobile traveling 30 miles per hour. This means that a car traveling at 60 miles per hour will skid four times as far when its

Fig. 4.4 *The potential energy of the elevated ram is converted to kinetic energy when released.*

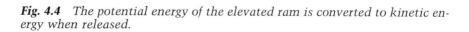

* If we multiply both sides of $F = ma$ (Newton's second law) by d, we get $Fd = mad$; since $d = \tfrac{1}{2}at^2$, we can say $Fd = ma(\tfrac{1}{2}\,at^2) = \tfrac{1}{2}m(at)^2$; and substituting $v = at$, we get $Fd = \tfrac{1}{2}\,mv^2$.

brakes are locked as a car traveling 30 miles per hour. This is because the velocity is squared for kinetic energy.

Question

When the brakes of a car traveling at 90 miles per hour are locked, how much farther will the car skid compared to locking the brakes at 30 miles per hour?

1. Underline the sentences that best define the terms *potential energy* and *kinetic energy.*

2. List the technical or specialized terms used in this selection. Define as many as possible.

   _____

   _____

3. List the abbreviations (notations) used in the article and give their meanings.

   _____

   _____

4. The writer uses examples as a means of explaining various ideas. List four of these examples and tell what each explains.

   _____

   _____

   _____

5. This excerpt contains two illustrations (Figures 4.3 and 4.4). The author does not discuss either in the text itself. Their use is left up to the reader. Describe when and how often you referred to each diagram.

   _____

   _____

   _____

6. What is Figure 4.3 intended to show?

   _____

7. What is Figure 4.4 intended to show?

   _____

8. What is the purpose of the Question at the end of the article? To what type of energy does this question refer?

_____

_____

9. In your own words, explain the difference between potential energy and kinetic energy.

_____

_____

SUMMARY

While textbooks are important sources of information, they are also valuable learning aids. Textbooks contain many features that are included to help the reader learn. At the beginning of a textbook, the preface, table of contents, and opening chapter provide information on the scope and focus of the book. Within each chapter, graphic aids (maps, graphs, charts, and pictures) and typographical aids (italic type, enumeration, headings and subheadings, and colored print) call attention to key information. At the end of each chapter, chapter questions and vocabulary lists provide an outline of important information and key words presented in the chapter. At the end of the textbook, the glossary provides a quick reference for important vocabulary presented in the book.

Textbooks are also organized so as to express ideas as clearly as possible. Through the use of headings and subheadings, chapters are divided into a number of sections that deal with different aspects of the subject covered in the chapter.

Technical material appears in textbooks for many courses. The distinguishing features of technical material include fact density, specialized vocabulary, abbreviations and notations, drawings and illustrations, and examples and sample problems.

Chapter 11

ORGANIZING AND REMEMBERING INFORMATION

THIS CHAPTER WILL SHOW YOU HOW TO

1. Underline and mark important information in textbook chapters

2. Outline information to show its organization

3. Summarize ideas for review purposes

Suppose you are planning a cross-country trip next summer. To get ready for the trip you begin to collect all kinds of information: maps, newspaper articles on various cities, places to visit, names of friends' friends, and so forth. After a while, you find that you have a great deal of information and that it is difficult to locate any one item. You begin to realize that the information you have collected will be of little or no use unless you organize it in some way. You decide to buy large envelopes and put different kinds of information into separate envelopes, such as information on individual states.

In this case, you found a practical, commonsense solution to a problem. The rule or principle that you applied was this: When something gets confusing, organize it.

This rule also works well when applied to college textbooks. Each text contains thousands of pieces of information—facts, names, dates, theories, principles. This information quickly becomes confusing unless it is organized. Once you have organized this information, you will be able to find in your memory the facts you need more easily than if your text were still an unassorted heap of information.

Organizing information requires sifting, sorting, and in some cases rearranging important facts and ideas. There are three common methods of organizing textbook materials.

- Underlining and marking

- Outlining

- Summarizing

In this chapter you will learn techniques for doing each. You will also see how to make study and review more effective.

UNDERLINING AND MARKING

Underlining and marking important facts and ideas as you read are effective methods of identifying and organizing information. They are also the biggest time-savers known to college students. Suppose it took you four hours to read an assigned chapter in sociology. One month later you need to review that chapter to prepare for an exam. If you did not underline or mark as you read the first time, then, in order to review the chapter once, you would have to spend another four hours rereading it. However, if you had underlined and marked as you read, then you could review the chapter in an hour or less—a savings of 300 percent. By this means you can save many hours each semester. More important, the less time you spend identifying what to learn, the more thoroughly you can learn the necessary information. This will pay off in your course grade.

Underlining Effectively

Here are a few basic suggestions for underlining effectively:

1. Read a paragraph or section first and then go back and underline what is important.

2. Underline important portions of the topic sentence and any supporting details you want to remember (see Chapter 7).

3. Be accurate. Make sure your underlining reflects the content of the passage. Incomplete or hasty underlining can mislead you as you review the passage and allow you to miss the main point.

4. Use a system for underlining. There are several systems you can use: (a) two or more different colors of ink or highlighters to dis-

tinguish between main ideas and details, (b) single underlining for details and double underlining for main ideas, and (c) placing a bracket around the main idea and using highlighter to mark important details. No one system is more effective than another. Try to develop a system that works well for you.

5. Underline as few words as possible in a sentence. Seldom should you underline an entire sentence. Usually, underlining the key idea along with an additional phrase or two is sufficient. Read the following paragraph. Notice that you can understand its meaning from the underlined parts alone.

    Example: The person who smokes <u>more than a pack</u> of cigarettes <u>a day</u> runs nearly <u>twice the risk</u> of <u>heart attack,</u> and nearly <u>five times the risk of stroke,</u> as does a non-smoker. <u>Abstaining</u> from smoking <u>lowers</u> your <u>risk</u> of heart attack <u>22 percent below the norm.</u> Smoking <u>more than a pack a day raises</u> your <u>risk</u> to <u>32 percent above the norm.</u> In addition, as explained in other chapters of this book, smoking greatly <u>increases susceptibility</u> to <u>lung cancer</u> and to such lung diseases as <u>bronchitis</u> and <u>emphysema.</u>

6. Use headings to guide your underlining (see Chapter 7). Use the headings to form questions that you expect to be answered in the section (see Chapter 4). Then underline the answer to each question.

Underlining the Right Amount

If you underline either too much or too little, you will defeat your purpose for underlining. By underlining too little, you will miss valuable information, and your review and study of the material will be incomplete. On the other hand, if you underline too much, you are not identifying the most-important ideas and eliminating less-important facts. The more you underline, the more you will have to reread when studying and the less of a time-saver the procedure will be. As a general rule of thumb, underline no more than 20 to 30 percent of the material.

Here is a paragraph underlined in three different ways. First, read the paragraph that is not underlined; then look at each underlined version. Try to decide which version would be most useful if you were rereading it for study purposes.

Outer space travel to distant planets has been limited by the human life span. Now, humans do not live long enough to reach faraway destinations. A proposed solution to this problem is human hibernation. Humans might hibernate in much the same way as certain animals do now. Scientists believe that humans who hibernate may live eight to ten times longer than if they do not. If this is so, humans might attain chronological ages of 800 years. The process is based on suspended animation. Bodily functions are slowed down to minimal levels needed to support life. Hibernation slows body time, allowing more clock time to elapse.[1]

Example 1:

> Outer space travel to distant planets has been limited by the human life span. Now, humans do not live long enough to reach faraway destinations. A proposed solution to this problem is human hibernation. Humans might hibernate in much the same way as certain animals do now. Scientists believe that humans who hibernate may live eight to ten times longer than if they do not. If this is so, humans might attain chronological ages of 800 years. The process is based on suspended animation. Bodily functions are slowed down to minimal levels needed to support life. Hibernation slows body time, allowing more clock time to elapse.

Example 2:

> Outer space travel to distant planets has been limited by the human life span. Now, humans do not live long enough to reach faraway destinations. A proposed solution to this problem is human hibernation. Humans might hibernate in much the same way as certain animals do now. Scientists believe that humans who hibernate may live eight to ten times longer than if they do not. If this is so, humans might attain chronological ages of 800 years. The process is based on suspended animation. Bodily functions are slowed down to minimal levels needed to support life. Hibernation slows body time, allowing more clock time to elapse.

Example 3:

> Outer space travel to distant planets has been limited by the human life span. Now, humans do not live long enough to reach faraway destinations. A proposed solution to this problem is human hibernation. Humans might hibernate in much the same way as certain animals do now. Scientists believe that humans who hibernate may live eight to ten times longer than if they do not. If this is so, humans might attain chronological ages of 800 years. The process is based on suspended animation. Bodily functions are slowed down to minimal levels needed to support life. Hibernation slows body time, allowing more clock time to elapse.

Example 3 is the best example of effective underlining. Only the most important information is underlined. Example 1 has too little underlining; it does not contain enough information. Example 2, on the other hand, has too much underlining to be useful for review.

EXERCISE 11-1

Directions: *Read and underline the following selection, using the guidelines presented in this section.*

WHAT CAN YOU EXPECT FROM YOUR MEMORY?

Some people have misconceptions about what is involved in improving their memories. It may be helpful to clear up some of these misconceptions, so that you will have a realistic idea of what to expect from your memory. The following are some considerations you should keep in mind with respect to improving your memory.

Remembering Is Hard Work

You probably do not need to be told that remembering is hard work, that it takes effort to learn and remember. But what many people do not realize is that principles and techniques for learning and remembering do not necessarily make remembering any *easier;* they just make it more *effective.* You will still have to work at it, but you will get more for your efforts.

Some people hope that memory training will reveal to them a simple "key"—one thing that they can do (with little effort) so they will never forget anything they see, hear, or do. There is no one key that provides a really easy way to improve memory. Remembering is a skill. Improving your memory is like acquiring any other skill. You have to learn the techniques and practice them.

Suppose you wanted to be good at golf, chess, math, or playing the piano. You would not expect to learn just one secret that would give you the skill. Rather, you would expect to learn techniques and principles, practice them, apply them, and thereby improve your skill. However, when it comes to memory, some people do not reason the same way. They do not want to work at it. When such a person finds out that improving memory takes effort, he may decide that he can make do with his memory as it is. . . .

There Is No One Best Method for Remembering Everything

This consideration is closely related to the previous one, but warrants separate attention. It has been noted that there is no single key to remember everything. . . . There are a number of circumstances that determine what method is best to learn material. For example: (a) Who is doing the learning? A chemistry professor and a beginning chemistry student may use different methods to study a new book on chemistry. (b) What is to be learned? Different methods may be used for learning word lists, nonsense syllables, numbers, poems, speeches, and book chapters. (c) How will remembering be measured? Preparing for a recognition task may require different methods than preparing for a recall task. (d) What kind of remembering is required? Rote remembering of facts may require a different method than understanding and applying the facts, and word-for-word memorizing may require a different method than remembering ideas and concepts. (e) How long will remembering be required? Preparing to recall the material immediately after learning it may require a different method than preparing to recall it a week later.

The practical implication of this consideration is that when a person asks how he can improve his memory, he cannot be given any useful answer until he makes his question more specific. What kinds of material does he want to remember? In what way? Under what circumstances? For how long? There are methods and principles in this book that apply to almost any kind of learning situation, but they do not all apply to all situations.

EXERCISE 11-2

Directions: *Read or reread and underline Chapter 4 in this book. Follow the guidelines suggested in this chapter.*

Testing Your Underlining

As you underline, check to be certain your underlining is effective and will be helpful for review purposes. To test the effectiveness of your underlining, take any passage that you have underlined and reread only the underlined portions. Then ask yourself the following questions:

- Does the underlining tell what the passage is about?

- Does it make sense?

- Does it indicate the most important idea in the passage?

EXERCISE 11-3

Directions: *Test the effectiveness of your underlining for the material you underlined in Exercises 11-1 and 11-2. Make changes, if necessary.*

Marking

In many types of textbooks, underlining alone does not clearly identify and organize information. Also, underlining does not allow you to react to or sort ideas. Try making notes in the margin as well as underlining. Notice how the markings in the following passage organize the information in a way that underlining cannot.

THE SOURCE OF ENERGY   Within the biosphere itself several forms of energy are produced: <u>hydraulic</u> energy, created by <u>water in motion</u> (a river pouring over a dam, storm waves striking a shoreline); <u>electrical energy</u> (lightning); and <u>geothermal</u> energy (underground <u>water</u> converted to <u>steam</u> by <u>hot rock</u> formations). Powerful as these sources of energy can be, they are insignificant compared with the huge flow of energy that comes to earth from the <u>sun</u>.

4 forms of energy
1. hydraulic
2. electrical
3. geothermal
4. sun

The sun's energy begins with reactions like that of a hydrogen bomb. Nuclear fusion deep in the <u>sun's core creates radiation</u>, which makes its way to the sun's surface and is then radiated away—most of it as visible light, some as ultraviolet light and infrared light and X rays (see Figure 1.3). This <u>sunlight</u> is the <u>dominant form of energy</u> in our world, one that primitive peoples recognized eons ago as the giver of life. All the energy humans produce in a single year from our many energy sources—coal, oil, hydraulic power, nuclear power— amounts, according to our present estimates, to only two ten-thousandths of the total energy coming to us each day from the sun.[2]

Radiation
↓
light
↓
energy

Here are a few examples of useful types of marking:

1. Circle words you do not know.

    Example: <u>Sulfur</u> is a yellow, solid substance that has several (allotropic) forms.

2. Mark definitions with an asterisk.

    Example: *<u>Chemical reactivity</u> is the tendency of an element to participate in chemical reaction.

3. Write summary words or phrases in the margin.

    Example: Some elements, such as aluminum (Al) or Copper (Cu), tarnish just from sitting around in the air. They react with oxygen (O_2) in the air.

    reaction w/air

4. Number lists of ideas, causes, and reasons.

    Example: Metallic properties include ①conductivity, ②luster, and ③ductility.

5. Place brackets around important passages.

   Example: In Group IVA, carbon (C) is a nonmetal, silicon (Si) and germanium (Ge) are metaloids, and tin (Sn) and lead (Pb) are metals.

6. Draw arrows or diagrams to show relationships or to clarify information.

   Example: Graphite is made up of a lot of carbon layers stacked on top of one another, like sheets of paper. The layers slide over one another, which makes it a good lubricant.

7. Make notes to yourself, such as "good test question," "reread," or "ask instructor."

   Example: Carbon is most important to us because it is a basic element in all plant and animal structures.

8. Put question marks next to confusing passages or when you want more information.

   Example: Sometimes an element reacts so violently with air, water, or other substances that an explosion occurs.

Try to develop your own code or set of abbreviations. Here are a few examples:

ex   example
T   good test question
sum   good summary
def   important definition
RR   reread later

EXERCISE 11-4

Directions: *Read each of the following passages and then underline and mark each. Try various ways of underlining and marking.*

Passage 1:

FLAVORS

"Natural flavors," "natural flavoring," "artificially flavored," "artificial flavor," "natural and artificial flavor" . . . Those are the words we will find on many food labels. What do they mean? What *is* a flavor, as the word is used to state an ingredient of a food product?

Flavors are the substances that impart taste and aroma to a food. 2
The sense of taste itself detects only sweet, sour, salty, and bitter, or
a blend of those. Only in its aroma, detected by the sense of smell,
does a food become truly unique in its flavor.

To see clearly and dramatically the difference between taste and 3
aroma, hold your nose and chew a piece of apple. Then repeat the
same process, this time with a piece of onion. Be sure to close your
nostrils tightly while you do this. All you will taste is sweet—in
both cases. Only the addition of the sense of smell enables you to distinguish the flavor difference between the onion and the apple.

The flavors present in foods such as fruits and spices can be sep- 4
arated from the food and used to impart the flavor to something else.
The flavor is carried in what is called the essential oil, so named because it contains the flavor essence characteristic of the food. For example, the flavor of nutmeg, in the form of oil of nutmeg, can be separated from the nutmeg and added to coffee-cake dough to delicately
flavor it. Similarly, essential oils of orange, lemon, grapefruit, and
many other fruits can be separated and used for flavoring purposes.

Why do processors bother to do such a thing? Some reasons are: 5
as a means of having the flavor available long after the source of the
oil has spoiled; and to provide a source of uniform flavor, much more
so than the original spice or fruit, and also in a very much more stable form.

These flavors are not pure chemical substances, but are a blend 6
of many substances. We had to learn what the precise composition
was that produced such strange and wonderful smells and tastes. During the nineteenth century, chemists were extraordinarily successful
in analyzing the components of many natural flavors and, even more
significant, learned to synthesize many of them. For example, extract
of vanilla contains vanillin, the principal component of vanilla flavor;
chemists soon were synthesizing and using vanillin as a flavor instead of the vanilla extract. Unfortunately, vanillin is not the only
substance in vanilla flavor, and we still don't have a synthetic dupli-
cation that tastes like the real thing. But synthetic vanillin is a precise duplicate of the vanillin found in vanilla extract from the vanilla
bean.

In some cases, the result has been ridiculous. Methyl anthra- 7
nilate is the principal material responsible for typical Concord grape
flavor. It is widely used as an artificial flavor in grape drinks, sodas,
and ice confections. Methyl anthranilate is not the only component
of grape flavor, and it has a very strong, coarse grape character. Children actually prefer grape drinks flavored with the synthetic anthranilate to the real thing, it is so much less subtle.

The labeling of flavors is not helpful enough to the consumer. 8
The mere word "artificial" tells us nothing since the substance may
be a synthetic duplicate of a component of natural flavor. Chances are

when the label says "artificial," the overall taste sensation will not be as smooth as a naturally flavored product, but this is not inevitably so at all.

There are over *seven hundred* synthetic flavors permitted as   9 food additives that are not GRAS [Generally Regarded as Safe by the Food and Drug Administration]. There are twenty-four synthetic flavors that are GRAS. The consumer has no way of telling which is in the food: the GRAS product or the non–GRAS additive.

Do not assume that because an extract is natural that it is safe.   10 One of the most dangerous materials is good old-fashioned oil of sassafras, out of which root beer was once made. It turned out that a natural substance in oil of sassafras, safrole, is a rather nasty cancer producer. This material is no longer permitted in foods; only safrole-free sassafras extract may now be used.

There is an enormous amount of ignorance on the subject of flavors.   11 One theory presented is that *all* additives and especially artificial flavors cause hyperactivity in children, but nobody has been able to duplicate the work reported. On the other hand, nobody has ever claimed that highly flavored, artificially flavored foods are good for you, and on the general principle of moderation, especially in the presence of ignorance, it is probably a good idea to avoid eating and feeding your children a great deal of artificially flavored, or even strong naturally flavored, foods or drinks.

Passage 2:

MELTING POINT

The particles (atoms or molecules) of a solid are held together by   1 attractive forces. . . . Heating up a solid, such as a piece of ice, gives its molecules more energy and makes them move. Pretty soon they are moving fast enough to overcome the attractive forces that were holding them rigidly together in the solid. The temperature at which this happens is the *melting point* of the solid. When a liquid, such as water, is cooled, the reverse process happens. We take energy away from the molecules, and pretty soon the molecules are moving slowly enough for their attractive forces to hold them rigidly together again and form a solid. The temperature at which this happens is the *freezing point* of the liquid. Melting point and freezing point are really the same thing, approached from opposite directions. To melt a substance, we supply heat; to freeze it, we remove heat. While a solid is melting, its temperature stays constant at its melting point. Even though we keep heating a solid as it melts, we won't increase its temperature until all of the solid has changed to liquid. When a solid starts to melt, all of the heat that is put into it from then on goes into breaking up the attractive forces that hold the atoms or molecules together in the solid. When the solid is all melted, then the heat that is put in can once more go into increasing the temperature of the substance. The amount of heat that it takes to melt one gram of any substance at its melting point is called the *heat of fusion*. If we let the substance freeze, then it will give off heat in the amount of the heat of fusion. Freezing is a process that releases energy.

Every substance has a melting (or freezing) point except diamond, which no one has been able to melt yet. The stronger the attractive forces that hold atoms or molecules together in the solid, the higher its melting (or freezing) point will be. The forces holding a diamond together in the solid state are so strong that they can't be overcome by heating. Most elements are solids at "room temperature," a vague term meaning a range of about 20°C to 30°C. A substance that's a solid at room temperature has a melting point higher than room temperature. Some substances are borderline, and they can be either liquids or solids depending on the weather: we've all seen tar melt on a hot day. Olive oil will solidify (freeze) on a cold day. . . .

OUTLINING

Outlining is a good way to create a visual picture of what you have read. In making an outline, you record the writer's organization and show the relative importance of and connection between ideas.

Outlining has a number of advantages:

1. It gives an overview of the topic and enables you to see how various subtopics relate to one another.

2. Recording the information in your own words tests your understanding of what you read.

3. It is an effective way to record needed information from reference books you do not own.

How to Outline

Generally, an outline follows a format like the one below.

I. First major idea

   A. First supporting detail
      1. Detail
      2. Detail

    B. Second supporting detail
      1. Detail
        a. Minor detail or example
        b. Minor detail or example

II. Second major idea
   A. First supporting idea

Notice that the most important ideas are closer to the left margin. Less important ideas are indented toward the middle of the page. A quick glance at an outline shows what is most important, what is less important, and how ideas support or explain one another.

Here are a few suggestions for using the outline format:

1. Do not be overly concerned with following the outline format exactly. As long as your outline shows an organization of ideas, it will work for you.

2. Write words and phrases rather than complete sentences.

3. Use your own words rather than lifting words from the text.

4. Do not write too much. If you need to record numerous facts and details, underlining rather than outlining might be more effective.

5. Be sure that all the information you place underneath a heading explains or supports that heading.

6. Every heading that is in the same left-right position on the page should be of equal importance.

Now read the following brief passage on poverty in America and then study its outline.

WHO'S GETTING THE LEAST? POVERTY IN AMERICA

To count the poor, we have to define *poverty*. But defining it is not easy. Poverty is meaningful only by comparison to something else. When we compare our poor to people in India, our poor families look well off. When we compare them to our rich families, they look very poor. Deciding where to draw the line between poor and nonpoor is difficult.

Often, we rely on the Bureau of the Census's **poverty line,** which takes into account what a family would need to spend for "austere" but minimally adequate amounts of nutrition, housing, and other needs. According to the bureau's poverty line, the percentage of Americans who were poor plummeted in the 1960s. But as stagflation set in during the 1970s, the decline in the poverty population leveled off.

In 1979, about 25.3 million people—11.6 percent of the population—were poor.

A careful, decade-long study of 5,000 American families showed that poverty may be even more extensive than the poverty line suggests. In this representative sample of American families, almost a third were below the poverty level at least once during the decade, suggesting that as many as 70 million Americans live close enough to the poverty line that some crisis can push them into poverty. About a fifth of the poor were poor in nine of the ten years studied; thus, about 4 to 5 million Americans were in the throes of permanent poverty. No distinctive set of attitudes—no "culture of poverty"—distinguished the poor from the nonpoor. Instead, it was more commonly some crisis or opportunity—losing a job, getting a divorce, working longer hours, "moonlighting," having a new mouth to feed—that accounted for movement into or out of the poverty class.

The poor are a varied group. Poverty, though, is more common among some groups—blacks, older Americans, female-headed families, and rural residents—than among others. Lots of things—the state of the economy, what people do for themselves, plus a large

I. POVERTY
   A. DEFINING POVERTY
      1. MEANINGFUL ONLY BY COMPARISON
         a. COMPARED TO INDIA, AMERICAN POOR ARE WELL OFF
      2. BUREAU OF CENSUS — POVERTY LINE
         a. CONSIDERS WHAT MONEY A FAMILY NEEDS FOR MINIMUM FOOD, HOUSING, ETC.
   B. EXTENT OF POVERTY
      1. BUREAU OF CENSUS
         a. '79 – 25.3 MILLION IN POVERTY
         b. 11.6 PERCENT OF POPULATION
      2. DECADE-LONG STUDY INDICATES CENSUS FIGURES MAY UNDERESTIMATE
         a. 1/3 POPULATION BELOW POVERTY LEVEL AT LEAST ONCE IN DECADE
         b. 70 MILLION CLOSE TO POVERTY
   C. CHARACTERISTICS OF POOR
      1. NO DISTINCTIVE ATTITUDES
      2. CRISIS OFTEN MOVES PEOPLE IN AND OUT OF POVERTY
      3. MOST COMMON AMONG BLACKS, OLDER AM., FEMALE-HEADED HOUSEHOLDS, AND RURAL

measure of luck—determine who gets what in the American scramble for income and wealth. But government and its policies are also crucial factors in determining who's poor and who's not.

EXERCISE 11-5

Directions: *Read the following passage and the incomplete outline that follows. Fill in the missing information in the outline.*

THE STRUCTURE OF THE MEDIA

Journalists divide the world of the media into two types: *print* and *broadcast*. The print media include newspapers and magazines. The broadcast side includes radio and the glamour stock of the journalistic trade, television.

About 1,700 newspapers are published daily in the United States. But in 1914 there were as many *foreign language* papers published in the United States as there are daily papers published today. Strikes, low profit margins, and fierce competition have all taken their toll. Today, less than 4 percent of all cities have competing daily newspapers. Many papers are owned by chains, making the fiercely independent editor-owner-publisher largely an image of the past. In addition, newspapers depend heavily on the two wire services, the Associated Press and United Press International, for their national and international coverage. Only the very largest papers—the *Washington Post*, the *Chicago Tribune*, the *New York Times*, the *Los Angeles Times*, and a few others—have their own far-flung bureaus generating news from around the nation and the world.

The magazine business, on the other hand, has blossomed. Newsstands overflow with the popular magazines of news and opinion—*Time, Newsweek, U.S. News & World Report, Atlantic, Harper's*, and others. Packed alongside them are dozens of specialized magazines. A handful of magazines are the major means of communication among elite intellectuals. When he examined the American intellectual elite, Charles Kadushin noted about twenty journals that were most widely read and most influential. Among them are the *New York Review of Books, Dissent, Daedalus, New Yorker, Hudson Review*, and *Commentary*. There are also magazines and journals appealing mainly to a political readership. *Public Opinion*, the *National Review, Public Interest, Foreign Affairs*, and others offer commentary, opinion, and even data about American politics and policy.

Network television is the latest, biggest, and most profitable entrant onto the media stage. Big it is. CBS news claims that its evening news was watched by an average of 17 million people a day in one six-month period. Conservative columnist Kevin Phillips has argued that the media, television especially, are part of an interlocking directorate controlling not only American news but the whole political agenda. CBS, he pointed out, ranked as number 102 among *Fortune's* list of the 500 biggest corporations in 1976; its sales were $2.25 billion. NBC, part of the massive RCA conglomerate, was number 31 on the *Fortune* 500 list, topping $5 billion in sales.

Regardless of whether the media are too big or too influential, as some conservatives claim, or an important part of our free press, as their defenders insist, they have a significant impact on the policy agenda. What we know about a crisis, how we perceive objective conditions, and whether we hear the voices of policy entrepreneurs will be mightily influenced by how the media define the news of the day.

I. Types of media

   A. Print
      1. Newspapers are declining.
         a. Fewer newspapers today
         b. Very few cities have competing papers
         c. Most heavily dependent on wire service

      2. _____

         a. _____

         b. _____

         c. _____

   B. Broadcast
      1. Television

         a. _____

         b. _____

   C. Influences of the media

      1. _____

      2. _____

MAPPING

Mapping is a visual method of organizing information. It involves drawing diagrams to show how ideas in an article or chapter are related. Some students prefer mapping to outlining because they feel it is freer and less tightly structured.

Maps can take numerous forms. You can draw them in any way that shows the relationships of ideas. Figure 11-1 shows two sample maps. Each was drawn to show the overall organization of Chapter 4 in this book. First, refer back to Chapter 4, then study each map.

MAP 1

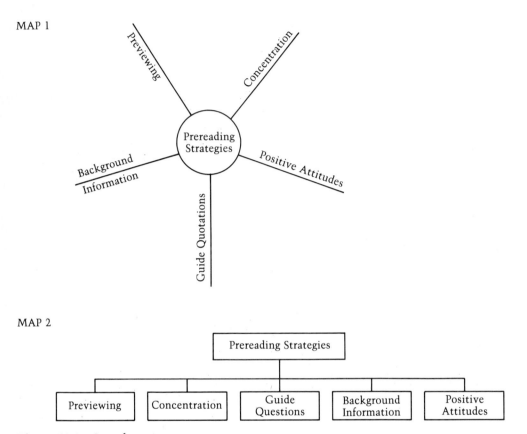

MAP 2

Figure 11-1   Sample maps.

How to Draw Maps

Think of a map as a picture or diagram that shows how ideas are connected. Use the following steps in drawing a map.

1. Identify the overall topic or subject and write it in the center or top of the page.

2. Identify major supporting information that relates to the topic. Draw each piece of information on a line connected to the central topic.

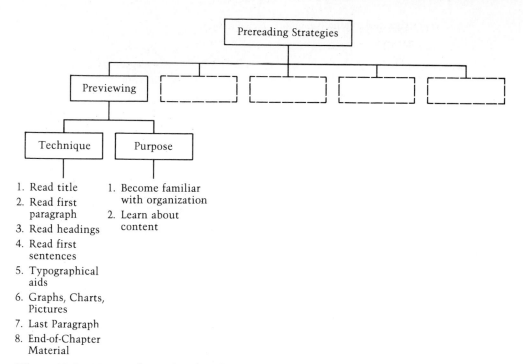

Figure 11-2 Map with greater detail.

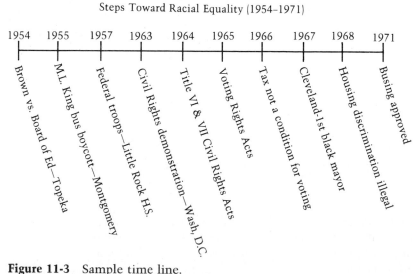

Figure 11-3 Sample time line.

Process: Selecting a Brand Name for a New Product

Figure 11-4 Sample process map.

3. As you discover details that further explain an idea already mapped, draw a new line branching from the idea it explains.

How you arrange your map will depend on the subject matter and how it is organized. Like an outline, it can be quite detailed, or very brief, depending on your purpose. A portion of a more detailed map of Chapter 4 is shown in Figure 11-2.

Once you are skilled at drawing maps, you can become more creative, drawing different types of maps to fit what you are reading. For example, you can draw a time line (see Figure 11-3) that shows historical events, or a process diagram to show processes and procedures (see Figure 11-4).

EXERCISE 11-6

Directions: *Draw a map of the article on "Melting Point" on p. 228–229.*

EXERCISE 11-7

Directions: *Draw a map of the article "Flavors" on p. 226–228.*

EXERCISE 11-8

Directions: *Draw a map of Chapter 5 in this book.*

SUMMARIZING

A summary is a brief statement that reviews the major idea of something you have read. Its purpose is to make a record of the most important ideas in condensed form. A summary is much shorter than an outline and contains less-detailed information.

A summary goes one step beyond recording what the writer says. It pulls together the writer's ideas by condensing and grouping them. There are numerous situations in college courses in which the ability to summarize is essential, such as:

- Answering an essay question

- Reviewing a film or videotape

- Writing a term paper

- Recording results of a laboratory experiment or demonstration

- Summarizing the plot (main events) of a short story before analyzing it

- Quickly reviewing large amounts of information

How to Write a Summary

Before writing a summary, be sure you understand the material and have identified the writer's major points.

1. As a first step, write a brief outline of the material or underline each major idea.

2. Write one sentence that states the writer's overall concern or most important idea (see thesis statements in Chapter 9). To do this, ask yourself what one topic the material is about. Then ask what point the writer is trying to make about that topic. This sentence will be the topic sentence of your summary.

3. Be sure to use your own words rather than those of the author.

4. Next, review the major supporting information that the author gives to explain the major idea (see Chapter 7).

5. The amount of detail you include, if any, will depend on your purpose for writing the summary.

6. Normally, present ideas in the summary in the same order in which they appeared in the original materials.

7. For other than textbook material, if the writer presents a clear opinion or expresses an attitude toward the subject matter, include it in your summary.

8. If the summary is for your own use only and not to be submitted as an assignment, do not worry about sentence structure. Some students prefer to write summaries using words and phrases rather than complete sentences.

Read the following summary of "The Structure of the Media," which appeared on pages 232–233.

Example:

> THE MEDIA ARE DIVIDED INTO TWO CATEGORIES: PRINT AND BROADCAST. PRINT MEDIA INCLUDE NEWSPAPERS AND MAGAZINES; BROADCAST REFERS TO RADIO AND TELEVISION. NEWSPAPERS ARE DECLINING IN NUMBERS AND THEIR COMPETITIVENESS IS DIMINISHED AS WELL. WHILE MAGAZINES HAVE GROWN AND BECOME AN IMPORTANT MEANS OF COMMUNICATION, TELEVISION IS THE LARGEST AND MOST INFLUENTIAL MEDIUM. THERE IS SOME CONCERN THAT THE MEDIA, ESPECIALLY TELEVISION, HAVE BECOME TOO POWERFUL AND INFLUENTIAL AND THAT THEY CONTROL NOT ONLY THE NEWS BUT THE POLITICS OF OUR COUNTRY.

Notice that this summary contains only the broadest, most-important ideas. Details are not included. The first two sentences state the basic structural division of the media. The next two sentences summarize the current trend of each of the major media. The last sentence states the writer's concern (attitude) about the media.

EXERCISE 11-9

Directions: *On a separate sheet, write a summary of a television show you viewed recently.*

EXERCISE 11-10

Directions: *On a separate sheet, write a summary of the selection "How Muzak Manipulates You," which appears on pages 163–165.*

EXERCISE 11-11

Directions: *Write a summary of the article "Who's Getting the Least: Poverty in America" on p. 230–231. When you have finished, compare it with the sample summary shown in Figure 11-5 on the next page. Then answer the following questions.*

1. How does your summary differ from the sample?

> POVERTY IS A MEANINGFUL WORD ONLY WHEN COMPARED TO A STANDARD. IN THE U.S. THE STANDARD USED IS THE POVERTY LINE, A STATISTIC THAT DEFINES THE MINIMUM INCOME A FAMILY CAN LIVE ON FOR A YEAR. THE POVERTY LINE IS NOT COMPLETELY ACCURATE IN DEFINING WHO LIVES IN POVERTY, ACCORDING TO A 10-YEAR STUDY OF POVERTY. THE STUDY REPORTS MUCH LARGER NUMBERS OF PEOPLE LIVE IN POVERTY AND MANY MORE LIVE VERY CLOSE TO POVERTY. THERE ARE NO DISTINCTIVE CHARACTERISTICS OF THOSE LIVING IN POVERTY. INSTEAD, PEOPLE SEEM TO MOVE IN AND OUT OF POVERTY DEPENDING ON CIRCUMSTANCE. POVERTY IS MOST COMMON AMONG BLACKS, RURAL DWELLERS, OLDER AMERICANS, AND FEMALE-HEADED HOUSEHOLDS.

Figure 11-5 Sample summary: "Who's Getting the Least: Poverty in America."

2. Did your summary begin with a topic sentence? How does it compare with the sample?

3. Did your summary include ideas in the order they were given in the article?

IMMEDIATE AND PERIODIC REVIEW

Once you have read and organized information, the last step is to learn it. Fortunately, this is not a difficult task if you have organized the information effectively. In fact, through underlining, outlining, and/or summarizing, you have already learned a large portion of the material. Review, then, is a way to fix, or store, information in your memory for later recall. There are two types of review, immediate and periodic.

How Immediate Review Works

Immediate review is done right after you finish reading an assignment or finish writing an outline or summary. When you finish any of these, you may feel like breathing a sigh of relief and taking a break. However, it is worth the time and effort to spend another five minutes going back over what you just read and refreshing your memory. The best way to do this is to go back through the chapter and reread the headings, graphic material, introduction, summary, and any underlining or marginal notes.

Immediate review works because it consolidates, or draws together, the material just read. It also gives a final, lasting impression of the content. Considerable research has been done on the effectiveness of immediate review. Results indicate that review done immediately rather than delayed until a later time makes a large difference in the amount remembered.

How Periodic Review Works

Although immediate review will increase your recall of information, it will not help you retain information for long periods of time. To remember information over time, you must periodically refresh your memory. This is known as periodic review. You must go back over the material on a regular basis. Do this by looking again at those sections that carry the basic meaning and reviewing your underlining, outlining, and/or summaries. Here is an example of a schedule one student set up to periodically review assigned chapters in a psychology textbook.

Week 1—Read ch. 1

Week 2—Review ch. 1
           Read ch. 2

Week 3—Review ch. 1 & 2
           Read ch. 3

Week 4—Review ch. 3
           Review ch. 1
           Read ch. 4

Week 5—Review ch. 4
           Review ch. 2
           Read ch. 5

You can see that this student reviewed each chapter the week after reading it and again two weeks later. This schedule is only an example. You will need to make a schedule for each course that fits the course requirements. For math and science courses, for example, you may need to include a review of previous homework assignments and laboratory work. In other courses, less- or more-frequent review of previous material may be needed.

EXERCISE 11-12

Directions: *Choose one of your courses that involves regular textbook reading assignments. Plan a reading and periodic review schedule for the next three weeks. Assume that new chapters will be assigned as frequently as in previous weeks and that you want to review whatever has been covered over the past three weeks.*

SUMMARY

This chapter presented three methods for organizing textbook information: underlining and marking, outlining, and summarizing.

Underlining is a way of sorting important information from less-important information. It eliminates the need to reread entire textbook chapters in order to review their major content. It also has the advantage of helping you stay active and involved with what you are reading. Marking involves using signs, symbols, and marginal notes to react to, summarize, or comment on the material.

Outlining is a method of recording the most-important information and, at the same time, showing the organization and relative importance of ideas. It is particularly useful when you need to see how ideas relate to one another or when you want to get an overview of the subject.

Mapping is a visual method of organizing information. It involves drawing diagrams to show how ideas in an article or chapter are related.

Summarizing is a way to pull together the most important ideas in condensed form. It provides a quick review of the material and forces you to take the writer's ideas and explain them in your own words.

PART FOUR REVIEW

MAKING YOUR SKILLS WORK TOGETHER

BUILDING A SYSTEM FOR READING AND STUDYING

Throughout Part Four and in previous sections of this book, you have seen that there is more to reading than simply opening a book, starting to read, and continuing until you finish. In Chapter 4 you learned that it is useful to preview and to form questions before you begin to read. In Chapters 5 through 10 you learned how to read to understand the writer's message and organization. Then, in Chapter 11 you learned that you should underline and mark as you read and/or outline, map, or summarize. Finally, you learned that it is important to review immediately after reading and to schedule periodic review to ensure long-term memory. These steps may at first seem to complicate your reading. However, you will find they are worth the extra effort. Both the amount you understand and the amount you remember will increase.

Now we will put these steps together in a list:

1. PREVIEW   Become familiar with the organization and content.

2. QUESTION   Decide what you need to find out as you read.

3. READ   Look for answers to your questions.

4. UNDERLINE/MARK/OUTLINE/MAP/SUMMARIZE   Record and organize the information.

5. REVIEW   Go back over the important ideas.

Together these techniques form a step-by-step method. The method is well tested and proven to be effective. As you try it, think of it as a way of learning while you read.

EXERCISE 1

Directions: *Read the following excerpt from a chapter on food additives in a nutrition textbook, following the steps listed.*

1. Preread the excerpt. Write a sentence describing what the chapter will be about.

   _____

2. Form several questions that you want to answer as you read. Write them in the space provided.

   _____

   _____

   _____

3. Read the excerpt and, on a separate sheet, write a brief outline or draw a map.

4. Review the excerpt immediately after you finish reading. Now look at your outline or map again and make any additions or changes.

FOOD ADDITIVES

Why Do We Use Additives?
1. *City living*: We live in cities and suburbs, not on farms. We shop infrequently, sometimes only once a week. Since food is produced far from the consumption point and must be kept fresh and wholesome until it reaches the consumer, added preservatives are often required.
2. *Modern lifestyle*: The need and desire for refined foods and lower caloric intake require some foods to be fortified with nutritional additives to assure adequate vitamin and mineral intake.
3. *New knowledge of the relationship of food to disease*—most significantly, of saturated fats and cholesterol to heart disease—has created a need and demand for new man-made foods, which require additives to make them acceptable.
4. *High-speed processing of foods* often requires additives to make the processing economical, or even possible.
5. *More women than ever are working*, creating an enormous demand for convenience foods: prepared, ready-to-eat, or heat-and-

eat foods. Additives preserve the flavor, texture, appearance, and safety of these products.

6. *Snacking* has become a national pastime. Many snacks are man-made—with additives required to make them.

What Additives Do

A food additive has been defined by the Food Protection Committee as "a substance or mixture of substances, other than a basic foodstuff, which is present in food as a result of any aspect of production, processing, storage or packaging. This term does not include chance contaminants."*

Substances are added to foods in order to accomplish one or more of the following things:

1. To preserve the product; that is, to prevent its deterioration from any cause.

2. To improve the texture of the food.

3. To improve the flavor, taste, or appearance of the food.

4. To improve the nutritional quality of the food.

5. To minimize the loss of quality during processing itself.

6. To protect the food during its growth, harvest, and storage. These are the incidental, rather than the deliberate, materials, such as pesticides.

How Additives Work

Let's take a closer look at the different types of food additives and how they work.

Preservatives function to slow down or prevent the growth of bacteria, yeasts, or molds. These microorganisms may merely spoil the flavor and texture of the food or may actually produce an end product that is dangerous for human consumption. Some of the more common preservatives used are sodium benzoate, sorbic acid (or potassium sorbate), and sodium nitrate.

Antioxidants slow down or prevent the reaction of components of a food with the oxygen in the air. Such reaction can produce undesirable flavors, such as rancidity in fats; unpleasant colors; and loss of vitamin value.

Emulsifiers are used for smooth blending of liquids or batters. Mono- and diglycerides are commonly used emulsifiers.

Stabilizers are often added to obtain a certain texture or to preserve a food's texture or its physical condition. For example, stabilizers are used to keep a liquid thick, to slow down the melting of ice cream, to prevent the fluid in a cheese from running off like water. Algin, xanthan gum, and other gums are stabilizers.

* Food Protection Committee, *Principles and Procedures for Evaluating the Safety of Food Additives*, National Academy of Science/National Research Council pub. no. 750 (Washington: U.S. Government Printing Office, 1959).

Sequestrants combine with trace amounts of metals that may be present in a product and prevent those metals from reacting with the foods to produce undesirable flavors or physical changes (to sequester means to keep in isolation). EDTA (ethylenediaminetetraacetic acid, a synthetically produced chemical) is a sequestrant.

Acids, alkalies, and buffers regulate the acidity of a food. We all know the difference between a tart cooking apple and a less tart (but still slightly acid) eating apple. In addition to its effect on taste, however, acidity is also very important to the preservation of food. Harmful bacteria usually do not grow in foods that are acid enough. Vitamins, including the natural vitamins present in food, tend to resist destruction more in foods that are acid, especially during the cooking process. In many foods, the preservation of the ideal flavor and color is helped by maintaining a specific acidity in the food. For these purposes, the acids make foods more acid, the alkalies make them less acid, and the buffers prevent change in acidity during storage. Citric acid is a typical acid, sodium citrate is a typical and common buffer, and sodium bicarbonate is a typical alkali.

Nutritional additives are the vitamins, minerals, and amino acids added to food either to enhance its nutritional value or to replace nutrients that might have been removed during processing. Some confusion has arisen now that vitamins are referred to by their chemical names rather than as *vitamins* in the ingredient list. It's unfortunate, but the listings of vitamins on the food label sometimes sound horrifying because their precise chemical names are given. "Vitamin B_1" is a lot more reassuring than "thiamine mononitrate."

Colors and flavors are added to make the food more appealing in appearance, smell, and taste.

Bleaching or maturing agents serve to oxidize wheat flour. While many foods must be protected against oxidation in order to preserve their quality, wheat flour used for baking must be oxidized in order to achieve the necessary quality.

Many years ago, it was possible to store flour for the necessary period of a month or longer to allow such oxidation to occur naturally with air. However, with bulk handling of flour and the massive bakeries that exist today, much flour is bleached in order to achieve artificial aging and to make the flour suitable for industrial use so that bread and cake can be produced uniformly at high speed. . . .

Non-nutritive sweeteners sweeten without calories. Until 1978, both calcium cyclamate and saccharin were used to replace sugar in foods for those people who were supposed to restrict their intake of ordinary sweets. When cyclamate was "found" to produce cancer in laboratory animals, it was prohibited under the Delaney Clause. Since 1978, saccharin alone has been used.

For years, saccharin was required to bear the statement "Contains *x* percent saccharin, an artificial sweetener to be used only by persons who must restrict their intake of ordinary sweets." Sometimes this statement was in type so small it could not be read without a magnifying glass.

Now, saccharin also has been "found" to produce cancer in laboratory animals. Under the Delaney Clause, it too would have been prohibited, but since it is the only usable artificial sweetener available, a delay in its prohibition has been granted, and even extended, to provide more time for confirmatory testing. (The granting of this delay actually required Congressional action.) In the meantime, saccharin must carry the warning: "Use of this product may be hazardous to your health. This product contains saccharin, which has been determined to cause cancer in laboratory animals."

The history of artificial sweeteners is an example of the seriousness with which our food labeling regulations are applied, and of the problems raised by the Delaney Clause. The rationale for the delay in the prohibition of saccharin is that the danger to people that would occur through its elimination (overweight and resultant cardiac disease and stroke) is greater than the danger of cancer. In the meantime, retesting of saccharin and cyclamates, and the testing of new substances, such as aspartame, is proceeding in the hope of finding that there is no confirmable cancer-producing hazard.

Miscellaneous materials such as leavening agents and those used for other special purposes will be explained as we go through the labels further on.

EXERCISE 2

Directions: *Choose a chapter from one of your textbooks, or use a later chapter in this book. Complete each of the following steps.*

1. Preview the chapter. Write a sentence describing what the chapter will be about.

   _____

2. Form several questions that you want to answer as you read. Write them in the space provided.

   _____

   _____

   _____

3. Read the first section (major heading) of the chapter and underline the important information.

4. Review the section immediately after you finish reading and underlining.

5. On a separate sheet, write a brief outline or map of the major ideas in this section of the chapter that you read.

PART FIVE

CRITICAL READING AND THINKING: Interpreting and Reacting

Catherine was taking a sociology course. One assignment directed her to find several articles on any controversial issue and to write a paper reacting to the writers' positions. Catherine chose the topic of legalized abortion. She easily located three articles on the topic and had no difficulty reading and taking summary notes on each article. Then she was ready to start writing her reaction paper.

After an hour or so, all Catherine had managed to create was a pile of crumpled sheets of paper. It was then she understood her problem—she had nothing to say. Although she had understood what each writer had said, she had not gone beyond the factual content to examine the author's ideas, sources, evidence, methods, or means of support. She realized that she had not only to understand the ideas, but to criticize and react to them.

Some college students and other adults accept much of what they read at face value. They assume that because something is in print, it must be true, be worth reading, have value, and contain reliable information. They fail to step back and examine the author's ideas, sources, evidence, and methods with a critical eye. Actually, much inaccurate information and many uninformed opinions appear in print every day. To be an alert, thinking, critical reader, you must approach everything you read with an open, questioning mind.

THIS PART OF THE TEXT WILL HELP YOU BECOME A MORE CRITICAL READER SO THAT

1. You will know how words can make positive or negative impressions on the reader. (Chapter 14)

2. You will be able to make logical inferences. (Chapter 12)

3. You will understand how writers use figurative language. (Chapter 12)

4. You will be able to identify the author's purpose for writing. (Chapter 13)

5. You will be familiar with seven critical questions to ask to evaluate what you read. (Chapter 14)

Chapter 12

INTERPRETING:
Understanding the
Writer's Message

THIS CHAPTER WILL SHOW YOU HOW TO

1. **Recognize words that suggest positive or negative attitudes**

2. **Make inferences about what you read**

3. **Understand figurative language**

Up to this point, we have been concerned with building vocabulary, understanding a writer's basic organizational patterns, acquiring factual information, and organizing that information for learning and recall. So far each chapter has been concerned with understanding what the author *says*, with factual content. Now our focus must change. To read well, you must go beyond what the author says and also consider what he or she *means*.

Many writers directly state some ideas but hint at others. It is left to the reader to pick up the clues or suggestions and use logic and reasoning skills to figure out the writer's unstated message. This chapter will explain several features of writing that suggest meanings. Once you are familiar with these, you will be able to understand better the writer's unstated message.

CONNOTATIVE MEANINGS

Which of the following would you like to be part of: crowd, mob, gang, audience, congregation, or class? Each of these words has the same basic meaning: "an assembled group of people." But each of these words has a different shade of meaning. *Crowd* suggests a disorganized, large group. *Audience,* on the other hand, suggests a quiet, controlled group. Try to decide what meaning each of the other words in the list suggests.

This example shows that words have two levels of meaning—a literal meaning and an additional shade of meaning. These two levels of meaning are called denotative and connotative. A word's *denotative meaning* is the meaning stated in the dictionary—its literal meaning. A word's *connotative meaning* is the additional implied meanings, or shadings, that a word may take on. Often the connotative meaning carries either a positive or negative, favorable or unfavorable impression. The words *mob* and *crowd* have a negative connotation because they imply a disorderly, disorganized group. *Congregation, audience,* and *class* have a positive connotation because they suggest an orderly, organized group.

Here are a few more examples. Would you prefer to be described as "slim" or "skinny"? as "intelligent" or "brainy"? as "heavy" or "fat"? as "particular" or "picky"? Notice that each pair of words has a similar literal meaning, but each word has a different connotation.

Depending on the words they choose, writers can suggest favorable or unfavorable impressions of the person, object, or event they are describing. For example, through the writer's choice of words, the two sentences below create two entirely different impressions. As you read them, underline words that have a positive or negative connotation.

The unruly crowd forced its way through the restraint barriers and ruthlessly attacked the rock star.

The enthusiastic group of fans burst through the fence and rushed toward the rock star.

When reading any type of informative or persuasive material, pay attention to the writer's choice of words. Often a writer may communicate subtle or hidden messages, or he or she may encourage the reader to feel positively or negatively toward the subject.

Read the following paragraph on violence in sports and, as you read, underline words that have a strong positive or negative connotation.

So it goes. Knifings, shootings, beatings, muggings, paralysis, and death become part of our play. Women baseball fans are warned to walk with friends and avoid taking their handbags to games because of strong-arm robberies and purse snatchings at San Francisco's Candlestick Park. A professional football coach, under oath in a slander case, describes some of his own players as part of a "criminal element" in his sport. The commissioner of football proclaims that playing field outlaws and bullies will be punished, but to anybody with normal eyesight and a working television set the action looks rougher than ever. In Europe and South America—and, chillingly, for the first time in the United States—authorities turn to snarling attack dogs to control unruly mobs at athletic events.[1]

EXERCISE 12-1

Directions: *For each of the following pairs of words, underline the word with the more positive connotation.*

1. request   demand
2. overlook   neglect
3. tease   ridicule
4. glance   stare
5. display   expose
6. garment   gown
7. gaudy   showy
8. awkward   clumsy
9. artificial fake
10. token   keepsake

EXERCISE 12-2

Directions: *For each word listed below, write a word that has a similar denotative meaning but a negative connotation. Then write a word that has a positive connotation. Use your dictionary, if necessary.*

	Negative	Positive
Example: eat	gobble	dine
1. take	_____	_____
2. ask	_____	_____
3. look at	_____	_____
4. walk	_____	_____
5. dress	_____	_____

6. music   _____   _____

7. car   _____   _____

8. laugh   _____   _____

9. large   _____   _____

10. woman   _____   _____

IMPLIED MEANINGS

An inference is an educated guess or prediction about something unknown based on available facts and information. It is the logical connection that you draw between what you observe or know and what you do not know.

Suppose that you arrive ten minutes late for your sociology class. All the students have papers in front of them, and everyone is busily writing. Some students have worried or concerned looks on their faces. The instructor is seated and is reading a book. What is happening? From the known information you can make an inference about what you do not know. Did you figure out that the instructor had given the class a surprise quiz? If so, then you made a logical inference.

While the inference you made is probably correct, you cannot be sure until you speak with the instructor. Occasionally a logical inference can be wrong. Although it is unlikely, perhaps the instructor has laryngitis and has written notes on the board for the students to copy. Some students may look worried because they do not understand what the notes mean.

Here are a few more everyday situations. Make an inference for each.

You are driving on an expressway and you notice a police car with flashing red lights behind you. You check your speedometer and notice that you are going ten miles over the speed limit.

A woman seated alone in a bar nervously glances at everyone who enters. Every few minutes she checks her watch.

In the first situation, a good inference might be that you are going to be stopped for speeding. However, it is possible that the officer only wants to pass you to get to an accident ahead or to stop someone driving faster than you. In the second situation, one inference is that the woman is waiting to meet someone who is late.

The following paragraphs are taken from a magazine article on the exchange of top-secret information with the Russians. First, read the article for factual content.

In a villa near Warsaw in June 1980, an American electronics engineer hands a top officer of the Polish Intelligence Service a huge bundle of secret documents about his country's first-line strategic weapon—the Minuteman intercontinental ballistic missile—as well as methods of defending it against nuclear attack. In return he receives an envelope stuffed with hundred-dollar bills.

Polish specialists rush the documents to the Soviet embassy in Warsaw. There, 20 KGB technical experts, flown in from Moscow, examine the papers. For a mere $100,000, the Russians have obtained U.S. secrets for which they had pried and probed all over the world for many years—secrets that are worth billions of dollars in research and development and are of incalculable strategic value.[2]

These paragraphs are primarily factual—they tell who did what, when, and where. However, some ideas are not directly stated and must be inferred from the information given. Here are a few examples. Some are fairly obvious inferences; others are not so obvious.

1. The engineer accepted a bribe. (You must infer from the engineer's acceptance of the envelope that he agreed to trade the documents for money.)

2. The engineer worked with top-secret information as part of his job.

3. The Polish and Russian governments are working together against the United States.

4. The United States is planning a course of action in the event of nuclear war.

5. The engineer is not concerned about national defense.

6. The engineer values money more than his country's defense.

7. The writer disapproves of the engineer's acceptance of the bribe.

Although none of the above ideas is directly stated, you can infer them from clues provided in the passage. Some of the statements could be inferred from actions, others by adding facts together, and still others by the writer's choice of words.

Now read the following passage to find out why Cindy Kane is standing on the corner of Sheridan and Sunnyside.

An oily midnight mist had settled on the city streets . . . asphalt mirrors from a ten-o'clock rain now past . . . a sleazy street-corner reflection of smog-smudged neon . . . the corner of Sheridan and, incongruously, Sunnyside . . . Chicago.

A lone lady lingers at the curb . . . but no bus will come.

She is Cindy Kane, twenty-eight. Twenty-eight hard years old. Her iridescent dress clings to her slender body. Her face is buried under a technicolor avalanche of makeup.

She is Cindy Kane.

And she has a date.

With someone she has never met . . . and may never meet again.

Minutes have turned to timelessness . . . and a green Chevy four-door pulls slowly around the corner.

The driver's window rolls down. A voice comes from the shadow . . .

"Are you working?"

Cindy nods . . . regards him with vacant eyes.

He beckons.

She approaches the passenger side. Gets in. And the whole forlorn, unromantic ritual begins all over again. With another stranger.

If you made the right inferences, you realized that Cindy Kane is a prostitute and that she is standing on the corner waiting for a customer. Let us look at the kinds of clues the writer gave that led to this inference.

1. DESCRIPTION   By the way the writer describes Cindy Kane, you begin to suspect that she is a prostitute. She is described as "hard." She is wearing an iridescent, clinging dress and "a technicolor avalanche of makeup." These descriptive details convey an image of a gaudy, unconventional appearance.

2. ACTION   The actions, although there are only a few, also provide clues about what is happening. The woman is lingering on the corner. When the car approaches, she gets in.

3. CONVERSATION   The only piece of conversation, the question, "Are you working?" is one of the strongest clues the writer provides.

4. WRITER'S COMMENTARY/DETAILS   As the writer describes the situation, he slips in numerous clues. He establishes the time as around midnight ("An oily midnight mist"). His reference to a "reflection of smog-smudged neon" suggests an area of bars or night clubs. The woman's face is "buried under . . . makeup." Covering or hiding one's face is usually associated with shame or embarrassment. In the last paragraph, the reference to a "forlorn, unromantic ritual" provides a final clue.

How to Make Inferences

Making an inference is a thinking process. As you read, you are following the author's thoughts. You are also alert for ideas that are suggested but not directly stated. Because inference is a logical thought process, there is no simple, step-by-step procedure to follow. Each inference depends entirely on the situation, the facts provided, and the reader's knowledge and experience with the situation.

However, here are a few guidelines to keep in mind as you read. These will help you get in the habit of looking beyond the factual level to the inferential.

1. *Be sure you understand the literal meaning.*   You should have a clear grasp of the key idea and supporting details of each paragraph.

2. *Notice details.*   Often a detail provides a clue that will help you make an inference. When you spot a striking or unusual detail, ask yourself: Why did the writer include this piece of information?

3. *Add up the facts.*   Consider all the facts taken together. Ask yourself: What is the writer trying to suggest from this set of facts? What do all these facts and ideas point toward?

4. *Watch for clues.*   The writer's choice of words and of detail often suggests his or her attitude toward the subject. Notice, in particular, descriptive words, emotionally charged words, and words with strong positive or negative connotations.

5. *Be sure your inference is supportable.*   An inference must be based on fact. Make sure there is sufficient evidence to justify any inference you make.

EXERCISE 12-3

Directions: *Read each of the following passages. Then answer the questions that follow. You will need to reason out, or infer, the answers.*

Passage 1:

Eye-to-eye contact and response are important in real-life relationships. The nature of a person's eye contact patterns, whether he or she looks another squarely in the eye or looks to the side or shifts his gaze from side to side, tells a lot about the person. These patterns also play a significant role in success or failure in human relationships. Despite its importance, eye contact is not involved in television watching. Yet children spend several hours a day in front of the television set. Certain children's programs pretend to speak directly to each individual child. (Mr. Rogers is an example, telling the child "I like you, you're special," etc.) However, this is still one-way communication and no response is required of the child. How might such a distortion of real-life relationships affect a child's development of trust, or openness, of an ability to relate well to other people?

a. How would the author answer the question asked in the last sentence of the paragraph?

b. What is the author's attitude toward television?

_____

c. To develop a strong relationship with someone should you look directly at him or her or shift your gaze?

_____

d. What activities, other than television, do you think this author would recommend for children?

_____

Passage 2:

Our clothes may disclose something about our behavior. If you have ever worn a uniform of any kind, you know how clothes can transform you and change your behavior. If we get dressed up for a job interview, we feel important; in our own mind our actions also take on importance. Because this occurs in our mind, it is also very likely to affect our behavior. We will be more calculated, purposeful, and dynamic. We may stand erect rather than slouch. We may tend to lower our voice, slow our rate of speaking, and use fewer nonfluencies ("uh's" and "um's"). Just as dress affects us, we are also likely to judge other people's behavior by the way they dress. What expectations do you have for a person dressed as a police officer, judge, nurse, or priest?

a. Answer the question asked in the last sentence of the paragraph.

_____

b. What behaviors would you expect of a person who did *not* dress appropriately for a job interview?

_____

c. Why do you think Burger King and McDonald's require their employees to wear a uniform?

_____

Passage 3:

John Thompson and Bill Russell, former teammates on the Boston Celtics and still friends, were talking about education the other day waiting for a celebrity golf tournament to begin.

Russell, now a businessman and television commentator, said that if the University of San Francisco had not made an exception for him, his daughter likely would not be attending Harvard Law School. Thompson, basketball coach at Georgetown University, agreed, saying that if Providence College hadn't made an exception for him, his son wouldn't be attending Princeton University.

Both men were the first in their families to attend college.

"What's that boy's name from Tulane? (Hot Rod) Williams?" Thompson said. "Don't tell me that Williams was exploited. Tell me what his child will do. I saw a little baby sitting in his lap (in a magazine article). I'm willing to bet that his son, as a result of Williams' experiences, will be better off. Education comes in a delayed effect sometimes.

"If I expose you to something, you may not get the degree. I've got a former player who was not responsive to education who is as responsive as hell to his child's education, because he's been exposed to some things."

a. What type of "exceptions" do you think the University of San Francisco and Providence College made for Thompson and Russell?

_____

b. Explain the statement, "Education comes in a delayed effect sometimes."

_____

c. To what kinds of things are students exposed that change their attitudes toward education?

_____

Passage 4:

People kill people, but handguns make it easier. When other weapons (knives, for instance) are used, the consequences are not so often deadly. Strangling or stabbing someone takes a different degree of energy and intent than pulling a trigger. Registration will not interfere with hunting and other rifle sports but will simply exercise control over who can carry handguns. Ordinary people do not carry handguns. If a burglar has a gun in his hand, it is quite insane for you to shoot it out with him, as if you were in a quick draw contest in the Wild West. Half of all the guns used in crimes are stolen; 70% of the stolen guns are handguns. In other words, the supply of handguns used by criminals already comes to a great extent from the households these guns were supposed to protect.*

a. Does the author favor or oppose gun control laws?

_____

b. Would the author agree or disagree with the following statements?
1. If a gun is not available, a murderer would use a knife or rope to kill his victim. _____

* From "Fifty Million Handguns" by Adam Smith, April, 1981, *Esquire*. Reprinted with permission from *Esquire*. Copyright © 1981 by Adam Smith.

2. All murders are basically the same. _____

3. Citizens living in high crime areas should keep a weapon in their bedrooms. _____

4. Registration of guns will significantly reduce crime. _____

c. How is strangling or stabbing different from shooting?

_____

EXERCISE 12-4

Directions: *Read each of the following articles and answer the questions that follow.*

THE FATHER AND HIS DAUGHTER

A little girl was given so many picture books on her seventh 1 birthday that her father, who should have run his office and let her mother run the home, thought his daughter should give one or two of her new books to a little neighbor boy named Robert, who had dropped in, more by design than by chance.

Now, taking books, or anything else, from a little girl is like tak- 2 ing candy from a baby, but the father of the little girl had his way and Robert got two of her books. "After all, that leaves you with nine," said the father, who thought he was a philosopher and a child psychologist, and couldn't shut his big fatuous mouth on the subject.

A few weeks later, the father went to his library to look up "fa- 3 ther" in the Oxford English Dictionary, to feast his eyes on the praise of fatherhood through the centuries, but he couldn't find volume F–G, and then he discovered that three others were missing, too—A–B, L–M, V–Z. He began a probe of his household, and learned what had become of the four missing volumes.

"A man came to the door this morning," said his little daughter, 4 "and he didn't know how to get from here to Torrington, or from Torrington to Winstead, and he was a nice man, much nicer than Robert, and so I gave him four of your books. After all, there are thirteen volumes in the Oxford English Dictionary, and that leaves you nine."

Moral This truth has been known from here to Menander: what's sauce for the gosling's not sauce for the gander.

1. In the first paragraph, the author gives the first clue that the father's actions are going to lead him into trouble. Underline the clue.

2. What does the writer think of the father? Support your answer with references to the article.

_____

_____

_____

3. What inference did the girl make from her father's actions?

_____

_____

4. Do you think the father approved of his daughter's action? Explain your reasons.

_____

_____

5. Explain the "Moral" at the end of the selection.

_____

THE NON-RUNNER

What kind of people are these non-runners? Who are these path-finders bold enough to drop out of the faddish rat race? Are they weirdos? buffoons? sociopaths? naive sycophants? craven toadies? harmless eccentrics? perverts? trolls? Medicaid cheaters? brainwashed zombies? Red spies? 1

Not at all. 2

Surprisingly, non-runners are very much like you and me. They include people from every walk of life. And there are not only walkers. There are sitters, leaners, nappers, starers, procrastinators, TV-watchers, popsicle-lickers, readers, sneezers, yawners, teasers, stumblers, lechers, stamp collectors, static-electricity gatherers, and, of course, the totally immobile. 3

This amazingly versatile group comprises people of all ages, races, and sexes. Non-running is accessible to young and old, rich and fat, the famous as well as the depressed. Whether you're an android or an aborigine, you can take part. Or you can take all. 4

Many non-runners have been doing it all their lives. Others have only recently kicked the running habit to join the swelling ranks of the unrun. Together, these non-runners spend an estimated $665 billion annually on products totally unrelated to running in any way. Without them and their non-running-related expenditures, the U.S. economy would fold up in a minute. 5

But the economic gain from non-running is only part of the picture. There is also the spiritual side. Non-runners are linked by a common bond; they feel a kinship that expresses itself in innumerable ways. Non-runners will often wave to other non-runners they 6 don't even know. Sometimes they will even invite them home to dinner and later go to bed with them.

And there is the well-known psychological lift that comes to non-runners. After the first half hour or so of not running, you become so elated by the realization that you are not out in the hot sun or in the rain pounding around a hard sidewalk or dusty track that you may find yourself uttering a restrained sigh. This indefinable sense of quiet satisfaction is one of the things that makes not running so pleasurable.

1. What do you infer that the authors think of runners?

   _____

   _____

2. Throughout the passage, the authors give clues about their attitude toward runners. What words and phrases suggest their attitude?

   _____

   _____

3. Are the authors completely serious about the values of nonrunning? Explain your answer by referring to the selection.

   _____

   _____

   _____

4. Part of the humor of this article comes from the way the authors take some of the benefits of running and apply them to the nonrunner. For example, in paragraph 6, they explain that nonrunners are linked by a common bond. This is a reverse of what is usually thought to be true —that runners share a common bond. Locate and describe other examples of this reversal technique.

   _____

   _____

   _____

FIGURATIVE LANGUAGE

Read each of the following statements:

The cake tasted like a moist sponge.

The wilted plants begged for water.

Jean wore her heart on her sleeve.

You know that a cake cannot really have the same taste as a sponge, that plants do not actually request water, and that a person's heart cannot really be attached to her or his sleeve. However, you know what message the writer is communicating in each sentence. The cake was soggy and tasteless, the plants were extremely dry, and Jean revealed her feelings to everyone around her.

Each of these sentences is an example of figurative language. Figurative language is a way of describing something that makes sense on an imaginative level but not on a factual or literal level. Notice that while none of the above expressions is literally true, each is meaningful.

In many figurative expressions, one thing is compared with another for some quality they have in common. Take, for example, the familiar expression in the following sentence:

Sam eats like a horse.

The diagram below shows the comparison being made in this figurative expression:

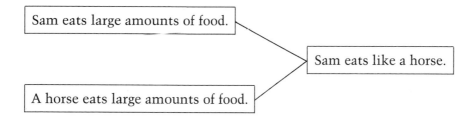

You can see that two unlike things—Sam and a horse—are compared because they are alike in one particular way—the amount they eat.

The purpose of figurative language is to paint a word picture—to help you visualize how something looks, feels, or smells. Figurative language is a device writers use to express an idea or feeling and, at the same time, allow the reader the freedom of imagination. Figurative language, since it is not factual, allows the writer to express attitudes and opinions without directly stating them. Depending on the figurative expression chosen, a writer can create a variety of impressions.

When reading an article that contains figurative language, be sure to pay close attention to the images and feelings created. Be sure you recognize that the writer is shaping your response to the topic or subject.

Figurative language is used in many types of articles and essays. It is also used in everyday speech and in slang expressions. Various types of literature, especially poetry, also use figurative language. Notice its use in the following excerpt from a poem by Emily Dickinson.

> My Life has stood—a Loaded Gun—
> In Corners—till a Day
> The Owner passed—identified—
> And carried Me away—

In the opening stanza of this poem, Dickinson compares her life to a loaded gun.

Here are a few more examples from other sources. Notice how each creates a visual image of the person, object, or quality being described.

> The red sun was pasted in the sky like a wafer.
> (Stephen Crane, *The Red Badge of Courage*)

> In plucking the fruit of memory,
> one runs the risk of spoiling its bloom.
> (Joseph Conrad)

> "I will speak daggers to her, but use none."
> (Shakespeare, *Hamlet*)

> Life, like a dome of many-colored glass,
> Stains the white radiance of Eternity.
> (Shelley, "Adonais")

> I am going to "float like a butterfly, sting like a bee."
> (Muhammad Ali)

> Like a bridge over troubled water,
> I will lay me down.
> (Paul Simon)

EXERCISE 12-5

Directions: *Each of the following sentences includes a figurative expression. Read each sentence and explain in your own words what the expression means.*

1. My psychology quiz was a piece of cake.

_____

_____

2. My life is a junkyard of broken dreams.

   _____

   _____

3. You took scissors and sheared my life to shreds.

   _____

   _____

4. Life is as tedious as a twice-told tale.

   (Shakespeare, *King John III*)

   _____

   _____

5. A sleeping child gives me the impression of a traveler in a very far country.

   (Ralph Waldo Emerson)

   _____

   _____

6. I refuse to accept the notion that nation after nation must spiral down a militaristic stairway into the hell of nuclear war.

   (Martin Luther King, Jr.)

   _____

   _____

EXERCISE 12-6

Directions: *Read each of the following selections and answer the questions that follow.*

LOVE IN THE AFTERNOON—IN A CROWDED PRISON HALL

Each time I visit my man in prison, I relive the joy of reunion— and the anguish of separation.   1

We meet at the big glass door at the entrance to the small visi-   2
tors' hall at Lompoc Federal Correctional Institution. We look at each other silently, then turn and walk into a room jammed with hundreds of molded fiberglass chairs lined up side by side. Finding a place in the crowded hall, we sit down, appalled that we're actually in a prison. Even now, after four months of such clocked, supervised, regulated visits, we still can't get used to the frustrations.

Yet, as John presses me gently to his heart, I feel warm and ten-   3 der, and tears well up inside me, as they do each weekend. I have seven hours to spend with the man I love—all too brief a time for sharing a lifetime of emotion: love and longing, sympathy and tenderness, resentment and anger.

The guard's voice jars us: "Please keep the chairs in order!"   4

We can't keep from laughing, for we're struck by the absurdity of   5 the scene: 60 couples, some with families, packed in a single room— each trying, somehow, to create an atmosphere of intimacy. And what's demanded by the single guard who's assigned to oversee us? *Chairs in a straight line.*

Nevertheless, John and I abide by the rules, holding each other   6 as close as we can—without moving our chairs—and the loneliness of the past week gradually subsides.

We break our silent communion with small talk much like the   7 kind we shared at home for the past three years. Like: *Should we have the van repaired, or sell it?*

Then we speak of our separate needs and fears. He feels de-   8 feated—by confinement, by prison life, by the 20 months left to serve on a two-year sentence for a drug-related charge that we think should never have come to trial. He feels deeply insecure, too, doubting my fidelity and hating himself for doubting me. He wants support and reassurance.

But what about me? *Doesn't he understand that this has been*   9 *an ordeal for me, too?* My whole life fell apart when he went to prison. Our wedding plans were canceled; I had to quit school, sell everything, find a job, and move in with relatives.

Prison has become my second full-time occupation. Each week-   10 end I spend 10 hours traveling. Always I must save money—money for my motel room in Lompoc, money for his collect phone calls to supplement the letters we write, money for his supplies at the prison commissary.

Worst of all, there's the almost unbearable burden of conducting   11 my home life alone. At least in prison he has no decisions to make, no meals to worry about, no rent. So I, too, need reassurance and emotional support.[3]

1. Answer each of the following questions by making an inference.

   a. Who is visiting the man in prison?

   _____

   b. Why is she there?

   _____

c. Does she go there often? How do you know?

_____

d. Why do they break the silence with small talk?

_____

e. Why does the guard insist that the chairs be kept in a straight line?

_____

f. Why did the woman have to quit school?

_____

g. Does the writer feel sorry for herself? How do you know?

_____

_____

2. List several words with negative connotations that suggest how the writer feels about the prison.

_____

3. List several words with positive connotations that suggest how the woman feels about the man she is visiting.

_____

4. What main point do you think the writer is trying to make?

_____

_____

FROM EITHER/OR TO MULTIPLE OPTION

Personal choices for Americans remained rather narrow and lim- 1
ited from the postwar period through much of the 1960s. Many of us
lived the simple lives portrayed in such television series as *Leave it
to Beaver* and *Father Knows Best*: Father went to work, mother kept
house and raised 2.4 children. There were few decisions to make; it
was an either/or world:

- Either we got married or we did not (and of course, we almost always did).

- Either we worked nine to five (or other regular full-time hours) or we didn't work, period.

- Ford or Chevy.

- Chocolate or vanilla.

Admittedly, we sometimes got a third choice: NBC, CBS, or ABC. *Look, Life,* or the *Post.* Strawberry ice cream. But it was still either/or, a society of mass markets and mass market advertising, where homogenized tastes were easily satisfied with few product choices.

Not anymore. The social upheavals of the late 1960s, and the quieter changes of the 1970s, which spread 1960s values throughout much of traditional society, paved the way for the 1980s—a decade of unprecedented diversity. In a relatively short time, the unified mass society has fractionalized into many diverse groups of people with a wide array of differing tastes and values, what advertisers call a market-segmented, market-decentralized society.

Remember when bathtubs were white, telephones were black, and checks green?

In today's Baskin-Robbins society, everything comes in at least 31 flavors.

There are 752 different models of cars and trucks sold in the United States—and that's not counting the choice of colors they come in. If you want a subcompact, you can choose from 126 different types. In Manhattan, there is a store called Just Bulbs, which stocks 2,500 types of light bulbs—and nothing else. Its most exotic bulb comes from Finland and emits light that resembles sunshine. Today, there are more than 200 brands (styles, as the industry calls them) of cigarettes on the U.S. market.

This is the analog for what is going on in society. Advertisers are forced to direct products to perhaps a million clusters of people who are themselves far more individualistic and who have a wide range of choices in today's world. The multiple-option society is a new ballgame, and advertisers know they must win consumers market by market, an approach some are calling "guerrilla warfare."

The either/or choices in the basic areas of family and work have exploded into a multitude of highly individual arrangements and lifestyles. But the basic idea of a multiple-option society has spilled over into other important areas of our lives: religion, the arts, music, food, entertainment, and finally in the extent to which cultural, ethnic, and racial diversity are now celebrated in America.[4]

1. What major change in American society does this selection describe?

_____

2. In paragraph 5 the writer lists the number of different models of trucks, types of light bulbs, and brands of cigarettes. Why does he list these facts? Infer what point the writer is making.

   _____

   _____

3. The writer requires you to make numerous inferences as you read. Answer these questions, based on the inferences you have made:

   a. What are *Look, Life,* and the *Post* choices of?

   _____

   b. What was life like on *Leave It to Beaver* and *Father Knows Best?*

   _____

   _____

   c. When were bathtubs white, telephones black, and checks green?

   _____

4. Is the author's statement that the American family raised 2.4 children a literal or a figurative expression? Why?

   _____

   _____

5. Identify a statement in the selection that makes sense on a figurative but not a literal level.

   _____

6. Did you notice the writer's choice of words throughout the selection? Tell whether each of the following words and phrases has a positive or negative connotation. Then write a sentence explaining your reasons.

   a. guerrilla warfare (paragraph 6)

   _____

   b. new ballgame (paragraph 6)

   _____

   c. exploded (paragraph 7)

   _____

   d. spilled over (paragraph 7)

   _____

    e. social upheavals (paragraph 3)

    _____

7. What do you think the writer's attitude is toward the change he describes in American society? Why do you think this?

    _____

    _____

SUMMARY

This chapter was concerned with the critical reading skills of inference and interpretation. Three features of writing were discussed through which writers suggest, but do not directly state, their ideas. These are connotative meanings, implied meanings, and figurative language. Connotative meanings refer to the shades of meaning a word may have in addition to its denotative (dictionary) meaning. Connotative meanings often convey either a positive or negative, favorable or unfavorable impression.

Implied meanings are ideas that are suggested but not directly stated. They are ideas that are left to the reader to infer, based on the facts and information provided by the writer.

Figurative language is a way of describing things that makes sense on an imaginative level but not on a factual or literal level.

Chapter 13

INTERPRETING: Understanding the Author's Purpose

THIS CHAPTER WILL SHOW YOU HOW TO

1. **Understand the author's purpose by considering style and intended audience**

2. **Identify the writer's tone**

3. **Recognize various types of language**

Writers have many different reasons or purposes for writing. Read the following statements and try to decide why each was written:

1. About 14,000 ocean-going ships pass through the Panama Canal each year. This averages about three ships per day.

2. *New Unsalted Dry Roasted Almonds*. Finally, a snack with a natural flavor and without salt. We simply shell the nuts and dry-roast them until they're crispy and crunchy. Try a jar this week.

3. Man is the only animal that blushes or has a need to.

4. If a choking person has fallen down, first turn him or her face up. Then knit together the fingers of both your hands and apply pressure with the heel of your bottom hand to the victim's abdomen.

5. If your boat capsizes, it is usually safer to cling to the boat than to try to swim ashore.

Statement 1 was written to give information, 2 to persuade you to buy almonds, 3 to amuse you and make a comment on human behavior, 4 to explain, and 5 to give advice.

In each of the examples, the writer's purpose was fairly clear, as it will be in most textbooks (to present information), newspaper articles (to communicate daily events), and reference books (to compile facts). However, in many other types of writing, authors have varied, sometimes less obvious, purposes. In these cases, an author's purpose must be inferred.

Often a writer's purpose is to express an opinion indirectly. Or the writer may want to encourage the reader to think about a particular issue or problem. Writers achieve their purposes by manipulating and controlling what they say and how they say it. This chapter will focus on techniques writers use and features of language that writers control to achieve the results they want.

STYLE AND INTENDED AUDIENCE

Are you able to recognize a friend just by his or her voice? Can you identify family members by their footsteps? You are able to do so because each person's voice and footsteps are unique. Have you noticed that writers have unique characteristics as well? One author may use many examples; another may use few. One author may use relatively short sentences, another may use long, complicated ones. The characteristics that make a writer unique are known as style. By changing their style, writers can create different effects.

Writers may vary their style to suit their intended audiences. A writer may write for a general-interest audience (anyone who is interested in the subject but is not considered an expert). Most newspapers and periodicals, such as *Time* and *Newsweek*, appeal to a general-interest audience. On the other hand, a writer may have a particular interest group in mind. A writer may write for medical doctors in the *Journal of American Medicine* or for skiing enthusiasts in *Skiing Today* or for antique collectors in *The World of Antiques*. A writer may also target his or her writing for an audience with particular political, moral, or religious attitudes. Articles in the *Atlantic Monthly* often appeal to the conservative political viewpoint, whereas *The Catholic Digest* appeals to a particular religious group.

Depending on the group of people for whom the author is writing, he or she will change the level of language, choice of words, and method of presentation. One step toward identifying an author's purpose, then, is to ask yourself the question: Who is the intended audience? Your response will be your first clue to determining why the author wrote the article.

EXERCISE 13-1

Directions: *Read each of the following statements and decide for whom each was written. Write a sentence that describes the intended audience.*

1. Chances are you're going to be putting money away over the next five years or so. You are hoping for the right things in life. Right now, a smart place to put your money is in mutual funds or bonds.

   _____

2. Think about all the places your drinking water has been before you drink another drop. Most likely it has been chemically treated to remove bacteria and chemical pollutants. Soon you may begin to feel the side effects of these treatments. Consider switching to filtered, distilled water today.

   _____

3. Introducing the new, high-powered Supertuner III, a stereo system guaranteed to keep your mother out of your car.

   _____

4. Bright and White laundry detergent removes dirt and stains faster than any other brand.

   _____

5. As a driver, you're ahead if you can learn to spot car trouble before it's too late. If you can learn the difference between drips and squeaks that occur under normal conditions and those that mean big trouble is just down the road, then you'll be ahead of expensive repair bills and won't find yourself stranded on a lonely road.

   _____

TONE

The tone of a speaker's voice helps you interpret what he or she is saying. If the following sentence were read aloud, the speaker's voice would tell you how to interpret it: Would you mind closing the door? In print you cannot tell whether the speaker is polite, insistent, or angry. In speech you could tell by whether the speaker emphasized the word *would*, *door*, or *mind*.

Just as a speaker's tone of voice tells how the speaker feels, so does a writer convey a tone, or feeling, through his or her writing. *Tone*, then, refers to the attitude or feeling a writer expresses about the subject. A writer may adopt a serious tone, an angry tone, a humorous tone, a sympathetic tone, an instructive tone, a persuasive tone, and so forth. Here are a few examples of different tones. How does each make you feel?

- Instructive

  Example: When purchasing a piece of clothing, one must be concerned with quality as well as with price. Be certain to check for the following: double-stitched seams, matched patterns, and ample linings.

- Sympathetic

  Example: The forlorn, frightened-looking child wandered through the streets alone, searching for someone who would show an interest in helping her find her parents.

- Persuasive

  Example: Child abuse is a tragic occurrence in our society. Strong legislation is needed to control the abuse of innocent victims and to punish those who are insensitive to the rights and feelings of others.

In the first example, the writer offers advice in a straightforward, informative style. In the second, the writer wants you to feel sorry for the child. This is done through description. In the last example, the writer tries to convince the reader that action must be taken to prevent child abuse. The use of such words as *tragic, innocent,* and *insensitive* establish this tone.

The tone of an article directly affects how the reader interprets and responds to it. If, for example, the writer's tone is humorous and you do not recognize this, you will miss the point of the entire selection. If the writer's tone is sympathetic, it is important to know that an appeal to your feelings is being made. You can begin to suspect, then, that you may not receive an objective, unbiased treatment of the subject.

The author's tone is intended to rub off on you, so to speak. If a writer's tone is humorous, the writer hopes you will be amused. If a writer's tone is persuasive, the writer hopes you will accept his or her viewpoint. You can see how tone can be important in determining an author's purpose. Therefore, a second question to ask when trying to determine an author's purpose is: What tone does the writer use? Or: How is the writer trying to make me feel about the subject?

EXERCISE 13-2

Directions: *Read each of the following statements, paying particular attention to the tone. Then write a sentence that describes the tone. Prove your point by listing some of the author's words that reveal his or her feelings.*

1. No one says that nuclear power is risk free. There are risks involved in all methods of producing energy. However, the scientific evidence is clear and obvious. Nuclear power is at least as safe as any other means used to generate electricity.

   _____

   _____

2. The condition of our city streets is outrageous. The sidewalks are littered with paper and other garbage—you could trip while walking to the store. The streets themselves are in even worse condition. Deep potholes and crumbling curbs make it unsafe to drive. Where are our city tax dollars going if not to correct these problems?

   _____

   _____

3. I am a tired American. I am tired of watching criminals walk free while they wait for their day in court. I'm tired of hearing about victims getting as much as or more hassle than criminals. I'm tired of reading about courts of law that even accept a lawsuit in which a criminal sues his or her intended victim.

   _____

   _____

4. Cross-country skis have heel plates of different shapes and materials. They may be made of metal, plastic, or rubber. Be sure that they are tacked on the ski right where the heel of your boot will fall. They will keep snow from collecting under your foot and offer some stability.

   _____

   _____

LANGUAGE

One important feature that writers adjust to suit their purpose is the kind of language they use. There are two basic types of language, objective and subjective.

Objective and Subjective Language

Objective language is factual, whereas subjective language expresses attitudes and feelings.

Read each of the following descriptions of the death penalty. As you read, decide how they differ.

The death penalty is one of the most ancient of all types of formal punishment for crime. In early criminal codes, death was the penalty for a wide range of offenses, such as kidnapping, certain types of theft, and witchcraft. Today, in the United States, the death penalty is reserved for only the most serious of crimes—murder, kidnapping and treason.

The death penalty is a prime example of man's inhumanity to man. The death penalty violates the Eighth Amendment to the Constitution, which prohibits cruel and unusual punishment.

You probably noticed that the first paragraph gave facts about the death penalty and that the second paragraph seemed to state a case against it. These two paragraphs are examples of two different types of writing.

The first paragraph is an example of objective language. The writer reported information without showing feelings. You cannot tell whether the writer favors or is opposed to the death penalty.

The second paragraph is an example of subjective language. Here, the writer expresses freely his or her own attitudes and feelings. You know exactly how the author feels about the death penalty. Through choice of words and selection of facts, a tone of moral disapproval is evident. Such words as *inhumanity, violate,* and *cruel* have negative connotations.

EXERCISE 13-3

Directions: *Choose a topic in which you are interested or use one of the topics listed below. On a separate sheet, write two brief paragraphs. In the first, use only objective, factual information. In the second, try to show your feelings about the topic by using subjective language.*

1. One of your college instructors

2. Managing your time

3. Current fashion fads

Descriptive Language

Descriptive language is a particular type of subjective language. It is the use of words that appeal to one or more of the reader's senses. Descriptive words help the reader create an imaginary picture of the object, person, or event being described. Here is a paragraph that contains numerous descriptive words and phrases. As you read, underline words and phrases that help you to imagine what the Oregon desert is like.

You can camp in the Oregon desert for a week and see no one at all, no more than the glow of headlights hovering over a dirt road miles distant, disappearing soundlessly over the curve of the Earth. You can see, as you wander over those dry flats, that man has been there, that vast stretches of sagebrush have replaced the bunchgrass grazed off by his cattle and sheep. Against a hill you can find the dry-rotting foundation of a scuttled homestead. But the desert is not scarred by man's presence. It is still possible to be alone out there, to stare at your hands for an hour and have no one ask why. It is possible to feel the cracks in the earth, to sense the enormity of space, to roll, between the tips of your fingers, the dust of boulders gone to pieces.[1]

Through descriptive language, a writer often makes you feel a certain way about the topic. In the preceding paragraph, the writer is trying to suggest that the desert is lonely, peaceful, and a good place to think or relax. Did you notice such words and phrases as *soundlessly, sensitive, enormity of space, distant, wander, vast stretches?*

EXERCISE 13-4

Directions: *Read each of the following selections and answer the questions that follow.*

AMERICANS AND THE LAND

I have often wondered at the savagery and thoughtlessness with which our early settlers approached this rich continent. They came at it as though it were an enemy, which of course it was. They burned the forests and changed the rainfall; they swept the buffalo from the plains, blasted the streams, set fire to the grass, and ran a reckless scythe through the virgin and noble timber. Perhaps they felt that it was limitless and could never be exhausted and that a man could move on to new wonders endlessly. Certainly there are many examples to the contrary, but to a large extent the early people pillaged the country as though they hated it, as though they held it temporarily and might be driven off at any time.[2]

1. Is this selection an objective or subjective account of the early settlement of America? Give examples to support your choice.

_____

_____

2. Describe the writer's tone. How does it make you feel?

_____

_____

3. Why do you think the author wrote this selection?

_____

"DOING" COCAINE: A VICTIM'S ROAD TO RUIN *

She had it all. Beautiful, bright and rich, she could do anything, and she knew it. Maybe that was the trouble.

She ended up "doing" cocaine.

Now, 10 years and hundreds of thousands of dollars are gone. At age 32, her face is scarred and so are her memories. She is fearful of meeting people, of going places. Most of all, she is afraid of herself.

With the understanding that her name wouldn't be printed, she agreed to tell her story, one not unlike those of thousands of other drug victims.

The first time I did cocaine was in Aspen, Colo. I was in the restroom of a nice restaurant and a girl dipped her fingernail in a vial and shoved it up my nose. I didn't know what was going on. I was with friends, and I remember them telling me it was an aphrodisiac.

After dinner, our group's host was doing it. He would take a snort and go, "Ooh, ahh." I wondered what he was "oohing" about, because it didn't do a thing for me. I spent the next decade investigating.

Every time that I heard someone had cocaine for sale, I would buy. Eventually I had two safety-deposit boxes full of it.

I had so much of the stuff that I used to keep a cookie jar filled with it for my friends. Of course, I know now that I was manipulated by those people. When I started running low, my friends quit coming around.

Tell-tale trunk. Then I got busted. A friend had put some in my trunk, and I didn't know about it when I waved down a cop to change a flat tire. He arrested me for possession.

The charge was expunged, though. The attorney general owed my lawyer a favor, and the case was delayed and delayed. To get off, part of the deal was that I go to a hospital in Connecticut for three months.

But by then I was really obsessive about cocaine, addicted to it.

* Reprinted from *U.S. News & World Report* issue of May 16, 1983. Copyright 1983, U.S. News & World Report, Inc.

It wasn't a secret to anybody because I stuttered, didn't eat, never slept. I had to snort probably every 10 minutes. One time I was in Hawaii when I ran out of coke, and I left in the middle of my vacation to come back and get more.

Then I met this guy who used a needle and I started "shooting" cocaine. It was totally different, an instant rush. It makes you crazy. You go on three and four-day binges. I was cooking up "hits" every 30 minutes, putting a little rock in a spoon, adding water and drawing it up through a cotton ball with a syringe.

However much coke you have, you use it, no holds barred. On one binge, I took too big a hit. I closed my eyes and was drifting off. When I opened my eyes, this guy I was with looked scared. He said I'd been having a seizure. I didn't believe it until I saw my blood all over the wall where I had spit up.

It got so I wouldn't buy coke unless I had Quaaludes to keep me from getting too crazy. Then bootleg Quaaludes came out. They make you even crazier.

I was beat up by this guy who was desperate to get more drugs.

When I didn't give him money, he knocked his fist through the wall, pulled the phones out of the wall, ripped a door off the hinge, dragged me across the floor by my hair, beating me. He was crazed, driving the car all over the yard. I crawled out of my kitchen, too weak to get up, and a girl who lived behind me called the police when she saw I was bleeding all over.

They say I kicked the door off the ambulance when they took me away. I woke up in the hospital with my mother and other people around who thought I was dying.

Even after all that, I just couldn't wait to get back to cocaine. It got to the point where I sold my furniture, some pieces several times before the first buyers could pick them up. I sold the jewelry I inherited from my grandmother. I sold my car, my stereo. In the last year I spent $100,000 on drugs—$80,000 in six months. As for the eight years before that, I can't even guess how much I spent.

Two years ago I weighed 80 pounds, and I'm 5 foot 4½. I was a skeleton. Then I got beat up again by this guy who said he was so concerned that I was trying to kill myself doing drugs. He broke my nose, gave me a black eye. Of course, he did drugs, too. Crazy.

My mother took one look at me and took me bodily to a drug-treatment center in Arizona. I was so crazy when walking through the airport that I tried to get a policeman's gun so I could go through the machine that sets off the alarm. Every chance I got, I lay down in the corridor. My mother dragged me onto the airplane, into first class.

Return trip. At the drug center, we had lectures and group therapy. I had bad withdrawal, the shakes. I didn't sleep for eight days.

They started getting me in touch with my feelings, feelings I'm not sure I ever felt before. I was at the point that I couldn't have given you one word for any feeling, whether it was pain, guilt, remorse, anything. I did a lot of justifying, anything but being honest with myself. But they force you to be honest.

That's made me well—or made me want to be well.

I haven't done coke now for 18 months. I don't think I have to fight the cocaine, but I haven't been around it, and I'm not associating with any people who do it, so it's hard to say. I know I wouldn't snort again, because after using a needle, snorting is like learning to read a book backwards.

I don't have cravings, but I sure would be scared to be around coke. I think that if it were right here with a syringe, I'd do it. I know I would.

My plans are just to take it one day at a time. I'm not making any plans.

1. Is this selection objective or subjective? Give some examples to support your answer.

   _____

   _____

2. The author uses descriptive language to help the reader understand the effects of cocaine. List words and phrases that you feel are particularly descriptive. Then describe the effect of these phrases.

   _____

   _____

   _____

3. What tone does this selection seem to express? What words are particularly effective in expressing this tone?

   _____

   _____

4. What other tone could the writer have used to tell the story? Explain whether it would be as effective as the tone the author actually used.

   _____

   _____

5. Why do you think the writer agreed to tell her story? Do you think it was effective?

   _____

   _____

6. Whom do you think the intended audience of this article might be? Give reasons for your answers.

_____

_____

SUMMARY

Writers may have a variety of purposes, including to present information, express opinions, give advice, or persuade the reader to accept the writer's ideas. Understanding an author's purpose was the focus of this chapter. It examined four features of writing that will help you decide why an author wrote a particular article or essay: style, audience, tone, and language.

A writer will change his or her style—level of language, choice of words, and method of presentation—to suit the intended audience. Analyzing the style and identifying the intended audience are the first steps toward identifying an author's purpose. A writer's tone—serious, humorous, angry, sympathetic—is a clue to how the writer wants you to feel about the topic and therefore also suggests the writer's purpose. A writer's language may be objective or subjective, depending on whether the writer is simply presenting facts or expressing an opinion or feelings, and this presents one more clue to the writer's purpose.

Chapter 14

EVALUATING:
Asking Critical Questions

THIS CHAPTER WILL SHOW YOU HOW TO

1. **Judge the accuracy and value of what you read**

2. **Ask questions to evaluate what you read**

If you were thinking of buying a used car from a private owner, you would ask a number of questions before deciding whether to buy it. You would ask about repairs, maintenance, gas mileage, and so forth. When it comes to buying something, most of us have learned the motto "Buyer beware." We have learned to be critical, and sometimes suspicious, of a product and/or its seller. We realize that often salespeople will tell us only what will make us want to buy the item. They will not tell what is wrong or whether the item compares unfavorably with a competitor's product.

Although many of us have become wise consumers, few of us have become wise, critical readers. We need to adopt a new motto: Reader beware. You can think of some writers as sellers and their written material as the product to be sold. Just as you would ask questions about a car before buying it, so should you ask questions about what you read before you accept what is said. You should ask questions about who wrote the material and where it came from. You need to decide whether the writer is selling you a one-sided view or an objective, unbiased viewpoint. You should evaluate whether the writer provides sufficient support for his or her ideas to allow you to accept them. This chapter will discuss these critical questions and show you how to apply them to articles and essays.

WHAT IS THE SOURCE OF THE MATERIAL?

Just as you might check the brand label on an item of clothing before you buy it, so should you check to see where an article or essay comes from before you read it. You will often be asked to read material that is not in its original form. Many textbooks, such as this one, include excerpts or entire selections borrowed from other authors. Instructors often photocopy articles or essays and distribute them or place them on reserve in the library for students to read.

A first question to ask before you even begin to read is: What is the source—from what book, magazine, or newspaper was this taken? Knowledge of the source will help you judge the accuracy and soundness of what you read. For example, in which of the following sources would you expect to find the most-accurate and up-to-date information about computer software?

- An advertisement in *Time*

- An article in *Reader's Digest*

- An article in *Software Review*

The article in *Software Review* would be the best source. This is a magazine devoted to the subject of computers and computer software. *Reader's Digest*, on the other hand, does not specialize in any one topic and often reprints or condenses articles from other sources. *Time*, a weekly newsmagazine, does contain information, but a paid advertisement is likely to provide information on only one line of software.

Knowing the source of an article will give clues to the kind of information the article will contain. For instance, suppose you went to the library to locate information for a research paper on the interpretation of dreams. You found the following sources of information. What do you expect each to contain?

- An encyclopedia-entry titled "Dreams"

- An article in *Woman's Day* titled "A Dreamy Way to Predict the Future"

- An article in *Psychological Review* titled "An Examination of Research on Dreams"

You can predict that the encyclopedia entry will be a factual report. It will provide a general overview of the process of dreaming. The *Woman's Day* article will probably focus on the use of dreams to predict future events. You can expect the article to contain little research. Most likely, it will be concerned largely with individual reports of people who accurately dreamt about the future. The article from *Psychological Review*, a journal that reports research in psychology, will present a primarily factual, research-oriented discussion of dreams.

EXERCISE 14-1

Directions: *For each set of sources listed below, place a checkmark next to the one that would be most useful for finding information on the stated topic. Then, in the space provided, give a reason for your choice.*

1. Topic: gas mileage of American-made cars

   Sources: _____ a. A newspaper article titled "Gas-Eating American Cars"

   _____ b. An encyclopedia article on "Gas Consumption of Automobile Engines"

   _____ c. A research report in *Car and Driver* magazine on American car performance

   Reason:_____

2. Topic: viruses as a cause of cancer

   Sources: _____ a. A textbook titled *Well-Being: An Introduction to Health*

   _____ b. An article in *Scientific American* magazine on controlling viruses

   _____ c. An issue of the *Journal of the American Medical Association* devoted to a review of current research findings on the causes of cancer

   Reason:_____

3. Topic: the effects of aging on learning and memory

   Sources: _____ a. An article in *Reader's Digest* titled "Older Means Better"

   _____ b. A psychology textbook titled *A General Introduction to Psychology*

   _____ c. A textbook titled *Adult Development and Aging*

   Reason:_____

WHAT IS THE AUTHORITY OF THE AUTHOR?

The qualifications of the author to write about the subject is another clue to the reliability of the information. If the author lacks expertise in or experience with a subject, the material may not be accurate or worthwhile reading.

In textbooks, the author's credentials may appear on the title page or in the preface. In nonfiction books and general market paperbacks, a summary of the author's life and credentials may be included on the book jacket or back cover. In many other cases, however, the author's credentials are not given. You are left to rely on the judgment of the editors or publishers about an author's authority.

If you are familiar with an author, then you can anticipate the type of material you will be reading and predict the writer's approach to and attitude toward the subject. If, for example, you have found an article on world banking written by former President Carter, you could predict it will have a political point of view. If you were about to read an article on John Lennon written by Ringo Starr, one of the other Beatles, you could predict the article might possibly include details of their working relationship from Ringo's point of view.

EXERCISE 14-2

Directions: *Read each statement and place a checkmark next to the individual who would seem to be the best authority on the subject.*

1. *General Hospital* is one of the best soap operas on TV.

    _____ Rick Levine, the new producer of *General Hospital*

    _____ Sally Jennings, a soap opera fan for fifteen years

    _____ Frances Hailey, a TV critic for the *New York Times*

2. The president's recent news conference was a success.

    _____ Peter Webb, a well-known NBC news commentator

    _____ Janet Ferrick, one of the president's advisors

    _____ Howard Summers, a professor of economics

3. Kurt Vonnegut is one of the most important modern American novelists.

    _____ James Toth, producer of a TV documentary on Vonnegut's life

    _____ John Vilardo, a *Time* magazine column writer

————Cynthia Weinstein, a professor of twentieth-century literature at Georgetown University

DOES THE WRITER MAKE ASSUMPTIONS?

An assumption is an idea, theory, or principle that the writer believes
to be true. The writer then develops his or her ideas based on that assumption. Of course, if the assumption is not true or is one you disagree with,
then the ideas that depend on that assumption are of questionable value.
For instance, an author may believe that the death penalty is immoral and,
beginning with that assumption, develop an argument for different ways to
prevent crime. However, if you believe that the death penalty is moral,
then from your viewpoint, the writer's argument is invalid.

Read the following paragraph. Identify the assumption the writer
makes, and write it in the space provided.

> The evil of athletic violence touches nearly everyone. It tar-
> nishes what may be our only religion. Brutality in games blasphemes
> play, perhaps our purest form of free expression. It blurs the clarity of
> open competition, obscuring our joy in victory as well as our dignity
> in defeat. It robs us of innocence, surprise, and self-respect. It spoils
> our fun.[1]

Assumption:_____

Here the assumption is stated in the first sentence—the writer assumes that athletic violence exists. He makes no attempt to prove or explain that sports are violent. He assumes this and goes on to discuss its effects. You may agree or disagree with this assumption.

EXERCISE 14-3

Directions: *For each of the following paragraphs, identify the assumption
that is made by the writer and write it in the space provided.*

1. Do you have any effective techniques that you use regularly to reduce
   your level of stress? If not, you may be among the many people who in-
   tellectually recognize the dangers of chronic stress—perhaps even have
   benefited from relaxation exercises—but somehow haven't made stress
   reduction part of their daily schedule. And you may be especially fas-
   cinated by a unique six-second exercise conceived and developed by
   Charles F. Stroebel, M.D., Ph.D., director of research at The Institute of
   Living in Hartford, Connecticut, and professor of psychiatry at the University of Connecticut Medical School.[2]

   Assumption:_____

2. Although fear of math is not a purely female phenomenon, girls tend to drop out of math sooner than boys, and adult women experience an aversion to math and math-related activities that is akin to anxiety. A 1972 survey of the amount of high school mathematics taken by incoming freshmen at Berkeley revealed that while 57 percent of the boys had taken four years of high school math, only 8 percent of the girls had had the same amount of preparation. Without four years of high school math, students at Berkeley, and at most other colleges and universities, are ineligible for the calculus sequence, unlikely to attempt chemistry or physics, and inadequately prepared for statistics and economics.[3]

Assumption:_____

IS THE AUTHOR BIASED?

As you evaluate any piece of writing, always try to decide whether the author is objective or one-sided (biased). Does the author present an objective view of the subject or is a particular viewpoint favored? An objective article presents both sides of an issue, while a biased one presents only one side.

You can decide whether a writer is biased by asking yourself these questions: Is the writer acting as a reporter, presenting facts, or as a salesperson, providing only favorable information? Are there other views toward the subject that the writer does not discuss?

Use these questions to determine whether the author of the following selection is biased:

Teachers, schools, and parent associations have become increasingly concerned about the effects of television on school performance. Based on their classroom experiences, many teachers have reported mounting incidences of fatigue, tension, and aggressive behavior, as well as lessened spontaneity and imagination.

So what have schools been doing? At Kimberton Farms School in Phoenixville, Pennsylvania, parents and teachers have been following written guidelines for five years which include no television *at all* for children through the first grade. Children in second grade through high school are encouraged to watch no television on school nights and to restrict viewing to a total of three to four hours on weekends. According to Harry Blanchard, head of the faculty, "You can observe the effects with some youngsters almost immediately. . . . Three days after they turn off the set you see a marked improvement in their behavior. They concentrate better, and are more able to follow directions and get along with their neighbors. If they go back to the set you notice it right away."

As Fiske has pointed out, "In the final analysis, the success of schools in minimizing the negative effects of television on their (children's) academic progress depends almost entirely on whether the parents share this goal."[4]

The subject of this passage is children's television viewing. It expresses concern and gives evidence that television has a negative effect on children. The other side of the issue—the positive effects or benefits—is not mentioned. There is no discussion of such positive effects as the information to be learned from educational television programs or the use of television in increasing a child's awareness of different ideas, people, and places. The author is biased and expresses only a negative attitude toward television.

IS THE WRITING SLANTED?

Slanting means the selection of details that suit the author's purpose and the omission of those that do not. Suppose you were asked to write a description of a person you know. If you wanted a reader to respond favorably to the person, you might write something like this:

> Alex is tall, muscular, and well built. He is a friendly person and seldom becomes angry or upset. He enjoys sharing jokes and stories with his friends.

On the other hand, if you wanted to create a less-positive image of Alex, you could omit the above information and emphasize these facts instead:

> Alex has a long nose and his teeth are crooked. He talks about himself a lot and doesn't seem to listen to what others are saying. Alex wears rumpled clothes that are too big for him.

While all of these facts about Alex may be true, the writer decides which to include.

Much of what you read is slanted. For instance, advertisers tell only what is good about a product, not what is wrong with it. In the newspaper advice column, Dear Abby gives her opinion on how to solve a reader's problem, but she does not discuss all the possible solutions.

As you read material that is slanted, keep these questions in mind:

1. What types of facts has the author omitted?

2. How would the inclusion of these facts change your reaction or impression?

EXERCISE 14-4

Directions: *Below is a list of different types of writing. For each item, decide whether it has little slant (L), is moderately slanted (M), or is very slanted (V). Write L, M, or V in the space provided.*

_____ 1. Help-wanted ads

_____ 2. An encyclopedia entry

_____ 3. A newspaper editorial

_____ 4. A biology textbook

_____ 5. A letter inviting you to apply for a charge account

_____ 6. A college catalog

_____ 7. An autobiography of a famous person

_____ 8. An insurance policy

_____ 9. *Time* magazine

_____10. *Catholic Digest*

HOW DOES THE WRITER SUPPORT HIS OR HER IDEAS?

Suppose a friend said he thought you should quit your part-time job immediately. What would you do? Would you automatically accept his advice, or would you ask him why? No doubt you would not blindly accept the advice but would ask why. Then, once you heard his reasons, you would decide whether they made sense.

Similarly, when you read, you should not blindly accept a writer's ideas. Instead, you should ask why by checking to see how the writer supports or explains his or her ideas. Then, once you have examined the supporting information, decide whether it is sufficient to accept the idea.

Evaluating the supporting evidence a writer provides involves using your own judgment. The evidence you accept as sufficient may be regarded by someone else as insufficient. The judgment you make depends on your purpose and background knowledge, among other things.

In judging the quality of supporting information a writer provides, you should watch for the use of (1) generalizations, (2) personal experience, and (3) statistics as evidence.

Generalizations

What do the following statements have in common?

Dogs are vicious and nasty.

College students are more interested in having fun than in learning.

Parents want their children to grow up to be just like them.

These sentences seem to have little in common. But although the subjects are different, the sentences do have one thing in common: each is a generalization. Each makes a broad statement about some group (college students, dogs, parents). The first statement says that dogs are vicious and nasty. Yet the writer could not be certain that this statement is true unless he or she had seen every existing dog. No doubt the writer felt this statement was true based on his or her observation of and experience with dogs.

A generalization is a statement that is made about an entire group or class of individuals or items based on experience with some members of that group. It necessarily involves the writer's judgment.

The question that must be asked about all generalizations is whether they are accurate. How many dogs did the writer observe and how much research did he or she do to justify the generalization? Try to think of exceptions to the generalization. Perhaps, for instance, you know of or own a dog that is neither vicious nor nasty.

As you evaluate the supporting evidence a writer uses, be alert for generalizations that are presented as facts. A writer may, on occasion, support a statement by offering unsupported generalizations. When this occurs, treat the writer's ideas with a critical, questioning attitude.

EXERCISE 14-5

Directions: *Read each of the following statements and decide whether it is a generalization. Place a checkmark next to the statements that are generalizations.*

_____1. My sister wants to attend the University of Chicago.

_____2. Most engaged couples regard their wedding as one of the most important occasions in their lives.

_____3. Senior citizens are a cynical and self-interested group.

_____4. People do not use drugs unless they perceive them to be beneficial.

_____5. Warning signals of a heart attack include pain or pressure in the left side of the chest.

EXERCISE 14-6

Directions: *Read the following paragraphs and underline each generalization.*

1. Teenagers need privacy; it allows them to have a life of their own. By providing privacy, we demonstrate respect. We help them disengage themselves from us and grow up. Some parents pry too much. They read their teenagers' mail and listen in on their telephone calls. Such violations may cause permanent resentment. Teenagers feel cheated and enraged. In their eyes, invasion of privacy is a dishonorable offense. As

one girl said: "I am going to sue my mother for malpractice of parent-hood. She unlocked my desk and read my diary."[5]

2. Farmers are interested in science, in modern methods, and in theory, but they are not easily thrown off balance and they maintain a healthy suspicion of book learning and of the shenanigans of biologists, chemists, geneticists, and other late-rising students of farm practice and management. They are, I think, impressed by education, but they have seen too many examples of the helplessness and the impracticality of educated persons to be either envious or easily budged from their position.[6]

3. Although the most commonplace reason women marry young is to "complete" themselves, a good many spirited young women gave another reason: "I did it to get away from my parents." Particularly for girls whose educations and privileges are limited, a *jailbreak marriage* is the usual thing. What might appear to be an act of rebellion usually turns out to be a transfer of dependence.[7]

Personal Experience

Writers often support their ideas by describing their own personal experiences. Although a writer's experiences may be interesting and reveal a perspective on an issue, do not accept them as proof. Suppose you are reading an article on drug use and the writer uses his or her personal experience with particular drugs to prove a point. There are several reasons why you should not accept the writer's conclusions about the drugs' effects as fact. First, the effects of a drug may vary from person to person. The drug's effect on the writer may be unusual. Second, unless the writer kept careful records about times, dosages, surrounding circumstances, and so on, he or she is describing events from memory. Over time, the writer may have forgotten or exaggerated some of the effects. As you read, treat ideas supported only through personal experience as *one person's experience.* Do not make the error of generalizing the experience.

Statistics

People are often impressed by statistics—figures, percentages, averages, and so forth. They accept these as absolute proof. Actually, statistics can be misused, misinterpreted, or used selectively to give other than the most objective, accurate picture of a situation.

Here is an example of how statistics can be misused. Suppose you read that magazine X increased its readership by 50 percent, while magazine Y had only a 10-percent increase. From this statistic, some readers might assume that magazine X has a wider readership than magazine Y. The missing but crucial statistic is the total readership of each magazine prior to the increase. If magazine X had a readership of 20,000 and this increased by 50 percent, its readership would total 30,000. If magazine Y's readership was already 50,000, a 10-percent increase, bringing the new total to 55,000, would still give it the larger readership despite the fact of the smaller increase. Even statistics, then, must be read with a critical, questioning mind.

Here is another example:

Americans in the work force are better off than ever before. The average salary of the American worker is $23,000.

At first, the above statement may seem convincing. However, a closer look reveals that the statistic given does not really support the statement. The term *average* is the key to how the statistic is misused. An average includes all salaries, both high and low. It is possible that some Americans earn $4,000 while others earn $250,000. Although the average salary may be $23,000, this does not mean that everyone earns $23,000.

EXERCISE 14-7

Directions: *Read each of the following statements and decide how the statistic is misused. Write your explanation in the space provided.*

1. Classrooms on our campus are not overcrowded. There are ten square feet of floor space for every student, faculty member, and staff member on campus.

   _____

   _____

2. More than 12,000 people have bought Dodge Dusters this year, so it is a popular car.

   _____

   _____

3. The average water pollution by our local industries is well below the hazardous level established by the Environmental Protection Agency.

   _____

   _____

DOES THE WRITER MAKE VALUE JUDGMENTS?

A writer who states that an idea or action is right or wrong, good or bad, desirable or undesirable is making a value judgment. That is, the writer is imposing his or her own judgment on the worth of an idea or action. Here are a few examples of value judgments:

Divorces should be restricted to couples who can prove incompatibility.

Abortion is wrong.

Welfare applicants should be forced to apply for any job they are capable of performing.

Premarital sex is acceptable.

You will notice that each statement is controversial. Each involves some type of conflict or idea over which there is disagreement:

1. Restriction versus freedom

2. Right versus wrong

3. Force versus choice

4. Acceptability versus nonacceptability

You may know of some people who would agree and others who might disagree with each statement. When a writer takes a position or side on a conflict, he or she is making a value judgment.

As you read, be alert for value judgments. They represent one person's view only and there are most likely many other views on the same topic. When you identify a value judgment, look behind it, so to speak, to determine whether the author offers any evidence in support of the position.

EXERCISE 14-8

Directions: *Read the following selection and answer the questions that follow.*

A WELFARE MOTHER

I start my day here at five o'clock. I get up and prepare all the children's clothes. If there's shoes to shine, I do it in the morning. About seven o'clock I bathe the children. I leave the baby with the baby sitter and I go to work at the settlement house. I work until twelve o'clock. Sometimes I'll work longer if I have to go to welfare and get a check for somebody. When I get back, I try to make hot food for the kids to eat. In the afternoon it's pretty well on my own. I scrub and clean and cook and do whatever I have to do. 1

Welfare makes you feel like you're nothing. Like you're laying back and not doing anything and it's falling in your lap. But you must understand, mothers, too, work. My house is clean. I've been scrub- 2 bing since this morning. You could check my clothes, all washed and ironed. I'm home and I'm working. I am a working mother.

A job that a woman in a house is doing is a tedious job— 3 especially if you want to do it right. If you do it slipshod, then it's not so bad. I'm pretty much of a perfectionist. I tell my kids, hang a towel. I don't want it thrown away. That is very hard. It's a constant game of picking up this, picking up that. And putting this away, so the house'll be clean.

Some men work eight hours a day. There are mothers that work 4 eleven, twelve hours a day. We get up at night, a baby vomits, you have to be calling the doctor, you have to be changing the baby. When do you get a break, really? You don't. This is an all-around job, day and night. Why do they say it's charity? We're working for our money. I am working for this check. It is not charity. We are giving some kind of home to these children.

I'm so busy all day I don't have time to daydream. I pray a lot. I 5 pray to God to give me strength. If He should take a child away from me, to have the strength to accept it. It's His kid. He just borrowed him to me.

I used to get in and close the door. Now I speak up for my right. I 6 walk with my head up. If I want to wear big earrings, I do. If I'm over-weight, that's too bad. I've gotten completely over feeling where I'm little. I'm working now, I'm pulling my weight. I'm gonna get off wel-fare in time, that's my goal—get off.

It's living off welfare and feeling that you're taking something 7 for nothing the way people have said. You get to think maybe you are. You get to think, Why am I so stupid? Why can't I work? Why do I have to live this way? It's not enough to live on anyway. You feel degraded.

The other day I was at the hospital and I went to pay my bill. 8 This nurse came and gave me the green card. Green card is for wel-fare. She went right in front of me and gave it to the cashier. She said, "I wish I could stay home and let the money fall in my lap." I felt rot-ten. I was just burning inside. You hear this all the way around you. The doctor doesn't even look at you. People are ashamed to show that green card. Why can't a woman just get a check in the mail: Here, this check is for you. Forget welfare. You're a mother who works.

This nurse, to her way of thinking, she represents the working 9 people. The ones with the green card, we represent the lazy no-goods. This is what she was saying. They're the good ones and we're the bad guys.

1. What do you think is the source of this selection?

_____

2. Do you consider this welfare mother to be an authority? Why or why not?

   _____

   _____

3. What assumptions does this welfare mother make? Do you agree or disagree? Why?

   _____

   _____

   _____

4. Do you think this view of a welfare mother is biased? Why or why not?

   _____

   _____

5. Is the writing in this article slanted? If so, give some examples.

   _____

   _____

6. How does this welfare mother support her ideas?

   _____

   _____

7. Does this welfare mother make any value judgments? If so, what are they?

   _____

   _____

8. Does this welfare mother make any generalizations? If so, underline them.

SUMMARY

Evaluating the accuracy and worth of an article or essay is an important part of reading critically. This chapter discussed seven questions that will help you evaluate what you read:

1. What is the source of the material?

2. What is the authority of the author?

3. Does the writer make assumptions?

4. Is the author biased?

5. Is the writing slanted?

6. How does the writer support his or her ideas?

7. Does the writer make value judgments?

PART FIVE REVIEW

MAKING YOUR SKILLS WORK TOGETHER

A GUIDE TO EFFECTIVE READING

Now that you have completed Part Five of this book, it is time to take all the skills you have learned and see how they fit together.

At first we were concerned with understanding the writer's basic messages expressed through words, sentences, and paragraphs (Parts One, Two, and Three). Then we moved to longer materials—articles, essays, and textbook chapters (Part Four). There, focus was on the structure of these materials and how to organize and remember the information they contain. Finally, in Part Five we were concerned with interpreting and evaluating these materials.

You have learned many new skills. Basically, these skills can be grouped into three levels or types of comprehension. Keep these levels in mind as you read. They will serve as a guide to help you read more effectively.

1. LITERAL LEVEL At this level, you are concerned with understanding the writer's basic message. You are reading to find out what the writer *said*. Here you use your basic vocabulary, sentence, and paragraph structure skills.

2. INTERPRETIVE LEVEL This second level assumes you understood the basic literal content—"Who did what, when, and

where?" Here you think and reason about what you are reading. You are concerned with what the writer *means*. You look for indirect or unstated meanings. You try to see how the writer has organized his or her ideas. You are also looking for *why* the writer wrote (author's purpose) and *how* the purpose was achieved.

3. EVALUATIVE LEVEL   At this level you examine the author's ideas, organization, and approach. Your purpose is to judge the worth, use, and value of what you are reading. Here you ask critical questions.

EXERCISE 1

Directions: *Read the following selection and answer the questions that follow.*

THE COMPANY MAN

—*Ellen Goodman*

He worked himself to death, finally and precisely, at 3:00 A.M. Sunday morning.   1

The obituary didn't say that, of course. It said that he died of a   2 coronary thrombosis—I think that was it—but everyone among his friends and acquaintances knew it instantly. He was a perfect Type A, a workaholic, a classic, they said to each other and shook their heads—and thought for five or ten minutes about the way they lived.

This man who worked himself to death finally and precisely at   3 3:00 A.M. Sunday morning—on his day off—was fifty-one years old and a vice-president. He was, however, one of six vice-presidents, and one of three who might conceivably—if the president died or retired soon enough—have moved to the top spot. Phil knew that.

He worked six days a week, five of them until eight or nine at   4 night, during a time when his own company had begun the four-day week for everyone but the executives. He worked like the Important People. He had no outside "extracurricular interests," unless, of course, you think about a monthly golf game that way. To Phil, it was work. He always ate egg salad sandwiches at his desk. He was, of course, overweight, by 20 or 25 pounds. He thought it was okay, though, because he didn't smoke.

On Saturdays, Phil wore a sports jacket to the office instead of a   5 suit, because it was the weekend.

He had a lot of people working for him, maybe sixty, and most of   6 them liked him most of the time. Three of them will be seriously considered for his job. The obituary didn't mention that.

But it did list his "survivors" quite accurately. He is survived by   7
his wife, Helen, forty-eight years old, a good woman of no particular marketable skills, who worked in an office before marrying and mothering. She had, according to her daughter, given up trying to compete with his work years ago, when the children were small. A company friend said, "I know how much you will miss him." And she answered, "I already have."

"Missing him all these years," she must have given up part of   8
herself which had cared too much for the man. She would be "well taken care of."

His "dearly beloved" eldest of the "dearly beloved" children is a   9
hard-working executive in a manufacturing firm down South. In the day and a half before the funeral, he went around the neighborhood researching his father, asking the neighbors what he was like. They were embarrassed.

His second child is a girl, who is twenty-four and newly married.   10
She lives near her mother and they are close, but whenever she was alone with her father, in a car driving somewhere, they had nothing to say to each other.

The youngest is twenty, a boy, a high-school graduate who has   11
spent the last couple of years, like a lot of his friends, doing enough odd jobs to stay in grass and food. He was the one who tried to grab at his father, and tried to mean enough to him to keep the man at home. He was his father's favorite. Over the last two years, Phil stayed up nights worrying about the boy.

The boy once said, "My father and I only board here."   12

At the funeral, the sixty-year-old company president told the   13
forty-eight-year-old widow that the fifty-one-year-old deceased had meant much to the company and would be missed and would be hard to replace. The widow didn't look him in the eye. She was afraid he would read her bitterness and, after all, she would need him to straighten out the finances—the stock options and all that.

Phil was overweight and nervous and worked too hard. If he   14
wasn't at the office, he was worried about it. Phil was a Type A, a heart-attack natural. You could have picked him out in a minute from a lineup.

So when he finally worked himself to death, at precisely 3:00   15
A.M. Sunday morning, no one was really surprised.

By 5:00 P.M. the afternoon of the funeral, the company president   16
had begun, discreetly of course, with care and taste, to make inquiries about his replacement. One of three men. He asked around: "Who's been working the hardest?"

1. Summarize the basic literal content of this selection by describing who it is about, what happened, and so forth.

   _____

   _____

   _____

2. Go beyond what Goodman says and think about what she means. What real message is the writer trying to express? Here are a few questions to lead you in the right direction. Answer these first.

   a. Why does Goodman wait until the third paragraph to tell us Phil's name?

   _____

   _____

   b. Why are we not told Phil's last name?

   _____

   _____

   c. Why does Goodman tell us what the obituary did *not* include?

   _____

   _____

   d. Why does Goodman keep repeating "3:00 A.M. Sunday morning"?

   _____

   _____

   e. Describe Phil's relationships with his wife and each of his children.

   _____

   _____

   _____

   f. Why are ages emphasized throughout the article?

   _____

   _____

3. To evaluate and react to this article, answer the following questions:

   a. How does the writer explain and support her ideas?

   _____

   _____

b. Is Goodman's article biased?

_____

c. Explain whether this article is a meaningful comment on your life or that of someone you know.

_____

_____

_____

PART SIX

READING SELECTIONS

Practice is an important part of most types of learning: training for a sport, learning to type, cook, change a tire, or solve a math problem. The same is true of reading: *practice is important*. To read well, you must apply and practice the skills you have learned. You must try out these skills on a variety of types of reading materials.

The purpose of Part Six is to give you practice in applying the reading skills presented in Parts One through Five. Each selection gives you the opportunity to use your skills in a slightly different way on a new topic written by a different author. A set of exercises accompanies each selection. These exercises are organized in the same way. Each set has seven parts. The following is a brief introduction to each of these parts and provides some advice on how to use them to learn as much as possible.

- INTRODUCTION Each selection begins with a brief introduction. This acquaints you with the topic of the selection and provides any background information you may need to know before you read the selection.

- VOCABULARY PREVIEW Each selection contains some difficult words or phrases. This section lists some of these and gives a brief definition of each as it is used in the selection. (Words may have other meanings that are not listed.) Before you read the selection, be sure to go through this word list, noticing words you do not know and studying their meanings. Later, as you read the selection, refer back to this list to check meanings as you need them. The paragraph in which the word appears is given in parentheses following the word.

- PREREADING   Prereading (see Chapter 4) is a way of getting ready to read. This portion of the exercise directs you to preview the selection and then ask questions that are intended to focus your attention on the article and help you discover what you already know about the subject.

- CHECKING YOUR COMPREHENSION   This exercise gives you a chance to see whether you have understood what you have read. You will notice that the type of question differs for each selection. Some are true-false questions; others may ask you to write an outline or summary. Regardless of the type, each question checks your ability to understand the writer's basic message. Specifically, the questions in this section test your ability to apply the skills taught in Chapters 4–11. Often, in order to answer the question or complete the directed activity, you will apply several of the skills contained in these chapters.

- CRITICAL READING AND THINKING   In this exercise you are asked to interpret and react to the author's ideas. You will find a variety of questions that give you the opportunity to apply the skills taught in Part Five. Each of these questions is open ended and requires an explanation. Always answer in complete sentences. That way, you will be certain you have expressed a complete idea in a clear, understandable form.

- WORDS IN CONTEXT   Although each selection has difficult words, you can figure some of them out using context clues (see Chapter 1). This exercise contains a list of words (along with the paragraph number in which they appear). You are asked to write a brief definition of each word. To do this, go back to the paragraph in which the word is used and reread, looking for meaning clues.

- VOCABULARY REVIEW   This exercise gives you practice with all or most of the words contained in the Vocabulary Preview section. It is an opportunity to work with these words in contexts other than those used in the selection.

SELECTION 1

A GUARD'S FIRST NIGHT ON THE JOB

William Recktenwald

A prison is a separate society with its own set of rules and behaviors. This selection describes one evening in a prison from the viewpoint of a new guard.

VOCABULARY PREVIEW

rookie (par. 1) beginner or novice

cursory (par. 4) hastily done with little attention to detail

tiers (par. 5) groups of cells, rooms, or items arranged above or behind each other

apprehensive (par. 16) worried, anxious, or concerned

ruckus (par. 17) noisy confusion or disturbance

mace (par. 22) chemical with the combined effect of tear gas and nerve gas used to stun its victims

equivalent (par. 25) equal to

PREREADING

Directions: *Preview the selection and answer the following questions.*

What fears and feelings would you have if you were just hired as a prison guard? What problems would you expect to face?

_____

_____

. . . When I arrived for my first shift, 3 to 11 p.m., I had not had a   1
minute of training except for a one-hour orientation lecture the previous
day. I was a "fish," a rookie guard, and very much out of my depth.

A veteran officer welcomed the "fish" and told us: "Remember, these   2
guys don't have anything to do all day, 24 hours a day, but think of ways
to make you mad. No matter what happens, don't lose your cool. Don't
lose your cool!"

I had been assigned to the segregation unit, containing 215 inmates   3
who are the most trouble. It was an assignment nobody wanted.

To get there, I passed through seven sets of bars. My uniform was my   4
only ticket through each of them. Even on my first day, I was not asked for
any identification, searched, or sent through a metal detector. I could have
been carrying weapons, drugs, or any other contraband. I couldn't believe
this was what's meant by a maximum-security institution. In the week I
worked at Pontiac, I was subjected to only one check, and that one was
cursory.

The segregation unit consists of five tiers, or galleries. Each is about   5
300 feet long and has 44 cells. The walkways are about 3½ feet wide, with
the cells on one side and a rail and cyclone fencing on the other. As I
walked along one gallery, I noticed that my elbows could touch cell bars
and fencing at the same time. That made me easy pickings for anybody
reaching out of a cell.

The first thing (they) told me was that a guard must never go out on a   6
gallery by himself. You've got no weapons with which to defend yourself,
not even a radio to summon help. All you've got is the man with whom
you're working.

My partner that first night was Bill Hill, a soft-spoken six-year   7
veteran who immediately told me to take the cigarettes out of my shirt
pocket because the inmates would steal them. Same for my pen, he said
—or "They'll grab it and stab you."

We were told to serve dinner on the third tier, and Hill quickly tried   8
to fill me in on the facts of prison life. That's when I learned about cookies
and the importance they have to the inmates.

"They're going to try and grab them, they're going to try to steal them   9
any way they can," he said. "Remember, you only have enough cookies for
the gallery, and if you let them get away, you'll have to explain to the guys
at the end why there weren't any for them."

Hill then checked out the meal, groaning when he saw the drippy rav-   10
ioli and stewed tomatoes. "We're going to be wearing this," he remarked,
before deciding to simply discard the tomatoes. We served nothing to
drink. In my first six days at Pontiac, I never saw an inmate served a
beverage.

Hill instructed me to put on plastic gloves before we served the meal.   11
In view of the trash and waste through which we'd be wheeling the food
cart, I thought he was joking. He wasn't.

"Some inmates don't like white hands touching their food," he   12
explained.

Everything went routinely as we served the first 20 cells, and I wasn't   13
surprised when every inmate asked for extra cookies.

Suddenly, a huge arm shot through the bars of one cell and began   14
swinging a metal rod at Hill. As he ducked away, the inmate snared the
cookie box.

From the other side of the cart, I lunged to grab the cookies—and was   15
grabbed in turn. A powerful hand from the cell behind me was pulling
my arm. As I jerked away, objects began crashing about, and a metal can
struck me in the back.

Until that moment I had been apprehensive. Now I was scared. The   16
food cart virtually trapped me, blocking my retreat.

Whirling around, I noticed that mirrors were being held out of every   17
cell so the inmates could watch the ruckus. I didn't realize the mirrors
were plastic and became terrified that the inmates would start smashing
them to cut me up.

The ordinary din of the cell house had turned into a deafening roar.   18
For the length of the tier, arms stretched into the walkway, making grabbing motions. Some of the inmates swung brooms about.

"Let's get out of here—now!" Hill barked. Wheeling the food cart be-   19
tween us, we made a hasty retreat.

Downstairs, we reported what had happened. My heart was thump-   20
ing, my legs felt weak. Inside the plastic gloves, my hands were soaked
with sweat. Yet the attack on us wasn't considered unusual by the other
guards, especially in segregation. That was strictly routine, and we didn't
even file a report.

What was more shocking was to be sent immediately back to the   21
same tier to pass out medication. But as I passed the cells from which we'd
been attacked, the men in them simply requested their medicine. It was as
if what had happened minutes before was already ancient history. From
another cell, however, an inmate began raging at us. "Get my medication,"
he said. "Get it now, or I'm going to kill you." I was learning that whatever you're handing out, everybody wants it, and those who don't get it frequently respond by threatening to kill or maim you. Another fact of prison
life.

Passing cell No. 632, I saw that a prisoner I had helped take to the   22
hospital before dinner was back in his cell. When we took him out, he had
been disabled by mace and was very wobbly. Hill and I had been extremely
gentle, handcuffing him carefully, then practically carrying him down the
stairs. As we went by his cell this time, he tossed a cup of liquid on us.

Back downstairs, I learned I would be going back to that tier for a   23
third time, to finish serving dinner. This time, we planned to slip in the
other side of the tier so we wouldn't have to pass the trouble cells. The
plates were already prepared.

"Just get in there and give them their food and get out," Hill said. I   24
could see he was nervous, which made me even more so. "Don't stop for
anything. If you get hit, just back off, 'cause if they snare you or hook you
some way and get you against the bars, they'll hurt you real bad."

Everything went smoothly. Inmates in the three most troublesome   25
cells were not getting dinner, so they hurled some garbage at us. But that's
something else I had learned: Getting no worse than garbage thrown at you
is the prison equivalent of everything going smoothly.

CHECKING YOUR COMPREHENSION

1. This selection describes the events that occurred during the guard's first
    night on the job. How is this selection organized?

    _____

    _____

2. What main point does the guard make? (Main idea: see Chapter 7)

    _____

    _____

3. Why did the guards wear gloves to serve the food?

    _____

    _____

4. Explain the prisoners' use of mirrors.

    _____

    _____

5. Does the selection end with a summary or a conclusion? (Summaries
    and conclusions: see Chapter 9)

    _____

6. Write a summary of the guard's experiences. (Summaries: see Chapter
    11)

    _____

    _____

    _____

    _____

    _____

CRITICAL READING AND THINKING

1. Using evidence from the selection, show why the guard did not feel prepared to begin his first shift.

   _____

   _____

   _____

2. Do you think the new guard disagreed with how some things are done in a prison? If so, list the things with which the guard seemed dissatisfied.

   _____

   _____

3. Explain the figurative expression "I was a 'fish,' a rookie guard, and very much out of my depth." (Figurative language: see Chapter 12)

   _____

   _____

4. What did you learn from this selection about life as a prisoner?

   _____

   _____

5. Why do you think the prisoner in Cell 632, whom the guards had treated gently on the way to the hospital, threw a cup of liquid at them later in the same evening?

   _____

   _____

6. Why are cookies so important to the prisoners? What might they represent?

   _____

   _____

7. This selection was reprinted in a textbook titled *Introduction to Criminology*. Why do you think the author of the textbook included this selection?

   _____

   _____

   _____

8. Decide whether this selection is a narrative or a descriptive essay. Defend your choice by referring to parts of the selection. (Types of essays: see Chapter 9)

_____

_____

9. Based on his limited experience of one evening, the guard formed some generalizations about the prisoners and prison life. Underline several of these generalizations. (Generalizations: see Chapter 14)

_____

_____

WORDS IN CONTEXT

Directions: *Locate each word in the paragraph indicated and reread that paragraph. Then, based on the way the word is used in the paragraph, write a synonym or brief definition for each.*

1. contraband (par. 4) _____

2. din (par. 18) _____

3. maim (par. 21) _____

VOCABULARY REVIEW

Directions: *Use the words listed in the Vocabulary Preview to complete each of the following sentences.*

1. A beginner on a professional hockey team is called a _____.

2. An instructor who spent little time reading essay exams could be said to have read them in a _____ manner.

3. One kilometer is _____ to .62 miles.

4. The students were _____ about their final grades in chemistry.

5. The class of kindergarten children visiting the zoo created a _____.

6. The police officer used _____ to stop the man who was attacking her.

7. The lobby of the new hotel had several _____.

SELECTION 2

LEISURE WILL KILL YOU
Art Buchwald

Do you have trouble deciding what to do with your leisure time? In this selection, Art Buchwald, a well-known humorist and newspaper columnist, complains about his leisure time.

VOCABULARY PREVIEW

Jacuzzi (par. 15)   hot tub with whirlpool of water

digital (par. 17)   relating to the fingers; done with a finger

encore (par. 22)   additional performance, usually done
upon request

PREREADING

Directions: *Preview the selection and answer the following questions.*

Americans today have more leisure time than previous generations. Why is this so? Do you think leisure time "will kill you", as the title suggests?

_____

_____

This country is producing so much leisure equipment for the home   1
that nobody has any leisure time anymore to enjoy it. A few months ago I
bought a television tape recorder to make copies of programs when I was
out of the house.

Last week I recorded the Nebraska-Oklahoma football game. When I   2
came home in the evening, I decided to play it back. But my son wanted to

311

play "Baseball" on the TV screen with his Atari Computer. We finished four innings when my wife came in the room and asked me if I would like to listen to the Vienna Opera on our hi-fi stereo set. I told her I was waiting to finish the baseball match so I could watch the football game I had recorded.

She said if I watched the football game for three hours, I would miss *Love Boat*. I told her I would record *Love Boat* and we could watch it later in the evening. She protested that *Casablanca* was showing on Channel 5 at 11:30 and she wanted to see it again. 3

"Don't worry," I assured her, "we can watch *Love Boat* late Saturday and *Casablanca* on Sunday morning when we get up." 4

"But if we watch *Casablanca* tomorrow morning when can we see the instant Polaroid movies you took of Ben yesterday afternoon?" 5

"We'll see them after we play backgammon on the new table." 6

"If we do that," my daughter said, "we won't be able to see the Washington Redskins–New York Giants football game." 7

"I'll record the Redskins-Giants football game and we'll watch it while *60 Minutes* is on the air. We can see *60 Minutes* at 11 o'clock." 8

"But," my son said, "you promised to play the pinball machine with me at 11." 9

"Okay, we'll play pinball at 11 and watch *60 Minutes* at midnight." 10

My wife said, "Why don't we listen to the Vienna Opera while we're eating and then we can save an hour to play computer golf?" 11

"That's good thinking," I said. "The only problem is I've rented a TV tape for *Cleopatra* and that runs for three hours." 12

"You could show it on Monday night," she suggested. 13

"I can't do that. I have to return the tape Monday afternoon or be charged for it another week. I have an idea. I won't go to work Monday morning and we'll watch it then." 14

"I was hoping to use our Jacuzzi Monday morning," my wife said. 15

"Okay, then I'll tape *Cleopatra* and you can see it Monday afternoon." 16

"I'm using the set Monday afternoon," my son said, "to play digital hockey on the TV screen." 17

"You can't do that," I said, "I have to watch the *Today* show in the afternoon if I'm going to watch *Cleopatra* in the morning." 18

"Why can't you watch the *Today* show at dinnertime?" my wife asked. 19

"Because the Wolfingtons are coming over to hear me play 'Tea for Two' on the electric organ." 20

"I thought we might play computer bridge at dinner," my wife said. 21

"We'll play it after my encore," I assured her. 22

"Then when will we see *Monday Night Football*?" my son wanted to know. 23

"Tuesday," I said. 24

"Does that mean you're not going to work on Tuesday?" my wife   25
asked.

"How can I go to work," I yelled, "when I've got so much leisure time   26
on my hands?"

CHECKING YOUR COMPREHENSION

Directions: *Buchwald says he has trouble finding enough time to do all the things he would like to do in his leisure time. Make a list of the different leisure-time activities mentioned in the selection.*

_____

_____

_____

_____

CRITICAL READING AND THINKING

1. Underline a sentence in the selection that best shows how the author really feels about leisure time.

2. What type of supporting information does Buchwald use to make his point? (Supporting ideas: see Chapter 13)

_____

_____

3. For what type of audience do you think Buchwald wrote the selection? (Audience: see Chapter 13)

_____

4. Explain why you agree or disagree with Buchwald's ideas about leisure-time equipment.

_____

_____

_____

5. At what point in the selection did you realize that Buchwald was not completely serious about everything he says? What clues did you find?

_____

_____

6. What tone does Buchwald use throughout the selection? (Tone: see Chapter 13)

_____

WORDS IN CONTEXT

Directions: *Locate each word in the paragraph indicated and reread that paragraph. Then, based on the way the word is used in the paragraph, write a synonym or brief definition for each.*

1. protested (par. 3) _____

2. assured (par. 4) _____

3. backgammon (par. 6) _____

VOCABULARY REVIEW

1. Name several situations in which an encore might be requested.

_____

_____

2. When do you think it would be enjoyable or relaxing to use a Jacuzzi?

_____

3. The article mentions digital hockey. What are some other types of digital games?

_____

_____

SELECTION 3

GREENPEACE AND THE PIRATES
Robert A. Wallace

Greenpeace is a group of volunteers who protect sea animals. Read the article to find out who the pirates are.

VOCABULARY PREVIEW

ethic (par. 1)   moral code, basic philosophy

roving (par. 1)   wandering without specific destination

profiteering (par. 1)   making a profit by charging ridiculously high prices for things that are difficult to obtain

zodiacs (par. 2)   round, balloon-like capsules

soundings (par. 2)   using sonar to detect the presence and location of objects under water

floe (par. 2)   a floating piece of ice

nurslings (par. 3)   young babies still nursing from their mothers

slipway (par. 4)   a platform sloping into the water serving as a landing place for smaller boats

hull (par. 6)   outer frame of a ship

PREREADING

Directions: *Preview the article. Next, write a sentence describing the issues you think the article will be concerned with.*

Greenpeace is an organization dedicated to the preservation of the sea   1
and its great mammals, notably whales, dolphins, and seals. Its ethic is
nonviolent but its aggressiveness in protecting our oceans and the life in
them is becoming legendary. In their roving ship, the *Rainbow Warrior*,
Greenpeace volunteers have relentlessly hounded the profiteering ships of
any nation harming the resources Greenpeace deems to be the property of
the world community. Whales, they believe, belong to us all and have a
right to exist no matter what the demand for shoe-horns, cosmetics, and
machine oil. (In 1985, the *Rainbow Warrior* was sunk in a New Zealand
harbor by French military saboteurs just before it was to sail into the
South Pacific to protest French nuclear testing there, killing one member
of the group.)

Greenpeace volunteers routinely place their lives in danger in many   2
ways, such as by riding along the backs of whales in inflatable zodiacs,
keeping themselves between the animal and the harpoons of ships giving
chase. They have pulled alongside Dutch ships to stop the dumping of dangerous toxins into the sea. They have placed their zodiacs directly in the
paths of ships disrupting delicate breeding grounds of the sea with soundings and have forced some to turn away or even abandon their efforts.
They have confronted hostile sealers on northern ice floes to try to stop
them from bludgeoning the baby seals in the birthing grounds, skinning
them on the spot, and leaving the mother sniffing at the glistening red
corpse of her baby as its skin is stacked aboard the ship on the way to
warm the backs of very fashionable people who gather where the bartender
knows their favorite drink. (The mother seal would be so proud to know
that her dead baby had nearly impressed some bartender.) They have peti-
tioned the International Whaling Commission to establish rules and enact
bans.

But some conservationists feel that peaceful efforts are not enough.   3
Such efforts did not, for example, stop a Japanese whaler called the *Sierra*
(of all things). The *Sierra* sailed for twelve years, subscribing to no code but
that of the merchant. It ruthlessly and efficiently killed every whale it encountered, including threatened species and nurslings. When accused or
formally reprimanded, it simply changed flags and continued the killing.

In 1967, the ship was converted to a processor ship and killer all in   4
one—the world's first factory-catcher. A long rear deck capable of holding
several whales was added with a sloping stern slipway for hauling the
whales aboard. Modifications below deck enabled it to move the tons of
meat that they carved from each whale. New huge freezer compartments
would accommodate the catch.

Renamed the *Run* and registered to the Atlantic Fishing Company   5
in Nassau, Bahamas, the ship set out in 1968 to kill whales along the
coast of southern Africa, an area totally off limits to IWC whaling. In the
next three years, its crew harpooned 1,676 whales, most of them Bryde's
whales, as well as humpbacks and the extremely rare southern right

whale. For the sake of speed and efficiency, they only took about half the meat. When whales became scarce in one area, the ship would move on, often wiping out entire herds as it went.

Conservationists of a different stripe began to track the *Run* using   6
everything from computers to bribery to keep it located. One group, aboard a vessel called the *Sea Shepherd*, apparently had enough of the wrist slapping. They wanted the killing stopped. Period. They encountered the *Run* one July day in 1979 off the coast of Portugal. With engines straining, they rammed the *Run*. It was rather unusual behavior for normally gentle conservationists, but although they failed to sink the killer ship, they had served a clear warning. But the point was not made absolutely clear until later. After the ramming, the *Run* had limped to port, unloaded its catch and then slowly made it back to Japan. Apparently the owners were not yet convinced. The boat was brought to Lisbon Harbor to be reoutfitted and resume its dreadful business. However, something strange happened. One dark night, powerful explosives managed to become attached to its hull and then somehow to become detonated. The *Run* found itself blown to smithereens and smiles found their way to faces around the world.

CHECKING YOUR COMPREHENSION

1. What is the primary purpose of the Greenpeace organization? List the activities the Greenpeace volunteers are trying to prevent.

2. For everything Greenpeace volunteers are trying to prevent, list the method they use.

3. How have Greenpeace volunteers risked their lives?

4. Why do Greenpeace volunteers feel it is important to protect sea animals?

5. What motivates owners of ships to send vessels to sea to kill sea animals?

6. What raw materials are used in the production of shoe-horns, cosmetics, and machine oil?

CRITICAL READING AND THINKING

1. Is the writing slanted for or against Greenpeace? Justify your answer with examples. (Slanted Writing: see Chapter 14)

   _____

2. Write a list of words used in the article that have negative connotations. (Connotations: see Chapter 13)

   _____

3. What action is implied (suggested) but not directly stated in the last paragraph?

   _____

4. Who is the intended audience of this article? (Audience: see Chapter 13)

   _____

5. Do you object to the use of furs in fashion clothing? Justify your response.

   _____

6. How do you think a Greenpeace volunteer would react to trapping mammals to obtain their pelts?

   _____

7. Locate the sentence in which the writer says the opposite of what he really means.

   _____

8. Who are the pirates mentioned in the title of the article?

   _____

WORDS IN CONTEXT

Directions: *Locate each word in the paragraph indicated and reread that paragraph. Then, based on the way the word is used in the paragraph, write a synonym or brief definition for each.*

1. preservation (par. 1)   _____

2. deems (par. 1)   _____

3. saboteurs (par. 1)   _____

  4. toxins (par. 2)   _____

  5. bludgeoning (par. 2)   _____

  6. enact (par. 2)   _____

  7. reprimanded (par. 3)   _____

  8. processor (par. 4)   _____

  9. modifications (par. 4) _____

 10. detonated (par. 6)   _____

VOCABULARY REVIEW

1. How would you describe a *zodiac*?

   _____

2. What would a college course in *ethics* involve?

   _____

3. What is a *hull*?

   _____

4. Describe the activity of a dog that *roves* the neighborhood.

   _____

5. Give an example of *profiteering*.

   _____

6. How would a fisherman be able to use *soundings*?

   _____

7. What is a *floe* made of?

   _____

8. Describe a *nursling* animal.

   _____

9. What is a *slipway* used for?

   _____

SELECTION 4

CHESTER WARD: "THERE WAS SO MUCH DEATH"

Peter Goldman and Tony Fuller

Many Vietnam veterans are still suffering the effects of their wartime experiences. This selection describes the impact of the war on one man's life.

VOCABULARY PREVIEW

aura (par. 1)   quality or feeling

melancholies (par. 1)   states of sadness or depression

mobile (par. 2)   able to move from place to place

bereaved (par. 2)   feeling loss as a result of someone's death

penetrate (par. 3)   enter or force a way into; understand

tantrums (par. 3)   fits of bad temper

intermittent (par. 3)   not happening regularly

sustained (par. 4)   experienced; suffered

PREREADING

Directions: *Preview the selection and answer the following question.*

Do you expect the effects of the war on Chester Ward to be positive or negative? Why?

_____

_____

Chester Ward got out of Vietnam early on a hardship reassignment 1
when his mother died, leaving his father alone in the Long Island resort
town of Southampton with a small taxicab business and eleven other kids
to feed. But it wasn't early enough, Ward's wife, Bertha, thought when she
saw him; it was as if a part of him had been killed in the war. He had gone
off a happy-go-lucky black teenager with a crooked smile, a lady-killing
manner, a passable high-school transcript and a developing gift for basketball. Girls had buzzed around him like bees around honey; he had fathered
three children with his sweetheart at Southampton High and a fourth with
Bertha before he went away to the Army. But he came home silent, sullen
and angry, *as if*, Bertha thought helplessly, *he was under some sort of pressure*. The crooked smile and the sunshine aura were gone, replaced by
quick spasms of temper and long, wordless melancholies afloat on rivers of
Scotch.

Sometimes, in her alarm, his wife wondered if he were taking some 2
sort of drug. He wasn't. The monkey on Chet Ward's back, as it turned
out, was death. He had seen a lot of it in Charlie Company's Vietnam, and
when he got his early out to help his father, the Army, by lot or Kafka-
esque design, had assigned him to its corps of professional mourners—
those mobile honor guards that traveled the country to stand with the colors at the gravesides of the American dead. He felt on those details like an
unwelcome presence, an intruder, though whether it was because he was a
black man, a soldier or a messenger of death was never clear. The bereaved
families never invited him into their homes. At one burial, the mother of a
fallen soldier had turned on Ward beside the open grave and, choked with
grief, had told him, "You should be lying in there, not my son! Why are
you here alive when he is dead?"

Ward came home shaken that day and seemed to slide deeper than 3
ever into his blank, liquid silences. He was drinking hard, at home and in
bars. He was helping out with the cab, but his father worried that his
boozing would offend the high-gloss Hampton summer people who made
up a major portion of their trade in season. His wife could not penetrate
his moods, the long blank passages and the sudden tantrums over nothing.
"I just don't want to talk about it," he would snap when she asked him
about the war. There were only the intermittent signals about what it
seemed to be doing to him inside. "We were over there fighting and dying," he told her once, "but no one knew what they were fighting and dying for." And again: "There was so much death and none of it meant anything."

He hadn't been back very long when he set out from his home one 4
rainy early morning in August 1969 and headed west along the Sunrise
Highway toward his post at Fort Hamilton in Brooklyn. It was 6:00 A.M.
Ward had been drinking as usual the night before, enough perhaps to leave
him heavy-lidded. No one could tell precisely what happened or why; the
police accident report recounted only that Ward's car ran out of control,

jumped the grassy median strip and collided with an oncoming auto in the eastbound lane. The other driver sustained only minor injuries. By the time they got Ward to a hospital in Bay Shore, he was dead.

The honor guard came to *his* funeral, this time. They assured his   5 widow that Ward had soldiered with great distinction in the war and that they would see to it that his medals were sent to her. Before they left, they gave her and her son the flag from Ward's coffin, folded into a crisp triangle. The medals, if they existed at all, never came, and Ward's name was not inscribed on the official roll of the casualties of Vietnam. The sort of bleeding wounds he suffered there were hidden even from his widow's view until the day he died of them.

CHECKING YOUR COMPREHENSION

1. Why was Chet Ward allowed to leave Vietnam early?

2. What job was Chet assigned to do by the Army when he returned to the United States after serving in Vietnam?

3. Describe Chet's personality before he entered the war.

4. Describe the changes that were evident in Chet's personality following his return from Vietnam.

5. What kept bothering Chet after the war was over?

CRITICAL READING AND THINKING

1. What do you think of the mother of the dead soldier who told Chet that he should be in the grave instead of her son? Try to explain her emotions.

2. Do you think the medals existed or not? Explain your reasons.

3. Should Ward's name have been inscribed on the official roll of casualties of Vietnam? Why or why not?

_____

_____

4. From your experience, do you feel Chet's wartime experiences and after-effects were unique or characteristic of many veterans?

_____

_____

5. What do you think the writer means by the last sentence of the selection: "The sort of bleeding wounds he suffered there were hidden even from his widow's view until the day he died of them"?

_____

_____

_____

WORDS IN CONTEXT

Directions: *Locate each word in the paragraph indicated and reread that paragraph. Then, based on the way the word is used in the paragraph, write a synonym or brief definition for each.*

1. sullen (par. 1)   _____

2. spasms (par. 1)   _____

3. intruder (par. 2)   _____

4. median (par. 4)   _____

VOCABULARY REVIEW

Directions: *Complete each of the following statements. Refer to the Vocabulary Preview if necessary.*

1. A tantrum is a _____ .

2. Someone who is melancholy is _____ .

3. A mobile home is one that _____ .

4. A bereaved mother just lost her _____ .

5. If a bomb penetrated a protective wall, what happened? _____

_____ .

6. If intermittent rain and sleet are forecast for tomorrow, you know it will

_____ .

7. If someone sustained serious injuries, what happened? _____

_____ .

8. An aura is a(n) _____ .

SELECTION 5

LIFE IN DEVASTATED AREAS
Barry Popkess

The possibility of nuclear war is one of the most serious threats we face today. This selection is taken from a book titled The Nuclear Survival Handbook, *which describes what life would be like after a nuclear war.*

VOCABULARY PREVIEW

aerial (par. 1)   of, in, or caused by air

orientation (par. 1)   general position or direction

gradient (par. 2)   incline or slope

excavating (par. 4)   making a hole; digging out

stunned (par. 5)   dazed; overcome with surprise or shock

refuse (par. 6)   trash; rubbish

spoor (par. 8)   tracks

PREREADING

Directions: *Preview the selection and answer the following question.*

What problems would survivors of a nuclear war face?

_____

Finding Our Way Around

A look at an aerial photograph of our town, just a mass of roofs and 1
roads from that unfamiliar angle, will suggest how difficult it may be to

pick our way through the rubble when the town hall clock, road intersections, and other landmarks are gone. Canal paths and railway lines, and perhaps sewers, may be the only unblocked routes through heavily damaged areas. Even orientation may present problems.

It need not, though, for few towns are built on entirely flat land. Yet, 2 because buildings hide its shape, we tend not to see a gradient as what it is—a hill: a hill whose height we can gauge from the town hall or other large building—that is, of course, while they are still standing.

But a hill presents different shapes from different directions. No mat- 3 ter how used we may become to seeing one of these, we may not recognize it from another direction. Before we wander from sight of the view we know, therefore, we should note how it lies in relation to other hills, embankments, and other features that seem likely to remain.

The Map

In the shelter there should be maps . . . of our town or area. On these 4 should be marked: our shelter; permanent landmarks; industrial hazards; prevailing winds . . . ; details of the local water table; built-over streams and wells; sand pits; main sewers; pharmacies; food shops and depots; locations of excavating equipment and fuel for it, for clearing debris and for the digging of mass graves; places from which looters may obtain weapons; places where radiation monitoring equipment is available; hospitals; homes and consulting rooms of doctors and vets; homes of district and other nurses, and of the nearest ambulance attendants; and likely strategic targets. . . .

Security

Possibly while still stunned by a situation we had known might come 5 but had not dared picture, the concealing of remaining stocks of food, water, and medical supplies from looters may require attention. In the period between the explosion of a nuclear weapon and arrival of heavy fallout, rubble should have been placed around the shelter, hiding at least its entrance.

The burning of damp wood or other smoke-producing fuels for cook- 6 ing or heating purposes should be avoided. Refuse should be buried. Noise and cooking smells should be minimized.

Bicycles are the best means by which to move about. They are silent, 7 can be carried over rubble, and shorten a journey through an area where there may be long-lived fallout.

When moving about outside the shelter, our routes should vary as we 8 come and go, so as not to leave a clear spoor to it. Walking should be with light steps, without speaking, and without equipment that rattles, and we should stop every few yards to listen.

We should be able to recognize the footsteps of those within our own   9
group, and the way they hold themselves and move so that they may be
known when they are too far away for their faces to be seen. We should get
used—it is not difficult—to "switching off" whatever it is that warns people we are watching them, and ourselves become more sensitive to being
watched by others.

This "sixth sense," of which most of us have never deliberately made   10
use before, may have to serve us as our other senses will; and this is not in
that low gear in which we move about in our usual part-daydream from
which we emerge to speak to others, perform unfamiliar tasks, or watch
something that we like to watch. As we talk with a stranger we will watch
his eyes, and everything else that is in our vision while we are doing so. At
each new sound we will ask ourselves what made it. When we lie down to
sleep, having strewn the ground around us with things that will snap or
rustle if walked on, we will tell that part of us that now wakes us if we
have an early train to catch, that it should do so at the first sound it does
not recognize.

If the wind direction has changed, does it now blow from where we   11
think fallout may have been heavy, perhaps brought down by rain and now
having had time to dry and blow about? Was there, near this cellar, a gas
main that may have fractured, or may we shelter there until the wind
drops? And as we move toward it, we will be judging what our reactions
must be to a threat appearing as we pass that wall or that fence. For these
questions always to be asked in time, we may need to reach and hold ourselves in a state of sensory top gear.

CHECKING YOUR COMPREHENSION

Directions: *Mark each of the following statements* T *for true or* F *for false
based on the content of the selection.*

———— 1. Survivors of a nuclear war are likely to be unable to find
their way around their own town.

———— 2. Burning of garbage is advisable.

———— 3. All mechanical means of transportation should be avoided.

———— 4. The "sixth" sense that may need to be developed is a sense
of caution and self-protection.

———— 5. Travel routes outside the shelter should be changed often
to avoid exposure to particular radioactive areas.

———— 6. A map that includes the locations of the homes of medical
doctors and nurses should be kept in the shelter.

_____ 7. A key part of survival is keeping your shelter secure.

_____ 8. Looting and theft are threats that survivors may have to face.

CRITICAL READING AND THINKING

1. Explain why you think the writer's view of life after a nuclear war is or is not accurate.

   _____

   _____

2. The writer believes that people's attitude toward and treatment of strangers will change after a nuclear war. Give examples from the selection that support this statement.

   _____

   _____

3. The author feels that nuclear war is a real enough possibility that a survival handbook needed to be written and published. Explain why you agree or disagree that nuclear war is a threat.

   _____

   _____

4. What other threats and problems not mentioned by the author do you feel survivors would face?

   _____

   _____

WORDS IN CONTEXT

Directions: *Locate each word in the paragraph indicated and reread that paragraph. Then, based on the way the word is used in the paragraph, write a synonym or brief definition for each.*

1. mass (par. 1)   _____

2. debris (par. 4)   _____

3. concealing (par. 5)   _____

4. emerge (par. 10)   _____

5. strewn (par. 10)   _____

VOCABULARY REVIEW

Directions: *Use the words listed in the Vocabulary Preview to complete each of the following sentences.*

1. Hunters often follow _____ to locate deer.

2. The woman was _____ by the sudden death of her husband.

3. Unless _____ is disposed of properly, it can become a health hazard.

4. The gentle _____ of the land was not immediately noticeable.

5. Earth-moving equipment was used for _____ the ditch for the pipeline.

6. Dizziness can cause people to lose their _____ in familiar places.

7. Planes that fly over Russia have been accused of _____ spying.

SELECTION 6

THAT LEAN AND HUNGRY LOOK
Suzanne Britt Jordan

Do you think heavy people act differently from thin people? The author of this selection says that each has a very different personality. Read the selection to find out how she describes each personality type and decide whether you agree.

VOCABULARY PREVIEW

menacing (par. 1)   threatening; dangerous

condescending (par. 1)   looking down upon; assuming an air of superiority

metabolisms (par. 3)   physical and chemical processes of the human body

inert (par. 3)   inactive; lifeless; slow

surly (par. 4)   bad tempered; rude

wizened (par. 4)   dried up; withered

nebulous (par. 5)   unclear; vague

elusive (par. 8)   hard to grasp; baffling

oppress (par. 10)   overpower; hold down

torsos (par. 10)   trunks of the human body

cerebral machinations (par. 10)   intellectual plots or schemes

loom (par. 10)   appear in a threatening way

convivial (par. 12)   sociable

PREREADING

Directions: *Preview the selection and answer the following question.*

Does a person's personality seem to match his or her physical appearance? Explain your answer using examples.

_____

_____

_____

Caesar was right. Thin people need watching. I've been watching 1
them for most of my adult life, and I don't like what I see. When these narrow fellows spring at me, I quiver to my toes. Thin people come in all personalities, most of them menacing. You've got your "together" thin person, your mechanical thin person, your condescending thin person, your tsk-tsk thin person, your efficiency-expert thin person. All of them are dangerous.

In the first place, thin people aren't fun. They don't know how to goof 2
off, at least in the best, fat sense of the word. They've always got to be adoing. Give them a coffee break, and they'll jog around the block. Supply them with a quiet evening at home, and they'll fix the screen door and lick S&H green stamps. They say things like "there aren't enough hours in the day." Fat people never say that. Fat people think the day is too damn long already.

Thin people make me tired. They've got speedy little metabolisms 3
that cause them to bustle briskly. They're forever rubbing their bony hands together and eyeing new problems to "tackle." I like to surround myself with sluggish, inert, easygoing fat people, the kind who believe that if you clean it up today, it'll just get dirty again tomorrow.

Some people say the business about the jolly fat person is a myth, 4
that all of us chubbies are neurotic, sick, sad people. I disagree. Fat people may not be chortling all day long, but they're a hell of a lot *nicer* than the wizened and shriveled. Thin people turn surly, mean, and hard at a young age because they never learn the value of a hot-fudge sundae for easing tension. Thin people don't like gooey soft things because they themselves are neither gooey nor soft. They are crunchy and dull, like carrots. They go straight to the heart of the matter while fat people let things stay all blurry and hazy and vague, the way things actually are. Thin people want to face the truth. Fat people know there is no truth. One of my thin friends is always staring at complex, unsolvable problems and saying, "The key thing is. . . ." Fat people never say that. They know there isn't any such thing as the key thing about anything.

Thin people believe in logic. Fat people see all sides. The sides fat 5
people see are rounded blobs, usually gray, always nebulous and truly not

worth worrying about. But the thin person persists. "If you consume more calories than you burn," says one of my thin friends, "you will gain weight. It's that simple." Fat people always grin when they hear statements like that. They know better.

Fat people realize that life is illogical and unfair. They know very well 6
that God is not in his heaven and all is not right with the world. If God was up there, fat people could have two doughnuts and a big orange drink anytime they wanted it.

Thin people have a long list of logical things they are always spouting 7
off to me. They hold up one finger at a time as they reel off these things, so I won't lose track. They speak slowly as if to a young child. The list is long and full of holes. It contains tidbits like "get a grip on yourself," "cigarettes kill," "cholesterol clogs," "fit as a fiddle," "ducks in a row," "organize," and "sound fiscal management." Phrases like that.

They think these 2,000-point plans lead to happiness. Fat people 8
know happiness is elusive at best and even if they could get the kind thin people talk about, they wouldn't want it. Wisely, fat people see that such programs are too dull, too hard, too off the mark. They are never better than a whole cheesecake.

Fat people know all about the mystery of life. They are the ones ac- 9
quainted with the night, with luck, with fate, with playing it by ear. One thin person I know once suggested that we arrange all the parts of a jigsaw puzzle into groups according to size, shape, and color. He figured this would cut the time needed to complete the puzzle by at least 50 percent. I said I wouldn't do it. One, I like to muddle through. Two, what good would it do to finish early? Three, the jigsaw puzzle isn't the important thing. The important thing is the fun of four people (one thin person included) sitting around a card table, working a jigsaw puzzle. My thin friend had no use for my list. Instead of joining us, he went outside and mulched the boxwoods. The three remaining fat people finished the puzzle and made chocolate, double-fudged brownies to celebrate.

The main problem with thin people is they oppress. Their good inten- 10
tions, bony torsos, tight ships, neat corners, cerebral machinations, and pat solutions loom like dark clouds over the loose, comfortable, spread-out, soft world of the fat. Long after fat people have removed their coats and shoes and put their feet up on the coffee table, thin people are still sitting on the edge of the sofa, looking neat as a pin, discussing rutabagas. Fat people are heavily into fits of laughter, slapping their thighs and whooping it up, while thin people are still politely waiting for the punch line.

Thin people are downers. They like math and morality and reasoned 11
evaluation of the limitations of human beings. They have their skinny little acts together. They expound, prognose, probe, and prick.

Fat people are convivial. They will like you even if you're irregular 12
and have acne. They will come up with a good reason why you never wrote the great American novel. They will cry in your beer with you. They will put your name in the pot. They will let you off the hook. Fat people

will gab, giggle, guffaw, gallumph, gyrate, and gossip. They are generous, giving, and gallant. They are gluttonous and goodly and great. What you want when you're down is soft and jiggly, not muscled and stable. Fat people know this. Fat people have plenty of room. Fat people will take you in.

CHECKING YOUR COMPREHENSION

Directions: *This selection compares and contrasts thin and fat people on the basis of personality traits. Therefore, an effective way to make notes would be to prepare a study sheet organized like the one below. List as many characteristics of thin people as you can recall from the article. Then list as many characteristics of fat people as you can remember.*

Thin People	*Fat People*
_____	_____
_____	_____
_____	_____
_____	_____
_____	_____

CRITICAL READING AND THINKING

1. Do you think the author is a thin person or a fat person? Why?

   _____

   _____

2. Is this selection biased or slanted? Why do you think so? (Bias: see Chapter 14)

   _____

   _____

3. Why do you think Jordan wrote the selection? (Author's purpose: see Chapter 13)

   _____

   _____

4. Do you think the writer wants you to take the selection seriously? How do you know?

   _____

   _____

5. What reactions does the writer want you to have to the selection? Explain your answer.

_____

_____

_____

6. On a separate sheet, write a paragraph that takes a different view of thin and fat people from Jordan's.

WORDS IN CONTEXT

Directions: *Locate each word in the paragraph indicated and reread that paragraph. Then, based on the way the word is used in the paragraph, write a synonym or brief definition for each.*

1. vague (par. 4)   _____

2. consume (par. 5)   _____

3. spouting (par. 7) _____

4. muddle (par. 9)   _____

VOCABULARY REVIEW

Directions: *Match each word in Column A with its meaning in Column B by writing the letter of the definition next to the number of the word it defines.*

Column A	Column B
_____ 1. condescending	a. dangerous
_____ 2. wizened	b. appear to threaten trouble
_____ 3. loom	c. difficult to grasp
_____ 4. convivial	d. dried up
_____ 5. nebulous	e. inactive
_____ 6. oppress	f. assuming a superior air
_____ 7. surly	g. sociable
_____ 8. metabolisms	h. intellectual schemes
_____ 9. elusive	i. unclear

_____ 10. inert   j. rude

_____ 11. menacing   k. upper parts of human bodies

_____ 12. torsos   l. chemical or physical processes
                                               of the human body

_____ 13. cerebral machinations   m. overpower

SELECTION 7

THE MEANINGS OF THE KISS
Carol Tavris and Leonore Tiefer

This selection traces the history of an important custom—kissing.
Read the selection to find out the basic meanings that a kiss may have.

VOCABULARY PREVIEW

icons (par. 1)   images, figures, or representations of a religious figure

reverence (par. 1)   feeling of respect for something sacred

bawdier (par. 2)   more indecent or obscene

subordinate (par. 4)   inferior; lower in rank or importance

deference (par. 4)   respect or high regard

reconciliation (par. 5)   settlement or resolution of a disagreement

pagan (par. 6)   not religious

adherence (par. 8)   attachment; staying firm in belief or support

solidarity (par. 9)   agreement or unity among a group for a common purpose, interest, or feeling

deceptive (par. 9)   misleading, untrue

PREREADING

Directions: *Preview the selection and then list as many meanings of a*
kiss as you can think of.

_____

_____

Throughout history, people have found occasion to kiss almost every 1
object that didn't fight back, and a few that did. We kiss icons, dice, the Bible and lottery tickets for luck: we kiss the Blarney Stone for the gift of gab; we kiss religious garments in reverence: we kiss to say hello, good-by, get well, get lost.

There have been so many kinds of kisses that from time to time 2
scholars feel obliged to try to sort them into categories. The ancient rabbis divided kisses into three kinds: greeting, farewell and respect. The Romans identified *oscula* (friendly kisses), *basia* (love kisses) and *suavia* (passionate kisses)—it appears that they were somewhat bawdier than the ancient rabbis. The German language had no fewer than 30 types of kisses at the turn of the century, from *Abschiedkuss* (farewell kiss) to *Zuckerkuss* (sweet kiss). They have since lost, unfortunately, *nachküssen*, which in 1901 meant "making up for kisses that have been omitted."

However many types of kisses one makes up, though, they boil down 3
into only a few basic messages:

"I am your subordinate and I respect you." The kiss as a symbol of 4
deference and duty has a long tradition. In the Middle Ages the location of the kiss was a precise clue to the status of the participants: one kissed the mouth or cheek of an equal, the hand of a political or religious leader, the hem of the robe of a truly great figure and—to express extreme respect— the foot or ground in front of a king, saint or revered hero. The further away one was in status from the kissee, the farther away from the face one kissed.

"I am your friend." To allow someone close enough to kiss you re- 5
quires a measure of trust; in its earliest form the kiss of greeting undoubtedly meant, "It's safe. I will not bite your ear or stab your back." The kiss of reconciliation preceded the handshake in many societies, and even today children—and sometimes grownups—are encouraged to "kiss and make up."

"The bargain is sealed." Originally the kiss exchanged between bride 6
and groom was a business kiss—a pagan practice that meant the couple were officially assuming their legal and economic obligations. When all the guests kissed the new wife, they were publicly recognizing the legality of the union.

"I will take care of you and ward off evil." Mothers kiss their chil- 7
dren's scraped knees, feverish foreheads and bruised arms to "make the hurt go away," just as faith healers "kiss away" the ailments of grown-up penitents. Belief in the magical powers of kisses has filtered into everyday superstition: When you kiss dice or a cross (or your crossed fingers) or any object "for luck," you are enlisting the aid of fortune, God or the fates.

"We are in and you are out." The "ins" may be family, a neighbor- 8
hood, community or religious fellowship. When St. Paul instructed the faithful to "salute one another with an holy kiss," he established a ritual that came to reflect public adherence to the faith. St. Paul's kiss of peace,

as it came to be known, was exchanged among Christians variously at services, baptism, confession, ordination and communion.

Because the kiss implies trust, solidarity and affection, deceptive   9
kisses are everywhere despised. Judas's betrayal of Christ in the garden of
Gethsemane was, of course, the most famous Western example. The Judas
kiss is practiced ritually even today. Among some Mafiosi, a man who has
betrayed the organization will be kissed on the mouth by his assassin—a
sign of loving farewell.

CHECKING YOUR COMPREHENSION

Directions: *Mark each of the following statements* T *for true or* F *for false
based on the content of the selection.*

_____ 1. Some people believe a kiss has magical powers.

_____ 2. A kiss is never used to bring good luck.

_____ 3. In some cultures a kiss is a sign of distrust and suspicion.

_____ 4. In the Middle Ages the place on which you kissed someone
depended on who he or she was.

_____ 5. Throughout history kissing has been a custom practiced only by
Christians.

CRITICAL READING AND THINKING

1. What was the author's purpose in writing this selection? (Author's purpose: see Chapter 13)

   _____

2. When a little girl on her way to kindergarten gives her mother a good-bye kiss, what basic message is the girl expressing?

   _____

3. Explain why you agree or disagree with the following statement: The authors cover all the basic messages a kiss can have.

   _____

4. What other social customs communicate a message?

   _____

5. For whom do you think this article was written? (Audience: see Chapter 13)

   _____

WORDS IN CONTEXT

Directions: *Locate each word in the paragraph indicated and reread that paragraph. Then, based on the way the word is used in the paragraph, write a synonym or brief definition for each.*

1. status (par. 4) _____

2. revered (par. 4) _____

3. preceded (par. 5) _____

4. enlisting (par. 7) _____

VOCABULARY REVIEW

Directions: *Use the words listed in the Vocabulary Preview to complete each of the following sentences.*

1. The woman who learned that her husband was not working late in the office as he had claimed accused him of being _____.

2. A couple who had filed for divorce agreed instead to a _____.

3. An X-rated film is _____ than one rated PG.

4. Many religious families have _____ in their homes.

5. The company executive regarded her _____ as a valuable member of the organization.

6. The man spoke to the court judge with _____.

7. Because the tribal members could not express their religious beliefs to the anthropologist, they were considered to be _____.

8. The teenagers' _____ to family customs made them seem old fashioned.

9. The union members showed strong _____ in their refusal to accept the contract offer.

10. During the prayer, everyone bowed his or her head in _____.

SELECTION 8

SELF-DEFENSE: CAN YOU PROTECT YOURSELF AND AVOID THE SLAMMER?

Arthur R. Miller

Are you afraid of being mugged when walking down a street or in a subway? How would you defend yourself if attacked? Would your action be legal? This selection discusses your legal rights with respect to self-defense.

VOCABULARY PREVIEW

justified (par. 3)   proved or shown to be just, right, or reasonable

retreat (pars. 4, 5)   escape or withdrawal to a safe place

aggressor (par. 4)   person who attacks

premium (par. 4)   very high value

dignity (par. 4)   pride; self-respect

exception (par. 5)   case or situation in which a rule does not apply

indisputably (par. 5)   without doubt or question

context (par. 5)   situation

diligently (par. 6)   carefully and steadily; through hard work

emerged (par. 9)   became visible

gesture (par. 11)   movement

PREREADING

Directions: *Preview the selection and then answer the following questions.*

What do you already know about your right to protect yourself if attacked? What information do you feel you need to know?

_____

_____

_____

Imagine you're a woman living alone in a big city. Lately, a number   1
of people in your apartment building have been mugged right in the neighborhood—the worst place is an unlighted section of street near where you get off the bus from work. Since you often stay late at the office, you have no choice but to walk there after dark. A neighborhood committee has approached the police about getting more protection, but the police say that they already are spread thin and can't spare the manpower. To make matters worse, the city is in financial trouble and will be laying off officers, so in the future you can count on even less protection.

It's becoming clear to you that the neighborhood isn't going to get any   2
safer, so you begin thinking about what you can do to protect yourself. Your thoughts grow more serious when you learn that the woman who lives across the hall was badly beaten by a mugger near the bus stop. Now you're really determined, but what's the first move? Should you learn karate, or buy a gun or a can of Mace? Are any of these measures illegal—will they get you into trouble? Now that you're actually considering self-defense, you realize you really don't know what you're allowed to do.

So the first thing you do is ask a lawyer friend what your rights are.   3
He tells you that the law differs from state to state, but that the basic rule is that you can use reasonable force to repel a real or apparent attack. The amount of force that is "reasonable" differs according to the circumstances, but you're generally justified in using the same amount of force against your assailant as he is using, or proposes to use, against you. And you are allowed to use deadly force (which is force likely to kill, even if it doesn't succeed) against an attack that could kill you or cause you serious bodily harm.

In some states, however, there is a duty to retreat before resorting to   4
deadly force: You must make an effort to escape, if it appears that you can do so safely, before you are entitled to use it. The classic case is the fight at the local saloon, in which the aggressor pulls a knife on the other man, who responds by pulling out a gun. Can he shoot if the knife wielder advances upon him? Not in a duty-to-retreat state if there's a back door to the saloon and he can safely run away. As you can see, the duty to retreat

places a higher premium on human life than on human dignity. Thus it is not surprising that the states that allow you to "stand your ground" are generally found in the South and West—regions where the notion of "a man's right to be a man" is more deeply rooted than it is in the East.

Even in states that require you to retreat before using deadly force, there's an exception to the rule: You're generally entitled to stand your ground in your own home if you are menaced by an intruder. This stems from the old idea that your home is your castle, and that you should not have to retreat from the one place that is indisputably yours. But even in this context, society's desire to preserve life and discourage "frontier justice" has led a few courts to limit the defense of the home by force.

So now that you know the rules, what do you do next? You enroll in a self-defense class given especially for women. You learn how to chop throats and gouge eyes and stomp insteps and throw all sorts of exotic punches and kicks. You work out diligently, practice hard, and after eight weeks you're given your diploma, which officially declares you a mistress of unarmed combat.

Now, let's suppose a week after graduation from self-defense school, you get off the bus late one night and start walking home. Suddenly a man comes up and grabs you and starts to wrestle you to the ground. You use your newly acquired expertise to knock him flat on his back. Obviously you can't be convicted of assault. This is a clear case of self-defense, since you acted to protect yourself from physical attack. A court most likely would conclude that you used reasonable force to repel the attacker, especially since you did not employ deadly force.

Let's say that when you knock him down he hits his head on the pavement and dies. Does that change anything? The answer is that it probably doesn't, since his death was not a result that could reasonably have been expected to follow from the amount of force you used in the course of legitimate self-defense. In other words, you did not use deadly force, even if death in fact resulted. Assuming that your use of force was justified, the law won't hold you responsible for any unforeseen injury to your opponent.

But what if the man hadn't actually gotten close enough to grab you? What if he had suddenly emerged from the shadows, and without waiting for more, you had delivered a kick that sent him sprawling? Suppose it turns out he's a perfectly respectable citizen who just wanted to ask you for directions?

The rule is that you can use force against what reasonably appears to be an attack, even if you were mistaken and weren't really being threatened. For example, if someone points a fake gun at you as a practical joke, you can use force, in this case even deadly force, if under the circumstances you reasonably believed that the gun was real and that the person was about to shoot you. Similarly, if you reasonably believed that the man approaching you was about to attack you, then you would be entitled to protect yourself, even if it turned out that your "assailant" only wanted directions. The key, of course, is whether you were reasonable in believing you were under attack. You are not allowed to let fly every time someone comes near you, or bumps you, or says something unpleasant.

So what happens when you flatten the man who wanted directions? If he did no more than walk toward you, you probably were not justified in using force. He would have had to have done more for you to say you believed he was about to attack you—for example, if he had said something, or had made a threatening gesture, or followed you for a ways before approaching you. But unless you can supply some reason for your "belief" that you were under attack, you can be charged with the crime of assault, and also can be sued by the man you knocked down for money damages to compensate him for his injuries. 11

How do you react to that? Not surprisingly, you might say that you are an unarmed woman and that if you wait for a potential assailant to make his intentions clear, it may well be too late for you to defend yourself. There may be some truth to your argument, but in addition to your safety, the law has to consider the well-being of innocent people who might want to use the city streets. Suppose that you weren't the woman who was approached on the street, but were the wife or close friend of the man who wanted directions. How would you feel about his being clobbered by someone who was so jumpy she struck him before even attempting to find out what he wanted? 12

CHECKING YOUR COMPREHENSION

1. Although rules vary from state to state, what is the basic rule about the use of force to fight off an attacker?

_____

2. How much force is considered "reasonable"?

_____

3. How does the author explain that retreat before use of deadly force is often required in the eastern part of the country but not in the South and West?

_____

_____

4. Explain how the rules about deadly force differ for attacks that occur in one's own home.

_____

_____

5. What would happen if you used force against what appeared to be an attack but was not?

_____

_____

CRITICAL READING AND THINKING

1. The writer asks you to imagine that you are living in a city where police protection is already "spread thin." The city is also in financial trouble and it is likely that the neighborhood will have less, rather than more, protection in the future. Why do you think the writer describes the city in this way?

_____

_____

2. The author, Arthur Miller, is a professor of law at Harvard University. He has had his own TV show, *Miller's Court*, and appeared on TV talk shows as a legal advisor. Evaluate his authority to write this selection. (Authority of the author: see Chapter 14)

_____

_____

3. How would you describe the organization of the selection?

_____

_____

4. Now that you are familiar with some of your rights in self-defense, explain whether you feel the law is fair and how well your rights are protected by law.

_____

_____

_____

5. Name several self-defense situations that this selection does not cover.

_____

_____

6. Do you think the need for self-defense is a growing concern of many residents of large cities? Give reasons for your answer.

_____

_____

_____

7. Explain whether you agree or disagree with the "retreat before resorting to deadly force" rule.

_____

_____

_____

WORDS IN CONTEXT

Directions: _Locate each word in the paragraph indicated and reread that paragraph. Then, based on the way the word is used in the paragraph, write a synonym or brief definition for each._

1. manpower (par. 1)   _____

2. assailant (par. 3)   _____

3. wielder (par. 4)   _____

4. expertise (par. 7)   _____

5. compensate (par. 11)   _____

VOCABULARY REVIEW

1. Give an example of something on which you have worked diligently.

   _____

2. What gesture represents a friendly "hello"?

   _____

3. Would you feel justified in leaving the scene of an automobile accident in which you were involved?

   _____

4. During an argument in a bar, one man punches another. Which one is the aggressor?

   _____

5. Mention a disagreement in which you knew indisputably that you were correct.

   _____

6. In what context, if any, do you feel it is appropriate to insult someone?

_____

7. Mention a rule for which you feel an exception should be made.

_____

8. Why would a rock-star retreat to a waiting car after a concert?

_____

9. Explain this statement: Many people place a premium on wealth.

_____

10. In what type of situation might a person lose his or her dignity?

_____

11. What would your reaction be if a strange creature emerged from a lake in which you were swimming?

_____

SELECTION 9

STRESS MANAGEMENT: PERSONALLY ADJUSTING TO STRESS

Richard L. Weaver II

Stress, or pressure, is common in our society. Read this article to find out how to cope with stress.

VOCABULARY PREVIEW

concurrently (par. 1)   happening at the same time

intensity (par. 2)   sharpness, strength

simultaneously (par. 6)   done at the same time

retrospect (par. 9)   looking at the past

relevant (par. 11)   attentive to important things occurring

overwhelmed (par. 11)   overcome with great emotion

subjective (par. 13)   changeable according to personal views, viewed differently by different people

unrequited (par. 13)   unreturned, not mutual

PREREADING

Directions: *Preview the article and then answer the following questions:*

1. What topics do you expect the article to cover?

2. What do you already know about stress, its causes, its effects, and its control?

_____

Stress is a state of imbalance between demands made on us from 1
outside sources and our capabilities to meet those demands.[10] Often, it
precedes and occurs concurrently with conflict. Stress, as you have seen,
can be brought on by physical events, other people's behavior, social situations, our own behavior, feelings, thoughts, or anything that results in
heightened bodily awareness. In many cases, when you experience pain,
anger, fear, or depression, these emotions are a response to a stressful situation like conflict.

Sometimes, in highly stressful conflict situations, we must cope with 2
the stress before we cope with the conflict. Relieving some of the intensity
of the immediate emotional response will allow us to become more logical
and tolerant in resolving the conflict. In this brief section, some of the
ways we have for controlling our physical reactions and our thoughts will
be explained.

People respond differently to conflict just as they respond differently 3
to stress. Some people handle both better than others do. Individual differences are not as important as learning how to manage the stress we feel.
The goal in stress management is self-control, particularly in the face of
stressful events.

Stress reactions involve two major elements: (1) heightened physical 4
arousal as revealed in an increased heart rate, sweaty palms, rapid breathing, and muscular tension, and (2) anxious thoughts, such as thinking you
are helpless or wanting to run away. Since your behavior and your emotions are controlled by the way you think, you must acquire skills to
change those thoughts.

Controlling physical symptoms of stress requires relaxation. Sit in a 5
comfortable position in a quiet place where there are no distractions. Close
your eyes and pay no attention to the outside world. Concentrate only on
your breathing. Slowly inhale and exhale. Now, with each exhaled breath
say "relax" gently and passively. Make it a relaxing experience. If you use
this method to help you in conflict situations over a period of time, the
word "relax" will become associated with a sense of physical calm; saying
it in a stressful situation will help induce a sense of peace.

Another way to induce relaxation is through tension release. The the- 6
ory here is that if you tense a set of muscles and then relax them, they will
be more relaxed than before you tensed them. Practice each muscle group
separately. The ultimate goal, however, is to relax all muscle groups simultaneously to achieve total body relaxation. For each muscle group, in
turn, tense the muscles and hold them tense for five seconds, then relax
them. Repeat this tension-release sequence three times for each group of
muscles. Next, tense all muscles together for five seconds, then release

them. Now, take a low, deep breath and say "relax" softly and gently to yourself as you breathe out. Repeat this whole sequence three times.

You do not need to wait for special times to practice relaxing. If, during the course of your daily activities, you notice a tense muscle group, you can help relax this group by saying "relax" inwardly. Monitor your bodily tension. In some cases you can prepare yourself for stressful situations through relaxation *before* they occur. Practice will help you call up the relaxation response whenever needed. 7

For other ways to relax, do not overlook regular exercise. Aerobic or yoga-type exercise can be helpful. Personal fitness programs can be tied to these inner messages to "relax" for a complete relaxation response. 8

Controlling your thoughts is the second major element in stress management. Managing stress successfully requires flexibility in thinking. That is, you must consider alternative views. Your current view is causing the stress! You must also keep from attaching exaggerated importance to events. Everything seems life-threatening in a moment of panic; things dim in importance when viewed in retrospect. 9

Try to view conflict from a problem-solving approach: "Now, here is a new problem. How am I going to solve this one?" (A specific problem-solving approach will be discussed in the next section.) Too often, we become stressed because we take things personally. When an adverse event occurs we see it as a personal affront or as a threat to our ego. For example, when Christy told Paul she could not go to the concert with him, he felt she was letting him know she disliked him. This was a blow to Paul because he had never been turned down—rejected—before. Rather than dwell on that, however, he called Heather, she accepted his invitation, and he achieved his desired outcome—a date for the concert. 10

One effective strategy for stress management consists of talking to ourselves. We become our own manager, and we guide our thoughts, feelings, and behavior in order to cope. Phillip Le Gras suggests that we view the stress experience as a series of phases. Here, he presents the phases and some examples of coping statements: 11

1. *Preparing for a stressor.* [Stressors are events that result in behavioral outcomes called stress reactions.] What do I have to do? I can develop a plan to handle it. I have to think about this and not panic. Don't be negative. Think logically. Be rational. Don't worry. Maybe the tension I'm feeling is just eagerness to confront the situation.
2. *Confronting and handling a stressor.* I can do it. Stay relevant. I can psych myself up to handle this, I can meet the challenge. This tension is a cue to use my stress-management skills. Relax. I'm in control. Take a low breath.
3. *Coping with the feeling of being overwhelmed.* I must concentrate on what I have to do right now. I can't eliminate my fear com-

pletely, but I can try to keep it under control. When the fear is overwhelming, I'll just pause for a minute.

4. *Reinforcing self-statements*. Well done. I did it! It worked. I wasn't successful this time, but I'm getting better. It almost worked. Next time I can do it. When I control my thoughts I control my fear.[11]

The purpose of such coping behavior is to become aware of and moni- 12 tor our anxiety. In this way, we can help eliminate such self-defeating, negative statements as "I'm going to fail," or "I can't do this." Statements such as these are cues that we need to substitute positive, coping self-statements.

If the self-statements do not work, or if the stress reaction is excep- 13 tionally intense, then we may need to employ other techniques. Sometimes we can distract ourselves by focusing on something outside the stressful experience—a pleasant memory, a sexual fantasy—or by doing mental arithmetic. Another technique is imaging. By manipulating mental images we can reinterpret, ignore, or change the context of the experience. For example, we can put the experience of unrequited love into a soap-opera fantasy or the experience of pain into a medieval torture by the rack. The point here is that love and pain are strongly subjective and personal, and when they are causing us severe stress we can reconstruct the situation mentally to ease the stress. In both these cases the technique of imaging helps to make our response more objective—to take it *outside* ourselves. The more alternatives we have to aid us in stress reduction, the more likely we are to deal with it effectively.

CHECKING YOUR COMPREHENSION

Directions: *Mark each statement as "True" or "False".*

_____ 1. The tension-release method for stress management does not bring about relaxation.

_____ 2. Relaxation should only be practiced when you feel a lot of stress.

_____ 3. Exercise is an important way to relax.

_____ 4. Talking to yourself about your problems increases stress and makes it difficult to relax.

_____ 5. It is not acceptable to control fears; one must eliminate them.

_____ 6. Imaging is a means of redirecting one's attention and making one's response more objective.

_____ 7. Stress reactions include sweaty palms, rapid breathing, and wanting to run away.

_____ 8. Sometimes it is possible to prepare yourself for a stressful situation ahead of time.

_____ 9. Physical symptoms of stress cannot be controlled or reduced.

_____ 10. Fantasies usually reinforce stressful experiences.

CRITICAL READING AND THINKING

1. Using the definition of stress given in paragraph 1, make a list of several stressful situations you have experienced. Next, from among the management techniques described, identify which might be most useful in reducing stress.

_____

2. Tests and exams are often stressful for college students. What types of reinforcing self-statements might help someone handle stress owing to exams?

_____

_____

3. A college student feels stressed and overwhelmed by numerous class assignments, tests, and papers. How might he cope with this feeling? Make specific suggestions.

_____

4. A student has just enrolled in a required speech communication class in which five brief speeches are required. The student is experiencing an intense stress reaction. Her instructor has recommended that she try the imaging technique. How should she use it and what should she do?

_____

_____

WORDS IN CONTEXT

Directions: *Locate each word in the paragraph indicated and reread that paragraph. Then, based on the way the word is used in the paragraph, write a synonym or brief definition for each.*

1. induce (par. 6) _____

2. flexibility (par. 9) _____

3. stressors (par. 11) _____

4. imaging (par. 11) _____

5. phases (par. 11) _____

VOCABULARY REVIEW

Directions: *Use the words listed in the Vocabulary Preview to complete each of the following sentences.*

1. Owing to its popularity, the same movie was being shown _____ _____ at two theatres in the movie complex.

2. When he proposed to her, she was _____ and began to cry.

3. After the patient described the _____ of the pain, the doctor decided to operate.

4. Because Ellen failed her psychology exam, she came to realize that _____ studying and watching television was not the way to succeed in college.

5. The love and respect the son showed for his father was _____.

6. In _____, Vanessa realized that putting the fragile wine glasses in the dishwasher was a mistake.

7. The student's comment about the professor's age did not seem _____ _____.

8. Grading an essay exam is _____; two professors may give the same paper slightly different grades.

SELECTION 10

THE 25-CENT ADDICTION
Geoffrey Loftus and Elizabeth Loftus

Have you ever played a video game? Did you enjoy it? Read this se-lection to find out what makes video games fun and why they are so popular.

VOCABULARY PREVIEW

dictated (par. 2)   controlled; guided

reinforcement (par. 2)   event that increases the likelihood that an action will happen again

confront (par. 3)   face; meet face to face

partial (par. 5)   affecting only a part; not complete or total

intuitive (par. 10)   knowing without conscious reasoning

magnitude (par. 10)   greatness, size, or measurable amount

opt (par. 10)   choose

incentive (par. 11)   something that encourages one to take action or work harder

feedback (par. 12)   knowledge of results

PREREADING

Directions: *Preview the selection and then place a checkmark in front of each of the following topics you expect the article to discuss.*

_____ Rewards in video games

_____ Video-game stores/rooms/arcades

_____ Computer programs that control video games

_____ Educational uses of video games

_____ Scoring points in video games

_____ Why people play video games

A young boy scanning the sky in search of shooting stars; a glassy-   1
eyed woman mechanically depositing nickels in a slot machine; a businessman spending lunch hour after lunch hour hunched over a favorite
video game.

Though seemingly unconnected, all three situations have a common   2
element: In each one, behavior is dictated by what psychologists refer to as
the partial-reinforcement effect. Video games—which are designed primarily to take your money—must and do make excellent use of this response.
In each of the preceding examples, reinforcement of some sort is involved.
For the aspiring astronomer, seeing a shooting star is the reinforcement.
For the gambler, it's the slot machine's payoff. For the video-game player,
it's beating a previous high score or winning a free game or shooting down
an enemy spaceship. Any video game that does something to make a
player feel good will be played again and again—until parents go berserk.

Designers confront many questions when trying to create a game peo-   3
ple will like. How often should a player be reinforced? Is it a good idea to
make sure that players never leave their first game without some kind of
reinforcement? Or should the games be created so that they are suffi-
ciently difficult that several plays are necessary before a single rewarding
event occurs?

Laboratory animals provide some valuable answers. Suppose a rat has   4
been taught that it will receive a food pellet every time it pushes a lever in
its cage. Suppose then that we change the reward schedule and provide pel-
lets only once in a while. What will the rat do? It will continue pressing, at
least for a while. Eventually, if another pellet appears, the behavior will be
reinforced anew.

Such partial reinforcement is a powerful method for hooking both rats   5
and people. They keep responding in the absence of reinforcement because
they are hoping that another reward is just around the corner.

Unpredictable Rewards

What this means in the world of video games is that rewards must be   6
unpredictable. If the game is too difficult, novices never get the hang of the
thing; if it's too easy, it becomes boring. Thus, the games' computers are
programmed to allow a beginning player to do at least respectably well after only a few tries. Only a handful of experts—who have literally played
thousands of games—are able to make it to the highest level of difficulty.

Knowing about the partial-reinforcement effect gives any video game   7 producer an edge in developing a particularly appealing game. But there is more that the designer needs to know. For example, Pac-Man gobbles yellow dots that are worth 10 points each. Why 10 points? Is this the optimum number of points to award for each dot devoured or should the figure be larger? The size of the reward is of critical importance.

There is no question that behavior is related to the nature of the 8 reinforcing event. Rats, for example, will run faster and more frequently if they are rewarded with more food rather than with less. People will play longer on a slot machine if they have a chance of winning $1,000 than if they have a chance of winning only $100.

It is thus to a game designer's advantage to allow even a first-time 9 Pac-Man player to score a few hundred or a few thousand points a game. But why did they stop where they did? Why not 100 points per Pac-Man dot? Why not 1,000?

The answer seems to be that, at some point, people stop having an in- 10 tuitive grasp of what magnitude means. Above some point, any amount is pretty much equal to any other similarly high amount. Imagine, for example, that you are a participant in a TV game show and you are given the following choice: (1) You can either have $1 for sure, or (2) a coin will be tossed and you will receive $10 if the coin comes up heads and nothing if it comes up tails. Almost invariably, people choose the second alternative. But now imagine that you either get a sure $1 million or a coin is tossed and you get $10 million if it comes up heads and nothing if it comes up tails. Now we find that people almost always choose the first alternative. For most people, $1 million and $10 million are psychologically pretty much the same thing—they're both "very large amounts of money." Thus it makes perfect sense to opt for the sure thing rather than the choice that involves a 50 percent chance of getting nothing.

Though scoring points is a powerful positive incentive, there is an- 11 other side to this motivational coin: regret over things you haven't managed to accomplish during a game. In most situations, regret is something you just have to live with. But that's not true of video games. Often, a video game ends because you've made a mistake, and you immediately know what you've done wrong. Instead of simply feeling frustrated, however, you can take some action: You can play the game again and correct your mistake. So in goes another quarter. But in the process of playing again, you make another mistake. And spend another quarter to correct *it*. Computer games provide the ultimate chance to eliminate regret; alternatives are available.

The final reason video games are so addictive is that they are so re- 12 sponsive. In a world in which people are often too wrapped up in themselves to give you the time of day, the games are just the opposite. As a player, you get feedback all the time. When we watch a movie or read a book we passively observe the fantasies. Whey we play a computer game, we actively participate in a fantasy world created by the game.

CHECKING YOUR COMPREHENSION

Directions: *Mark each of the following statements* T *for true or* F *for false based on the content of the selection.*

_____ 1. The size of the reward is of little importance in video games.

_____ 2. Business people as a group are among the most frequent video-game players.

_____ 3. A video-game player wants to continue playing because it makes him or her feel good.

_____ 4. Partial reinforcement means that a reward is given each time.

_____ 5. The feeling of regret is an important part of video games.

_____ 6. The fact that the player can actively participate is another advantage of video games.

CRITICAL READING AND THINKING

1. Suppose a video-game player obtained a perfect score the first time he or she played a new game. Explain why he or she would or would not want to play it again.

   _____

   _____

2. What other games or sports use some of the same motivaters as video games? Explain how each is similar.

   _____

   _____

3. What reasons other than those mentioned in the article explain why people play video games?

   _____

   _____

4. Explain why you agree or disagree with the following statement: The authors are video-game players.

   _____

   _____

5. Do you play video games? If so, what particular motivating feature makes you want to continue playing?

_____

_____

WORDS IN CONTEXT

Directions: *Locate each word in the paragraph indicated and reread that paragraph. Then, based on the way the word is used in the paragraph, write a synonym or brief definition for each.*

1. scanning (par. 1)   _____

2. unpredictable (par. 6) _____

3. novices (par. 6)   _____

4. optimum (par. 7)   _____

5. responsive (par. 12)   _____

VOCABULARY REVIEW

Directions: *Match each word in Column A with its meaning in Column B by writing the letter of the definition next to the number of the word it defines.*

Column A	*Column B*
_____ 1. confront	a. increased likelihood of recurrence
_____ 2. dictate	b. size
_____ 3. incentive	c. reward
_____ 4. intuitive	d. stand up to
_____ 5. magnitude	e. knowing by unconscious feeling
_____ 6. partial	f. incomplete
_____ 7. opt	g. control
_____ 8. feedback	h. choose
_____ 9. reinforcement	i. knowledge of results

SELECTION 11

A DEGREE OF DETACHMENT
Bruce Shragg

Should medical doctors become emotionally involved with patients?
This article describes a doctor's struggle to remain uninvolved.

VOCABULARY PREVIEW

CT (computed tomography) scan technologist (par. 1)   person who takes
   x-rays so that body organs can be seen clearly without the surrounding
   organs, bones, or muscles appearing on the x-ray.

biopsy (par. 1)   removing cells or fluids from the body for testing

pathologist (par. 3)   a medical expert dealing with disease-related changes
            of the body

radiologist (par. 3)   a medical doctor who reads x-rays

malignant (par. 6)   cancerous

tranquil (par. 7)   calm and quiet

aspirate (par. 9)   to use suction to remove fluid from a part of the body

cavalier (par. 10)   indifferent and easy-going about important things

discernment (par. 19)   the ability to recognize clearly

havoc (par. 19)   destruction, turmoil, confusion

PREREADING

Directions: *Preview the article and then answer the following question:*

   Think about the experiences you have had with medical doctors. Are
   they sensitive to your needs and feelings? Why or why not?

_____

_____

It's 10:15 on a Tuesday morning. I'm at my desk, dictating out a stack 1
of X-rays, when the phone rings. It's Carol, our C.T. (computed tomography) scan technologist. "Dr. Shragg, we're ready to do the biopsy."

"I'll be right over," I tell her. 2

A woman has a tumor in her pancreas. Her internist has asked me, 3
the radiologist, to do a needle biopsy. A pathologist will study the biopsy
under the microscope and render a final diagnosis.

I put on my white doctor's coat, call the pathologist, who must be in 4
the room at the time of biopsy, and mosey on over to the C.T. room. As
I'm walking, I think about all sorts of things—my forthcoming trip up the
California coast, the dinner I had with a friend last night, the tires I need
for the car. I'm not particularly thinking about the needle I'm about to
stick into a patient's abdomen. I walk into the room smiling.

"Hi, Mrs. Chambers," I say to a fairly robust, fiftyish woman lying on 5
a gurney. "How are you feeling this morning?"

She does her best to smile. "Fine. Well, good as can be expected, I 6
guess." If she were more truthful, she'd probably tell me she's scared to
death. She knows, from what her doctor has told her, that there's a tumor
in her pancreas, and that it might be malignant.

I put on my sterile gloves and make reassuring small talk. She asks 7
me if I think it's cancer. The question makes me uncomfortable. Maybe
one of the reasons I chose the relatively detached and tranquil field of diagnostic radiology is that we don't have to give patients bad news very often.
We let the internists and surgeons be the purveyors of doom. But I know
from experience that the odds that this tumor is malignant are very high. I
tell her there's no way of knowing for sure whether something is benign or
malignant without looking at it under the microscope. This isn't very reassuring to her, but it gets me off the hook.

Mrs. Chambers is slid into the large doughnutlike machine. As the 8
preliminary scans are taken, I think about the impact of computers on
medicine, about how amazing the C.T. scanner is. It allows us to see detailed cross-sectional anatomy. C.T. scans were new 10 years ago, when I
was a student. We called them CAT scans back then. Today, we take C.T.
for granted, as an indispensable tool of modern medicine.

As the computer processes the scans of Mrs. Chamber's abdomen, 9
the images are painted, one by one, on the television screen. The first
image reveals part of the tumor. The next one, about a centimeter away,
shows more of it. On the screen, I measure the distance from the skin
to the center of the tumor—seven centimeters, straight down. I mark
the skin, cleanse the area, inject a local anesthetic and make a small incision. By this time, the pathologist has arrived with her glass slides and
the solutions she needs to stain the cells I'm about to aspirate from the
tumor.

It's funny how cavalier we physicians are with needles. We stick so 10
many needles into people, we forget that needles hurt. I sometimes joke
with patients as I'm about to stick them. "This won't hurt me a bit." I

think I'm being funny. But I know, from having been on the receiving end, that there's nothing funny about it.

Biopsy needles come in all sizes. The one I'm using is nine centimeters long and very skinny. I ask Mrs. Chambers to hold her breath as I insert the needle into her abdomen. Once more, she is positioned into the scanner—this time to get a picture of the tumor with the needle in place. The scan shows the needle tip to be precisely in the center of the tumor. "Not bad," I think. I attach a syringe to the biopsy needle, aspirating as I rotate the needle, gently moving it several millimeters up and down. I pull out the needle and syringe, handing them to the pathologist. My work, I hope, is done. 11

"You all right?" I ask Mrs. Chambers. 12

"Fine," she says. "I'm surprised how little it hurt." 13

I tell her it'll take about 10 minutes for the pathologist to stain the slides, to see if we have an adequate specimen. If the slides are good, the procedure is over. If not, we may have to repeat it one or two more times. 14

"I hope the slides are good," she says. 15

Hmm, I think. A good slide. What does that mean? To me, it means that the specimen will be adequate to make the diagnosis—in this case, probably cancer. And indeed, 10 minutes later, while the pathologist and I are reviewing the freshly stained slides, she says to me: "You got it. It's definitely malignant." 16

I feel a slight rush of exhilaration at having made the diagnosis. But as I saunter back to the C.T. room, I remind myself that this woman has just been given a sentence of death. I rationalize: somebody had to make the diagnosis. Maybe I'm saving her from extensive surgery for an incurable tumor. Maybe that will allow her a better quality of life during her remaining days. 17

I walk into the room, trying to be pleasant. "We're finished," I tell her. "The specimen is adequate. After the pathologist studies the slides, she'll contact your doctor. You should have the results later this afternoon. Are you feeling O.K.?" She nods, smiles, and thanks me. I feel a twinge of guilt for not telling her the result of the biopsy. It's her body. She has a right to know. But, again, I rationalize: It's not my job. After all, her internist has a better rapport with her. She's his patient and, if I were Mrs. Chambers, I wouldn't want someone I hardly knew to tell me I had cancer. My guilt eases a bit. 18

Yet, as I return to my desk, the conflicting emotions linger. I did my job, and I did it well, which is all a man can really hope to do. Like a judge, like a financial analyst, like a nuclear physicist, I exercised reason, discernment, skill—and like their efforts, the result of my work can sometimes create havoc in other people's lives. Maybe a certain degree of detachment is necessary in order to do an optimal job. 19

Then I think of Mrs. Chambers. She will soon be faced with the task 20 of putting her affairs in order, saying goodbye to her husband, her two sons, her daughter, her 2-year-old granddaughter.

I pick up my microphone and resume dictating out my stack of 21 X-rays.

CHECKING YOUR COMPREHENSION

1. To what profession does the author belong?

2. What is one of the reasons why he chose this profession?

3. Describe the author's reactions and feelings toward Mrs. Chambers.

4. How does the author justify not telling Mrs. Chambers that she has cancer?

5. Why is the author pleased when he learns Mrs. Chambers' diagnosis?

6. Does the author feel he has helped Mrs. Chambers in any way? Explain.

7. What message is the writer trying to communicate through the article?

CRITICAL READING AND THINKING

1. Do you think a degree of detachment is necessary to be a good doctor?

2. Do you think the author should have told Mrs. Chambers that she had cancer? Justify your answer.

3. The author compares himself to a judge and a financial analyst. Is the comparison accurate? Explain your answer.

4. Is the language used in this article objective or subjective? Cite exam-
    ples from the article to support your answer. (Objective and Subjective:
    see Chapter 13)

    _____

5. Do you think Mrs. Chambers knows or suspects the diagnosis?

    _____

6. Do you feel this article is descriptive? If so, identify several particularly
    descriptive words. (Descriptive Language: see Chapter 13)

    _____

WORDS IN CONTEXT

Directions: *Locate each word in the paragraph indicated and reread that
paragraph. Then, based on the way the word is used in the paragraph,
write a synonym or brief definition of each word.*

1. render (par. 3)   _____

2. diagnosis (par. 3)   _____

3. indispensable (par. 8) _____

4. exhilaration (par. 17) _____

5. rationalize (par. 17) _____

6. rapport (par. 18)   _____

7. detachment (par. 19)   _____

VOCABULARY REVIEW

1. Using your knowledge of these professions, match the person with the
    job he or she might perform in the diagnosis of cancer

    _____ a. reads the x-rays   1. CT scan technologist

    _____ b. explains the way in which   2. radiologist
                 cancer affects the body

    _____ c. sets up and performs the   3. pathologist
                 x-rays

2. Describe something you might *rationalize* about to yourself.

    _____

3. What is a *biopsy*?

   _____

4. If a person felt *tranquil*, how might they act?

   _____

5. What is a *malignant* tumor?

   _____

6. If a professor acted *cavalier* about your failing a class, how would you feel and why?

   _____

7. Name an event that could easily be described as creating *havoc*.

   _____

SELECTION 12

YOUR NAME IS YOUR DESTINY
Joe Bodolai

    Do you like your name? Do you think it affects how people react to you? This selection discusses how people form opinions of others on the basis of their names.

VOCABULARY PREVIEW

appellation (par. 1)   name or title

urbane (par. 1)   smooth; polished

deplored (par. 2)   regretted; regarded as unfortunate

coup (par. 3)   sudden successful move or action

allure (par. 3)   attraction

subliminally (par. 3)   below the level of consciousness

prominent (par. 4)   widely known

connotation (par. 5)   association; suggestion

stereotyping (par. 6)   creating a fixed idea that does not allow for change
                 or interpretation

peers (par. 7)   persons of the same rank, or equal status

arbitrary (par. 8)   not controlled by rules; based on a chance decision

antiquated (par. 8)   out of date

bestowed (par. 10)   gave, usually as a gift or present

esthetic (par. 10)   sensitive to art and beauty; showing good taste

PREREADING

Directions: *Preview the selection and answer the following question.*

From your experience, are certain names positive or favorable while others are negative or unfavorable? If so, give examples.

_____

_____

For her first twenty-four years, she'd been known as Debbie—a perky little appellation that didn't suit her dark, willowy, good looks and urbane manner. "My name has always made me think I should be a cheerleader, or go blonde," she complained. "I just don't *feel* like a Debbie!" 1

One day, while filling out an application form for a publishing job, the young woman impulsively substituted her middle name, Lynne, for the long-deplored Debbie. "That was the smartest thing I ever did," she says now. "As soon as I stopped calling myself Debbie, I felt more comfortable with myself . . . and *other* people started to take me more seriously." Two years after her successful job interview, the former waitress is a successful magazine editor—friends and associates call her Lynne. 2

Naturally, the name change didn't *cause* Debbie Lynne's professional coup—but it surely helped, if only by adding a crucial bit of self-confidence to her already abundant talents. Social scientists say that what you're called *can* affect your life. Throughout history, names have not merely identified people but also *described* them. ". . . As his name is, so is he . . ." says the Bible (I Samuel 25:25), and Webster's Dictionary includes the following definition of *name*: "a word or words expressing some quality considered characteristic or descriptive of a person or thing, often expressing approval or disapproval." Note well "approval or disapproval": For better or worse, qualities such as friendliness or reserve, athletic ability or a bookish bent, homeliness or allure may be suggested by your name and subliminally conveyed to other people before they even meet you. 3

What's in an Image?

Names become attached to specific images, as anyone who's been called "a plain Jane" or "just an average Joe" can attest. The latter epithet particularly galls me since *my* name is Joe, which some think makes me more qualified to be a shortstop than, say, an art critic. Yet, despite this disadvantage, I did manage to become an art critic for a time. Even so, one prominent magazine consistently refused to print "Joe" in my by-line, using my first initials, J.S., instead. I suspect that if I were a more refined Arthur or Adrian, the name would have appeared complete. 4

Of course, names with a *positive* connotation can work *for* you —even encouraging new acquaintances. A recent survey showed that 5

American men thought Susan to be the sexiest female name, while women believed Richard and David were the most attractive for men. One woman I know turned down a blind date with a man named Harry because "he sounded dull." Several evenings after passing up the date, she sidled up to me at a party, pressing for an introduction to a devastating Richard Gere look-alike; they'd been exchanging glances all evening. "Oh," I said. "You mean *Harry*?" She squirmed.

Though most of us would like to think ourselves free from such pre- 6
conceived notions, we're all guilty of name stereotyping to some extent. Confess: Wouldn't *you* be surprised to meet a construction worker named Nigel? A fashion model called Bertha? A Pope Mel? Often, we *project* name-based stereotypes on people, as one woman friend discovered while minding a day-care center's group of four-year-olds. "There I was, trying to get a little pepperpot named Julian to sit quietly and read a book—and pushing a pensive creature named Rory to play ball. I had their personalities confused just because of their names!"

Apparently, such prejudices can affect classroom achievement as 7
well. In a study conducted by Herbert Harari of San Diego State University, and John McDavid of Georgia State University, teachers gave consistently lower grades on essays supposedly written by boys named Elmer and Hubert than they awarded to the *same* papers when the authors' names were given as Michael and David. However, teacher prejudice isn't the only source of classroom differences: Dr. Thomas V. Busse and Louisa Seraydarian of Temple University found that girls with names such as Linda, Diane, Barbara, Carol, and Cindy performed better on objectively graded IQ and achievement tests than did girls with less appealing names. (A companion study showed that the girls' popularity with their peers was also related to the popularity of their names—although the connection was less clear for boys.)

Changing Fashions

How did your parents arrive at the "sound symbol" that so relent- 8
lessly types you? Their method may have been as arbitrary as pointing to a Bible page at random, or as deliberate as a tribute to a favorite ancestor. Not surprisingly, the process of choosing names varies widely from culture to culture. The custom of several tribes of Indians, for example, was to name a baby for a memorable event in one of the parent's lives. In China, an elder dictates names for the next seven generations. As children are born into the family the parents select a name from the list. Even within a culture, names may go through distinct trends. Prudence, Maude, or Agatha—once as stylish for girls as the current Michelle or Lisa—now seem as antiquated as corsets. Interestingly, girls' names fall in and out of fashion more rapidly than do those of boys, who are often named after fa-

thers or grandfathers—keeping the same names in the family for generations of males.

Even appellations of *recent* vintage can date you. If you're named   9
Debbie or Sherry, for example, you're probably in your midtwenties. In the
midfifties, these two names rose to the top of the popularity lists like hit
songs—and faded just as fast. (Although in 1950 neither name was in the
top *100*, by 1956 Debbie and Sherry were first and second in popularity
for newborn girls. By 1960 both names had dropped from the top ten.) A
longer-lasting fifties fad was the name Kimberly, no doubt inspired by actress Kim Novak. Newborn Kimberlies abounded until well into the seventies. For boys Kevin followed a similar pattern. At one time, I didn't
know a single Kevin who was more than six, and I still won't vote for any
candidate named Kevin because part of me insists he's too young to hold
office.

In the sixties, babies were bestowed with imaginative names meant   10
to reflect their parents' spirituality, individuality, or alternate life style.
Daycare centers were full of little Sunshines, Frees, Moons, Chastitys, and
Geminis. Many such names now carry the same esthetic impact as black
light posters. (One child I know announced upon arriving the first day of
school, "My real first name is Tree, but I'd like to be called George, if you
don't mind.")

Currently, names beginning with *J* are the rage; Jennifer or Jessica for   11
girls; Jason or Jeremy for boys. (You'd be hard-pressed, though, to find a
plain Jane or an average Joe.) Androgynous, "designer" names—Dale, Brit,
Brooke, Lane—are also popular for both boys and girls. Despite recent innovations, however, one of the most common female names among all age
groups is still Mary: over three-and-a-half million women answer to that
well-loved choice, more than twice as many as were christened with the
runners-up, Elizabeth and Barbara.

CHECKING YOUR COMPREHENSION

Directions: *Mark each of the following statements* T *for true or* F *for false
based on the context of the selection.*

_____ 1. Certain names are associated with certain personalities.

_____ 2. Teachers' prejudices about names can affect students' grades in
school.

_____ 3. The process of choosing a name for a baby is the same in all
countries.

_____ 4. Certain names have been popular in certain time periods.

_____ 5. One of the three most common female names is Susan.

CRITICAL READING AND THINKING

1. Do you feel that your name suits your personality? What images are usually associated with your name?

   _____

2. If you could choose a new name, what name would you choose and why? What images does this name suggest?

   _____

3. List five names that you feel have negative images and five with positive images.

   Negative   *Positive*

   _____   _____

   _____   _____

   _____   _____

   _____   _____

   _____   _____

4. What names do you think are currently in fashion?

   _____

5. How does the author prove the central point of the selection? (Thesis statement: see Chapter 9)

   _____

WORDS IN CONTEXT

Directions: *Locate each word in the paragraph indicated and reread that paragraph. Then, based on the way the word is used in the paragraph, write a synonym or brief definition for each.*

1. abundant (par. 3) _____

2. conveyed (par. 3) _____

3. attest (par. 4) _____

4. epithet (par. 4) _____

5. sidled (par. 5) _____

6. androgynous (par. 11) _____

VOCABULARY REVIEW

Directions: *Use the words listed in the Vocabulary Preview to complete each of the following sentences.*

1. A person who is sophisticated, smooth, and polished could be described as _____.

2. A businessperson who made a quick, successful decision to sell a new product is said to have made a(n) _____.

3. A name or title is sometimes called a(n) _____.

4. A(n) _____ person is well known.

5. A beautiful woman is said to have _____.

6. An out-of-date custom is _____.

7. A name that suggests that someone is dull and boring has a negative _____.

8. A decision made without regard to rules is _____.

9. Other students in your class are your _____.

10. If you regretted doing something, you could say you _____ the action.

11. Advertising that is intended to reach your subconscious level works _____.

12. My grandmother _____ the family silver on me when I got married.

13. The carefully designed room pleased my _____ sense.

SELECTION 13

HOW NOT TO GET THE FLU THIS YEAR
Susan Goodman

Read this article to find out how to use exercise to stay healthy.

VOCABULARY PREVIEW

vulnerable (par. 1)   open to an attack

bolster (par. 1)   strengthen, add to

primed (par. 1)   prepared, ready

stationary (par. 2)   unmoving

devour (par. 2)   take in and destroy greedily

components (par. 3)   parts, pieces

reinforce (par. 4)   improve and strengthen, prepare for an attack

lymph nodes (par. 6)   bodily structures that produce a fluid that fills the spaces between cells and is given off by inflamed tissue

speculate (par. 7)   think about and make guesses

predators (par. 7)   creatures that hunt other animals for food

anticipatory (par. 7)   waiting for, expecting

enhance (par. 8)   improve or increase

antibodies (par. 9)   produced by the body in response to contact with germs in order to fight them

PREREADING

Directions: *Preview the selection and answer the following questions.*

1. What do you know about causes of the flu?

   _____

2. What preventive measures have you found effective in avoiding getting the flu?

   _____

   _____

3. Does exercise seem to affect your health?

   _____

We've heard about the bad health habits that beat up on our immune systems, making us vulnerable to the flu (and worse): stress, lack of sleep, a lousy diet. But now there's good news about disease prevention: By exercising, we may be able to bolster our immune systems and keep them primed to ward off infection and disease.

1

Warming up the Body's Defenses

Research in this area is so new that scientists are still collecting the pieces of the puzzle. But consider the following:

2

- Laurel Traeger Mackinnon, Ph.D., at the University of New Mexico in Albuquerque, put well-trained athletes through a vigorous two-hour workout on a stationary bicycle. She then measured the activity of their immune systems' natural "killer" cells, which defend the body against viruses and tumor cells. Dr. Mackinnon found that these Rambo-like cells' ability to wipe out tumor cells rose to about 40 percent above normal for at least one hour after a workout.

- James E. Wilkerson, Ph.D., former director of the Exercise Physiology Laboratory at Indiana University in Bloomington, put healthy men through a workout and found that the men's neutrophils—which devour intruders like an immune-system version of Pac-man—increased in proportion to the length and intensity of exercise.

- Matthew J. Kluger, Ph.D., when working with fellow physiologist Joseph G. Cannon, Ph.D., at the University of Michigan in Ann Arbor, found that 60 minutes of cycling elevated subjects' blood levels of Interleukin-1, which plays an important role in the body's inflammatory response—a sign that the immune system is fighting an infection.

How to Activate Your Immune System

All these immune-system components must travel through the 3 bloodstream to reach infected or diseased body tissue. The above experiments indicate that exercise increases the number of these "warrior" cells coursing through the blood, ready for action. But how?

One theory is that exercise spurs the brain to activate certain 4 hormones—which in turn carry a message to immune components to reinforce their ranks.

Other researchers in the field believe that exercise causes the body's 5 internal temperature to rise and that the body may mistake this increase in temperature for the onset of fever. It responds by releasing Interleukin-1, which raises one's body temperature even further and also stimulates the immune system.

Yet another theory suggests that exercise acts a bit like Liquid Plumr 6 or Drāno, working to flush immune cells off blood-vessel walls and into the bloodstream. Most of the body's immune cells are normally "in storage," explains Dr. Mackinnon, either inside the tissues and lymph nodes or adhering to the walls of the body's smallest veins. These cells, she believes, are actually sticky. "When you exercise, your need for oxygen opens up your blood vessels," Dr. Mackinnon says. "And the increased blood circulation may knock the sticky immune cells into movement in the bloodstream."

As for *why* exercise mobilizes the immune system, scientists can 7 only speculate about this also. Many turn to evolution as an explanation. "Back at the beginning of our history," suggests Dr. Kluger, "we 'exercised' only to acquire food or to escape from predators. Both activities carried potential harm. Perhaps it made sense to have an increase of these immune markers as an anticipatory defense response."

Easy Exercise Does It

Experts still cannot say whether this exercise-induced rush of im- 8 mune cells into the bloodstream will actually improve your chances of avoiding disease, but a number of them believe it can do so. Like Dr. Mackinnon, they think that a sensible routine of moderate aerobic exercise can help maintain your health. "The exercise an average person does, be it swimming or aerobics classes three times a week, may actually help enhance the immune response," she says.

Her research also suggests, however, that you can get too much of a 9 good thing. Dr. Mackinnon found that the level of antibodies that present a frontline defense against viruses in the nose, throat and upper respiratory system decreases after an exhaustive workout. So, if you're out to escape the flu bug this year, your best strategy may be to stick to moderate exercise instead.

CHECKING YOUR COMPREHENSION

1. List the effects exercise has on the immune system.

   _____

2. Give three explanations (theories) of *how* exercise affects the immune system.

   _____

3. Explain *why* exercise seems to activate the immune system.

   _____

4. How might excessive exercise affect you?

   _____

CRITICAL READING AND THINKING

1. What type(s) of evidence does the author use to support the value of exercise?

   _____

2. What further information would you like to have about the three experiments described in paragraphs 2 to 4 in order to evaluate them?

   _____

3. Is the article biased or objective about the value of exercise?

   _____

4. What type(s) of experiments could scientists conduct to find out whether too much exercise is harmful?

   _____

5. As they conduct experiments, scientists often make inferences (Inferences: see Chapter 12). What inferences were made in the experiments described in this article?

   _____

   _____

WORDS IN CONTEXT

Directions: *Locate each word in the paragraph indicated and reread that paragraph. Then, based on the way the word is used in the paragraph, write a synonym or brief definition for each.*

1. vigorous (par. 2)   _____

2. neutrophils (par. 2) _____

3. elevated (par. 2)   _____

4. coursing (par. 3)   _____

5. onset (par. 5)   _____

6. mobilizes (par. 7)   _____

7. acquire (par. 7)   _____

VOCABULARY REVIEW

Directions: *Use the words listed in the Vocabulary Preview to complete each of the following sentences.*

1. During the three day heavy snowstorm, many cars remained _____.

2. Elephants are not _____; they eat vegetation instead of other animals.

3. Both teams were _____ for the Superbowl; they had practiced for several weeks.

4. The lion felt very unprotected in the middle of the cage, but he didn't feel so _____ in the corner.

5. I knew Alfred was hungry after I saw him _____ a whole pizza.

6. Because the frame for the barn was unsteady, the carpenter had to _____ it with steel braces.

7. Because the flight was delayed an hour, I began to _____ about çauses.

8. Assembling the _____ of a stereo system is very complicated.

9. Adding bulbs of higher wattage will certainly _____ the lighting in this room.

10. The army decided to _____ its resources by adding 30 tanks and 100 missiles.

SELECTION 14

ON TRIAL: LIE DETECTION BY POLYGRAPH
Philip G. Zimbardo

This selection, taken from a psychology textbook, describes how lie detection tests work and questions their accuracy.

VOCABULARY PREVIEW

emissary (par. 2)   a government person representative

autonomic nervous system (par. 4)   controls the functioning of the lungs, heart, intestines, and other internal organs

sympathetic (par. 4)   part of the autonomic nervous system that increases heart rate and raises blood pressure in response to alarm

intuition (par. 7)   ability to know something without having actually learned it

statistical (par. 7)   factual or numerical evidence

validity (par. 7)   extent to which a test measures what it is intended to measure

dispositional (par. 10)   of a person's frame of mind

anecdotal (par. 11)   information based on individual personal histories

pathological (par. 11)   compulsive, driven by irrational impulse

PREREADING

Directions: *Preview the article and answer the following questions:*

1. In what situations are lie detector tests given?

_____

2. How would you feel about being asked to take one as part of a job interview? Would you worry about failing it?

_____

People lie. They often deceive others, distorting the truth while claiming to be truthful. We also know that people accuse of lying others who, in fact, are honest when they claim to be telling the truth. How can we tell the difference? Why is it important to do so, and what are the consequences of erring in making the decision that someone is or is not lying? 1

Adolf Hitler convinced British emissary Neville Chamberlain that he had no intentions of starting a war—just before World War II. The political careers of Senator Edward Kennedy and Presidents Richard Nixon and Ronald Reagan were tainted by public doubts of their truthfulness in attempting to cover up suspected illegal actions. Recently, spy ring leader Anthony Walker, Jr., was found guilty of having deceived the Navy for nearly 20 years while he passed top secrets to the Soviets. Walker had received "top clearance" to handle classified material, but somehow was able to "beat the system" at its own intelligence game. Gary Dotson was sentenced to prison for the rape of Cathy Webb; despite his claim of innocence, Webb's courtroom testimony persuaded the jury and judge of Dotson's guilt. Several years later, she recanted, saying that she had lied about the rape, that Dotson had told the truth. If so, how can the judge believe a confessed liar when she is allegedly telling the truth? 2

Lie Detection Theory

In earlier times, tests of lie detection were based on the assumption that emotionality is associated with lying: a liar's nervousness will be revealed in bodily reactions that change under stress. Thus, the Bedouins of Arabia made conflicting witnesses lick hot irons—the liar was the one whose tongue stuck to the iron. The Chinese are reputed to have had suspects chew rice powder and then spit it out—the guilty party's rice was dry. During the Inquisition, suspected witches swallowed a slice of bread and cheese—the deceptive person was the one whose bread stuck in the throat. These tests share the belief that saliva will dry up when a person who is lying is frightened of being caught. Although less dramatic, modern tests of lying use the same theory about the relationship between lying, emotions, and physiology (Kleinmuntz & Szucko, 1984). 3

Modern lie detection theory assumes that if lying is deliberate and   4
purposeful, a person aware of his or her attempted deception will become
emotionally aroused as the sympathetic branch of the autonomic nervous
system is activated. These changes in the autonomic nervous system can
be tracked by attaching to the subject electrodes or sensors that detect a
wide range of bodily functions such as breathing, heart rate, skin temperature, and GSR (galvanic skin response). Printouts of these changes are used
as an index of emotionality. The graphed results of these channels of physiological information is what the *polygraph* is designed for.

Polygraph Uses

More than a million polygraph tests are given annually by private   5
agencies, businesses, police departments, and federal agencies, including
the military and the CIA (Lykken, 1981). In many states polygraph evidence is admissible as evidence in civil and criminal trials. A fifth of the
nation's major corporations and about half of the fast-food companies,
such as McDonald's, use preemployment polygraph tests to screen prospective employees, attempting to identify those who can be expected to
carry out their jobs honestly and faithfully. The Chief of Naval Intelligence told a Senate subcommittee on investigations that it is Navy policy
to use this test for national security purposes. "The polygraph is a valuable
and effective tool for specific personnel security purposes . . . particularly
useful in assessing candidates for access to our most sensitive information" (Rear Admiral John Butts quoted in Squires, 1985, p. 9). It is reasonable to assume that the general public also believes in the validity of the
polygraph test for lie detection.

Polygraph Testing

If you were to undergo a polygraph test, to what procedures would   6
you be subjected? First there would be an initial structured interview designed to get biographical data, to evaluate your attitudes toward dishon-
esty, and to judge your views toward the test situation. The interviewer
would also be trying to get leads to use during the next phase when you
were hooked up to the electrodes that measure a half dozen or so of your
physiological reactions. You would be asked a series of questions to be answered yes or no, and the answers would be reviewed prior to the actual
testing. Three types of questions are asked: (a) case-irrelevant, about established biographical data; (b) case-relevant, about the specific issues being
investigated; and (c) control questions that encourage lying or mild emotional arousal. Answers to these control questions are used to compare
your reactions to the predicted greater arousal when lying to relevant questions.

The tester then evaluates your polygraph record using intuition to de-   7 tect signs of greater autonomic disturbance to relevant questions, predicted if you are lying or the opposite if you are being truthful. In some cases this "clinical" interpretation is replaced by statistical analysis based solely on an objective evaluation of the numerical scores assigned to each difference in autonomic functioning. Statistical evaluation has been shown to be superior to the clinical evaluation—but neither technique meets acceptable standards of validity.

Polygraph Misuses

Despite the fact that polygraph testing has become standard operating procedure in many areas of society, is itself a big business for polygraph experts, and has been written about in thousands of books and articles, the best recent evidence clearly indicates that the polygraph test is *not valid* for systematically detecting those who are truthful. It is a psychological test with moderately high reliability and poor validity (Barland & Raskin, 1976; Horvath, 1977; Kleinmuntz & Szucko, 1984; Lykken, 1979, 1981, 1984). 8

Validity is assessed in laboratory studies where subjects are instructed to lie or tell the truth during polygraph testing, and in field studies where polygraph charts of those previously found to be innocent or confessed to a suspected crime are evaluated by polygraph experts. Using signal detection analysis (recall chapter 5), researchers found a *high false alarm rate*, or *false positives*, of truthful subjects classified as liars by the polygraphers. The best "experts" call innocent people guilty about 20 percent of the time, while some studies have found over 50 percent of truthful subjects misclassified as deceptive. Organizations are willing to tolerate these false positive errors in order to catch a few risky job candidates or dishonest employees, because only the victim suffers. Then, of course, there are the Anthony Walker, Jr.-type *false negative errors* in which liars pass polygraph tests with "flying colors." 9

Although a polygraph test reliably detects changes in human involuntary responses associated with emotions, there is no known direct relationship between deception and emotionality. Measureable physiological changes can be produced by a great many situational and dispositional variables which have nothing to with lying. "The polygraphic pens do no special dance when we are lying" concluded one reviewer of the evidence (Lykken, 1981). 10

Conclusion

At a 1987 congressional hearing on the use of polygraph technology, psychologist Edward Katkin presented the conclusion on behalf of the 11

American Psychological Association that "other than anecdotal data, we have no basis to assume such tests to be valid" (APA News Brief, 1987, March 11). This does not mean that lying cannot sometimes be detected by physiological changes or that liars cannot be betrayed by changes in voice, facial expressions, word usage, or body movement, as shown in research by Paul Ekman (1985). No test can do so with sufficient precision to protect the innocent from false accusation and the associated negative consequences nor unmask the talented, trained, or pathological liars among us. Polygraph results are not only fallible, they are also fakable. The practical application of this information is never to submit to a polygraph test if you know you are innocent, but take a chance on the validity of the test to misclassify you if you are guilty.

CHECKING YOUR COMPREHENSION

1. Describe the types of reactions a lie detector test measures.

2. Why are polygraph tests considered invalid or not very useful?

3. If polygraph test results are so often incorrect, why do some organizations continue to use them?

4. What sorts of lie detection tests existed before the modern polygraph was invented? How are they similar to the polygraph?

5. Can polygraph tests show if a person is unintentionally lying?

CRITICAL READING AND THINKING

1. Do you agree or disagree with the author's advice about who should submit to a lie detector test? Explain.

2. Is the article biased or does it present an objective view of lie detector tests? (Bias: see Chapter 14)

3. Under what circumstances would you agree to take a lie detector test?

_____

4. On what assumptions are modern polygraph tests based?

_____

5. Does the skill of the tester have a bearing on the results? Do you think the examiner's attitudes toward the subject can influence the results? How?

_____

6. What variables could influence how you score on a polygraph test?

_____

WORDS IN CONTEXT

Directions: *Locate each word in the paragraph indicated and reread that paragraph. Then, based on the way the word is used in the paragraph, write a synonym or brief definition of each word.*

1. tainted (par. 2)   _____

2. recanted (par. 2)   _____

3. electrodes (par. 4)   _____

4. polygraph (par. 4)   _____

5. physiological (par. 4) _____

6. clinical (par. 7)   _____

7. fallible (par. 11)   _____

VOCABULARY REVIEW

Directions: *Complete each of the following statements using one of the words from the Vocabulary Preview.*

1. As an _____ of the U.S. to China, she was expected to learn Chinese customs.

2. Jane was sure the baby would be a boy. When it turned out that she was right, her husband was shocked at her _____.

3. _____ evidence has shown that people who smoke have a high risk of developing lung cancer.

4. The boss would smile at his employees one minute and snap at them the next. His behavior was very _____.

5. The attorney questioned the _____ of the lie detector test.

6. _____ records are considered important in psychological analysis.

7. A _____ murderer commits crimes impulsively.

SELECTION 15

THE PSYCHOLOGY OF BUYING: THE PURCHASE-DECISION PROCESS

Hal B. Pickle and Royce L. Abrahamson

Why do you buy a particular brand of cereal? What influences your decision to purchase a VCR? This selection, taken from a business textbook, describes buyer motivation.

VOCABULARY PREVIEW

consumer (par. 1) a person who purchases goods, a buyer

motives (par. 2) reasons driving you to do something

insight (par. 2) ability to understand something fully and clearly

emulate (par. 7) imitate out of admiration

esteem (par. 7) respect

norms (par. 7) standards

breadth (par. 8) wide range

reinforcement (par. 9) strengthening of a decision

merits (par. 9) value or worthfulness

deliberation (par. 7) carefully think out alternatives before coming to a judgment or decision

PREREADING

Directions: *Preview the article and answer the following question.*

List as many factors as you can think of that influence your decision to purchase a particular item.

_____

_____

We have stressed that one of the chief concerns of marketing managers is to try to understand the psychology of consumer behavior. No single formula exists to explain why consumers make the purchases they do. For example, a shopper may purchase a radio for individual use, general family use, or as a gift. The complex issue is summed up concisely by Britt: 1

> What actually determines buying decisions? It may not be possible to obtain answers to such broad questions. The task is enormous. The answers are complex. Each of us has almost infinite likes and dislikes, and there are more likes and dislikes than there are people. And each individual's likes and motives are subject to change with different circumstances.[1]

Consumers are influenced by a wide variety of motives when making purchases. Sometimes consumers are unaware of their purchase motives or are unwilling to discuss them. Consumers have three levels of awareness with regard to purchases: conscious, subconscious, and unconscious. *Conscious motives* are those motives of which the consumer is aware and which the consumer is willing to talk about. *Subconscious motives* are the motives that a consumer may be aware of but not willing to talk about with others. If a consumer is unaware of what motivated a purchase, this is an *unconscious motive*. While these difficulties of understanding consumer behavior do exist, the purchase-decision process discussed below provides some insight into the psychology of consumer behavior. 2

We learned that each of us has primary and secondary needs. Before we are motivated to make a purchase, we must be aware that we have an unfulfilled need that must be satisfied. For example, if we are hungry (a need), we will be motivated to buy some type of food to satisfy our hunger. The motives that prompt a consumer to purchase a particular kind of product to satisfy needs are **primary buying motives**. A consumer may recognize a need for a new TV to replace a worn-out set. 3

Once the consumer makes a decision to buy a new television set, he or she must consider a number of alternatives before making the purchase. One alternative is the brand (Zenith, G.E., RCA, Sony). Other alternatives include choices such as color vs. black-and-white, portable vs. cabinet model, screen size, furniture style for cabinet models, the manufacturer's guarantee, and the price. The motives that underlie the consumer's choice of which television set to buy are **selective buying motives**. 4

[1] S. H. Britt, *The Spenders* (New York: McGraw-Hill Book Co., Inc., 1960), p. 20.

When the consumer decides to make the purchase, several other mo- 5
tives influence the kind of product he or she buys (rational or emotional)
and where he or she makes the purchase (patronage).

Rational Motives. Rational buying motives involve conscious thought 6
and deliberation by the consumer on the purchase decision. He or she tries
to learn as much as possible about the product. In a rational buying decision, the individual seeks to justify to himself or herself the purchase of
the merchandise. Common motivations that influence a rational decision
to buy include economy, dependability, and convenience in the use of the
product.

Emotional Motives. Sometimes a purchase is made on impulse, 7
meaning little or no preplanning goes into the decision to buy, as when
purchasing a convenience good. In fact, an individual may not even be
aware of the actual reasons prompting the purchase. Such buying motives
are identified as **emotional buying motives**. Some of the factors that influence an emotional purchase include the desire to emulate well-known
personalities who use the product, to fulfill a need for esteem from one's
fellow workers and social acquaintances by purchasing a distinctive or expensive product; to be socially accepted by conforming to group norms by
purchasing current styles; and the need for self-expression by purchasing
products that allow the individuals to express their creativity.

Patronage Motives. The variety of factors that influence where cus- 8
tomers will make their purchases are **patronage motives**. No one motive is
more significant than any of the others. Instead, shoppers usually consider
a combination of motives simultaneously when deciding just where and
from whom to buy. Some of the important patronage motives that affect
shoppers are courteous and helpful sales personnel; reputation of the
seller; convenience of location; the types of customer services (i.e., delivery) and product related services (i.e., service after the sale) offered by the
seller; the variety and breadth of assortment of merchandise available; and
the fairness and competitiveness of prices charged for the merchandise. For
some consumers, the ownership of the establishment is a significant patronage motive. Some may prefer large chain stores while others prefer the
personal service they often receive in small business establishments.

When consumers begin to use a product after its purchase, they form 9
opinions about it. Frequently, they try to find ways of gaining approval or
reinforcements for their purchase decision. They may seek approval from
their friends or read literature that explains the merits of the product.

CHECKING YOUR COMPREHENSION

This article was taken from a business textbook. Assume you are taking a
business course and this chapter was assigned. Complete the following
outline so that it would be useful as a study aid.

Outline

I. The Purchase-Decision Process

   A. Buyer Awareness Motives
       1.
       2.
       3.

   B. Buying Motives
       1.
       2.
       3.
       4.
       5.

   C. Purchase Feedback

CRITICAL READING AND THINKING

1. Identify which type of buying motives each of the following situations illustrates:

   a. ordering a pizza from the same shop you usually call

   _____

   b. buying a famous name handbag

   _____

   c. buying a compact disk player because your best friend owns one

   _____

   d. buying a car because it is fuel efficient

   _____

   e. buying gas at a particular service station because the attendants are friendly.

   _____

2. What buying motives might be involved in the purchase of a stereo system for your car?

   _____

3. Give an example of a purchase that involves purchase feedback.

   _____

4. A teenager who, when asked why she shops at the Gap, shrugs her shoulders and says "Just because" illustrates what level of buyer awareness?

_____

WORDS IN CONTEXT

Directions: *Locate each word in the paragraph indicated and reread that paragraph. Then, based on the way the word is used in the paragraph, write a synonym or brief definition of each.*

1. infinite (par. 1)   _____

2. alternatives (par. 4) _____

3. distinctive (par. 7) _____

4. patronage (par. 8)   _____

VOCABULARY REVIEW

1. What is a *consumer*?

_____

2. If you held your parents in high *esteem*, how would you treat them?

_____

3. If you had *insight* about your friend's behavior, what would you know?

_____

4. Name a *motive* that explains why you are attending college.

_____

5. If you were asked to list the *merits* of a particular instructor, what would you include?

_____

6. Why would someone *emulate* another person?

_____

7. If a jury spent three days in *deliberation*, what would they be doing?

_____

SELECTION 16

THE FAST-FOOD PHENOMENON
Lila Perl

Have you ever driven down a street lined with fast-food restaurants and wondered how they all stay in business? How nutritious is the food they serve? Read this selection and find out.

VOCABULARY PREVIEW

token (par. 7)   something that serves as a sign or symbol

ration (par. 7)   fixed amount given out on a regular basis

rancid (par. 7)   spoiled or decomposed, especially fats or oils

binge (par. 9)   excessive eating or drinking; give in to a desire, especially for food or drink

common denominator (par. 11)   characteristic or quality that is held in common

unauthentic (par. 11)   not real; fake

blandness (par. 11)   dullness; lack of character

PREREADING

Directions: *Preread the selection and answer the following question.*

What features of fast-food restaurants make them so popular?

Americans have been described as a people who are always "on the   1
move." Speed that up a little to "on the run," and you can easily see why
fast food has become a way of life for most of us.

The Eating-Out Society

What makes Americans spend nearly half their food dollars on meals   2
away from home? The answers lie in the way Americans live today. During the first few decades of the twentieth century, canned and other convenience foods freed the family cook from full-time duty at the kitchen
range. Then, in the 1940s, work in the wartime defense plants took more
women out of the home than ever before, setting the pattern of the working wife and mother.

Today about half of the country's married women are employed out-   3
side the home. But, unless family members pitch in with food preparation,
women are not fully liberated from that chore. Instead many have become,
in a sense, prisoners of the completely cooked convenience meal. It's easier to pick up a bucket of fried chicken on the way home from work or
take the family out for pizzas, heroes, or burgers than to start opening cans
or heating up frozen dinners after a long, hard day.

Also, the rising divorce rate means that there are more single working   4
parents with children to feed. And many young adults and elderly people,
as well as unmarried and divorced mature people, live alone rather than as
part of a family unit and don't want to bother cooking for one.

Fast food is appealing because it *is* fast, it doesn't require any dressing   5
up, it offers a "fun" break in the daily routine, and the outlay of money
seems small. It can be eaten in the car—sometimes picked up at a drive-in
window without even getting out—or on the run. Even if it is brought
home to eat, there will never be any dirty dishes to wash because of the
handy disposable wrappings. Children, especially, love fast food because
it's finger food, no grappling with knives and forks, no annoying instructions from adults about table manners.

As for traveling Americans, a traditionally mobile people in a very   6
large country, the familiar golden arches, Mexican "taco" hats, and "lean-
ing towers" of pizza are reassuring signs that make them feel at home
away from home. Even boring, repetitious food is okay, Americans seem to
have decided, as long as it is recognizable and dependable. No wonder
Ray Kroc unashamedly titled his McDonald's success-story autobiography
Grinding It Out.

Fast Food Nutrition

What about the nutrition in a standard fast food meal of a burger,   7
fries, and a Coke or shake? Fast feeders argue that the meat patty, lettuce
and tomato, enriched bun, and potatoes are honest foods offering protein,
carbohydrates, vitamins, and minerals. But let's take a closer look. The
beef patty is shockingly expensive protein on a cost per ounce basis, the
lettuce and tomato are minimal, a token gesture toward supplying a ration
of salad for the guilt-ridden, the bun is basically bleached white flour and

air, and the fries are overloaded with grease and salt. They are also low in the nutriment that a baked or boiled potato would supply because high-heat frying and long standing tend to destroy their vitamin C and other nutrients. One particular fast food risk is the too-often reheated fat used in deep frying. Smoking or rancid oil commonly causes only indigestion, but recent studies indicate that it may also have carcinogenic effects.

No one seems able to defend the cola drink with its sugar (or saccharin) and caffeine. And the fast food shake, which is carefully *not* called a milkshake, contains mainly water, saturated fat, emulsifiers, thickeners, sugar, and artificial flavoring. Nor do the brine-soaked pickle slices or "special" sauces thickened with gum tragacanth add any nutritive pluses. In short, the typical fast food meal is high in sugar, salt, saturated fat, and additives. Although it may offer some protein, it is generally low in calcium, iron, fiber, and vitamins A, C, D, and E. 8

At the same time, it contributes about 1,000 calories to our daily intake, more than one-third of the average requirement for males eleven years and up, and nearly half of the daily requirement for females aged eleven and up. An occasional binge at the burger stand isn't going to ruin one's health, but it's pretty clear that a too-steady fast food diet is poorly balanced and carries a lot of empty calories—far too many for the food value it provides. 9

Of course, all fast food isn't hamburgers. But it's questionable whether the typical fried chicken, fried fish, hot dog, chili, or taco meal can be any better balanced nutritionally, for most lack whole grains, fresh fruits and vegetables, and milk. 10

In addition, the flavors of the food specialties presented tend to have been processed out by design. In order to appeal to the widest possible range of eaters, the industry has had to find an acceptable common denominator. So fish, which has had a bad name with many Americans because of its "fishy" taste, has been rendered almost flavorless by the seafood chains and is served up in slabs that taste more of breading and fat than of fish. And Mexican food, which the chains considered too "hot" for the average American taste, has lost its character and been "de-spiced" into an unauthentic blandness. 11

Eating the Scenery

What their food may lack in the way of flavor and character, many of the new sit-down eateries try to make up for in the decor. The "theme restaurant" is one of the latest developments in the fast food industry. A fish-and-chips outlet may be done up as a sea pirate's lair, or a family-style steak house may be a replica of an Old West gambling parlor. English pubs, Mexican haciendas, and even Victorian railroad stations are among today's most popular "dinner house" themes. Usually molded plastic masquerades as rough oak beams, yet the scenery tries hard to make the food taste more 12 authentic than it is. Nevertheless, the chain-run dinner houses serve the same kind of assembly-line meals that the fast food takeouts do. Food arrives in the restaurant kitchen prepackaged, in individual portions, and often precooked, requiring just a quick browning or a few seconds heating in a microwave oven. No chef presides over the kitchen, merely a staff of attendants who work from printed timing instructions.

Even some of the more elite restaurants, with fancy menus, formal   13
waiters, and high prices are not above serving prefrozen beef burgundy and lobster à al Newburg supplied by the same corporate kitchens that prepare airline meals.

How can you tell, short of visiting the kitchen, if you're getting mass-   14
produced glop at gourmet prices? Small, family-run restaurants more often prepare honest food from scratch. And critical taste buds, not dulled by a regular diet of unimaginative, standardized food, can usually spot the difference between the thinly disguised TV dinner and a well-cooked meal prepared with quality ingredients.

To help restaurant patrons know what they're paying for, several   15
American cities have recently proposed "truth-in-menu" bills. Restaurants would have to indicate on their menus any dish that wasn't made in their own kitchens, and would also have to reveal the additives they used, such as MSG, in preparing various dishes. Such proposals may not pass easily into law, but through alerting the public to deceptive practices they may help to stem the advance of high-priced fast food served on white tablecloths.

CHECKING YOUR COMPREHENSION

1. List as many reasons as you can recall that explain the popularity of fast-food restaurants.

   _____

   _____

2. Find and underline the two sentences in the article that summarize the nutritional values and content of most fast foods.

3. Does the writer think fast food is high or low in calories? Underline the sentence in which this information is stated.

4. Why are french fries a fast-food risk?

   _____

5. Describe the quality of the food served at chain-run dinner houses.

   _____

6. From this article, what do you know about the average American's taste preferences?

_____

CRITICAL READING AND THINKING

1. Why do you think the author chose the heading "Eating the Scenery" to describe theme restaurants?

_____

2. Do you think the author eats at fast-food restaurants regularly? Why or why not?

_____

3. Would you favor a "truth-in-menu" law in your town or city? Explain your reasons.

_____

4. Do you go to fast-food restaurants often? If so, will the information contained in this article influence your choice of restaurants in the future? Why or why not?

_____

WORDS IN CONTEXT

Directions: _Locate each word in the paragraph indicated and reread that paragraph. Then, based on the way the word is used in the paragraph, write a synonym or brief definition for each._

1. grappling (par. 5)   _____

2. minimal (par. 7)   _____

3. replica (par. 12)   _____

4. masquerades (par. 12)   _____

5. presides (par. 12)   _____

6. elite (par. 13)   _____

VOCABULARY REVIEW

Directions: *Match each word in Column A with its meaning in Column B by writing the letter of the definition next to the number of the word it defines.*

Column A	*Column B*
_____ 1. rancid	a. spoiled
_____ 2. binge	b. excessive eating or drinking
_____ 3. token	c. common characteristic
_____ 4. ration	d. fixed amount
_____ 5. denominator	e. fake
_____ 6. unauthentic	f. dullness
_____ 7. blandness	g. sign or symbol

SELECTION 17

LIVING AS A "BLACK IN BLUE"
Lena Williams

The life of a black *man or woman in a* blue *police uniform is very different from a "white in blue." Read this article to learn about these differences.*

VOCABULARY PREVIEW

civilian (par. 1)   a person who does not belong to a military or police force

reconcile (par. 3)   settle differences, make things work together

underscores (par. 4)   emphasizes

stereotype (par. 4)   fixed idea or view

pervasive (par. 4)   common, widespread

ambiguities (par. 5)   confusions, things that are unclear

shunned (par. 8)   purposely avoided and made an outcast

slurs (par. 11)   remarks intended to harm a reputation

ostracized (par. 11)   banned, outcast

forensic (par. 12)   dealing with law

fraternity (par. 13)   a group of people (usually men) joined by some common interest or belief

rhetorically (par. 18)   asking a question to emphasize a point

concede (par. 26)   admit or acknowledge

PREREADING

Directions: *Preview the article, then write a list of questions you expect the article to answer about the problems black police officers experience.*

_____

_____

James Hargrove remembers the time he saw a robbery in progress in   1
Manhattan. As a police officer, he wanted to jump out of his patrol car. As
a black man in civilian clothes, carrying a weapon, he knew better.

So Patrolman Hargrove did what most other off-duty black police offi-   2
cers have been trained by instinct and by the job to do in such situations:
he stayed in the car and radioed for help.

The episode, recalled recently by Mr. Hargrove, who is now an Assis-   3
tant Police Commissioner in New York City, reflects some of the special
problems faced by black police officers as they try to reconcile their race
with their work.

Conflicts and Ambiguities

It also underscores a more complex issue: how the pervasive stereo-   4
type of criminals as young black males may influence police officers'
responses. That point was illustrated in December in Prince Georges
County, Md., when a black Washington, D.C., police officer was shot and
killed in his home by a white county police officer who mistook him for
an armed burglar.

In interviews around the country, black police officers said the con-   5
flicts and ambiguities that arise from being "black in blue" can be humil-
iating and demoralizing. "When the white guys finish work, they go home
to their white neighborhoods and the black guys go home to the black
community," said Ronald Hampton, a black Washington police officer
who lives in a predominantly black section of the capital.

Another black officer in Washington said: "You may be their partner   6
on the job, but the minute you're off duty, it's a different story. It's like
you'll find a bunch of white cops hovering in the locker room snickering at
something—then when you walk in they stop. Now what are you supposed to think?"

A Belief in Opportunities

Despite such problems, most of those interviewed said that their jobs   7
were satisfying and that they believed there were opportunities to advance.
The number of black police officers nationwide has more than doubled
since 1972, to 42,000 from 20,000. There are 12 black police chiefs in cities including New York, Chicago, Washington and Houston.

The black officers also overwhelmingly expressed the belief that, re-   8 gardless of personal likes, dislikes or prejudice, white officers would come to their aid and they would aid white officers. All shared the view that the relationship between black police officers and the black community, where the black officer is sometimes regarded as a "traitor" and often shunned, has improved in recent years, in part because of attempts by black police officers to control the high incidence of crime in black neighborhoods.

"We're tied to the black community by this umbilical cord," said Mr. 9 Hampton, who is also the information director for the National Black Police Association, which has 35,000 members. "We can't sever it because we have a commonality, and that is our color. We know that if we take off our uniforms, whites would treat us the same as they do other blacks in Anacostia," a predominantly, low-income black community in the District of Columbia.

"On the one hand, we're asked to think of ourselves as being blue, not 10 black," Sgt. Donald Jackson of the Los Angeles Police Department said in a telephone interview. "I had one fellow officer, who was white, tell me that if he calls blacks niggers it shouldn't offend me because I'm blue, not black."

But when Mr. Jackson began to speak out against such racial slurs, 11 first to his superior officers and then to the local news media, he said he was virtually ostracized by whites in the department.

Integration Vs. Solidarity

Charles Bahn, professor of forensic psychology at the John Jay College 12 of Criminal Justice in New York City, said the comments of these and other black officers illustrated the contradictory nature of the job.

"The police fraternity has not stretched to the point of fully 13 embracing blacks or women," said Mr. Bahn. "It is true, in part, because black officers have segregated themselves to be a force for their own people. Self-integration interferes with the issue of solidarity, which says anyone in blue is your brother or sister."

In his book "Black in Blue: A Study of the Negro Policeman," 14 Nicholas Alex wrote: "The black policeman can never escape his racial identity while serving in his official role. He attempts to escape his uniform as soon as possible after his tour of duty. He avoids the friends of his youth in order to avoid learning of their criminal behavior. He does not socialize with white cops after duty hours. In short, he is drawn into an enclave of black cops and becomes a member of a minority group within a minority group."

Most law-enforcement officials acknowledge that racial prejudice ex- 15 ists in their profession, but they say it is no more pervasive than in the rest of American society. "The police department is not much different than broader society to the extent that you have racism in the broader society," said Police Chief Lee P. Brown of Houston, Tex. He is black.

Shift in Training Emphasis

To combat this, nearly all the nation's 19,000 police departments are 16
shifting some emphasis from training at the firing range to training in
judgment and sensitivity. A few have brought in outside experts in an attempt to identify racially biased officers.

Criminologists and experts in law enforcement say such measures 17
have helped officers understand and appreciate cultural differences, but
they disagreed about the measures' effect on influencing police responses.

Referring to the police shooting in Maryland, Sergeant Jackson of the 18
Los Angeles police said rhetorically: "Had an armed white man been in
that house, would he have been shot? I doubt it. He would have been given
the benefit of the doubt by any officer, black or white."

That is vigorously disputed by other police organizations. "That's gar- 19
bage," said Buzz Sawyer, president of the Prince Georges County's Frater-
nal Order of Police, a social and professional organization that is the bar-
gaining unit for the 915-member force. "When someone turns at you with
a gun, you don't sit there and determine what color he is. Color has nothing to do with the fact that a person is armed." Mr. Sawyer is white.

Statistics do not support the notion that race is a significant factor 20
when police officers decide to shoot. A 1986 study by the Crime Control
Institute, a nonprofit research organization in Washington, reported a
sharp decline from 1971 to 1984 in killings by police officers in cities with
populations over 250,000. The researchers concluded that the 39 percent
reduction was "almost entirely" a result of fewer blacks' being killed.

In 1971, the peak year in the report, 353 people were killed by police 21
officers. In 1984, 172 were killed, the lowest number in the study. The
number of black civilians killed dropped by nearly 50 percent, from an average of 2.8 per 100,000 in 1971 to 1.4 per 100,000 in 1984.

Assignments and Promotions

Black officers frequently complain that they are treated differently 22
from whites in assignments and promotions. In a 1981 study, Dr. James J.
Fyfe, chairman of the Department of Justice, Law and Society at American
University in Washington, a white former New York City police officer,
concluded that black police officers were more likely to be assigned to
high crime areas in which minority groups live.

"Fewer than one in three white police officers or detectives is as- 23
signed to narcotics, street crime and A precincts," those where violent
crime is likely, said Dr. Fyfe, "while nearly half the blacks and more than
4 of 10 Hispanics work in these units. On the other hand, whites are more
than three times as likely to work in traffic or emergency as are blacks or
Hispanics."

Some of the black officers interviewed said they preferred to work in 24
minority communities, even with the greater potential for danger.

"We serve a dual purpose in the black community in that we are seen   25
as protectors of the community and in some respects as role models," said
Inspector Harold Washington of the Detroit Police Department. He is the
president of the National Organization of Black Law-Enforcement Executives.

Most black police officers say they have learned how to respond to   26
the pressures they face on and off the job, and most also concede that constant stress may eventually begin to take its toll.

"It was destroying me as a black man," said Sergeant Jackson, who is   27
29 years old, a graduate of California Lutheran College and the son of a retired Los Angeles police officer. "When I joined the force eight years ago I
went along with the racial slurs in order to be accepted by the police fraternity. It began to turn me against my own people. I began to see fellow
blacks as untrustworthy, as thieves and criminals. I began to shut myself
off from my family and friends."

Officer Jackson said he did not begin to feel better until he started to   28
speak out against racists in the department. Three months ago he formed
an organization of black police officers to address racism in the Los Angeles Police Department. Last month the department began a racial sensitivity program and established up [sic] a panel to examine acts of racism
and discrimination in the department.

CHECKING YOUR COMPREHENSION

1. Why did the black police officer who saw a robbery in progress stay in his car?

   _____

2. Summarize the problems of living as a "black in blue".

   _____

3. According to the article, how do white police officers treat black officers?

   _____

4. What kind of purpose do black officers serve in black communities?

   _____

5. What actions have been taken as a result of black officers' complaints
   about discrimination and prejudice?

   _____

6. According to Mr. Hampton, black officers are tied to the black community. Do you agree with this?

   _____

CRITICAL READING AND THINKING

1. Two opposing views on the police shooting incident are presented by Sergeant Jackson and Buzz Sawyer. Which opinion do you agree with?

   _____

2. In paragraph 9, the term "umbilical cord" is used figuratively. Explain its meaning. (Figurative language: see Chapter 12)

   _____

3. How does being a police officer affect the lives of off-duty black police officers?

   _____

4. In what other careers or occupations, if any, do you expect blacks face similar problems? Explain.

   _____

5. What solutions do you see to the problems discussed in the article?

   _____

6. Explain why Sergeant Jackson felt being a police officer was destroying him as a black man.

   _____

WORDS IN CONTEXT

Directions: *Locate each word in the paragraph indicated and reread that paragraph. Then, based on the way the word is used in the paragraph, write a synonym or brief definition of each.*

1. episode (par. 3)   _____

2. mistook (par. 4)   _____

3. predominantly (par. 5)   _____

4. solidarity (par. 13)   _____

5. enclave (par. 14)   _____

6. reduction (par. 20)   _____

VOCABULARY REVIEW

Directions: *Complete each of the following statements using words from the Vocabulary Preview.*

1. Scientists involved in studying and investigating criminal behavior are called _____.

2. Because the _____ was not a member of a military or police force, he was not permitted to enter the air force base.

3. After their argument, Jason made _____ that damaged Janet's reputation.

4. A _____ attitude that is widespread among Americans is that the United States is the best country in the World.

5. The seagull was _____ from its flock as an outcast because it had only one eye.

6. The anthropology professor was able to get her belief in God to work with her understanding of biological evolution; she was able to _____ the two.

7. Her husband could never _____ that he had lost an argument.

8. There were _____ about Pat's early home life as a child that could never be made clear.

9. The child's extreme fear of water in any form _____ his need for counseling.

10. A common _____ of professors is that they are absent-minded and forgetful.

SELECTION 18

WOULD YOU OBEY A HITLER?
Jeanne Reinert

Do you think you could be influenced to do things you normally do not believe in? This selection may make you question your self-control.

VOCABULARY PREVIEW

qualms (par. 2)   feelings of doubt or misgiving; uneasiness

thesis (par. 4)   proposition; idea to be discussed or tested

reinforcement (par. 6)   event that increases the likelihood that an action
will happen again

electrode (par. 10)   device that gives off electrical charges

merits (par. 16)   earns; deserves

cahoots (par. 18)   secret partnership

hoaxed (par. 18)   tricked; fooled

blithely (par. 21)   cheerfully; casually; in a carefree way

designations (par. 21)   markings, distinguishing names, signs, or titles

appalled (par. 23)   horrified; frightened

dumbfounded (par. 27)   astonished; stunned; extremely surprised

compliance (par. 27)   act of yielding to the wishes of others

dubious (par. 28)   questionable; doubtful

reconciliation (par. 33)   settlement or resolution of a disagreement

PREREADING

Directions: *Preview the selection and then answer the following questions.*

1. Is the article about Hitler?

_____

2. Recall what you know about Hitler. What crimes and atrocities were committed during his reign?

_____

Who looks in the mirror and sees a person ready and willing to inflict 1
pain and suffering on another in his mercy? Even if commanded? All of our
senses revolt against the idea.

The drama of a clearcut choice between obeying orders or qualms of 2
conscience seems clearest for a man in uniform. He must *decide* to pull
the trigger.

Being behind the trigger is very dramatic, but obeying orders is an ev- 3
eryday event for all of us. Seldom do we have a chance to test our actions
when confronted with a clearcut choice between hurting a person and
obeying orders.

In the early 1960s, Stanley Milgram, a psychologist at Yale Univer- 4
sity, devised an experimental setup to give that choice to subjects. He
wanted to measure obedience. He had been taken with the historian's
thesis that the Germans shared an extreme trait—a willingness to obey orders. This character flaw was, the theory goes, responsible for the Germans' carrying out Hitler's mad plan against the Jews. Dr. Milgram wanted
to test this theory by comparing obedience in America and in Germany.
He disguised his obedience tests as experiments in learning.

Imagine yourself as a subject in Dr. Milgram's setup. You walk into a 5
laboratory on the Yale campus after answering an ad that asked for paid
volunteers ($4.50 per hour) for an educational experiment.

At your appointment, you and another volunteer, a nervous man in 6
his 50's, are told that the experiment in which you will participate is set
up to test the effect of negative reinforcement on the human learning process. Jack Williams, the experimenter conducting the tests, explains that if
punishment makes you learn faster, that's negative reinforcement—as opposed to learning faster when rewarded (positive reinforcement). In this experiment the punishment is an electric shock.

Williams also states, "The money is yours for coming to the labora- 7
tory. It's yours no matter what happens."

Then Williams takes two pieces of paper, shakes them together in a 8
hat and each of you draw one to see who will be the teacher and who the

learner. The nervous volunteer announces he is the learner; your slip of paper says "teacher."

The experimenter seats the learner in a chair and explains the procedure: "We have to strap down your arms to avoid excessive movement during the experiment. 9

"This electrode," he continues, "is connected to the shock generator in the next room. Do either of you have any questions before we go into the next room?" 10

"Are these shocks strong, are they dangerous?" asks the learner. 11

"No," replies Williams, "although they may be extremely painful, they cause no permanent tissue damage." 12

The experiment involves word pairing (e.g., nice-day, fat-pig, etc.). You, the teacher, read a word to the learner and ask him to match it with one of the four other words. The learner pushes one of four switches to indicate which of the four answers he believes is correct. If he is right, you go on to the next set of words. If he is wrong, you push a switch that buzzes and gives him an electric shock. Then you go to the next group of words. 13

Your position is before the electric shock generator, 30 levers in a row across the instrument panel. Each lever is clearly labelled in 15-volt jumps from 15 to 450 volts. When a lever is pushed down, a pilot light turns bright red, a buzzer sounds, a blue light flashes under the label "voltage energizer," the dial on the meter swings about and mechanical clicks are heard. 14

To be sure you know what is going on, you are given a sample shock, activated by the third switch, on the wrist. This 45-volt shock lets you know how the shock feels. 15

You are instructed to call out the voltage level before pressing the lever each time the learner merits a shock. You note that the levers are marked from left to right in broad categories, "slight shock, moderate shock, strong shock, very strong shock, intense shock, extreme intensity shock, danger: severe shock," and the two switches on the far right are simply marked "XXX." 16

When the lesson begins, the learner makes a lot of mistakes. In fact, he answers about three wrong answers to one right one. As the shocks get stronger, you are, of course, unhappy about their level. It quickly is apparent that the learner is going to give a lot more wrong answers. So you appeal to Williams, who responds, "Please go on." You protest and he says, "The experiment requires that you continue." 17

The learner is strapped in, he cannot get free. You have already been assured that the money is yours regardless. The experimenter has no actual authority over you. But he is requesting you to obey his commands. Would you do it? Would you injure the learner just because someone told you to do so? You know from your own experience that the shocks are painful. What you do *not* know is that the experiment is rigged. The 18 learner is not being shocked: in fact, he is in cahoots with the experimenter. He is part of a play, and you are the only person hoaxed in the setup.

Before the pilot study, Dr. Milgram took the idea to a class of senior 19 Yale psychology students and asked them to predict the distribution of behavior among 100 subjects. The entire class predicted that only a very small number of people would go to the extreme 450-volt shock. They predicted from none to three percent of any 100 people. Dr. Milgram's colleagues also thought few, if any, subjects would go beyond the shock labeled "very strong shock."

But they did go beyond. In fact, Dr. Milgram got such complete obedi- 20 ence that there was nothing to measure. He was, after all, interested in getting people to *disobey*. His first 40 people went beyond the expected breakoff point. Not one stopped before 300 volts. Only 14 persons stopped shocking the strapped-in learner before going to the very end of the shocks.

In the pilot studies, no noise was heard from the strapped-in learner. 21 Dr. Milgram had thought that the labels and voltage designations would stop the teachers. But instead virtually everyone "went blithely to the end of the board, seemingly indifferent to the verbal designations."

Dr. Milgram never expected such obedience. So he began to vary the 22 props and scripts in his private play to see what changes would encourage the teacher to rebel.

The first change was to add protests from the victim. Mild protests 23 did no good. Then the victim began to put up a vigorous fight. Dr. Milgram was appalled that many subjects, nonetheless, went to the end of the board, giving the harshest punishment. But at least some subjects did break off and give the experimenters something to measure. It also proved that obedience was much, much stronger than suspected. The victim's cries were tape-recorded so all subjects heard the same protests.

Finding in pilot studies that the teacher turned his eyes away from 24 the victim who could be seen dimly behind a silvered glass, various ways were devised to make it more difficult for the teacher to ignore his victim.

Voice protests were heard. The victim was in another room, but the 25 door was left ajar. At 75 volts, the learner grunted when shocked, also at 90 and 105 volts. At 120 volts, he shouted that the shocks were painful. At 135 volts, he groaned and at 150 he screamed, "Get me out of here! I won't be in the experiment anymore! I refuse to go on!" At 180 volts, he screamed, "I can't stand the pain." Still, 37.5 percent of the teachers went to 450 volts.

Each successive scheme brought the teacher and learner into more 26 personal contact until in the final scheme the victim received a shock only when his hand rested on the shockplate. The experimenter then ordered the teacher to push the subject's hand down on the plate. The teacher actually had to physically subdue the victim against his will to give him the shock. No one was more surprised than Milgram that the very first person so commanded reached over and fell upon the victim's arm. Thirty out of every 100 were still willing to go all the way with the shock level when commanded.

Dumbfounded by this high compliance, Dr. Milgram then decided the prestige of Yale was causing his subjects to be especially obedient. So the experiment was moved to Bridgeport, 20 miles away. There a modest suite of offices was rented in a run-down section. The sign on the door said, "Research Associates of Bridgeport," a deliberately vague title. If anyone asked what the work was for, they were told, "for industry." 27

Yet, even with this dubious authority, the levels of obedience were high, although not as high as on the Yale campus. Forty-eight percent of the people were totally obedient to the commands versus 65 percent under the same conditions at Yale. 28

What these scores do not show is the torment that accompanied the teacher's task. Subjects would sweat, tremble, stutter, bite their lips and groan as they were caught up in the web of conflict—to obey the calm experimenter's commands or the call of the poor man being shocked. The teachers often broke out in hysterical laughter. 29

Persons would argue with the experimenter, asking if he would take the responsibility. They wondered aloud if the victim had a heart condition. Some would exclaim, "You keep the money," but many times they kept on pulling the levers, despite all of their words to the contrary. They would complain that the other guy was suffering, that it was a hell of an experiment. Some got angry. Some just stood up and proceeded to leave the laboratory. 30

No teacher was kept at the controls once they had reached 450 volts. People either stopped before 350 volts, or carried on to the end, proving there was no limit to their obedience. Hateful as they found it to obey, it must have seemed better for them than to break off. 31

When those who pressed the levers to the end finished their task, the experimenter called a halt. The obedient teachers were relieved. They would mop their brows. Some fumbled for cigarettes. 32

Then Mr. Williams rushed to assure the teachers that it wasn't as bad as it seemed. Most important, the teachers met their screaming victim and had a reconciliation. The real purposes of the experiment were explained, and the participants were promised that the full results of the experiment would be sent to them when it was complete. They were asked to describe how they felt and how painful they believed the shocks to be. Also they were to rate on a scale how tense they were during the experiment. Dr. Milgram wanted to be sure that the persons understood that they had been hoaxed and that a man was only acting as he screamed in agony. 33

Dr. Milgram never imagined that it would be so hard to get people to defy the commands. As he explains, "With numbing regularity good people were seen to knuckle under the demands of authority and perform actions that were callous and severe. Men who in everyday life are responsible and decent were seduced by the trappings of authority. . . ." 34

To date, Dr. Milgram has tested 1,000 people with the steady 35
results—very, very obedient. Of course, if people were not willing to conform to the many rules that link us in a broader society, chaos would pre-
vail. But Milgram's results suggest quite the opposite, that perhaps we
have forgotten the formula for saying no. It looks as though few outrages
are so grand as to force us to be defiant. "I was only following orders" is
going to be with us for a long time.

CHECKING YOUR COMPREHENSION

Directions: *This selection describes Dr. Milgram's experiments in the order in which he conducted them. In each experiment conducted, the subjects' responses are described. An effective way to organize the factual
content of an article of this sort is to use a summary chart, such as the
one below. Complete the chart by filling in the missing information.*

Event	*Results*
1. Discussed idea for experiment with psychology students	_____
2. Pilot studies—no noise from victim	_____
3. _____	_____
4. _____	_____
5. _____	_____
6. _____	_____
7. _____	_____
8. _____	_____

CRITICAL READING AND THINKING

1. Why were the results of Dr. Milgram's experiments alarming? What do
they suggest about our society?

_____

_____

2. Why do you think the "teachers" in the experiment continued the punishment even though they thought it was painful to the subjects?

   _____

   _____

3. Why were some of the "teachers" relieved when they learned that they had not really hurt the "learners"?

   _____

   _____

4. Name some real-life situations in which people are expected to follow directions given by someone in authority.

   _____

5. What was Dr. Milgram's attitude toward the "teachers" who followed orders?

   _____

6. Explain why you agree or disagree with the following statement: This experiment proved that people will blindly obey orders.

   _____

   _____

7. In what instances do you think it is right to disobey orders?

   _____

   _____

8. Why is Hitler's name included in the title?

   _____

WORDS IN CONTEXT

Directions: *Locate each word in the paragraph indicated and reread that paragraph. Then, based on the way the word is used in the paragraph, write a synonym or brief definition for each.*

1. flaw (par. 4)   _____

2. excessive (par. 9)   _____

3. apparent (par. 17)   _____

4. rebel (par. 22)   _____

5. torment (par. 29)   _____

VOCABULARY REVIEW

Directions: *Use the words listed in the Vocabulary Preview to complete each of the following sentences.*

1. The _____ of my paper concerned women's rights.

2. After a period of separation, the married couple agreed to a _____.

3. _____ with speed laws is often checked by radar.

4. Chris was _____ when she learned her friends had planned a surprise birthday party for her.

5. Peter began climbing the dangerous mountain without any _____.

6. A painting by an unknown artist is of _____ value.

7. The instructor was _____ when half his class failed the exam.

8. The popular singer walked _____ onto the stage.

9. Everyone feels that George _____ an award because of his efforts.

10. The team members were in _____ when they played a trick on their coach.

11. The coach was annoyed when she learned she had been _____.

12. Because the child's temper tantrums were given positive _____, it is likely that they will continue.

13. _____ on each desk indicated the occupants' ranks in the company.

SELECTION 19

AIDS BRINGS EXPANDED DEBATE ON RIGHTS OF TERMINALLY ILL

Andrew H. Malcolm

AIDS is a continuing threat to healthy Americans. It raises many issues about life, interpersonal relationships, and death. This article focuses on the issue of the right to die.

VOCABULARY PREVIEW

forgo (par. 1)   to make do without

comatose (par. 1)   in a prolonged state of unconsciousness owing to illness or injury

ethical (par. 2)   having to do with standards of right and wrong

confrontations (par. 2)   direct oppositions

culpability (par. 2)   ability to be blamed

proxy (par. 3)   a person given the authority to act in place of another

incontinent (par. 5)   unable to control one's bodily functions

chronic (par. 6)   long-lasting and recurring often

notarized (par. 7)   certified as genuine

legislative (par. 10)   of the law or of official government bodies

resolution (par. 12)   statement by a governing body

lethal (par. 12)   fatal, deadly

PREREADING

Directions: *Preview the article and answer the following question.*

What questions, issues, and problems does the terminally ill patient face?

_____

_____

It seemed the stuff of a nightmare from fiction: a fatal disease ravaging the man's body from within, his decision to forgo heroic, life-prolonging steps and the doctors' decision to ignore those wishes and perform their medical magic on the comatose body. 1

But the nightmare came true in recent weeks for Thomas Wirth, a New Yorker who became a victim not only of AIDS but also of the ethical and moral fog that surrounds many of modern medicine's confrontations with the end of life. Should doctors ignore a patient's wishes and treat pneumonia or other serious infections because they can, knowing that they are "saving" the patient only so he can die later from something much worse? When and how can a terminally ill patient say, "Enough!" without exposing doctors and hospitals to legal and moral culpability in allowing a death? 2

Last week New York State took a first step toward giving competent patients the ironclad right to authorize in advance a proxy to make such life-and-death decisions if the patient becomes incompetent. The legislative proposal by the Governor's Task Force on Life and the Law could be introduced as soon as January. 3

Who can make such decisions is hardly a new question. But it is one certain to be faced increasingly with the inevitable spread of the inevitably fatal AIDS, which destroys the body's defenses against many otherwise treatable infections. 4

'You Know the Outcome'

"It's different from other diseases because you—and every patient—know the outcome from the start," said one New York physician who treats many AIDS patients and who asked to remain anonymous. "You both know he'll be dead within two years, weighing perhaps 65 pounds, incontinent, in severe pain, with 80 percent experiencing mental changes." 5

"AIDS telescopes what we all will go through. Most of us will not have the luxury of living until 80 and then being hit by a truck. Most of us will die of a chronic, progressive disease that will be painful to experience, painful to watch, expensive and ultimately fatal." 6

Mr. Wirth, 47 years old, had watched friends die slow, painful deaths from acquired immune deficiency syndrome. To avoid that, Mr. Wirth 7

signed a living will with notarized instructions saying he wished to be allowed to die with dignity and without "extraordinary measures." He even
designated a friend to make medical decisions in the event that he became
incapacitated.

Mr. Wirth did become ill. He fell into a coma in Bellevue Hospital.   8
His friend sought to halt aggressive medical treatment. Doctors refused,
saying that while the AIDS would certainly prove fatal over time, the immediate medical problem, a brain infection, was treatable. In July, a state
court judge agreed. Treatment was continued. Mr. Wirth died the next
month.

"That case should never have happened," said Giles Scofield, a staff   9
attorney for Concern for Dying, a right-to-die group, "But I'm afraid there
will be many others that shouldn't happen, either."

Mr. Wirth's designation of a proxy to make decisions, an arrangement   10
authorized by last week's legislative proposals, is not now recognized under New York law. But part of the problem stemmed from the wording of
Mr. Wirth's will. He spoke of ill-defined "extraordinary measures" at a
time when today's amazing technology can become tomorrow's ordinary
treatment. Better, Mr. Scofield said, to specify "a reasonable hope of recov-
ery," which is easier for doctors to agree on.

Competent patients have the legal right to refuse life-support sys-   11
tems, in theory. But emergency medical crews may not know an accident
victim's wishes. And, as the Wirth case demonstrated, once begun, such
treatment may prove impossible to stop.

Methods of decision-making are developing anyway. Court decisions,   12
hospital ethics committees and medical associations provide guidelines,
which increasingly stress the patient's rights. California's bar association
has approved a resolution that would allow doctors to give terminally ill
patients lethal drugs under some circumstances, as is done in the Nether-
lands.

The Hastings Center, a private research group specializing in ethics   13
issues, recently published guidelines on terminating treatment, favoring
the patient's choices. "I think the AIDS crisis is provoking a lot of thought
on advance planning," said Susan M. Wolf, who directed the project. "The
worst place to make these decisions is in the emergency room or the hall-
way when the doctor needs to know what to do immediately."

A Matter of Negotiation

Not every state recognizes living wills, and only Nevada, California   14
and Rhode Island specifically recognize the delegation of medical authority. With 80 percent of the average day's 5,750 deaths in this country
occurring in institutions, many are quietly negotiated between doctor, patient and family, and are becoming more open discussions and less open
secrets.

The New York doctor, for instance, tells every AIDS patient, "I will do as much as you want, but any time you want to call it quits, you'll get no argument from me." He said he has had more than 400 such patients. After long, painful periods of treatment and heavy medication, only four have opted out. 15

The doctor recalled: "They say 'would 20 of these pills kill me?' And I say, 'No, 30 would.' Too many doctors have reserved to themselves the right to give up medical treatment, but they don't give that right to the patient himself. I do." 16

CHECKING YOUR COMPREHENSION

1. Why did Mr. Wirth sign a living will refusing treatment?

2. Why was Mr. Wirth's will not carried out by doctors?

3. What problems do doctors face in deciding when and how to treat a terminally ill patient?

4. What trend or pattern seems to be developing on the issue of treatment of the terminally ill?

5. Explain how AIDS has affected the debate on rights of the terminally ill.

CRITICAL READING AND THINKING

1. Underline words used in the article with particularly strong connotations. (Connotative meanings: see Chapter 12)

2. Should doctors be allowed to give lethal drugs to terminally ill patients who desire them? Justify your answer.

3. Suppose the patient who was told that 30 pills would kill him took the 30 pills. Would the doctor who told him be in any way responsible for the patient's death?

4. What issues and problems would you face if you were asked to become a proxy for a dying friend or family member? Would you agree to do so? Explain.

_____

5. If you became terminally ill, would you write a living will?

_____

6. Is the article biased? If so, what is the other side of the issue? (Bias: see Chapter 14)

_____

WORDS IN CONTEXT

Directions: *Locate each word in the paragraph indicated and reread that paragraph. Then, based on the way the word is used in the paragraph, write a synonym or brief definition for each.*

1. terminally (par. 2) _____

2. telescopes (par. 6) _____

3. incapacitated (par. 7) _____

4. negotiated (par. 14) _____

VOCABULARY REVIEW

Directions: *Match the word in Column A with its meaning in Column B.*

Column A	Column B
_____ 1. comatose	a. governing body's decision
_____ 2. forgo	b. person acting for another
_____ 3. confrontation	c. opposition
_____ 4. culpability	d. fatal
_____ 5. proxy	e. unconscious owing to medical reasons
_____ 6. chronic	f. blamability
_____ 7. legislative	g. recurring
_____ 8. resolution	h. do without
_____ 9. lethal	i. having to do with governing bodies

SELECTION 20

BLUE HIGHWAYS
William Least Heat Moon

Have you ever felt as if you needed to be alone, completely away from everything and everyone you know? This selection is taken from the first few pages of a book titled Blue Highways. *It is the story of a man, part Sioux, who tries to sort out his life by leaving everything behind and going on the road.*

VOCABULARY PREVIEW

askew (par. 1)   out of order; disorganized

remote (par. 1)   far away

jeopardy (par. 3)   great danger or peril

skeins (par. 5)   flocks of geese or birds in flight

undulating (par. 5)   moving in a wavy manner; weaving

configuration (par. 5)   arrangement; outline

vernal equinox (par. 6)   day in spring when night and day are of equal
length

cartographer (par. 7)   map-maker

contaminated (par. 13)   impure; infected; polluted

perfidious (par. 13)   not trustworthy; disloyal

rendered (par. 15)   made; caused to be

delusion (par. 15)   false belief; misleading or deceiving idea

futility (pars. 15, 16)   sense of hopelessness or uselessness

PREREADING

Directions: *Preview the selection and answer the following question.*

List as many reasons as you can think of that explain why a person might want to travel through the United States alone.

_____

_____

Beware thoughts that come in the night. They aren't turned properly; they come in askew, free of sense and restriction, deriving from the most remote of sources. Take the idea of February 17, a day of canceled expectations, the day I learned my job teaching English was finished because of declining enrollment at the college, the day I called my wife from whom I'd been separated for nine months to give her the news, the day she let slip about her "friend"—Rick or Dick or Chick. Something like that.   1

That morning, before all the news started hitting the fan, Eddie Short Leaf, who worked a bottomland section of the Missouri River and plowed snow off campus sidewalks, told me if the deep cold didn't break soon the trees would freeze straight through and explode. Indeed.   2

That night, as I lay wondering whether I would get sleep or explosion, I got the idea instead. A man who couldn't make things go right could at least go. He could quit trying to get out of the way of life. Chuck routine. Live the real jeopardy of circumstance. It was a question of dignity.   3

The result: on March 19, the last night of winter, I again lay awake in the tangled bed, this time doubting the madness of just walking out on things, doubting the whole plan that would begin at daybreak—to set out on a long (equivalent to half the circumference of the earth), circular trip over the back roads of the United States. Following a circle would give a purpose—to come around again—where taking a straight line would not. And I was going to do it by living out of the back end of a truck. But how to begin a beginning?   4

A strange sound interrupted my tossing. I went to the window, the cold air against my eyes. At first I saw only starlight. Then they were there. Up in the March blackness, two entwined skeins of snow and blue geese honking north, an undulating W-shaped configuration across the deep sky, white bellies glowing eerily with the reflected light from town, necks stretched northward. Then another flock pulled by who knows what out of the south to breed and remake itself. A new season. Answer: begin by following spring as they did—darkly, with neck stuck out.   5

The vernal equinox came on gray and quiet, a curiously still morning not winter and not spring, as if the cycle paused. Because things go their own way, my daybreak departure turned to a morning departure, then to an afternoon departure. Finally, I climbed into the van, rolled down the window, looked a last time at the rented apartment. From a dead elm spar-   6 row hawks used each year came a high *whee* as the nestlings squealed for more grub. I started the engine. When I returned a season from now—if I did return—those squabs would be gone from the nest.

Accompanied only by a small, gray spider crawling the dashboard (kill 7 a spider and it will rain), I drove into the street, around the corner, through the intersection, over the bridge, onto the highway. I was heading toward those little towns that get on the map—if they get on at all—only because some cartographer has a blank space to fill: Remote, Oregon; Simplicity, Virginia; New Freedom, Pennsylvania; New Hope, Tennessee; Why, Arizona; Whynot, Mississippi; Igo, California (just down the road from Ono), here I come.

A pledge: I give this chapter to myself. When done with it, I will shut 8 up about *that* topic.

Call me Least Heat Moon. My father calls himself Heat Moon, my el- 9 der brother Little Heat Moon. I, coming last, am therefore Least. It has been a long lesson of a name to learn.

To the Siouan peoples, the Moon of Heat is the seventh month, a 10 time also known as the Blood Moon—I think because of its dusky midsummer color.

I have other names: Buck, once a slur—never mind the predominant 11 Anglo features. Also Bill Trogdon. The Christian names come from a grandfather eight generations back, one William Trogdon, an immigrant Lancashireman living in North Carolina, who was killed by the Tories for providing food to rebel patriots and thereby got his name in volume four of *Makers of America*. Yet to the red way of thinking, a man who makes peace with the new by destroying the old is not to be honored. So I hear.

One summer when Heat Moon and I were walking the ancestral 12 grounds of the Osage near the river of that name in western Missouri, we talked about bloodlines. He said, "Each of the people from anywhere, when you see in them far enough, you find red blood and a red heart. There's a hope."

Nevertheless, a mixed-blood—let his heart be where it may—is a 13 contaminated man who will be trusted by neither red nor white. The attitude goes back to a long history of "perfidious" half breeds, men who, by their nature, had to choose against one of their bloodlines. As for me, I will choose for heart, for spirit, but never will I choose for blood.

One last word about bloodlines. My wife, a woman of striking mixed- 14 blood features, came from the Cherokee. Our battles, my Cherokee and I, we called the "Indian wars."

For these reasons I named my truck Ghost Dancing, a heavy-handed 15 symbol alluding to ceremonies of the 1890s in which the Plains Indians, wearing cloth shirts they believed rendered them indestructible, danced for the return of warriors, bison, and the fervor of the old life that would sweep away the new. Ghost dances, desperate resurrection rituals, were the dying rattles of a people whose last defense was delusion—about all that remained to them in their futility.

A final detail: on the morning of my departure, I had seen thirty-eight   16
Blood Moons, an age that carries its own madness and futility. With a nearly desperate sense of isolation and a growing suspicion that I lived in an alien land, I took to the open road in search of places where change did not mean ruin and where time and men and deeds connected.

CHECKING YOUR COMPREHENSION

Directions: *In this article, Least Heat Moon explains why he is leaving everything behind and beginning a two- to three-month trip. List below as many reasons as you can recall that explain why Least Heat Moon is beginning this trip.*

_____

_____

_____

CRITICAL READING AND THINKING

1. What do you think Least Heat Moon means by "Chuck routine. Live the real jeopardy of circumstance"? (par. 3)

   _____

   _____

2. In paragraphs 4 and 5, the author asks a question and then answers it. First, underline the question and answer. Then, in your own words, explain what the answer means.

   _____

   _____

3. Explain Least Heat Moon's statement, "As for me, I will choose for heart, for spirit, but never will I choose for blood." (par. 13)

   _____

   _____

4. Why did Least Heat Moon name his truck "Ghost Dancing"?

   _____

   _____

5. What does the last sentence of the selection tell you about Least Heat Moon's life so far?

_____

_____

6. What do you think will be the results of Least Heat Moon's trip? Why do you think this?

_____

_____

WORDS IN CONTEXT

Directions: *Locate each word in the paragraph indicated and reread that paragraph. Then, based on the way the word is used in the paragraph, write a synonym or brief definition for each.*

1. declining (par. 1) _____

2. remake (par. 5) _____

3. pledge (par. 8) _____

4. alluding (par. 15) _____

VOCABULARY REVIEW

Directions: *Each of the following words has been formed from a root word and a suffix or verb ending. For each word, write the root word. Then, using a dictionary if necessary, write the meaning of the root word.*

Word	Root Word	Meaning of Root Word
Example: futility	futile	useless; worthless
1. undulating	_____	_____
2. contaminated	_____	_____
3. configuration	_____	_____
4. rendered	_____	_____
5. perfidious	_____	_____
6. delusion	_____	_____
7. cartographer	_____	_____

SELECTION 21

AN AMATEUR MARRIAGE
Steve Tesich

Getting married is an important step in most people's lives. Weddings are planned for months, sometimes years, ahead. This writer presents a different, more casual attitude toward marriage.

VOCABULARY PREVIEW

mythical (par. 2)   imaginary; not real

milestones (par. 2)   important events or turning points in life

rituals of passage (par. 2)   ceremonial events signifying changes or important acts

tidal (par. 7)   naturally forceful

ludicrous (par. 8)   obviously absurd or ridiculous

endeavor (par. 10)   careful effort; honest attempt

aimlessness (par. 12)   pointlessness; the state of being without direction or purpose

PREREADING

Directions: *Preview the selection and answer the following question.*

Try to think of events that have changed your life, or that are usually thought of as important events by others. Make a list of these events.

Everyone told me that when I turned 16 some great internal change   1
would occur. I truly expected the lights to go down on my former life and

come up again on a new, far more enchanting one. It didn't work. Nothing happened. When asked by others, I lied and said that, yes, I did feel a great change had taken place. They lied and told me that they could see it in me.

They lied again when I turned 18. There were rumors that I was now a "man." I noticed no difference, but I pretended to have all the rumored symptoms of manhood. Even though these mythical milestones, these rituals of passage, were not working for me, I still clung to the belief that they should, and I lied and said they were. 2

My 21st birthday was the last birthday I celebrated. The rituals weren't working, and I was tired of pretending I was changing. I was merely growing—adding on rooms for all the kids who were still me to live in. At 21, I was single but a family man nevertheless. 3

All these birthday celebrations helped to prepare me for the greatest myth of all: marriage. Marriage comes with more myths attached to it than a six-volume set of ancient Greek history. Fortunately for me, by the time I decided to get married I didn't believe in myths anymore. 4

It was a very hot day in Denver, and I think Becky and I decided to get married because we knew the city hall was air-conditioned. It was a way of hanging around a cool place for a while. I had forgotten to buy a wedding ring, but Becky was still wearing the ring from her previous marriage, so we used that one. It did the job. She had to take it off and then put it back on again, but it didn't seem to bother anyone. The air-conditioners were humming. 5

I felt no great change take place as I repeated our marriage vows. I did not feel any new rush of "commitment" to the woman who was now my wife, nor did I have any plans to be married to her forever. I did love her, but I saw no reason why I should feel that I had to love her forever. I would love her for as long as I loved her. I assumed she felt the same way. The women I saw on my way out of city hall, a married man, did not look any less beautiful than the women I saw on my way in. It was still hot outside. We walked to our car carrying plastic bags containing little samples of mouthwash, toothpaste, shampoo and aspirin, gifts from the Chamber of Commerce to all newlyweds. 6

And so my marriage began—except that I never really felt the beginning. I had nothing against transforming myself into a married man, but I felt no tidal pull of change. I assumed Becky had married me and not somebody else, so why should I become somebody else? She married a family of kids of various ages, all of them me, and I married a family of kids of various ages, all of them her. At one time or another I assumed some of them were bound to get along. 7

Marriage, I was told, required work. This sounded all wrong to me from the start. I couldn't quite imagine the kind of "work" it required, what the hours were, what the point was. The very idea of walking into my apartment and "working" on my marriage seemed ludicrous. My apart- 8 ment was a place where I went to get away from work. The rest of life was full of work. If marriage required "work," I would have to get another apartment just for myself where I could go and rest. Since I couldn't afford that at the time, I said nothing to Becky about working on our marriage. She said nothing about it herself. We were either very wise or very lazy.

We are led to believe that the harder we try, the better we get. This "aerobic dancing theory" of life may apply to certain things, but I don't think marriage is one of them. You can't go to a gym and pump marriage. It can't be tuned-up like a car. It can't be trained like a dog. In this century of enormous scientific breakthroughs, there have been no major marriage breakthroughs that I know of.   9

Progress junkies find this a frustrating state of affairs. They resist the notion that marriage is essentially an amateur endeavor, not a full-time profession, and they keep trying to work on their marriages and make them better. The only way to do that is to impose a structure on the marriage and then fiddle and improve the structure. But that has nothing to do with the way you feel when the guests have left the house and it's just the two of you again. You are either glad you're there with that person or you're not. I've been both.   10

This need to improve, the belief that we can improve everything, brings to mind some of my friends who are constantly up-dating their stereo equipment until, without being aware of it, they wind up listening to the equipment and not to the music. You can do the same thing to friendship, to marriage, to life in general. Let's just say I have chosen to listen to the music, such as it is, on the equipment at hand.   11

The best trips that I have taken were always last-minute affairs, taken as a lark. When I've sent off for brochures and maps, the trips always turned into disappointments. The time I invested in planning fed my expectations, and I traveled to fulfill my expectations rather than just to go somewhere I hadn't been. I consider my marriage one of those trips taken as a lark. I have become rather fond of the sheer aimlessness of the journey. It's a choice. I know full well that people do plan journeys to the Himalayas, they hire guides, they seek advice, and when they get there, instead of being disappointed, they experience a kind of exhilaration that I never will. My kind of marriage will never reach Mount Everest. You just don't go there as a lark, nor do you get there by accident.   12

I'm neither proud nor ashamed of the fact that I've stayed married for 13 years. I don't consider it an accomplishment of any kind. I have changed; my wife has changed. Our marriage, however, for better or worse, is neither better nor worse. It has remained the same. But the climate has changed.   13

I got married on a hot day a long time ago, because it was a way of cooling off for a while. Over the years, it's also become a place where I go to warm up when the world turns cold.   14

CHECKING YOUR COMPREHENSION

Directions: *Mark each of the following statements* T *for true or* F *for false based on the content of the selection.*

_____ 1. On his eighteenth birthday, the author felt that a change had occurred in his life.

_____ 2. The author bought his wife a wedding ring before they were married.

_____ 3. When the author got married, he did not feel any new commitment or change in his feelings toward his wife.

_____ 4. The author disagrees with the idea that people have to "work" on a marriage.

_____ 5. The author believes that last-minute, unplanned trips are often the best.

_____ 6. The author was married when he was twenty.

_____ 7. The author did not love his wife at the time he married her.

CRITICAL READING AND THINKING

1. Do you think the author gave more thought to the decision to get married than he admits in the article? Did he really get married, as he said, because the city hall was air-conditioned? If not, why did he say he did?

   _____

   _____

2. Did the author expect to feel different after he was married? How do you know?

   _____

   _____

3. Do you agree or disagree with the principle that "the harder we try, the better we get"? Are there some situations in which that statement might apply and others in which it does not? If so, give several examples.

   _____

   _____

4. What things about life did the author use this article to comment on or criticize?

_____

_____

5. Can you think of other events or milestones in life when everyone expects a change to occur or for you to feel or act differently?

_____

_____

6. Think of an event or milestone in your life (if you are or were married, think of the day you were married). Did people expect you to feel or act differently? Did you feel different that day?

_____

_____

7. The writer uses figurative language to express his ideas in several places in the article. Explain what Tesich means by each of the following statements. (Figurative language: see Chapter 12)

   a. I was merely growing—adding on rooms for all the kids who were still me to live in. (par. 3)

   _____

   b. At 21, I was single but a family man nevertheless. (par. 3)

   _____

   c. She married a family of kids of various ages, all of them me, . . . (par. 7)

   _____

8. Does the title reflect the content of the article? Why or why not?

_____

_____

WORDS IN CONTEXT

Directions: _Locate each word in the paragraph indicated and reread that paragraph. Then, based on the way the word is used in the paragraph, write a synonym or brief definition for each._

1. transforming (par. 7) _____

2. lark (par. 12) _____

3. exhilaration (par. 12) _____

VOCABULARY REVIEW

1. Name a milestone in your life.

_____

2. Give an example of something mythical.

_____

3. Describe a ritual of passage in your family's customs or in your religion.

_____

4. Give an example of an action or behavior you think is ludicrous.

_____

5. Name an endeavor that has been taking a lot of your time recently.

_____

6. Give an example of something that you have done in an aimless way.

_____

SELECTION 22

NONVERBAL COMMUNICATION
Anthony F. Grasha

How do you express your feelings to and about others? The primary way we communicate with others is through words. This excerpt from a psychology textbook discusses an alternate form of communication.

VOCABULARY PREVIEW

enhance (par. 1)   make greater in value, worth, or quantity

verbal (par. 1)   concerning or associated with words; having to do with speech

violate (par. 2)   interrupt; disturb

norms (par. 2)   standard models or patterns

manipulate (par. 7)   manage or control

utterances (par. 7)   speech sounds

converse (par. 8)   talk; engage in conversation

elaborate (par. 8)   explain more fully; give details

PREREADING

Directions: *Preview the selection and answer the following questions.*

What two aspects or types of nonverbal communication does this selection discuss? What do you already know about these two forms of communication?

_____

_____

Nonverbal Messages and Interpersonal Communication

The way we dress, our mannerisms, how close we stand to people, 1
eye contact, touching, and the ways we mark our personal spaces convey
certain messages. *Such nonverbal behaviors communicate certain messages by themselves and also enhance the meaning of our verbal communications.* Pounding your fist on a table, for example, suggests anger without anything being spoken. Holding someone close to you conveys the
message that you care. To say "I don't like you" with a loud voice or
waving fists increases the intensity of the verbal message. Let us examine
the concepts of *personal space* and *body language* to gain additional insights into the nonverbal side of interpersonal communication.

Nonverbal Messages: The Use of Personal Space

Edward Hall notes that we have personal spatial territories or zones 2
that allow certain types of behaviors and communications. We only allow
certain people to enter or events to occur within a zone. Let us look at
how some nonverbal messages can be triggered by behaviors that violate
the norms of each zone. The four personal zones identified by Hall are as
follows:

1 *Intimate distance.* This personal zone covers a range of distance 3
from body contact to one foot. Relationships between a parent and child,
lovers, and close friends occur within this zone. As a general rule, we only
allow people we know and have some affection for to enter this zone.
When someone tries to enter without our permission, they are strongly repelled by our telling them to stay away from us or by our pushing them
away. Why do you think we allow a doctor to easily violate our intimate
distance zone?

2 *Personal distance.* The spatial range covered by this zone extends 4
from one to four feet. Activities like eating in a restaurant with two or
three other people, sitting on chairs or the floor in small groups at parties,
or playing cards occur within this zone. Violations of the zone make people feel uneasy and act nervously. When you are eating at a restaurant, the
amount of table space that is considered yours is usually divided equally
by the number of people present. I can remember becoming angry and generally irritated when a friend of mine placed a plate and glass in my space.
As we talked I was visibly irritated, but my anger had nothing to do with
the topic we discussed. Has this ever happened to you?

3 *Social distance.* Four to twelve feet is the social distance zone. 5
Business meetings, large formal dinners, and small classroom seminars
occur within the boundaries of the social distance zone. Discussions concerning everyday topics like the weather, politics, or a best seller are
considered acceptable. For a husband and wife to launch into a heated argument during a party in front of ten other people would violate the ac-

cepted norms for behavior in the social zone. This once happened at a formal party I attended. The nonverbal behaviors that resulted consisted of several people leaving the room, others looking angry or uncomfortable, and a few standing and watching quietly with an occasional upward glance and a rolling of their eyeballs. What would violate the social distance norms in a classroom?

4 *Public distance.* This zone includes the area beyond twelve feet. 6 Addressing a crowd, watching a sports event, and sitting in a large lecture section are behaviors we engage in within this zone. As is true for the other zones, behaviors unacceptable for this zone can trigger nonverbal messages. At a recent World Series game a young male took his clothes off and ran around the outfield. Some watched with amusement on their faces, others looked away, and a few waved their fists at the culprit. The respective messages were, "That's funny," "I'm afraid or ashamed to look," and "How dare you interrupt the game." What would your reaction be in this situation?

Nonverbal Messages: The Use of Body Language

Body language refers to the various arm and hand gestures, facial ex- 7 pressions, tone of voice, postures, and body movements we use to convey certain messages. According to Irving Goffman, they are the things we "give off" when talking to other people. Goffman notes that our body language is generally difficult to manipulate at will. Unlike our verbal utterances, we have less conscious control over the specific body gestures or expressions we might make while talking. Unless we are acting on a stage or purposely trying to create a certain effect, they occur automatically without much thought on our part.

Michael Argyle notes that body language serves several functions for 8 us. *It helps us to communicate certain emotions, attitudes, and preferences.* A hug by someone close to us lets us know we are appreciated. A friendly wave and smile as someone we know passes us lets us know we are recognized. A quivering lip tells us that someone is upset. Each of us has become quite sensitive to the meaning of various body gestures and expressions. Robert Rosenthal has demonstrated that this sensitivity is rather remarkable. When shown films of people expressing various emotions, individuals were able to identify the emotion correctly 66 percent of the time even when each frame was exposed for one twenty-fourth of a second. *Body language also supports our verbal communications.* Vocal signals of timing, pitch, voice stress, and various gestures add meaning to our verbal utterances. Argyle suggests that we may speak with our vocal organs, but we converse with our whole body. *Body language helps to control our conversations.* It helps us to decide when it is time to stop talking, to interrupt the other person, and to know when to shift topics or elaborate on something because our listeners are bored, do not understand us, or are not paying attention.

CHECKING YOUR COMPREHENSION

Directions: *Assume that you are enrolled in a psychology course for which the textbook from which this selection was taken is used. Your next exam will cover the material presented in this excerpt as well as several other chapters. On a separate sheet, write an outline of this selection. Include information you would need to review to prepare for a multiple-choice exam.*

CRITICAL READING AND THINKING

1. How does this author let you know what is important (make his important points stand out)?

2. Do you think that such names as Irving Goffman and Michael Argyle are important to remember? Give your reasons.

3. If an exam on this material included an essay question, what question might you predict?

4. How would you answer the questions at the end of paragraphs 3, 5, and 6?

   Par. 3:

   Par. 5:

   Par. 6:

5. Describe personal situations in which body language was more important than verbal communication.

WORDS IN CONTEXT

Directions: *Locate each word or phrase in the paragraph indicated and reread that paragraph. Then, based on the way the word is used in the paragraph, write a synonym or brief definition for each.*

1. intensity (par. 1)

2. spatial territories (par. 2)

3. culprit (par. 6)

VOCABULARY REVIEW

Directions: *Match each word in Column A with its meaning in Column B by writing the letter of the definition next to the number of the word it defines.*

Column A	Column B
_____ 1. verbal	a. models
_____ 2. violate	b. control
_____ 3. utterances	c. increase in value
_____ 4. converse	d. talk
_____ 5. elaborate	e. explain more fully
_____ 6. norms	f. break in on
_____ 7. enhance	g. having to do with words
_____ 8. manipulate	h. sounds of someone talking

SELECTION 23

MALE HUMOR
Isaac Asimov

Have you noticed that men often tell off-color jokes, but women seldom do? This article discusses how and why men tell such jokes and what makes them funny.

VOCABULARY PREVIEW

glee (par. 2)   liveliness; joy; gaiety

roundabouts (par. 5)   actions that are not direct or straightforward

austerely (par. 7)   very plainly, strictly, or severely

innocuous (par. 8)   harmless; dull or uninspiring

distortions (par. 9)   things that are twisted out of shape or changed

hypocrisy (pars. 9, 10)   pretending to be what one is not

unabashed (par. 11)   not embarrassed or self-conscious

scatology (par. 11)   interest in or obsession with obscenity or excrement

tyrannized (par. 12)   controlled or ruled with absolute power

tantalized (par. 13)   teased or tormented by the promise of something desirable that is withheld

catharsis (par. 15)   release of tension or emotions

PREREADING

Directions: *Preview the selection and answer the following questions.*

What makes a joke funny? Think of jokes you have heard or told and analyze why they make people laugh.

_____

_____

Most of us, if we are male, have gathered in groups that happened to 1
be exclusively masculine. On those occasions, at least according to my
experience, it is extremely common to have conversation turn to an exchange of off-color jokes.

Such is the glee with which such jokes are told, and such the delight 2
with which they are received, that one of the most serious objections to
admitting women to the gatherings is that the presence of the female of
the species would inhibit these exchanges and destroy much of the joy of
the occasion.

But think about it. Why should jokes of this sort be told at all? Why 3
should they be considered funny and why *are* they (when told well) unfail-
ingly funny at that? Why do even the most respectable and well-mannered
men tell them and listen to others tell them? We might almost paraphrase
Shakespeare and say, "One touch of smut makes the whole male world
kin."

But is it really a mystery? Sex and elimination—the two basic staples 4
of such jokes—are unmentionable in polite society (in theory) and yet are
always with us. They are simply unavoidable, though the rules of the eti-
quette books tell us they don't exist.

What a horror is introduced into life by refusing to mention what we 5
cannot escape. What a torture of roundabouts we are plunged into as a
result.

Have you ever watched television commercials push laxatives and 6
talk about the dread disease of "irregularity"? Irregularity of what? In fact,
even irregularity has become suspect, and no abnormal condition at all is
mentioned by name. It has all sunk into a tight-lipped look of gentle concern. The tight lips give it away, I think.

When you dash for the washroom, is it a wild desire to wash your 7
hands that fills you? Is it for a nice rest that you go to the rest room, for a
chance to lounge about that you retreat to the lounge, a last-minute adjustment to the top hat that makes it necessary to retire to the little room austerely marked "Gentlemen"? No civilized man from Mars could possibly
guess the function of such rooms from the names we give them.

And is there a married couple (or an unmarried one, for that matter) 8
that doesn't invent some coy and innocuous phrase to serve as a signal
that indicates a desire for sex? What's yours? A meaningful clearing of the
throat?

What relief it is, then—what sheer release of tension—to tell some 9
story that involves the open admission that such things exist. Add that re-

lease of tension to the natural humor such a joke might contain and the laugh can be explosive. It might even be argued that, given the distortions introduced by our social hypocrisy, the dirty joke is an important contributor to the mental health of males.

But don't women suffer from the same social hypocrisy as men do?   10
Aren't women repressed even more than men, since women are supposed to be "ladylike" and "pure"? Of course! And it is my experience that women laugh as hard at dirty jokes as men do, and show even greater tolerance for those that are not really very funny, but *are* very dirty.

Why, then, do men persist in believing that the presence of women   11
will spoil their fun? Partly, I suppose, it is because they are victims of the myth of feminine purity, but partly it is because one of the important components of the dirty joke is unabashed male chauvinism. Women are almost always the butts and victims of such jokes, and, indeed, a male chauvinist joke can be extremely successful even when there is no hint of any element of either sex or scatology.

Again, it's no mystery. Men are tyrannized by women from birth (or   12
feel themselves to be—which comes to the same thing, of course). The young boy is hounded unmercifully and continually by his mother, who is perpetually at him to do what he does not want to do, and to *not* do what he *does* want to do. (The father is inevitably a more distant creature and, unless he is a monster, is more easily handled.)

The young man in love is constantly tantalized by the young woman   13
he desires, and the young groom is harried to fulfill his campaign promises to his young bride. And, eventually, as married life settles down, the husband is hounded unmercifully and continually by his wife, who is perpetually at him to do what he does not want to do; and to *not* do what he *does* want to do. (At least, this is how it seems to him to be.)

Naturally, then, the male gathering is the one place (it seems to the   14
man) where he can escape from this unending, lifelong feminine domination, and where he can retaliate, in safety, by telling jokes in which women get what they deserve.

You might argue that there's no harm in it. When all the jokes are   15
done, he goes back home, having undergone a useful catharsis, and says his "Yes, dear" with far greater efficiency than he would have otherwise. Here again, such jokes may be essential to male mental health.

Do I approve?   16

No. I don't like male chauvinism—but let's not repress the jokes that   17
serve a useful psychological purpose. I would, instead, prefer to invite women into the charmed circle and have them tell their jokes, too, which perhaps will help remove some of *their* hang-ups.

The trouble is that they leave the jokes to the men. Women by the   18
hundreds have said to me, after having laughed fiendishly at some joke I have told: "Oh, I wish I could repeat it, but I never seem to be able to remember jokes, and when I do, I can't tell them."

Haven't we all heard that line?   19

Well, *why* can't women remember jokes? Have they poor memories?   20

Nonsense! They remember the price of every garment they have ever   21
bought, and the exact place they have bought it. They know where everything in the kitchen is, including the mustard jar that any husband will
swear, after a thorough search, is nowhere in the house.

They're just defaulting on their responsibilities, and, as long as they   22
do, they encourage us men to put our heads together and tell our chauvinist jokes after a nervous glance hither and thither assures us that no
woman can hear us.

CHECKING YOUR COMPREHENSION

Directions: *Mark each statement* T *for true or* F *for false based on the*
content of the selection.

_____ 1. The author feels that men used to be but are no longer controlled by women.

_____ 2. One reason men gather together is to escape from women.

_____ 3. The author states that most dirty jokes are about or make
fun of women.

_____ 4. Some men object to telling jokes in the presence of women
because it might destroy the fun of the occasion.

_____ 5. Women tell as many off-color jokes as men.

_____ 6. The author encourages women to develop their own off-
color jokes and make men the victims of the jokes.

_____ 7. Sex and male-female relationships are the two main topics
with which off-color jokes are concerned.

_____ 8. Calling a bathroom a restroom is an example of how
women control society.

_____ 9. Dirty jokes contribute to the mental health of males.

CRITICAL READING AND THINKING

1. Do you agree or disagree with Asimov's analysis of why dirty jokes are
funny? Give your reasons.

_____

_____

2. Do you believe the author when he invites women to join men and share their jokes with them? Why or why not?

   _____

3. Why do you think the author wrote the article? (Author's purpose: see Chapter 13)

   _____

4. What do you think the writer's attitude toward women is?

   _____

5. Name other instances or situations in which a euphemism, or cover-up word, is used to refer to the body or to a bodily function?

   _____

   _____

6. Review paragraphs 13–15. Underline the words that Asimov uses to describe women and their actions. Do these words have positive or negative connotations? (Connotation: see Chapter 12)

   _____

WORDS IN CONTEXT

Directions: *Locate each word in the paragraph indicated and reread that paragraph. Then, based on the way the word is used in the paragraph, write a synonym or brief definition for each.*

1. inhibit (par. 2)   _____
2. tolerance (par. 10)   _____
3. harried (par. 13)   _____
4. retaliate (par. 14)   _____

VOCABULARY REVIEW

Directions: *Use the words listed in the Vocabulary Preview to complete each of the following sentences.*

1. The senator's most recent speech was _____ because it did not discuss any of the key issues.

2. My brother _____ me by holding out his ice-cream cone and then slowly licking it.

3. The child felt _____ by his strict parents.

4. The child's eyes shone with _____ when she saw her new bicycle.

5. The farmer's directions to the country store proved to be a _____ way of getting there.

6. The woman was _____ dressed; she wore a black suit and black shoes.

7. The jury felt that the witness's testimony was full of _____ made to protect the defendant.

8. Breaking into tears in the therapist's office served as a _____ for the parents of a child who died of cancer.

9. We were shocked by the student's _____ demand for a higher grade.

10. _____ is common in our society; many people claim to be religious but do not practice the beliefs they profess to hold.

11. _____ plays a large role in the appeal of X-rated films.

SELECTION 24

COMPUTER CRIME
Michael Crichton

This selection discusses one of the newest types of crime—computer crime.

VOCABULARY PREVIEW

medieval (pars. 2, 3)   characteristic of the Middle Ages (A.D. 476–1450)

remnants (par. 3)   remainders, what is left over

embezzles (par. 3)   steals property that one is entrusted with

misperception (par. 5)   misunderstanding

humiliation (par. 5)   feeling of injured pride or dignity

depredations (par. 7)   acts of robbing or laying waste

leniency (par. 9)   mildness; mercifulness

vulnerable (par. 9)   open to criticism or attack; easily hurt

naïveté (par. 11)   innocence; unsophistication

disgruntled (par. 12)   displeased; not content

mitigating (par. 14)   softening or lessening; becoming less severe

PREREADING

Directions: *Preview the selection and answer the following questions.*

What types of crime can be committed using computers?

In what ways do they differ from other types of crimes?

In seventeenth-century England, more than two hundred crimes were 1
punishable by hanging. The great majority of those felonies were crimes
against property; stealing goods worth more than a shilling [a British coin]
was sufficient for the death sentence.

The only way to avoid hanging was by royal pardon or "benefit of 2
clergy"—a convicted criminal had the right to call for a Bible, and if he
could read it aloud to the court, he was branded on the thumb and released. Benefit of clergy was originally a medieval notion, dating from the
time when priests were the only literate members of society, and were
subject to their own ecclesiastical courts.

But remnants of this medieval tradition persist to this day in modern 3
attitudes toward white-collar crime. We are reluctant to define white-
collar crime as crime at all; the milk-toast bank clerk who embezzles, or
the corporate high roller with a Bahamas bank account, is likely to get off
with a slap on the wrist, if he is prosecuted at all.

Such criminals appear to us quite different from the brutal street 4
mugger who presses a gun to his victim's head. White-collar "criminals"
are nicely dressed, responsible, and educated. They steal from large, face-
less institutions, such as banks and insurance companies, which can afford
the losses. Privately, we resent the large institutions of society; anybody
who rips off the IRS or the telephone company is likely to be viewed as a
clever, praiseworthy person.

It is into this protective misperception of white-collar crime that the 5
computer criminal neatly fits. The computer criminal enjoys further advantages. Few like computers and fewer still understand them; the computer criminal is perceived as unusually bright and smart. Furthermore,
the computer criminal is often young and without serious criminal intent.
When a teenager taps into Defense Department data banks, we perceive
humiliation of the government, and we're delighted. The fact that it costs
the DOD $24 million to untangle the mess is hardly worth mentioning.
And if another teenager taps into the high-school records to change his
girlfriend's grades, that's just a youthful prank. We remember how it was.

Of course this is all nonsense. 6

Institutions pass their losses on; ultimately we pay for the depreda- 7
tions of computer criminals—an amount estimated at from $5 billion to
$30 billion a year.

If we stopped to think about it, we would not be amused by Alec 8
Guinness as the embezzling bank clerk, Liza Minnelli as the shoplifter, or
Peter Ustinov as the computer criminal.

In fact, the long-standing leniency toward white-collar crime is about 9
to undergo a startling revision. A company like Citibank uses computers
to process transactions amounting to $30 billion a day for customers in a

hundred different countries. American banks move $400 billion a day by computer just within the United States. Our society is now simply too vulnerable to disruption to view white-collar crime tolerantly. Among the changes:

Institutions will lose their embarrassment about their self-image—   10 the chief reason computer prosecutions are rare. Computer crime is not evidence of mismanagement; it's evidence of crime.

Companies will abandon their naïveté about employee honesty. Many   11 companies seem to think that their employees won't steal because they're good Americans and loyal to the company. Yet a substantial body of psychological data suggests that people will do whatever they can get away with. The best guarantee of employees' honesty is a system that doesn't tempt them.

We will be less inclined to regard computer crime as clever. Most   12 computer crime is rather stupidly simpleminded. The welfare worker who programs the computer to make out checks to himself isn't smart. (If he were smart, he wouldn't send the checks to his own house.) Nor is computer crime innocent. The disgruntled employee who programs a logic bomb in the computer to shut down the system a month after he leaves is no better than an arsonist.

Further, as more people become skilled in the use of computers, the   13 vulnerability of individuals will increase. It's one thing to read that someone ripped off the phone company. It's another thing to have an argument with your neighbor, who then taps into data banks and destroys your credit rating, eliminates bank records of your mortgage payments, or orders your car repossessed.

Finally, age will cease to be a mitigating factor. The ability of some   14 kid to shut down a large computer system in another city or another country for a week or two will simply be intolerable—no matter how much he explains that he didn't mean it. After a period of education in these matters, there will be several highly publicized cases in which twelve-year-olds go to jail. Everybody's going to feel uncomfortable about it, but society won't really have a choice.

CHECKING YOUR COMPREHENSION

1. What is white-collar crime?

   _____

2. Explain the historical beginnings of our lenient attitude toward white-collar crime.

   _____

   _____

3. Give some examples of computer crime.

4. Why is the computer criminal not thought of as a "real" criminal?

5. Why are computer criminals rarely prosecuted?

6. What evidence (reasons) does the author give to indicate that our attitude toward computer crime is about to change?

CRITICAL READING AND THINKING

1. In paragraph 5, what does the author mean by the phrase *protective misperception*?

2. Do you think computer crime is as serious as other types of crime? Why or why not?

3. What other types of white-collar crime can you think of?

4. What was the author's purpose in writing the article? (Author's purpose: see Chapter 13)

5. Do you think that a teenager who commits a computer crime should be punished as severely as an adult who commits the same crime? Why or why not?

6. Does the author of this selection seem to think that people are basically honest? How do you know? Do you agree or disagree with him?

WORDS IN CONTEXT

Directions: *Locate each word in the paragraph indicated and reread that paragraph. Then, based on the way the word is used in the paragraph, write a synonym or brief definition for each.*

1. ecclesiastical (par. 2) _____

2. perceived (par. 5) _____

3. mismanagement (par. 10) _____

4. prepossessed (par. 13) _____

VOCABULARY REVIEW

Directions: *Complete each of the following statements. Refer to the Vocabulary Preview if necessary.*

1. A word that describes a person who is not naïve is _____.

2. Someone who is vulnerable is _____.

3. A disgruntled diner in a restaurant might have had _____.

4. An example of a mitigating circumstance that could prevent a serious student from attending class is _____.

5. A word that means the opposite of *vulnerable* is _____.

6. A judge who is not lenient is _____.

7. A person who steals from the company that employs him or her might be called a(n) _____.

8. Knights lived in _____ times.

9. When you misperceive something, you _____ it.

10. If you tripped and fell down a flight of stairs, you might feel _____.

11. Depredations are _____.

12. A tailor who shortened your pants might save the _____ for you.

SELECTION 25

THE POSSIBILITY OF NUCLEAR WAR
Robert L. Lineberry

The threat of nuclear war is frightening, but, according to this article, taken from an American Government textbook, an event for which the United States has developed policies and procedures.

VOCABULARY PREVIEW

scenario (par. 2)   an outline of possible events

arsenal (par. 2)   collection or group of weapons

failsafe (par. 2)   preventing unintentional use or malfunctioning

console (par. 2)   a panel containing controls and screens

elaborate (par. 6)   develop detail, add to, explain further

assess (par. 5)   determine and evaluate

simulated (par. 5)   fake, unreal

irradiation (par. 5)   being exposed to radiation

allocate (par. 6)   distribute according to a plan

priority (par. 6)   order of importance

implementing (par. 8)   carrying out, completing

assumption (par. 7)   something accepted as true

PREREADING

Directions: *Preview the article and then answer the following questions:*

1. Have you considered the possibility of nuclear war?

   _____

2. How real a threat do you think nuclear war is?

   _____

3. How can you imagine a nuclear war beginning?

   _____

There are two kinds of war in the modern world. Conventional war, 1
fought without nuclear weapons, was the only sort of war we knew before
1945. Since the first use of nuclear weapons against Japan in 1945, nuclear
war has been an awesome possibility.

Contrary to our popular imagery, nuclear wars are not started by 2
pushing a button, but by turning a key. Sitting underneath the earth in
large egg-shaped containers in the North Dakota wheat fields are numerous pairs of young Air Force officers. These are our "missile men," the
lieutenants, captains, and majors whose job it would be to launch our nuclear arsenal toward the Soviet Union or other targets. Each officer sits at a
separate console and carries only a revolver for protection. The console
contains a computer terminal, a video display screen, collections of codes,
and failsafe procedures. The consoles are so placed that one officer cannot
reach two keyboards. If the order to launch came, each pair of officers
would have to insert their keys and turn them almost simultaneously.
That is how it would begin. Here is what would happen under one scenario.

If all goes according to plan, missiles would be launched from thou- 3
sands of silos in the Dakotas and other plains and southern states. Aging
B-52 bombers would also take off, flying only a few hundred feet above the
ground (to avoid Soviet radar detection), winging their way to Moscow and
other strike sites. No doubt missiles and bombers would be flying from the
other direction as well. Showers of nuclear bombs would rain on the earth.
Cities would disintegrate; radiation would stick to the skins of the survivors; forests would be in flames. According to American war plans, Moscow
would be hit with 60 nuclear warheads, Leningrad with more than 40, and
the next largest forty Soviet cities with an average of 14.4 warheads each.
Eighty percent of all Soviet cities with a population greater than 25,000
would be hit. Each would be in flames. Presumably, American cities would
suffer similar fates.[1]

The effects of this nuclear outburst are not entirely clear, but very 4
likely, a "nuclear winter" would follow within hours or days. If only 40
percent of the superpowers' warheads struck, igniting forests, cities, people, farms—literally everything—the total smoke emission would exceed

[1] Thomas Powers, "Nuclear Winter and Nuclear Strategy," *Atlantic* (November 1984):63.

100 million metric tons. And "one hundred million tons of smoke, if it were distributed as a uniform cloud over the entire globe, could reduce the intensity of sunlight reaching the ground by as much as 95 percent."[2] Probably, the smoke would be concentrated mainly in the northern hemisphere, reaching perhaps to the tropics. In the northern hemisphere, "local freezing could occur within two or three days." Over a longer period, "practically no area of the globe, north or south, would be safe from nuclear winter."[3]

We do not know for certain all the effects of nuclear war. The Pentagon, however, maintains the Defense Nuclear Agency (DNA), headquartered next to a golf course in northern Virginia. It spends about $400 million annually to assess the effects of nuclear weapons on military capacity. It conducts research and publishes military manuals on the effects of radiation on soldiering. As a result of DNA studies of radiation after-effects, the combat commander now confidently knows that tank loaders exposed to 1000 "rads" of radiation (about 1000 times as much as a chest X-ray) will remain "combat effective" for about 100 minutes. Within a day, they will be "combat ineffective"; within about a month, they will die. DNA also maintains a massive underground explosive unit in White Oak, Maryland, where virtually every military weapon is exposed to simulated nuclear explosions—10 million volts of gamma rays—to see how it performs after irradiation.[4] Someone, after all, has to find out whether those B-52 pilots could keep flying to Moscow after they and their planes have been radiated.

Planning for nuclear war is but one part of the United States' overall planning for war. The president as commander in chief is responsible for all war plans and preparations. Typically, the president will sign a short document, perhaps ten pages in length, which will outline military goals and strategies in case of war. (President Reagan's was called National Security Decision Directive 13.) The Pentagon will elaborate it further. The Strategic Air Command (SAC) in Omaha, Nebraska, is responsible for the nuclear component of the strategy. It is SAC which aims the missiles and orders the specific bombing routes.[5] The Pentagon made public the broad outlines (not, of course, specific details) of its war plan in May 1982. The 125-page document would be the basis for its congressional budget requests in the coming years. The document itself sketched the broad picture of United States strategy in a nuclear war.[6] First, emphasized the De-

5

6

[2] Richard P. Turco, et al., "The Climatic Effects of Nuclear War," *Scientific American* (August 1984):37.
[3] Ibid., p. 42. See also Paul R. Ehrlich, et al., *The Cold and the Dark: The World after Nuclear War* (New York: W.W. Norton. 1985).
[4] Rick Atkinson, "Rehearsing for Nuclear War: How Long Could an Irradiated Pilot Keep Flying?," *Washington Post Weekly Edition*, June 18, 1984, pp. 6–8.
[5] Powers, "Nuclear Winter and Nuclear Strategy," p. 64.
[6] Richard Halloran, "Pentagon Draws up First Strategy for Fighting a Long Nuclear War," *New York Times*, May 30, 1982, pp. 1ff.

partment of Defense (DOD), the United States should be prepared for what the document called a "protracted" conflict, that is, a war that could go on for days, weeks, or months beyond an initial nuclear exchange. Here are some principles DOD spelled out for such a war:

- An American nuclear attack on the Soviet Union would target key political and military leadership and communication lines.

- The conventional (nonnuclear) strategy would allocate military forces in priority order, first to the defense of the United States homeland, next to the defense of Western Europe, and then to protecting oil resources in the Persian Gulf; Asia, the Pacific, and Latin America would have low priority.

- Some military assistance would go to the People's Republic of China, hoping that a Chinese-Soviet conflict would reduce Soviet abilities to fight elsewhere.

The plan outlined in the document depends on the critical assumption that nuclear war can begin and then go on. The beginnings, though, are the easy part. The Congressional Office of Technology Assessment reviewed a scenario for the beginnings of a "limited nuclear war," that is, one devoted only to strikes at missile sites.[7] A limited attack, confined only to key missile sites, could kill from 2 million to 20 million people.   7

War and peace are serious business. Much of the energy of our foreign-policy makers is devoted to pursuing peace and planning for war, and such plans and pursuits have become ever more important in the interdependent world we live in. Military policy is the making and implementing of policies devoted to war. Foreign policy is the making and implementing of policies devoted—we hope—to peace.   8

[7] Cited in *Newsweek*, October 5, 1981, p. 37.

CHECKING YOUR COMPREHENSION

1. What steps are involved in initiating a nuclear attack?

_____

2. How would a nuclear winter occur?

_____

3. Explain three principles or plans the U.S. government has for a protracted conflict.

_____

4. What would a "limited nuclear war" be?

_____

5. What does the Defense Nuclear Agency (DNA) do? Do you feel its job is important? Why?

_____

6. Who is the primary person responsible for nuclear war planning and preparation?

_____

7. Describe some of the effects of a nuclear bomb explosion.

_____

CRITICAL READING AND THINKING

1. Do you think the system for beginning a nuclear war is trustworthy? Explain.

_____

2. Why does the author include the information that the DNA is located next to a golf course? What is implied, but not stated? (Implied meanings: see Chapter 12)

_____

3. Do you detect a note of sarcasm (saying one thing, but meaning another) at the end of paragraph 5? Explain.

_____

4. What do you think the author's attitude is toward the government's planning for nuclear war?

_____

5. Evaluate the connotative language used by the author. Cite several examples that reveal his attitude toward nuclear war. (Connotative language: see Chapter 12)

_____

6. Why do you think the author wrote the article? (Author's purpose: see Chapter 13)

WORDS IN CONTEXT

Directions: *Locate each word in the paragraph indicated and reread that paragraph. Then, based on the way the word is used in the paragraph, write a synonym or brief definition for each.*

1. disintegrate (par. 3) _____

2. presumably (par. 3) _____

3. protracted (par. 6) _____

4. conventional (par. 6) _____

5. initial (par. 6) _____

6. document (par. 7) _____

VOCABULARY REVIEW

Directions: *Use the words listed in the Vocabulary Preview to complete each of the following sentences.*

1. An outline of a possible occurrence is a _____.

2. An operation that is _____ prevents malfunctioning and misuse.

3. We visited an army _____, or collection of weapons.

4. A _____ diamond is one that is not real.

5. Determining the damage of a housefire is to _____ it.

6. If a friend asked you to add to or develop in detail a story, you would _____.

7. The college administration will _____ funds to departments.

8. To arrange your assignments in _____ order is to arrange them from most to least important.

9. Carrying out a plan of action is the same as _____ it.

SELECTION 26

TELEVISION ADDICTION
Marie Winn

We know that drugs, alcohol, and gambling can be addictive, but can television be addictive?

VOCABULARY PREVIEW

wryly (par. 1)   jokingly, kiddingly

surge (par. 1)   sudden increase

denote (par. 1)   indicate, stand for

dismaying (par. 3)   troubling, alarming

essence (par. 3)   basic quality; most important feature

pursue (par. 4)   try to obtain, strive for

passive (par. 7)   taking no active part, not involved

inchoately (par. 7)   unclearly, incompletely

enervated (par. 8)   weakened, having no strength

ruefully (par. 10)   regretfully, sadly

renders (par. 11)   makes or causes

sated (par. 12)   satisfied completely

PREREADING

Directions: *Preview the article and then write a list of 3 to 4 questions that you have about television addiction.*

_____

_____

The word "addiction" is often used loosely and wryly in conversation. People will refer to themselves as "mystery book addicts" or "cookie addicts." E. B. White writes of his annual surge of interest in gardening: "We are hooked and are making an attempt to kick the habit." Yet nobody really believes that reading mysteries or ordering seeds by catalogue is serious enough to be compared with addictions to heroin or alcohol. The word "addiction" is here used jokingly to denote a tendency to overindulge in some pleasurable activity.

People often refer to being "hooked on TV." Does this, too, fall into the lighthearted category of cookie eating and other pleasures that people pursue with unusual intensity, or is there a kind of television viewing that falls into the more serious category of destructive addiction?

When we think about addiction to drugs or alcohol, we frequently focus on negative aspects, ignoring the pleasures that accompany drinking or drug-taking. And yet the essence of any serious addiction is a pursuit of pleasure, a search for a "high" that normal life does not supply. It is only the inability to function without the addictive substance that is dismaying, the dependence of the organism upon a certain experience and an increasing inability to function normally without it. Thus a person will take two or three drinks at the end of the day not merely for the pleasure drinking provides, but also because he "doesn't feel normal" without them.

An addict does not merely pursue a pleasurable experience and need to experience it in order to function normally. He needs to *repeat* it again and again. Something about that particular experience makes life without it less than complete. Other potentially pleasurable experiences are no longer possible, for under the spell of the addictive experience, his life is peculiarly distorted. The addict craves an experience and yet he is never really satisfied. The organism may be temporarily sated, but soon it begins to crave again.

Finally a serious addiction is distinguished from a harmless pursuit of pleasure by its distinctly destructive elements. A heroin addict, for instance, leads a damaged life: his increasing need for heroin in increasing doses prevents him from working, from maintaining relationships, from developing in human ways. Similarly an alcoholic's life is narrowed and dehumanized by his dependence on alcohol.

Let us consider television viewing in the light of the conditions that define serious addictions.

Not unlike drugs or alcohol, the television experience allows the participant to blot out the real world and enter into a pleasurable and passive mental state. The worries and anxieties of reality are as effectively deferred by becoming absorbed in a television program as by going on a "trip" induced by drugs or alcohol. And just as alcoholics are only inchoately aware of their addiction, feeling that they control their drinking more than they really do ("I can cut it out any time I want—I just like to have three or four drinks before dinner"), people similarly overestimate their control over television watching. Even as they put off other activities to spend hour after hour watching television, they feel they could easily resume living in a different, less passive style. But somehow or other while the television set is present in their homes, the click doesn't sound. With television pleasures available, those other experiences seem less attractive, more difficult somehow.

A heavy viewer (a college English instructor) observes: 8

"I find television almost irresistible. When the set is on, I cannot ignore it. I can't turn it off. I feel sapped, will-less, enervated. As I reach out to turn off the set, the strength goes out of my arms. So I sit there for hours and hours."

The self-confessed television addict often feels he "ought" to do other   9
things—but the fact that he doesn't read and doesn't plant his garden or sew or crochet or play games or have conversations means that those activities are no longer as desirable as television viewing. In a way a heavy viewer's life is as imbalanced by his television "habit" as a drug addict's or an alcoholic's. He is living in a holding pattern, as it were, passing up the activities that lead to growth or development or a sense of accomplishment. This is one reason people talk about their television viewing so ruefully, so apologetically. They are aware that it is an unproductive experience, that almost any other endeavor is more worthwhile by any human measure.

Finally it is the adverse effect of television viewing on the lives of so   10
many people that defines it as a serious addiction. The television habit distorts the sense of time. It renders other experiences vague and curiously unreal while taking on a greater reality for itself. It weakens relationships by reducing and sometimes eliminating normal opportunities for talking, for communicating.

And yet television does not satisfy, else why would the viewer con-   11
tinue to watch hour after hour, day after day? "The measure of health," writes Lawrence Kubie, "is flexibility . . . and especially the freedom to cease when sated."[1] But the television viewer can never be sated with his television experiences—they do not provide the true nourishment that satiation requires—and thus he finds that he cannot stop watching.

[1]Lawrence Kubie, *Neurotic Distortion and the Creative Process* (Lawrence: University of Kansas Press, 1958).

CHECKING YOUR COMPREHENSION

1. How does the author define an addiction?

_____

_____

2. What is the difference between often experiencing an activity that is greatly enjoyable and being addicted to that activity?

_____

3. How does television addiction affect people's lives? Why do people become addicted to television?

_____

4. Does the author seem to have any positive feelings about television viewing? If so, what are they?

_____

5. How is television addiction similar to drug or alcohol addiction?

_____

6. Why is the television viewer never completely satisfied with his or her watching?

_____

CRITICAL READING

1. Does television have a negative or positive effect on your life? Explain.

_____

2. What kinds of destructive addictions other than television, drugs, and alcohol can you think of?

_____

3. List several words with negative connotations that are used to describe television addiction. (Connotative meanings: see Chapter 12)

_____

4. Does the author present an objective or subjective description of television addiction? (Objective and subjective: see Chapter 13)

_____

5. What type(s) of evidence does the writer use to support her claim that television is addictive? Evaluate the quality of this evidence. (Supporting evidence: see Chapter 14)

_____

6. What negative affects of television watching have you experienced or observed in others?

_____

WORDS IN CONTEXT

Directions: *Locate each word in the paragraph indicated and reread that paragraph. Then, based on the way the word is used in the paragraph, write a synonym or brief definition for each.*

1. tendency (par. 1)   _____

2. craves (par. 4)   _____

3. distinguished (par. 5) _____

4. deferred (par. 7)   _____

5. overestimate (par. 7) _____

6. sapped (par. 8)   _____

7. endeavor (par. 9)   _____

8. adverse (par. 10)   _____

VOCABULARY REVIEW

Directions: *Mark each statement T for true or F for false.*

_____ 1. To do something *ruefully* is to do it slowly.

_____ 2. The word "cat" *denotes* a small four legged animal.

_____ 3. If a student answers a question totally and clearly, then he answers it *inchoately.*

_____ 4. A *surge* of sea water can cause shoreline flooding.

_____ 5. To *wryly* say something is to say it in a joking or ironic way.

_____ 6. A man who takes charge of his life is very *passive.*

_____ 7. To *pursue* a career in accounting, a student should like working with numbers.

_____ 8. If you felt *enervated*, you would feel energetic and lively.

_____ 9. Feeling *sated* is the same as feeling angry.

SELECTION 27

WINNING THE WAR AGAINST TERRORISTS

Gayle Rivers

The author of this article is a member of a Special Forces team that fights terrorists.

VOCABULARY PREVIEW

perpetrates (par. 1)   does, performs, usually criminally

foremost (par. 5)   most importantly, first

clandestinely (par. 5)   secretly, hiddenly

strongholds (par. 5)   a place that is strongly defended and protected

alliance (par. 6)   association and agreement

proliferate (par. 7)   reproduce, multiply quickly

volition (par. 7)   will or conscious decision

adhering (par. 7)   sticking to, supporting

destabilize (par. 7)   unbalance or upset

rationale (par. 9)   reasoning or way of making a decision

tactician (par. 9)   an expert in planning and/or carrying out actions

culvert (par. 11)   a large underground pipe or drain

intent (par. 12)   meaning or purpose

escalation (par. 12)   a rapid rise or increase

PREREADING

Directions: *Preview the article and answer the following questions*:

1. List recent acts of world terrorism.

2. What do you know about their cause or outcome?

If one is about to clean house, a good first step is to get rid of the garbage. But one man's garbage is another man's keepsake. Garbage is what a person wants to get rid of. What I want to get rid of is the human garbage that willfully perpetrates outrages against the rest of humanity and whom we have come to call terrorists. 1

A victim who has looked a terrorist in the eyes often learns more in those few seconds than other people can by reading about terrorism in newspapers for years. Leon Klinghoffer, the 69-year-old American invalid in his wheelchair, knew what the terrorist is really like in those seconds before he was shot in the chest and face and thrown overboard from the *Achille Lauro*, his wheelchair flung into the sea after him. If, as it was reported by a witness, he bit one of the terrorists just before being shot, he certainly knew.[1] 2

Judge Stanley Kubacki of Philadelphia, a passenger on the *Achille Lauro*, reported that the hijackers forced his wife, Sophia, and two other women to hold hand grenades with the pins removed. Other hostages were forced to sit close to the women and watch. "If one of these women fell asleep or fainted," the judge said, "we would all have been blown up." These people, crowded around three middle-aged ladies with grenades, and the women themselves, of course, know what terrorists are like. 3

As a counterterrorist hunting and eliminating terrorists for fifteen or more years, I have looked terrorists in the eyes many times. In some instances, I saw a glint in their eyes when they thought my life was in their hands. I have also seen their eyes split seconds before I shot them. 4

As a counterterrorist I am foremost a highly trained and experienced specialist soldier. My enemies are terrorists of any nationality. My enemies are also those governments and people who give terrorists arms, money, and safe havens to train in and flee to. I have worked, almost always clandestinely, for the United States, Great Britain, Spain, and some of their allies. My missions have taken me to China, Iran, Greece, Africa, 5

---

[1] In October 1985, four Palestinian gunmen seized the Italian cruise ship *Achille Lauro* off the coast of Egypt while on a pleasure tour of the Mediterreanean. Before surrendering to Egyptian authorities 51 hours later, the hijackers killed Leon Klinghoffer, a 69-year-old, wheelchair-bound American passenger, by shooting him in the head and throwing him overboard.

the Lebanon, and into less exotic strongholds of terrorists in Western Europe.

My alliance is with the victims of terrorism. My highly specialized 6
job has been to prevent further victims, usually by killing terrorist leaders. What the reader of this book will have to decide is whether these terrorists are his enemies also, for there are ways of putting a stop to the terrorist war. . . .

There are people on this earth who think of all life as sacred and who 7
will not step on a roach. The fact is that roaches and their kindred insects have proved their ability to survive the centuries much better than man has. Similarly, rats have in every century outwitted mere men in survival techniques. To me, terrorists are like roaches and rats; if we let them proliferate, we will lose the war in which we have been pitted against them by their volition. They initiated the war against us, and not vice versa. Therefore, I remember hearing stories about captured SS killers who claimed immunity from prosecution because they were "only following orders." Moral mankind asserted that following orders to participate in the murder of innocent people is not an acceptable excuse. I remind my readers that terrorists are not following orders unwillingly. They are *volunteers*. And what they have volunteered to do is not to fight conventionally by adhering to Geneva conventions or whatever—they have volunteered to kill innocent bystanders and hostages in order to destabilize civilized societies.

A man will fiercely defend himself, his wife, his child from attack. 8
Societies whose populations believe in them will defend themselves fiercely. Or they will hire counterterrorists to do their dirty work.

As a counterterrorist by conviction, my aim is to win the terrorist 9
war by the best means available. These will be detailed in due course. My job has not been that of a strategist but of a tactician on the ground. And my function has been to kill terrorists. My rationale will be clear from the following example.

A few years ago I had an assignment in Spain. I was advised in a 10
briefing that two Basque terrorists were at a certain location, a private and otherwise unoccupied dwelling. I had to consider the following questions. If the intelligence information given me was incorrent, there might have been more than two terrorists in hiding in the "safe house" location. And I was given as my team two members of the Guardia Civil, who are law enforcement officers. I have the highest respect for good law enforcement officers around the world, but the fact is that only a very small number of them have had any training at all in dealing with terrorists, and those who have been trained have received instruction and practice at a level far lower than have the special forces such as SAS, Delta, GSG9, and their counterparts in other countries. Therefore it is most unusual for me to have to use policemen on an antiterrorist assignment, but in this case I had no choice.

The plan was for the two policemen to force their way into the front   11
of the house. I stationed myself in a wide culvert at some distance from
the rear of the house, where I could observe the back door and deal with an
exiting terrorist, whichever direction he chose to take.

As it happened, one of the terrorists did flee through the back door   12
and headed straight into the wide culvert in my direction. When he saw
me, his first instinct was to reach for the gun in his belt while still running, but he must have seen that my gun was already in my hand and he
changed his arm movements, raising them sideways. I must suppose that
he might have raised his hands all the way up into the surrender position,
but he lacked that opportunity because I shot and killed him. In most societies, a law enforcement official could be subjected to punishment for killing a criminal instead of taking him prisoner. But a counterterrorist must
have a completely different mind-set. This terrorist had killed innocents
brutally. He had made his own rules. It is amazing how he and others like
him expect a choice when the time comes to face the consequences of
being a terrorist. *A terrorist who is allowed to live and goes to prison
quickly becomes the direct cause of another terrorist act designed to free
him.* The further act may—and frequently does—involve taking hostages
and killing one or more as a demonstration of intent. Therefore the only
way to stop the escalation of terrorist acts is to kill known terrorists, not
take them prisoner.

CHECKING YOUR COMPREHENSION

1. Describe the author's occupation.

   _____

2. List two reasons why the narrator thinks terrorists should be killed.

   _____

3. Why does the author think terrorists should not be taken hostage?

   _____

4. Who are the author's enemies (aside from terrorists)?

   _____

5. According to the author, what is the way to really learn about a terrorist?

   _____

6. Explain how a terrorist is different from an SS killer.

   _____

CRITICAL READING AND THINKING

1. Identify words with negative connotations used to describe terrorists. (Connotations: see Chapter 12)

2. Does the author present an objective or subjective picture of world terrorism? Justify your answer. (Objective and subjective language: see Chapter 13)

3. The author describes terrorists as human garbage. Do you agree or disagree with the comparison? Why?

4. Do you believe you can evaluate or "read" a person by looking at their eyes? Explain.

5. Why might Klinghoffer have bitten the terrorists before he was killed?

6. Do terrorists deserve immunity from their actions?

7. Do you think the author should have killed the terrorist in the culvert who seemed about to surrender? Justify your position.

8. Defend or criticize the author's seeming disregard for the value of human life.

WORDS IN CONTEXT

Directions: *Locate each word in the paragraph indicated and reread that paragraph. Then, based on the way the word is used in the paragraph, write a synonym or brief definition for each.*

1. keepsake (par. 1)

2. counterterrorist (par. 4)

3. exotic (par. 5)

4. asserted (par. 7) _____

5. opportunity (par. 12) _____

VOCABULARY REVIEW

Directions: *Answer each of the following questions. Refer to the Vocabulary Preview, if necessary.*

1. If you are *adhering* to college policy, what are you doing?

   _____

2. What might an *alliance* between two countries be concerned with?

   _____

3. Rabbits *proliferate* quickly. What do they do?

   _____

4. If you purchased an item *clandestinely*, how did you buy it?

   _____

5. If you declare your *intent* to marry someone, what have you done?

   _____

6. If you *initiated* a conversation with a stranger in the subway, how might he react?

   _____

7. If a medical doctor explained the *rationale* behind his diagnosis, what would he explain?

   _____

8. If attending college is *foremost* in your mind, is it more or less important than your part-time job?

   _____

9. If you sign a contract on your *volition*, would you be doing it purposefully?

   _____

10. If a political uprising in a foreign country *escalates*, what is happening?

    _____

SELECTION 28

THE MIND–BODY LINK

Susan Seliger

Can the way you think influence how you feel physically? This selection explores the connection between mental and physical health.

VOCABULARY PREVIEW

terminal (par. 1)   ending in death; fatal

immune system (par. 4)   system of the body that enables it to resist or fight disease

dawning (par. 10)   beginning to appear or develop

hormone (par. 11)   chemical produced by the body

burgeoning (par. 12)   growing or expanding rapidly; flourishing

voodoo (par. 13)   ancient religion in which spells and rituals were believed to affect a person's health or safety

fringes (par. 13)   outer edges; minor, unimportant parts

disparaged (par. 14)   lowered in importance; discredited

innocuous (par. 16)   harmless

trauma (par. 20)   shocking or painful experience

emotional deprivation (par. 20)   lack of emotional relationships

incest (par. 21)   sexual relations with close relatives

PREREADING

Directions: *Preview the selection and answer the following question.*

The title of the article refers to a mind-body link. What links or connections between the mind and the body can you think of?

_____

_____

Gregory was ten years old and all the doctors gave him six months to 1 live. He'd had radiation treatment, but the tumor in his brain was growing bigger. They could not operate. He was terminal, they said. That was September 1978.

Then he went to the Menninger Clinic in Kansas, where the doctors 2 tried the only possibility left—they told Gregory that he would have to try to fix his brain by using his brain.

Gregory became the Blue Leader in his fantasy, the leader of a squad- 3 ron of fighter planes. He thought of his brain as the solar system and the tumor as an invading planetoid which he said was threatening to kill him.

Each night, the Blue Leader would close his eyes, breathe deeply, set- 4 tle into his cockpit, and take off into the solar system to do battle. And each night, soon after takeoff, the entire squadron would zero in on the invading planetoid, fire torpedoes and laser beams—those represented the killer lymphocytes in his immune system—until gradually they blew the foe to bits.

Gregory got worse for the first few months after he began this visuali- 5 zation therapy, but he stuck with it. Then, eight months after he began —two months beyond the doctors' expectations—he noticed he was regaining some control over his hands, and his eye stopped troubling him. Soon after, he was able to take off the leg brace without falling down. Then his walking began to improve—he walked with greater ease than he could remember for a long time. He felt good again.

Then one night when the Blue Leader took off, for the first time he 6 could not find his target. "Dad, it's gone," he yelled. His father calmed him down and urged him to try again. "Dad, there are only some funny white spots where the planetoid is supposed to be."

In February 1980, the Menninger Clinic's CAT scan of Gregory's 7 brain showed that the tumor was indeed gone—the only unusual thing in the picture, according to Dr. Patricia Norris, was a cluster of bony white chips, a little calcium deposit, exactly where the tumor used to be.

The Blue Leader is gone—Gregory is with us today. 8

MBL—The Mind-Body Link—Past and Present

The mind and body are inseparable, inextricably bound, interdepen- 9 dent—they are joined, they are one. It is a marriage more permanent than any made on this earth—not in sickness or in health, not till death do they part.

It is only in the last decade that the scientific and medical communities have begun to come back around to this idea—after over three centuries in which the Cartesian mind-body split has held sway. And even today, though the realization is dawning, doctors are reluctant to encourage patients to think that their attitudes, thoughts, and emotions can play a large role in the state of their health or the progress of their illnesses.   10

Today we know it is so: every illness from a cold to cancer to heart disease can be affected—for better or for worse—by our moods, personalities, attitudes about whether we will get better or not. With each passing day brain researchers are learning more about how our conscious thoughts and emotions influence hormone levels, organ functions, and the most powerful weapon in the defense of our health—the immune system.   11

There is even a new name for this burgeoning field of research—psychoneuroimmunology—the study of the interplay of the mind, the nervous system, and the immune system. It is one of the fastest-growing fields of research, likely to be one of the most important fields of health to be pursued in the coming years.   12

The Power of Suggestion Gains Acceptance

The power of the mind to influence the body has been recognized for thousands of years—in practices ranging from voodoo to chicken soup "therapy" and to the magic of a mother's kiss. But this healing force has been invoked most often on the fringes of the healing profession. Only recently have scientific studies been done that demonstrate the reliable potency of these healing powers we all possess.   13

But we have much to learn about how to use this internal force. Even today this proof of the mind's power over the body is still disparaged as "only the placebo effect."   14

We Aim to Please

The placebo effect—the process whereby someone feels better and gets better without being given "real" medication—rather a sugar pill or salt solution—has been shown to help patients in an average of one-third of cases.   15

Placebo, in Latin, means "I shall please." The result of taking a placebo is sometimes a belief so strong that a patient can reverse the effects of even very potent drugs. One doctor at New York Hospital tested this possibility while treating women suffering nausea in the early stages of pregnancy because their muscles were contracting abnormally. He offered a pill to soothe them—and the nausea vanished. The pill, far from an innocuous sugar tablet, was actually ipecac—one of the most powerful emetics used to induce vomiting in those who have swallowed poisons.   16

The women's belief, however, was stronger than the drug. . . .   17

Attitude, Emotions Can Make Us Flourish . . . or Wither

Our attitude about ourselves can have a critical effect on how we feel 18
and function. It determines whether we are under stress—. . . stress is not
an external event working on us but an internal series of bodily responses
triggered by our perception of events and our judgment about whether or
not we are comfortably in control of them.

If we harbor the fear that our lives are forever just beyond our control, 19
then we constantly trigger the stress response within us. Stress, negative
emotions such as anger and hostility, grief, anxiety, depression, can stimu-
late the release of hormones that damage arteries and lower the activity of
lymphocytes and other elements of the immune system that fight off in-
fectious agents. The mind can sabotage the body.

Children's physical growth can even be affected by emotional trauma. 20
A child deprived of loving emotional support—one with abusive parents,
for example, or indifferent institutional guardians—can actually stop
growing. The emotional deprivation retards not only mental development
but physical development as well. The condition is called "psychosocial
dwarfism" and is not as uncommon as we might wish.

Psychologists have also reported cases in which young girls who were 21
victims of incest—and who developed a great fear of growing up into even
more vulnerable womanhood—have actually kept themselves from developing women's bodies. Not until they begin psychotherapy and come to
grips with much of their haunting pasts do they begin—sometimes even
as late as in their twenties and thirties—finally to develop breasts and
hips. First they heal their minds, then their bodies.

The mind is a powerful force—the mind and body are a powerful 22
team. The medical profession is finally facing the realization that the way
we live—how happy and settled or stressful we feel—can have the greatest influence on whether we get sick or get well.

CHECKING YOUR COMPREHENSION

Directions: *Assume you have been assigned to read this selection for a
psychology class you are taking.*

1. Your instructor has said that the next exam will cover this selection
   among others. Reread the selection and mark and underline important
   information you would want to review and remember for the exam.
   (Underlining: see Chapter 11)

2. You suspect that on the exam you will be asked to summarize several
   articles you have read and comment on their importance. As preparation, write a summary of "The Mind-Body Link." (Summarizing: see
   Chapter 11)

CRITICAL READING AND THINKING

1. What is the author's purpose for writing the article? (Author's purpose: see Chapter 13)

   _____

   _____

2. Explain why you agree or disagree with the following statement: The source of this selection and the authority of the author are important in evaluating the selection. (Source and authority: see Chapter 14)

   _____

   _____

   _____

3. For whom do you think this article was written? (Intended audience: see Chapter 13)

   _____

   _____

4. What types of supporting information does Seliger use? (Supporting ideas: see Chapter 14)

   _____

   _____

5. What critical questions would you ask in evaluating this article? (Critical questions: see Chapter 14)

   _____

   _____

6. Are you convinced of the mind-body connection, or do you need further information? Explain your answer.

   _____

   _____

WORDS IN CONTEXT

Directions: *Locate each word in the paragraph indicated and reread that paragraph. Then, based on the way the word is used in the paragraph, write a synonym or brief definition for each.*

1. visualization therapy (par. 5)   _____

2. inseparable (par. 9)   _____

3. psychoneuroimmunology (par. 12)   _____

4. potency (par. 13)   _____

5. triggered (par. 18)   _____

6. harbor (par. 19)   _____

7. sabotage (par. 19)   _____

VOCABULARY REVIEW

1. Give an example of an emotional trauma.

   _____

2. The selection mentions emotional deprivation. List several other types of deprivation.

   _____

   _____

3. What is a disparaging remark?

   _____

4. Give an example of an innocuous remark.

   _____

5. Explain what the phrase "dawning of the Age of Rock Music" means.

   _____

6. Name several diseases that are often terminal.

   _____

7. If you were on the fringes of a crowd, where would you be?

   _____

8. Give an example of two people who, if they became sexually involved, would be guilty of incest.

   _____

SELECTION 29

DRUGS
Gore Vidal

This selection offers a surprising solution to the growing drug addiction problem in the United States. It is a solution with which many people disagree. Read the selection and evaluate the author's argument.

VOCABULARY PREVIEW

heroic (par. 1)   showing great strength and courage

enslave (par. 2)   make a slave of; control

exhortation (par. 3)   plea; urgent warning; strong encouragement and advice

persecuting (par. 3)   troubling, harassing, or annoying

zombies (par. 5)   walking corpses; people who look and act more dead than alive

mainliners (par. 6)   addicts who inject drugs directly into a large vein.

perennially (par. 6)   yearly; occurring again and again

moralist (par. 7)   person who tries to regulate others' morals; person who teaches, studies, or writes about right and wrong principles and behavior

repression (par. 8)   severe and strict control

vested interest (par. 10)   close involvement to promote selfish goals, usually at the expense of others

irresistible (par. 12)   unable to be resisted

463

PREREADING

Directions: *Preview the selection and take a few minutes to think about what you already know about drug addiction. What are its causes? How does it affect people? What possible solutions have you heard of?*

It is possible to stop most drug addiction in the United States within 1 a very short time. Simply make all drugs available and sell them at cost. Label each drug with a precise description of what effect—good and bad —the drug will have on the taker. This will require heroic honesty. Don't say that marijuana is addictive or dangerous when it is neither, as millions of people know—unlike "speed," which kills most unpleasantly, or heroin, which is addictive and difficult to kick.

For the record, I have tried—once—almost every drug and liked 2 none, disproving the popular Fu Manchu theory that a single whiff of opium will enslave the mind. Nevertheless many drugs are bad for certain people to take and they should be told why in a sensible way.

Along with exhortation and warning, it might be good for our citizens 3 to recall (or learn for the first time) that the United States was the creation of men who believed that each man has the right to do what he wants with his own life as long as he does not interfere with his neighbor's pursuit of happiness. (That his neighbor's idea of happiness is persecuting others does confuse matters a bit.)

This is a startling notion to the current generation of Americans. 4 They reflect a system of public education which has made the Bill of Rights, literally, unacceptable to a majority of high school graduates (see the annual Purdue reports) who now form the "silent majority"—a phrase which that underestimated wit Richard Nixon took from Homer who used it to describe the dead.

Now one can hear the warning rumble begin: if everyone is allowed 5 to take drugs everyone will and the GNP [Gross National Product (a measure of economic growth)] will decrease, the Commies will stop us from making everyone free, and we shall end up a race of zombies, passively murmuring "groovy" to one another. Alarming thought. Yet it seems most unlikely that any reasonably sane person will become a drug addict if he knows in advance what addiction is going to be like.

Is everyone reasonably sane? No. Some people will always become 6 drug addicts just as some people will always become alcoholics, and it is just too bad. Every man, however, has the power (and should have the legal right) to kill himself if he chooses. But since most men don't, they won't be mainliners either. Nevertheless, forbidding people things they like or think they might enjoy only makes them want those things all the more. This psychological insight is, for some mysterious reason, perennially denied our governors.

It is a lucky thing for the American moralist that our country has al- 7
ways existed in a kind of time-vacuum: we have no public memory of anything that happened before last Tuesday. No one in Washington today re-
calls what happened during the years alcohol was forbidden to the people
by a Congress that thought it had a divine mission to stamp out Demon
Rum—launching, in the process, the greatest crime wave in the country's
history, causing thousands of deaths from bad alcohol, and creating a general (and persisting) contempt among the citizenry for the laws of the
United States.

The same thing is happening today. But the government has learned 8
nothing from past attempts at prohibition, not to mention repression.

Last year when the supply of Mexican marijuana was slightly cur- 9
tailed by the Feds, the pushers got the kids hooked on heroin and deaths
increased dramatically, particularly in New York. Whose fault? Evil men
like the Mafiosi? Permissive Dr. Spock? Wild-eyed Dr. Leary? No.

The Government of the United States was responsible for those 10
deaths. The bureaucratic machine has a vested interest in playing cops and
robbers. Both the Bureau of Narcotics and the Mafia want strong laws
against the sale and use of drugs because if drugs are sold at cost there
would be no money in it for anyone.

If there was no money in it for the Mafia, there would be no friendly 11
playground pushers, and addicts would not commit crimes to pay for the
next fix. Finally, if there was no money in it, the Bureau of Narcotics
would wither away, something they are not about to do without a struggle.

Will anything sensible be done? Of course not. The American people 12
are as devoted to the idea of sin and its punishment as they are to making
money—and fighting drugs is nearly as big a business as pushing them.
Since the combination of sin and money is irresistible (particularly to the
professional politician), the situation will only grow worse.

CHECKING YOUR COMPREHENSION

Directions: *Vidal presents an argument for the legalization of drugs and
their sale at cost. On a separate sheet, write an outline of the major points
of his argument. Include the reasons and evidence he gives to support his
idea that legalizing drugs will nearly eliminate the problem of drug addiction.*

CRITICAL READING AND THINKING

1. How would you describe the tone of the article? (Tone: see Chapter 13)

2. Describe Vidal's attitude toward the U.S. government. Refer to specific parts of the article to substantiate what you say.

_____

_____

3. What is the basic assumption Vidal makes in building his argument? (Assumptions: see Chapter 14)

_____

4. Explain why you agree or disagree with the writer's basic assumption.

_____

5. What type of evidence does Vidal offer in support of his argument? (Supporting evidence: see Chapter 14)

_____

_____

6. Describe any other types of evidence that Vidal might have used that would have strengthened his argument.

_____

_____

7. Is there evidence that would have weakened his argument? If so, what?

_____

_____

8. Explain the expression, "We have no public memory of anything that happened before last Tuesday." Decide whether it is a literal or figurative expression and explain your reasons. (Figurative language: see Chapter 12)

_____

_____

WORDS IN CONTEXT

Directions: *Locate each word in the paragraph indicated and reread that paragraph. Then, based on the way the word is used in the paragraph, write a synonym or brief definition for each.*

1. precise (par. 1)   _____

2. launching (par. 7)   _____

3. contempt (par. 7)   _____

4. citizenry (par. 7)   _____

VOCABULARY REVIEW

Directions: *Each of the following words has been formed from a root word and a suffix or verb ending. For each word, underline the root word. Then form a new word by adding a different or additional ending. Write a sentence using a new word.*

	New Word	*Sentence*
1. heroic	_____	_____
2. exhortation	_____	_____
3. persecuting	_____	_____
4. perennially	_____	_____
5. moralist	_____	_____
6. repression	_____	_____
7. irresistible	_____	_____

SELECTION 30

WHY DON'T WE COMPLAIN?
William F. Buckley, Jr.

*Have you ever been annoyed by a situation but did nothing about it?
In this selection, the author examines our willingness to put up with in-
conveniences rather than try to correct them.*

VOCABULARY PREVIEW

virile (par. 2)   vigorous; active; forceful

resolution (par. 2)   decision; determination

sibilant (par. 2)   making a hissing sound

stupor (par. 2)   state in which senses are dull or not working

gauntlet (par. 3)   rows or lines of people

supine (par. 4)   sluggish; inactive

dissolution (par. 4)   breaking up; ending of life

rectify (par. 4)   to correct; adjust; set right

irrational (par. 4)   not reasonable; senseless

vexations (par. 4)   annoyances; small things that annoy or trouble

contortions (par. 6)   movements that twist out of shape

unobtrusive (par. 8)   not forceful or noticeable

ambiguous (par. 8)   unclear; open to different interpretations

passive compliance (par. 8)   act of inactively or quietly giving in to or going along with the wishes of others

▸ PREREADING

Directions: *Preview the selection and answer the following questions.*

1. List several situations in which you were annoyed or inconvenienced but took no action to correct or did not complain.

_____

2. Why didn't you complain?

_____

It was the very last coach and the only empty seat on the entire train, so there was no turning back. The problem was to breathe. Outside, the temperature was below freezing. Inside the railroad car the temperature must have been about 85 degrees. I took off my overcoat, and a few minutes later my jacket, and noticed that the car was flecked with the white shirts of the passengers. I soon found my hand moving to loosen my tie. From one end of the car to the other, as we rattled through Westchester County, we sweated; but we did not moan.   1

I watched the train conductor appear at the head of the car. "Tickets, all tickets, please!" In a more virile age, I thought, the passengers would seize the conductor and strap him down on a seat over the radiator to share the fate of his patrons. He shuffled down the aisle, picking up tickets, punching commutation cards. *No one addressed a word to him.* He approached my seat, and I drew a deep breath of resolution. "Conductor," I began with a considerable edge to my voice. . . . Instantly the doleful eyes of my seatmate turned tiredly from his newspaper to fix me with a resentful stare: what question could be so important as to justify my sibilant intrusion into his stupor? I was shaken by those eyes. I am incapable of making a discreet fuss, so I mumbled a question about what time we were due in Stamford (I didn't even ask whether it would be before or after dehydration could be expected to set in), got my reply, and went back to my newspaper and to wiping my brow.   2

The conductor had nonchalantly walked down the gauntlet of eighty sweating American freemen, and not one of them had asked him to explain why the passengers in that car had been consigned to suffer. There is nothing to be done when the temperature *outdoors* is 85 degrees, and indoors the air conditioner has broken down; obviously when that happens there is nothing to do, except perhaps curse the day that one was born. But when the temperature outdoors is below freezing, it takes a positive act of will on somebody's part to set the temperature *indoors* at 85. Somewhere a valve was turned too far, a furnace overstocked, a thermostat maladjusted: something that could easily be remedied by turning off the heat and allowing the great outdoors to come indoors. All this is so obvious. What is not obvious is what has happened to the American people.   3

It isn't just the commuters, whom we have come to visualize as a 4
supine breed who have got on to the trick of suspending their sensory fac-
ulties twice a day while they submit to the creeping dissolution of the railroad industry. It isn't just they who have given up trying to rectify irrational vexations. It is the American people everywhere.

A few weeks ago at a large movie theatre I turned to my wife and said, 5
"The picture is out of focus." "Be quiet," she answered. I obeyed. But a few
minutes later I raised the point again, with mounting impatience. "It will
be all right in a minute," she said apprehensively. (She would rather lose
her eyesight than be around when I make one of my infrequent scenes.) I
waited. It was *just* out of focus—not glaringly out, but out. My vision is
20-20, and I assume that is the vision, adjusted, of most people in the
movie house. So, after hectoring my wife throughout the first reel, I finally
prevailed upon her to admit that it *was* off, and very annoying. We then
settled down, coming to rest on the presumption that: a) someone connected with the management of the theatre must soon notice the blur and
make the correction; or b) that someone seated near the rear of the house
would make the complaint in behalf of those of us up front; or c) that—
any minute now—the entire house would explode into catcalls and foot
stamping, calling dramatic attention to the irksome distortion.

What happened was nothing. The movie ended, as it had begun, *just* 6
out of focus, and as we trooped out, we stretched our faces in a variety of
contortions to accustom the eye to the shock of normal focus.

I think it is safe to say that everybody suffered on that occasion. And I 7
think it is safe to assume that everyone was expecting someone else to
take the initiative in going back to speak to the manager. And it is probably true even that if we had supposed the movie would run right through
the blurred image, someone surely would have summoned up the purpo-
sive indignation to get up out of his seat and file his complaint.

But notice that no one did. And the reason no one did is because we 8
are all increasingly anxious in America to be unobtrusive, we are reluctant
to make our voices heard, hesitant about claiming our rights; we are afraid
that our cause is unjust, or that if it is not unjust, that it is ambiguous; or
if not even that, that it is too trivial to justify the horrors of a confrontation with Authority; we will sit in an oven or endure a racking headache
before undertaking a head-on, I'm-here-to-tell-you complaint. That tendency to passive compliance, to a heedless endurance, is something to
keep one's eyes on—in sharp focus.

CHECKING YOUR COMPREHENSION

Directions: *Mark each statement* T *for true or* F *for false based on the
content of the selection.*

_____ 1. When riding on the overheated train, Buckley planned to
complain to the conductor but was discouraged by his seatmate.

_____ 2. The conductor seemed concerned about the heat in the train.

_____ 3. Buckley thinks it is mainly commuters who do not complain when they should.

_____ 4. Buckley's wife becomes embarrassed when he makes a scene and complains.

_____ 5. Everyone in the theater expected someone else to complain.

_____ 6. The film that was out of focus was finally adjusted when Buckley complained to the management.

_____ 7. Buckley thinks Americans do not complain because they do not know how to.

CRITICAL READING AND THINKING

1. Describe how Buckley felt about his seatmate on the train.

_____

_____

2. What tone does Buckley use in the article? (Tone: see Chapter 13)

_____

3. Underline several sentences that best suggest Buckley's purpose for writing the article. (Author's purpose: see Chapter 13)

4. Buckley uses personal examples to make the point that Americans are afraid to complain. Explain why this is an effective approach.

_____

_____

5. Describe a situation you have observed in which everyone expected someone else to complain.

_____

_____

_____

6. Explain why you agree or disagree with Buckley's idea that Americans are afraid to complain.

_____

_____

7. Buckley uses descriptive language to help the reader visualize the situations and to make his points amusing but convincing. Underline several

words or phrases that you feel were particularly effective. (Descriptive language: see Chapter 13)

WORDS IN CONTEXT

Directions: *Locate each word in the paragraph indicated and reread that paragraph. Then, based on the way the word is used in the paragraph, write a synonym or brief definition for each.*

1. coach (par. 1) _____

2. flecked (par. 1) _____

3. consigned (par. 3) _____

4. maladjusted (par. 3) _____

5. mounting (par. 5) _____

6. hectoring (par. 5) _____

VOCABULARY REVIEW

Directions: *Each of the following words has been formed from a root word and a suffix or verb ending. For each word, underline the root word. Then form a new word by adding a different or additional ending. Write a sentence using the new word.*

	New Word	Sentence
1. resolution	_____	_____
2. vexations	_____	_____
3. unobtrusive	_____	_____
4. compliance	_____	_____
5. contortions	_____	_____
6. irrational	_____	_____
7. dissolution	_____	_____

Endnotes

Chapter 5

1. Paul R. Lohnes and William W. Cooley, *Introduction to Statistical Procedures* (New York: John Wiley and Sons, 1968), p. 11.
2. Brenda Kemp and Adele Pilliteri, *Fundamentals of Nursing* (Boston: Little, Brown, 1984), p. 776.
3. Roger Chisholm and Marilu McCarty, *Principles of Economics* (Glenview, Ill.: Scott, Foresman, 1981), pp. 483–484.
4. Knut Norstog and Andrew J. Meyerricks, *Biology* (Toronto: Charles E. Merrill, 1985), p. 193.
5. Norstog and Meyerricks, p. 315.
6. Chisholm and McCarty, p. 443.

Chapter 6

1. Philip G. Zimbardo, *Psychology and Life* (Glenview, Ill.: Scott, Foresman, 1985), p. 40.
2. High D. Barlow, *Introduction to Criminology* (Boston: Little, Brown, 1984), p. 422.
3. Chisholm and McCarty, p. 138
4. Walter S. Jones, *The Logic of International Relations*, 5th ed. (Boston: Little, Brown, 1985), p. 406.
5. Elliot Currie and Jerome H. Skolnick, *America's Problems: Social Issues and Public Policy* (Boston: Little, Brown, 1984), p. 294.

Chapter 7

1. Richard George, *The New Consumer Survial Kit* (Boston: Little Brown, 1978) p. 212.
2. K. Warner Schaie and James Geiwetz, *Adult Development and Aging* (Boston: Little, Brown, 1972), pp. 371–372.
3. Charles T. Brown, *Rock and Roll Story* (Englewood Cliffs, N.J.: Prentice-Hall, 1983), p. 109.
4. Edward S. Fox and Edward W. Wheatley, *Modern Marketing* (Glenview, Ill.: Scott, Foresman, 1978), p. 142.
5. Joyce Brothers, "What Dirty Words Really Mean," *Good Housekeeping*, May, 1973.
6. Brown, pp. 20–21.
7. William F. Smith and Raymond D. Liedlich, *From Thought to Theme* (New York: Harcourt Brace Jovanovich, 1983), pp. 281–282.
8. Fox and Wheatley, p. 26.
9. "Trees Talk to One Another," *Science Digest*, January 1984, p. 47.
10. John Naisbitt, *Megatrends* (New York: Warner Books, 1982), p. 23.
11. Frans Gerritsen, *Theory and Practice of Color* (New York: Van Nostrand, 1975), p. 9.
12. George, p. 114.
13. "ABC's of How a President Is Chosen," *U.S. News & World Report*, 18 February 1980, p. 45.
14. Paul G. Hewitt, *Conceptual Physics* (Boston: Little, Brown, 1985), p. 15.
15. Hewitt, pp. 234–235.
16. Hewitt, p. 259.
17. Edward H. Reiley and Carroll L. Shry, *Introductory Horticulture* (Albany, N.Y.: Delmar Publishers, 1979), p. 114.

Chapter 8

1. Hewitt, p. 21.
2. Hewitt, p. 56.
3. Hewitt, p. 224.
4. Thomas E. Garman, Sidney W. Eckert, and Raymond E. Forgue, *Personal Finance* (Boston: Houghton-Mifflin, 1985), pp. 15–16.
5. Hewitt, pp. 82–84.
6. Bowman O. Davis, et al., *Conceptual Human Physiology* (Columbus, Oh.: Charles E. Merrill, 1985), p. 213.
7. Hewitt, p. 233.
8. Barlow, p. 332
9. Hewitt, p. 252.
10. T. Walter Wallbank, Civilization Past and Present, Vol. II, 6th ed. (Glenview, Ill.: Scott, Foresman, 1987), p. 957.

Chapter 9

1. Richard Selzer, *Mortal Lessons* (New York: Simon & Schuster, 1976), pp. 45–46.
2. Howard Temin, "A Warning to Smokers," *Wisconsin State Journal*, 3 March 1976.

Chapter 10

1. Ellis Herwig/Stock Boston
2. Elliot Currie and Jerome H. Skolnick, *America's Problems* (Boston: Little, Brown, 1984), p. 202.
3. Henry L. Roediger III, J. Philippe Rushton, Elizabeth D. Capaldi, and Scott G. Paris, *Psychology* (Boston: Little, Brown, 1984), p. 104.
4. *Budget of the United States Government, Fiscal Year 1983*–(Washington, D.C.: U.S. Government Printing Office, 1982), page 64. Figures are given in constant 1983 dollars.
5. (3) Federal Bureau of Investigation, *Uniform Crime Reports, 1981* (Washington, D.C.: U.S. Government Printing Office, 1982), p. 339.
6. Kenneth Budinski, *Engineering Materials: Properties and Selection* (Reston, Va.: Reston Publishing Co., 1979), p. 15.
7. Herbert E. Ellinger, *Auto-Mechanics*, 2nd ed. (Englewood Cliffs, N.J.: Prentice-Hall, 1977), p. 183.
8. Hewitt, pp. 54–56.

Chapter 11

1. Molly Wantz and John E. Gay, *The Aging Process: A Health Perspective* (Cambridge, Mass.: Winthrop, 1981), p. 62.
2. Watson M. Laetsch, *Plants: Basic Concepts in Botany* (Boston: Little, Brown, 1979), p. 8.

Chapter 12

1. Robert C. Yeager, *Seasons of Shame: The New Violence in Sports* (New York: McGraw-Hill, 1979), p. 6.
2. Ralph K. Bennett, "The Great Russian Raid on U.S. Technology," *Reader's Digest*, March 1984, pp. 56–57.
3. Sara King, "Love in the Afternoon—In a Crowded Prison Hall," *Los Angeles Times*, 5 November 1976.
4. Naisbitt, pp. 231–232.

Chapter 13

1. Barry Lopez, "Weekend," *Audubon*, July 1973.
2. John Steinbeck, *America and Americans* (New York: Viking Press, 1966), pp. 127–128.

Chapter 14

1. Yeager, p. 4.
2. Barbara Stern, "Calm Down in Six Seconds," *Vogue*, October 1981.
3. Sheila Tobias, *Overcoming Math Anxiety* (New York: W. W. Norton, 1978).
4. Mary Gander and Harry W. Gardiner, *Child and Adolescent Development* (Boston: Little, Brown, 1981).
5. Haim Ginott, *Between Parent and Teenager* (New York: Macmillan, 1969), pp. 39–41.
6. E. B. White, *One Man's Meat* (New York: Harper & Row, 1944), pp. 305–306.
7. Gail Sheehy, *Passages* (New York: E. P. Dutton, 1976), p. 68.

(*continued from page iv*)

Page 72–74   Selection in Exercise 5–1. From *Biology: The World of Life* by Robert Wallace, p. 185. Copyright © 1986. Reprinted by permission of Scott, Foresman and Company.

Page 76   "Product Life-Cycle." From *Principles of Marketing* by Thomas C. Kinnear and Kenneth L. Bernhardt, pp. 271–273. Copyright © 1986. Reprinted by permission of Scott, Foresman and Company.

Page 80   Eugene H. Methvin, "TV Violence: The Shocking New Evidence." Reprinted with permission from the January 1983 *Reader's Digest*. Copyright © 1983 by The Reader's Digest Assn., Inc.

Pages 95, 156–158   From *Communication for Management and Business* by Norman B. Sigband. Copyright © 1982 by Scott, Foresman and Company. Reprinted by permission.

Pages 104, 108, 109, 111   From pages 22, 118, 58, 110–11 of *Jobs for the 21st Century*. Reprinted with permission of Macmillan Publishing Company from *Jobs for the 21st Century* by Bob Weinstein. Copyright © by Bob Weinstein.

Pages 105, 106, 108   From *Well-Being: An Introduction to Health* by John Dorfman et al. Copyright © 1980 by Scott, Foresman and Company. Reprinted by permission.

Page 125   From Sydney B. Newell, *Chemistry: An Introduction*, 2nd ed., p. 11. Copyright © 1980 by CompEditor. Reprinted by permission of Sydney B. Newell.

Pages 126, 134, 143, 144, 145, 258   From Richard L. Weaver, II, *Understanding Personal Communication*. Pages 24, 85, 113–114, 123, 185, 291. Scott, Foresman and Company 1987. Reprinted by permission of Scott, Foresman and Company.

Pages 129, 130, 140, 143   From Hal B. Pickle and Royce L. Abrahamson, *Introduction to Business*. Scott, Foresman and Company 1987. Pages 40, 119, 123, 222. Reprinted by permission of Scott, Foresman and Company.

Pages 135, 211, 214   From Robert C. Nickerson, *Fundamentals of Structured COBOL*, pp. 2, 7, 271. Copyright © 1984 by Robert C. Nickerson. Reprinted by permission of Scott, Foresman and Company.

Pages 139, 143–145   From *The World Book Encyclopedia*. © 1985 World Book, Inc. Reprinted by permission.

Pages 163–165   "How Muzak Manipulates You" by Andrea Dorfan, May 1984 issue of *Science Digest*. Copyright 1984 The Hearst Corporation. Reprinted with permission by Hearst Magazines.

Pages 166–168   From *Science Digest*, February 1984. Reprinted by permission of Ann Field.

Pages 170–172   From *The Buffalo News*, Thursday, 22 November 1984. "Why Grannie Set a Bountiful Thanksgiving Table" by Patricia Gaines-Carter. © *The Washington Post*. Reprinted with permission of *The Washington Post*.

Page 174   Excerpt from *A Higher Form of Killing* by Robert Harris and Jeremy Paxman. Copyright © 1982 by Robert Harris and Jeremy Paxman. Reprinted by permission of Farrar, Straus and Giroux, Inc., Chatto & Windus and the authors.

Pages 175–178   "In Idaho: Living Outside of Time" by Gregory Jaynes. Copyright 1985 Time Inc. All rights reserved. Reprinted by permission from *Time*.

Pages 180–182   "The Workplace Is In For a Revolution" by Barbara S. Moffet. From *The Buffalo Evening News*, Saturday, 20 October 1984. Reprinted by permission of the National Geographic News Service.

Pages 184–185   "I Want a Wife" by Judy Syfers. From *MS.*, Spring 1972. Copyright © 1971 by Judy Syfers. Reprinted by permission of the author.

Pages 187–188   From "A Black Looks at Education" by Arthur Ashe, February 6, 1977. *The New York Times*. Copyright © 1977 by The New York Times Company. Reprinted by permission.

Pages 188–190   "Salvation" from *The Big Sea* by Langston Hughes. Copyright 1940 by Langston Hughes, copyright renewed © 1968 by Arna Bontemps and George Houston Bass. Reprinted by permission of Farrar, Straus and Giroux, Inc.

Page 194   From Bijan Mashaw, *Programming Byte by Byte: Structured FORTRAN 77*, pp. xi–xii. American Computer Press. Copyright © 1983 by Bijan Mashaw. Reprinted by permission of Bijan Mashaw.

Page 200 From Louis Berman and J. C. Evans, *Exploring the Cosmos*, 4th ed., p. 145. Copyright © 1983 by Louis Berman and J. C. Evans. Reprinted by permission of Scott, Foresman and Company.

Pages 201, 204, 231–232, 233–234 From Robert L. Lineberry, *Government in America: People, Politics, and Policy*, 2nd ed. Copyright © 1983 by Robert L. Lineberry. Reprinted by permission of Scott, Foresman and Company. Pages 430, 61, 156, 162, 189–190, 190–191.

Page 205 Definition of "power": Copyright © 1980 by Houghton Mifflin Company. Reprinted by permission from *The American Heritage Dictionary of the English Language, New College Edition.*

Pages 216–219 From Paul G. Hewitt, *Conceptual Physics*, 5th ed. Copyright © 1985 by Paul G. Hewitt. Reprinted by permission of Scott, Foresman and Company.

Pages 224–225 From the book, *Your Memory: How It Works and How to Improve It* by Kenneth L. Higbee, Ph.D. © 1977. Reprinted by permission of the publisher, Prentice-Hall, Inc., Englewood Cliffs, N.J. 07632.

Pages 227–229, 244–247 From Zenas Block, *It's All on the Label* (Boston: Little, Brown, 1981). Reprinted by permission of the author.

Pages 229–230 From Sydney B. Newell, *Chemistry: An Introduction*, 2nd ed., pp. 47–48. Copyright © 1980 by CompEditor. Reprinted by permission of Sydney B. Newell.

Pages 255–256 Excerpt from *Paul Harvey's The Rest of the Story* by Paul Aurandt, edited and compiled by Lynne Harvey. Copyright © 1977 by Paulynne, Inc. Reprinted by permission of Doubleday and Co., Inc.

Pages 258–259 From *The Washington Post*. "Thompson: 'The Rule Doesn't Kill the Problem' " by Mark Asher. June 18, 1985. *The Washington Post*. Reprinted with permission of *The Washington Post.*

Page 259 From "Fifty Million Handguns" by Adam Smith, April 1981, *Esquire*. Reprinted with permission from *Esquire*. Copyright © 1981 by Adam Smith.

Page 260 "The Father and His Daughter" by James Thurber. Copyright © 1956, James Thurber. Copyright © 1984, by Helen W. Thurber & Rosemary A. Thurber. From *Further Fables for Our Time*, published by Simon & Schuster, Inc. Reprinted by permission.

Pages 261–262 From *The Non-Runners Book*. Reprinted with permission of Macmillan Publishing Company from *The Non-Runners Book* by Vic Ziegel and Lewis Grossberger. Copyright © 1978 by Macmillan Publishing Company.

Page 264 First stanza of poem #754 from *The Complete Poems of Emily Dickinson* edited by Thomas H. Johnson. Copyright 1929 by Martha Dickinson Bianchi, copyright © renewed 1957 by Mary L. Hampson. Reprinted by permission of Little, Brown and Company.

Page 264 Two Lines from *Bridge Over Troubled Waters*. Copyright © 1969 by Paul Simon. Used by permission.

Pages 288–290 " 'Doing' Cocaine: A Victim's Road to Ruin." Reprinted from *U.S. News & World Report*, issue of May 16, 1983. Copyright, 1983, *U.S. News & World Report.*

Pages 293–294 From *Working: People Talk about What They Do All Day and How They Feel about What They Do*, by Studs Terkel. Copyright © 1972, 1974 by Studs Terkel. Reprinted by permission of Pantheon Books, a Division of Random House, Inc.

Pages 298–299 "The Company Man" from *At Large* by Ellen Goodman. Copyright © 1981 by The Washington Post Company. Reprinted by permission of Summit Books, a division of Simon & Schuster, Inc.

Reading Selections, Part Four

1. "A Guard's First Night on the Job" by William Recktenwald. From *St. Louis Globe–Democrat*, 13 November 1978. Reprinted by permission: Tribune Media Services.
2. "Leisure Will Kill You" by Art Buchwald. Reprinted by permission of the Putnam Publishing Group and the author from *Laid Back in Washington* by Art Buchwald. Copyright © 1978–81 by Art Buchwald.
3. "*Greenpeace and the Pirates* by Robert Wallace. From *Biology: The World of Life* by

Robert Wallace, pp. 518–519. Scott, Foresman 1986. Reprinted by permission of Scott, Foresman and Company.

4. "Chester Ward: 'There Was So Much Death' " from *Charlie Company: What Vietnam Did to Us* by Peter Goldman and Tony Fuller. Copyright © 1983 by Newsweek, Inc. By permission of William Morrow & Co., Inc.

5. "Life in Devastated Areas." Reprinted with permission of Macmillan Publishing Company and Century Hutchinson Ltd. from *The Nuclear Survival Handbook*, rev. ed. by Barry Popkess. Copyright © 1980, 1982 by Barry Popkess.

6. From *Newsweek*, 9 October 1978. Reprinted by permission by Suzanne Britt.

7. "Everything You Ever Wanted to Know about the Kiss." Copyright © 1979 by Carol Tavris and Leonore Tiefer. Originally appeared in *Redbook*. Reprinted by permission of Lescher & Lescher, Ltd.

8. From *Miller's Court* by Arthur Miller. Copyright © 1982 by Arthur R. Miller. Reprinted by permission of Houghton Mifflin Company.

9. From *Understanding Interpersonal Communication* by Richard L. Weaver, II. Scott, Foresman, 1986, pp. 261–264. Reprinted by permission of Scott, Foresman and Company.

10. Adapted from *Mind at Play: The Psychology of Video Games* by Geoffrey R. Loftus and Elizabeth F. Loftus. Copyright © 1983 by Basic Books, Inc. Reprinted by permission of the publisher.

11. "A Degree of Detachment" by Bruce Shragg, July 26, 1987, *The New York Times Magazine*, p. 48. Copyright © 1987 by The New York Times Company. Reprinted by permission.

12. From *Cosmopolitan*, October 1980. Reprinted by permission of the author.

13. From *Mademoiselle*, February 1988, p. 98. Copyright © 1988 by The Conde Nast Publications, Inc. Reprinted with permission of the author.

14. From *Psychology and Life* by Philip G. Zimbardo, pp. 458–459. Scott, Foresman, 1986. Reprinted with permission of Scott, Foresman and Company.

15. From *Introduction to Business* by Hal B. Pickle and Royce L. Abrahamson. Scott, Foresman, 1987, pp. 231–239. Reprinted by permission of Scott, Foresman and Company.

16. From *Junk Food, Fast Food, Health Food* by Lila Perl, Copyright © 1980 by Lila Perl. pp. A-1, A-26. Reprinted by permission of Ticknor & Fields/Clarion Books, a Houghton Mifflin Company.

17. "Police Officers Tell of Strains of Living as a 'Black in Blue' " by Lena Williams, February 14, 1988, *The New York Times*, pp. A-1, A-26. Copyright © 1988 by The New York Times Company. Reprinted by permission.

18. From "Would You Obey a Hitler?" by Jeanne Reinert. *Science Digest*, May 1970. Copyright 1970 The Hearst Corporation. Reprinted with permission by Hearst Magazines.

19. "AIDS Brings Expanded Debate on Rights of the Terminally Ill" by Andrew H. Malcolm, October 4, 1987, *The New York Times*, p. E6. Copyright © 1987 by The New York Times Company. Reprinted by permission.

20. From *Blue Highways: A Journey into America* by William Least Heat Moon. Copyright © 1982 by William Least Heat Moon. By permission of Little, Brown and Company, in association with the Atlantic Monthly Press.

21. "About Men: Amateur Marriage" by Steve Tesich, September 23, 1984, *The New York Times Magazine*. Copyright © 1984 by The New York Times Company. Reprinted by permission.

22. From Anthony F. Grasha, *Practical Application of Psychology*, 2nd ed., pp. 248–250. Copyright © 1983 by Anthony F. Grasha. Reprinted by permission of Scott, Foresman and Company.

23. "About Men: Male Humor" by Isaac Asimov, June 5, 1983, *The New York Times Magazine*. Copyright © 1983 by The New York Times Company. Reprinted by permission.

24. From *Electronic Life* by Michael Crichton. Copyright © 1983 by Michael Crichton. Reprinted by permission of Alfred A. Knopf, Inc.

25. From Robert L. Lineberry, *Government in America: People, Politics, and Policy*, 2nd ed., pp. 600–602. Copyright © 1983 by Robert L. Lineberry. Reprinted by permission of Scott, Foresman and Company.

Index

Note: Italicized numbers indicate illustrations.

TO THE STUDENT:

As educational publishers, it is our job to continually improve our texts and make them more useful to instructors and students. One way to improve a book is to revise it, taking into account the experience of people who have used it. We need to know what you learned and what you found confusing, as well as what you enjoyed and what you disliked. Your instructor may be asked to comment on *Guide to College Reading Second Edition* later, but right now we want to hear from you, the person who paid for this book and read it.

Please help us by completing the questionnaire and returning it to College English Developmental Group, Scott, Foresman College Division, 1900 East Lake Avenue, Glenview, Illinois, 60025.

School: _____

Instructor's Name: _____

Title of Course: _____

1. Which of chapters 1 to 14 did you read for class? _____

   _____

2. Which chapter did you find the most interesting? _____

   Why? _____

3. Which chapter did you find the least interesting? _____

   Why? _____

4. What useful skills have you learned from this text? _____

   _____

5. Please give us your reactions to the Reading Selections.

   _____

	Keep	Delete
1. A Guard's First Night on the Job	_____	_____
2. Leisure Will Kill You	_____	_____
3. Greenpeace and the Pirates	_____	_____
4. Chester Ward: "There Was So Much Death"	_____	_____
5. Life in Devastated Areas	_____	_____
6. That Lean and Hungry Look	_____	_____
7. The Meanings of the Kiss	_____	_____
8. Self-Defense: Can You Protect Yourself and Avoid the Slammer?	_____	_____
9. Stress Management	_____	_____
10. The 25-Cent Addiction	_____	_____
11. A Degree of Detachment	_____	_____
12. Your Name Is Your Destiny	_____	_____
13. How Not To Get the Flu This Year	_____	_____
14. On Trial: Lie Detection by Polygraph	_____	_____
15. The Psychology of Buying: The Purchase-Decision Process	_____	_____
16. The Fast-Food Phenomenon	_____	_____
17. Living as a "Black in Blue"	_____	_____
18. Would You Obey a Hitler?	_____	_____
19. AIDS Brings Expanded Debate on Rights of Terminally Ill	_____	_____
20. Blue Highways	_____	_____
21. An Amateur Marriage	_____	_____
22. Nonverbal Communication	_____	_____
23. Male Humor	_____	_____
24. Computer Crime	_____	_____
25. The Possibility of Nuclear War	_____	_____
26. Television Addiction	_____	_____
27. Winning the War Against Terrorists	_____	_____
28. The Mind–Body Link	_____	_____
29. Drugs	_____	_____
30. Why Don't We Complain?	_____	_____

6. Do you intend to keep this book for your personal library?

_____ Yes _____ No

7. If you have any additional comments, questions, or concerns about *Guide to College Reading Second Edition*, please tell us about them.

Signature (optional) _____ Date: _____

Address (optional) _____